Conceiving a
New Republic

AMERICAN POLITICAL THOUGHT

edited by
Wilson Carey McWilliams and Lance Banning, Founding Editors

Conceiving a New Republic

The Republican Party and the Southern Question, 1869–1900

Charles W. Calhoun

 University Press of Kansas

Published by the University Press of Kansas (Lawrence, Kansas 66045), which was organized by the Kansas Board of Regents and is operated and funded by Emporia State University, Fort Hays State University, Kansas State University, Pittsburg State University, the University of Kansas, and Wichita State University

Library of Congress Cataloging-in-Publication Data

Calhoun, Charles W. (Charles William), 1948-
  Conceiving a new republic : the Republican Party and the southern question, 1869–1900 / Charles W. Calhoun.
    p.   cm. — (American political thought)
  Includes bibliographical references and index.
  ISBN 0-7006-1462-1 (cloth : alk. paper)
  1. Republican Party (U.S. : 1854–   )—History—19th century.   2. Southern States—Politics and government—1865–1950.   3. Reconstruction (U.S. history, 1865–1877)   4. United States—Politics and government—1865–1900.   5. Republicanism—United States—History—19th century.   I. Title.   II. Series.
  JK2356.C29 2006
  973.8—dc22   2006013433

British Library Cataloguing-in-Publication Data is available.

Printed in the United States of America

10 9 8 7 6 5 4 3 2 1

The paper used in this publication meets the minimum requirements of the American National Standard for Permanence of Paper for Printed Library Materials Z39.48–1984.

For Bonnie

CONTENTS

ACKNOWLEDGMENTS

As I look back over the years of researching and writing this book, I find the debts I owe to individuals and institutions simply staggering. Mention here cannot begin to compensate for all the help I have received.

Numerous librarians and archivists have greatly aided this enterprise. For the harried researcher with limited time, nothing was more useful (and comforting) than the efficient help these professionals cheerfully provided. Topping the list is Jeff Flannery whose encyclopedic knowledge of the manuscripts at the Library of Congress eased my examination of those vast holdings. Ed Schamel performed similar service at the National Archives, especially in tracking down the diverse incarnations of the Lodge Federal Elections bill. I extend special thanks to Dr. Benjamin Harrison Walker for making available his family's indispensable collection of Benjamin Harrison manuscripts.

In addition, I am deeply grateful for the superb assistance provided by the librarians and archivists at the Chicago Historical Society, the Cincinnati Historical Society, the Historical Society of Pennsylvania, the Huntington Library, the Indiana Historical Society, the Indiana State Library, the Louisiana State University Library, the Massachusetts Historical Society, the Nevada Historical Society, the New Hampshire Historical Society, the New York Public Library, the Ohio Historical Society, the Rutherford B. Hayes Presidential Center, the State Historical Society of Iowa, the Tulane University Library, the Western Reserve Historical Society, the Wisconsin Historical Society, and the Yale University Library, among others. I also thank the capable staff of the Inter-Library Loan Office of Joyner Library at East Carolina University.

Lewis L. Gould and R. Hal Williams read the entire manuscript and offered abundant and valuable suggestions. In addition, over the years Lew has been unstinting in sharing research materials and in lending encouragement at every step. Hal gave me the benefit of his deep understanding of James G. Blaine, as did Ed Crapol. In conversation, through correspondence, and in other ways I have profited from the insights of Michael Les Benedict, Roger Biles, Roger D. Bridges, Ballard Campbell, Vincent De Santis, Michael F. Holt, Ari Hoogenboom, H. Wayne Morgan, Anthony J. Papalas, Michael Perman, Alan Peskin, Brooks D. Simpson, and Mark Summers. I am grateful to all these individuals, but I alone bear responsibility for what I have written.

Fred Woodward, director of the University Press of Kansas, has been a stalwart champion of this enterprise. In addition, I very much appreciate the superb assistance that Larisa Martin and Susan Schott provided at the Press, and also the work of the copy editor, Karen Hellekson.

A fellowship from the National Endowment for the Humanities enabled me to spend an uninterrupted year doing research for this book. I am also thankful for an Albert J. Beveridge Grant from the American Historical Association and for a research grant from the Dirksen Congressional Center. East Carolina University supported this work through several grants, including a College of Arts and Sciences Research Award and designation as the History Department's Lawrence F. Brewster Scholar for 2003–2004. I wish also to thank my department chair, Michael A. Palmer, for his generous support and encouragement.

I owe my greatest debt to my family—for their love and encouragement and for their endless sacrifices. My daughter Elizabeth, much wiser than her fourteen years, constantly enlightens me about the complexity of human nature. My wife Bonnie, who encouraged me to become a historian in the first place, was a valuable assistant on many research trips. For more than three decades she has enriched my life in countless ways. This book's dedication to her is small compensation indeed.

INTRODUCTION

In the summer of 2005, leaders of the Republican party launched an effort to capture wider support among African Americans. In the mid-twentieth century, when the Democrats became the champions of blacks' political rights, Republicans had adopted a "southern strategy" designed to appeal to the racial intolerance of southern whites. Their aim was to build a new Republican majority in the nation at large, and the strategy worked. The Republicans built a party of whites in the South that became indispensable to their election victories. In doing so, the GOP consciously wrote off the vote of African Americans, whose support for the party became minuscule.

Now, in July 2005, the party's national chairman, Ken Mehlman, proclaimed to the national convention of the NAACP that Republicans "were wrong" in "trying to benefit politically from racial polarization." At least one black commentator dismissed the statement as an "empty apology" for what continued to be the party's "successful divide-and-conquer strategy." Nonetheless, the statement marked a moment of great historical irony, for by it, Republicans confessed to having capitalized on the very politics of bigotry and exclusion against which their late nineteenth-century ancestors had struggled mightily. Then, in the aftermath of the Civil War and Emancipation, southern Democrats had worn the robes of intolerance while Republicans had stood for liberty and defended blacks as citizens and voters. In that earlier time, Republicans dealing with the southern question had labored to build a national majority for their party, but they had also labored to erect a new Republic based on equality and inclusion. Ultimately, after years of travail, the effort failed and southern blacks were excluded from the polity. That earlier endeavor by the Republicans—particularly its republican ideological foundation—is the subject of this book.[1]

This work has its origins in a larger study investigating more generally the thought of the Republican party in the last three decades of the nineteenth century. In my original design, I expected the southern question to occupy no more than a chapter or two in the more general work, which would deal primarily with ideas related to political economy. But the more deeply I delved into Republicans' thinking about the southern question in the years 1869 to 1900, the more I realized how central it was to the party's sense of itself and its mission, even in the years after 1877. What to do about the South was a matter of vast

bedeviled Republicans for decades
waning northern will

complexity and one that bedeviled the Republicans for decades. I concluded that to do the subject justice required a book of its own.

The Republican Party's southern policy in these years is hardly uncharted territory. Numerous historians have examined the subject or phases of it. Two pioneering works by Vincent De Santis and Stanley Hirshson focused on the post-1877 period and portrayed the Republicans' course as one designed primarily to build a southern party in a bid to hold onto power. William Gillette and Richard Abbott saw a similar motivation at play in the pre-1877 period, although Abbott found the Republicans willing to let the South go if necessary to secure their more important electoral base in the North. Heather Richardson's study, centered on the opinions expressed in select periodicals rather than the actions or ideas of party leaders, concluded that the "death of Reconstruction" resulted from Republican fears that enfranchised blacks would enlist in working-class political movements and thus threaten the standing economic order.

In his examination of the Reconstruction presidents, Brooks Simpson presented a more sympathetic portrait of Ulysses S. Grant's and Rutherford B. Hayes's efforts both to conciliate southern whites and protect blacks' rights—efforts that ultimately could not surmount the effects of white southern intransigence and waning northern will. In a study of the legal and constitutional history of the question of black suffrage in the late nineteenth century, Xi Wang ascribed Republicans' southern policy not only to partisan imperatives but also to a genuine commitment to the ideal of democracy, although that commitment ebbed over the years.[2]

My aim here is not to present a comprehensive recapitulation of the Republicans' southern policy over a span of thirty years. Instead, my interest is in the party's ideas. My emphasis is less on what Republicans did than on what they thought about what they were doing. What I have tried to do is to pursue an analysis that locates Republicans' actions and motives in a fundamental ideological context, with primary regard to their beliefs about the meaning and nature of the American Republic. It is a truism that the Republicans, like any politicians, sought to win power, but beyond their quest for party advantage, GOP leaders in the postwar decades envisioned an essential reordering of the polity itself.

The attempted secession of the South in the 1860s and the preservation of national unity by force of arms presented the opportunity for a profound transformation in the country's republican edifice. Viewing their party as chiefly responsible for saving the Union and freeing the slaves, Republicans believed that they also should determine the shape of the postwar nation and blacks' role in it. Securing an equitable reconstruction required constructing an essentially new Republic. But the task of reconstruction and the persistent southern

perplexing

labored and failed

question proved enormously perplexing, and Republicans' unity of purpose in winning the war was never matched in their efforts to fashion the peace. This book, which concentrates on the three decades from the presidency of Ulysses S. Grant to that of William McKinley, examines the ideological struggle among Republicans as they labored—and eventually failed—to reinvent the American Republic. The book's central focus is on how party thought, especially regarding the concept of republicanism, determined the contours of that effort and was in turn shaped by it.

The rubric republicanism subsumes a range of notions about society, government, and public life. Republicans applied the term in a variety of ways and sometimes used it interchangeably with "equality," "free institutions," "liberty," "virtue," "majority rule," and other ideals. Most fundamentally, they defined it as rule by the people through the instrument of representative government. They traced its roots centuries back in human experience, but they also believed that a particular set of circumstances led to an exceptional development of republicanism in the United States. In sublime passages of unsurpassed power, the Declaration of Independence had distilled the essence of liberty, equality, and self-rule, and the Constitution had provided the blueprint for their practical application. But it was not until the war to preserve the Union and abolish slavery that the Founders' work was complete. Viewing their party as responsible for the Union victory, Republicans easily cast themselves as successors to the Founders, and set about to forge a new Republic.

At stake in the Republicans' reimagining of the Republic were values that were complex and sometimes contradictory. What was the meaning of republicanism as it applied to the reconstructed South? Should Republicans emphasize the broadest suffrage—extending it to former slaves as well as former Confederates—to ensure that the "people" did in fact rule? Or should the party give higher priority to the republicanism of civic virtue, leaving the task of political regeneration to the South's better sort, men of property and education? What now was the meaning of federalism? Secession was dead and notions of state "sovereignty" nearly so, but where lay the new boundaries between the national government and the states? What were the implications of the new citizenship set forth in the Reconstruction amendments, and what was the national government's role in shielding the rights inherent in that new citizenship? If the outcome of the war betokened a nationalism of federal government supremacy, how did that doctrine intersect with a different sort of nationalism borne of the impulse toward sectional "reconciliation"? To what degree, Republicans must also ask, would white southerners be willing to accede to the new order of things in their society? Was the South truly ready to accept the results of the war, or would northerners lose the peace to a desperate twilight struggle by southerners to preserve as much of the old order as they could? Underlying everything was the inescapable conundrum of race.

In exploring the evolution of Republican thinking on these questions, the book follows an essentially chronological structure. I have not retraced the well-worn path of early Reconstruction, whose titanic institutional struggle between the Republican Congress and President Andrew Johnson other scholars have fully explored. Instead, the examination here begins with the Republicans' assumption of united control of the national government and the concurrent framing of the Fifteenth Amendment. On the eve of Grant's inauguration, Republicans hammered out the terms of the suffrage amendment, reordering the body politic in order, they hoped, to truly effect the Republic's rebirth. In the early years of his administration they enacted an enforcement structure to try to fulfill the Fifteenth Amendment's republican promise. In Charles Sumner's words, they aimed at "nothing less than the regeneration of the Nation according to the promises of the Declaration of Independence."[3]

But even while they were creating that structure, Republicans began to argue about the meaning of republicanism and how it should be achieved in the formerly rebellious region. As time wore on, those disagreements accelerated. The Grant administration struggled with implementing the new order in the South but met with limited success, in part because of the failings and inadequacies of the supposed agents of change in the South and in part because of growing criticism from within the Republican ranks. But most detrimental to the new Republic's success was the unyielding resistance of southern whites and the Democratic Party generally. In 1874 the Democrats captured the House of Representatives, and for the next decade and a half, divided government at the national level inhibited forward movement in the republican project. The advent of Rutherford B. Hayes in 1877 did not represent an abandonment of the effort so much as a change of tactics, and his Republican successors similarly cast about for ways to keep the project alive.

When the Republicans at last regained control of Congress and the presidency in 1889, they made a valiant effort to salvage the republican experiment in the South with the Lodge Federal Elections bill. But it was too late. Attitudes and public concerns had shifted. The bill lost narrowly, and four years later, the Democrats repealed Reconstruction-era election legislation wholesale. With the federal defense of suffrage gutted and the triumph of disfranchisement in the South, Republicans came to recognize that a reinstatement of republicanism could not succeed until decades had effaced what Benjamin Harrison termed the "deep glacial lines" of race prejudice.[4] Republicans were reduced to encouraging African Americans to bide their time and improve themselves for republican citizenship yet to come—and they welcomed Booker T. Washington's sanction of that conclusion. Moreover, the Supreme Court, dominated by Republicans, countenanced the emergent racial caste system in *Plessy v. Ferguson*, which condoned the "separate but equal" doctrine, and in *Williams v. Mississippi*, which upheld the southern states' disfranchisement schemes.

The republican experiment also fell victim to the heightened nationalism of the 1890s, which placed greater stress on the equality of sections—North and South—than on the equality of men. The chief Republican apostle of that nationalism was President William McKinley, for whom the key to perpetuating republicanism lay not in black suffrage or other rights but in sectional reconciliation. As for African Americans, McKinley advised "patience, moderation, self-control, knowledge, [and] character," and thus in the spirit of the Atlanta Compromise, he touted not republican participation but republican virtues.[5] In the end, most party leaders found ways to accommodate themselves intellectually and morally to the defeat of their earlier ideals, although for others, the loss of the new Republic wrought a profound sense of failure.

In researching this book, I have consulted a wide variety of sources: congressional debates, presidential messages and addresses, judicial opinions, campaign speeches, party platforms, newspapers, campaign "textbooks," and other political publications and documents. I have read numerous memoirs, books, articles, and pamphlets written by late nineteenth-century Republicans. I have quoted extensively from their writings, believing that their own idiom best conveys the flavor of their ideas and the intensity of their beliefs.

Inevitably one confronts the question of how sincere these leaders and opinion makers were in the positions they espoused. Hence, I have tried to test their public rhetoric against the professions and intimations found in their private writings. Personal correspondence, memoranda, diary notes, and the like offer a valuable measure of the sincerity of politicians' public pronouncements and often provide a clearer insight into their thinking and motivation. Moreover, collections of politicians' papers contain countless letters from the party rank and file and from ordinary citizens, whose commentary on issues shows unmistakably that political discourse was not an empty or "false" argument among the elite but in considerable measure a continuing dialogue between leaders and the led.

In the end, the very fact that rhetoric in some measure partakes of contrivance underscores its importance. Political discourse is often a crystallized amalgam of what speakers believe and what they think will accord with their listeners' values. That Republican leaders sought power is a truism, but the premise here is that ideas and ideals figured in their strategy. They were politicians, not political philosophers, yet their belief systems, whether constructed explicitly or assimilated implicitly, influenced their political calculations and hence in part constituted their motivation. It may be true, as cynics would have it, that politicians use their rhetoric to try to fool the public, but it is a matter of no little significance that they make the attempt with one set of notions rather than another.

Regeneration of a Nation

[handwritten: bare-knuckled factionalism among southern Republicans]

"The Rebellion is at last Dead! Thank God," exclaimed a Tennessee Republican at the election of Ulysses S. Grant to the presidency in 1868. This latest triumph by the great Union general, said Boston lawyer E. H. Derby, "is the one thing needed to secure the results of the war & with him I hope for eight years of order, tranquility & progress."[1] It was not to be.

At the time Grant ascended to the presidency, a program of reconstruction was in place, but he and the Republicans in Congress still confronted enormous obstacles to a successful resolution of the southern question. As time wore on, national party leaders grew increasingly dissonant over what measures to apply to the South, and bare-knuckled factionalism among southern Republicans compounded the strife. Moreover, the enormous variation among the southern states ensured that no single policy was appropriate for all or likely to succeed. Congressional legislation was by its nature universal and hence relevant to the exigencies arising in only some of the states at any given time. More flexibly, the administration could tailor its actions to the circumstances of each state, but such varied approaches led to charges of inconsistency that obscured the larger aims of reconciliation and justice for the South at large. Most important, white conservatives' determination to regain control betrayed a tenacity that no policy could deflect. Their willingness to engage in egregious violence, coupled with

[handwritten: — enormous variation among southern states —]

their confident belief in the finite nature of northern will to back reconstruction, augured an eventual triumph of the Democratic white conservatives.

Even before Grant took office, the course of events since Appomattox had given stark notice of how difficult it would be to establish a lasting settlement based on a new republican project in the South. Enactment of the Reconstruction measures had occasioned the severest test ever of the Founders' wisdom in creating a national government of separate and countervailing powers. For nearly four years the Republican Congress and President Andrew Johnson had engaged in bitter political and institutional warfare that went to the brink of Johnson's removal from office. Out of that struggle emerged a blueprint for rebuilding the edifice of nation and states. The Fourteenth Amendment defined national as well as state citizenship, conferred its privileges upon the former slaves, guaranteed equal protection of the law, and temporarily reduced the political influence of leading ex-Confederates. In addition, while ratification of the amendment was pending, Congress passed a series of Reconstruction acts that set the procedure for reinstituting loyal governments in the southern states and for renewing their participation in the national polity. Congress also mandated the right to vote for southern black men. Whites in the South bridled at these changes, but by the end of June 1868, seven states had won readmission and thus stood eligible to participate in that year's presidential election.

Encouraged by this progress, delegates to the Republican National Convention that year "congratulate[d] the country on the assured success of the reconstruction policy of Congress." But party leaders conducted the fall election campaign as if sectional peace and effective reunification remained very much in jeopardy. They did so largely because they perceived a continuing defiance by the white conservative South, given voice by the southern and northern Democratic Party. That party's national convention in New York featured prominent ex-Confederates, and its platform accused the Republicans of oppressing the South with "military despotism and negro supremacy." For vice president, the Democrats nominated Frank Blair, a former Union general who had soured on Reconstruction and had publicly asserted that a Democratic president should declare the Reconstruction acts "null and void." Presidential nominee Horatio Seymour employed rhetoric less incendiary, but Republicans could not forget that as governor of New York during the antidraft and race riots in the dark days of July 1863 Seymour had addressed the rioters as "my friends."[2]

In response, Republicans characterized their opponents as the party of unrepentance. Massachusetts Senator Charles Sumner, a leading abolitionist before the war and now the preeminent champion of blacks' rights, told a Boston audience that the election choice was "whether loyalty or rebellion shall prevail." Carl Schurz, the foremost leader of German Americans who soon would

Ulysses S. Grant
(Library of Congress)

turn against Reconstruction, in 1868 stoutly defended "the liberal ideas of the North" against the "treasonable sentiments" of the Democrats.[3] Republican orators sprinkled their campaign speeches with battlefield triumphs, but experience since Appomattox, especially recent southern defiance, suggested that the Union victory was less than secure. As Ohio Congressman James A. Garfield put it, "the Democratic platform and leaders mean war."[4]

In this atmosphere, Republicans believed that the election of Grant presented the nation the best hope of real peace. The general himself had closed his letter of acceptance with the memorable phrase, "Let us have peace," and Republican campaigners consistently returned to that theme. Not the least of the war hero's assets as a candidate was that his election seemed to offer the surest avenue to genuine sectional reconciliation. Just as he was the embodiment of northern victory, Grant was the symbol of northern magnanimity. His generous treatment of Robert E. Lee at Appomattox signaled a willingness by the North to treat the humbled South charitably. From St. Louis, General William T. Sherman reported that southerners welcomed Grant's election "because they regard it as ending the political quarrel incident to the close of the war."

Grant: symbol of northern magnanimity

— Grant's inaugural —
Bring 1868 election onto JLC

Republicans high and low believed, as the economist and businessman Edward Atkinson put it, "the election of Genl Grant practically settles the southern question."[5]

As time would quickly tell, such declarations proved not only premature but wholly unwarranted. Still, in his inaugural address, Grant encouraged this spirit. Noting that the country had "just emerged from a great rebellion," he urged that remaining questions "be approached calmly, without prejudice, hate, or sectional pride." In tandem with fairness in dealing with the South, Grant would exercise firmness, to ensure "security of person, property, and free religious and political opinion in every part of our common country, without regard to local prejudice. All laws to secure these ends will receive my best efforts for their enforcement." Grant used the occasion to endorse the Fifteenth Amendment, barring discrimination in suffrage based on race, which Congress had passed just a week earlier. He argued that "this question should be settled now," because the "question of suffrage is likely to agitate the public so long as a portion of the citizens of the nation are excluded from its privileges in any State."[6]

A variety of influences had moved Republicans in the waning days of the Fortieth Congress to take this momentous step.[7] Many saw it as necessary to provide greater security to the right of black men to vote in the South. Despite the mandate of such suffrage by congressional legislation and southern state constitutions, the campaign in 1868 had witnessed widespread violence against blacks and their white allies by the Ku Klux Klan and similar organizations. Employing terrorist tactics, including murder, these groups intimidated untold numbers of southern Republicans from voting and thereby influenced the outcome in at least two states, Louisiana and Georgia. In the words of Louisiana Congressman J. P. Newsham, blacks were "shot down and murdered as if they were swine in the butcher's pen—simply because they were true to the country and party who had given them their liberties."[8]

Nor had blacks been the only victims. When Republicans in Congress returned to Washington in December, they mourned the loss of one of their colleagues, Representative James Hinds, an Arkansas carpetbagger, killed in broad daylight by a local Democratic Party secretary two weeks before the election. Hinds was the first victim of assassination in the history of the House, and Republicans portrayed him as a martyr "pleading for the rights of all."[9] The violence that claimed Hinds and scores, if not hundreds, of other victims occurred in states ostensibly governed by Republican regimes erected by congressional reconstruction. Once the Democrats regained control in the South, Republicans could only ask, what fate awaited southern blacks without a constitutional amendment authorizing federal intervention to protect the right of suffrage?

But even with the violence in 1868, the total black vote was estimated at

If black suffrage had not been limited in New York Grant's narrow loss would have been a narrow win.

Charles Sumner
(Library of Congress)

500,000. Since Grant's popular vote margin over Seymour nationwide was 300,000, black suffrage clearly held considerable potential, and many Republicans recognized the political utility of extending it nationwide. In 1868 black men had no right to vote in sixteen states of the twenty-six outside the former Confederacy, states that held more than 15 percent of the nation's black population.[10] In some states, such as New York, where black suffrage was restricted, unlimited suffrage might have reversed Grant's narrow loss of the popular vote that cost him all the state's electoral vote. Thus some historians have seen a cynical, self-serving political motive to gain this northern black vote as uppermost in Republicans' drive for nationwide black suffrage. They are fond of quoting Charles Sumner, who frankly counseled his fellow senators that black votes would help them carry closely contested northern states: "Where you most need them, there they are."[11]

1868 election

But these accounts miss the sarcasm in what Sumner was saying. "Pardon me," he needled his fellow senators, "but if you are not moved by considerations of justice under the Constitution, then I appeal to that humbler motive which is found in the desire for success." In fact, Sumner underestimated the altruism of his colleagues. According to Kansas Senator Edmund Ross, who still championed black rights despite his notorious vote to acquit Andrew Johnson, "The first great and sufficient reason why the negro should be admitted to the right of suffrage in all the States is that it is right." In their 1868 platform the Republicans had endorsed federal imposition of black suffrage only in the South while leaving the question to state determination in the North. Soon afterward, House member James G. Blaine later wrote, party leaders had become "heartily ashamed" of this "evasive and discreditable" stand. Such double-dealing, said Ohio's Samuel Shellabarger, not only violated Americans' "sense of fair play" but also shocked "the moral sense of mankind. . . . The decisive argument for the [Fifteenth] amendment is that it is right."[12]

In the protracted congressional debate during January and February 1869, Republicans struggled to define the republican project that the Fifteenth Amendment would proclaim. Party members generally agreed that something should be done to secure the vote by black men nationwide, but they disagreed about how best to do that and whether suffrage protection should extend beyond a ban against racial discrimination. Some, such as Oliver P. Morton, Indiana's intrepid wartime governor who now served in the Senate, thought it should. Crippled by a stroke, Morton had been relatively conservative early in Reconstruction, but by 1869 he had emerged as a champion of blacks' rights. He presciently argued that limiting the amendment to barring the disqualifiers of race, color, or previous condition of servitude left the way open for states to enact other means to keep blacks from voting. At one point, Massachusetts Radical Henry Wilson convinced the Senate to prohibit discrimination by education, property, nativity, or creed as well. A few Republicans in Congress even argued for women's suffrage. Sumner took the position that no new amendment at all was required, because the right of suffrage already inhered in American citizenship under the Constitution, especially since the adoption of the Fourteenth Amendment with its definition of citizenship and its guarantee of citizens' privileges and immunities. Avowing that "anything for Human Rights is constitutional," Sumner believed that Congress should simply pass the necessary legislation to uphold the constitutional right to vote, an approach that would obviate the delay and uncertainty of the ratification process necessary for an amendment. For their part, Democrats opposed all these various measures and argued that the matter of suffrage remained strictly within the province of the states.[13]

While Republicans grappled with the amendment's precise formula, their central focus was on the nature and composition of the electorate in the Republic. "In our Government," said Alabama carpetbag Senator Willard Warner, "the sovereignty is in the people; hence the question, 'Who are the people?' is of practical and vital importance. When you settle that you settle the basis of

"For most Republicans the good society entailed political equality but not social equality!

government." These discussions went to the heart of the meaning of republicanism. Among the most remarkable features of the debate was the degree to which Republicans looked back beyond the Constitution and appealed to the principles set forth in the Declaration of Independence. The Declaration stood not merely as a statement of the reasons for separation from England but also as the founding charter of the American Republic. According to first-term Iowa Representative William Loughridge, the Founders inserted into the Constitution "the same principles which were so conspicuous in the Declaration of Independence." Other Republicans, however, argued that the Framers had meant to implant the Declaration's creed in the Constitution but had failed in their purpose. Now the nation must act decisively to correct the omission by fully protecting the right of suffrage. As Sumner put it, only this "complete recognition" of the "great principles of the Declaration of Independence" could erect "the cap-stone of our Republic."[14]

In elucidating those "great principles," Republicans located the foundation of the right to vote for black men in the Declaration's bedrock ideal that all men are created equal. According to South Carolina Congressman C. C. Bowen, a former Confederate turned Republican, the "equality of man" lay at the core of "the political philosophy underlying American republicanism." Moreover, because equality represented a central tenet in Christian teaching, there could be no moral legitimacy in denying the suffrage to any man simply because of his race. By transcending "the prejudice of race," said Connecticut Senator Orris Ferry, the Fifteenth Amendment would open the way to "that state of society toward which the nations have been struggling since the beginning of the Christian civilization."[15]

For most Republicans, however, that good society entailed political equality but not social equality. Fears of race mixing, they insisted, were groundless. They noted that even though all whites possessed the right to vote, they were nonetheless arrayed in a wide variety of social divisions. No one need fear, said Representative William Higby of California, "that placing the ballot in the colored man's hand will be his passport to all ranks and conditions of society." On the other hand, Republicans drew a close connection between blacks' military performance and their claims to the suffrage. During the war black troops had distinguished themselves for fidelity and bravery at Fort Pillow, Fort Wagner, and elsewhere; as citizens, black men remained liable for future military service. To bar veterans and potential soldiers from voting on the basis of race would be the grossest ingratitude.[16]

Underlying such reasoning was Republicans' belief that black men possessed the capacity to cast the vote. Senator Samuel Pomeroy, a native of Massachusetts and one of the original Free State leaders of Bleeding Kansas, conceded that blacks "were unlearned and, for the most part, ignorant men. But," he insisted, "instinct is wiser than logic." Hundreds of thousands of them had voted in the South in 1868, and they had not disappointed "reasonable expectations." During the campaign, the Republican national committee distributed to black voters campaign badges described as "rewards of merit." According to a Tennessee campaign official, the black voters "regarded those badges with as much veneration and affection as ever Napoleon's veterans did the famous Crosses of the Legion of Honor. . . . Poor, noble hearted, generous creatures! What grand capacities for good they have exhibited and retained in spite of all the degradation of their race!" Simeon Corley, a Republican scalawag who represented a district in South Carolina, a state with a black majority population, believed that the nation faced "more danger from the machinations of intelligent traitors" than "from the ignorance of its loyal masses." In any event, he argued, "the ballot is the best educator. By its use all citizens may readily learn how to guard against its abuse."[17]

Republicans in general were willing to trust in what South Carolina Senator Frederick Sawyer called the black man's "powers of development." A Harvard graduate and an educator, Sawyer argued that the black man had already "gained a great degree of civilization since he was brought from his native barbarism in Africa" and he could now "be rendered a freeman with safety to the State." Sawyer, denying that blacks' backwardness was innate, speculated that if whites had been enslaved by blacks for two centuries and "deprived of every means of cultivation and self-development," they would have experienced the same difficulties in adjustment.[18] Florida carpetbag Senator Adonijah Welch took this separation of race and capacity to the farthest degree. A graduate of the University of Michigan and also an educator, Welch was about to assume the presidency of Iowa State Agricultural College. In Senate debate he cut to the heart of the issue with a scientific logic that has a modern ring.

[That] intelligence and virtue are indispensable to the safe exercise of the right of suffrage . . . [is] an axiom lying at the basis of our republican Government and national prosperity. But intelligence and virtue are not the distinctive characteristics of races; they are not peculiar to any race; they are not monopolized by nor wholly excluded from any people on the round earth. Intelligence and virtue are individual possessions, inconstant qualities varying *ad infinitum* among the individuals of every people. . . . Those constant qualities which make the different races are mainly physical, consisting of peculiarities of color, feature, figure, and the like; but as these peculiarities are not the qualifications for the voter, nor indicate the presence or absence of such qualifications, they cannot without absurdity be assumed as the ground for withholding or bestowing the right of suffrage. I do not share the prejudice of Senators against race; my prejudices are for or against individuals according to their merits or demerits.

If many Republicans hesitated to go as far as Welch in his theorizing on the comparative abilities of the races, all could accept his assertion that "the crowning virtue of American citizenship" was not "intellectual or social status" but patriotism. Even if the black man "never had a dozen thoughts in all his life and never changed their course, his steady unflinching love of this Union would render him a safer depository of the right of suffrage than he who has compassed all knowledge and all science and hates his country."[19]

While Republicans pointed to the Declaration of Independence as an official certification of the ideal of equality at the nation's founding, they saw further justification for the expansion of black suffrage in the document's second major premise: that to be legitimate, government must have the consent of the governed. "If this be true," said William Loughridge, "then that cannot be a just Government or exercise just powers which denies absolutely to one fifth of its citizens any voice or participation in the Government." The Revolutionary battle cry of "no taxation without representation," said Charles Sumner, was the first "definition of a republican government."[20]

Republicans also noted that Article Four of the Constitution specifically required that the "United States shall guarantee to every State in this Union a Republican Form of Government," a provision that Sumner described as the document's "most important clause" after the preamble. Linking government by consent to republicanism was thus central to Republicans' defense of an expanded suffrage. George S. Boutwell of Massachusetts, who sponsored the Fifteenth Amendment in the House, appealed to the original intent of the Framers, citing the assertion of Pennsylvania's James Wilson that "the right of suffrage is fundamental to republics." In Boutwell's view, "none of those States in which men are denied the elective franchise for themselves and for all their posterity are republican." Indeed, he insisted, "if certain persons are included and certain others excluded, not for themselves merely but for all their posterity, you have an aristocracy," and not a republic. Frederick Frelinghuysen, scion of a prominent New Jersey family who had just lost reelection to the Senate, deemed it a "singular paradox" that the Democrats, "who claim for themselves devotion to the principle of democracy, which is a government nearer to the people," should "oppose an amendment which will give the power of manifesting sovereignty to four million free native-born, arms-bearing, taxed citizens of the United States." Other Republicans likewise identified "democracy" as the goal they sought. South Carolina's C. C. Bowen spoke of "the American idea of democratic republicanism" and of completing the Fathers' work of "establishing for themselves and their posterity what they regarded as a genuine democracy." "Our end," said Willard Warner, "is a pure democracy."[21]

Many of the arguments Republicans adduced to support the expansion of black manhood suffrage nationwide could with equal logic and force apply to all adult citizens, and some Republicans were willing to carry the suffrage guarantee beyond the question of race. A few northern states still set property qualifications for voting, and this gave rise to the suggestion that the word *property* be inserted in the amendment as a prohibited category of discrimination. "It is property more than complexion that dictates the fate of mankind," Indiana Representative J. P. C. Shanks argued, "and republics can only stand when the ballot-box is secured to the poor as well as the rich." Noting that it was "the great laboring, industrial classes" that had "placed the Republic in her present proud rank among the nations," Warner cautioned that the safety of society demanded that "we will have no disfranchised, disaffected, clamoring classes always ready and ripe for tumult, rebellion, and revolution. Then the will of the people, legally and peacefully expressed, will have a weight and a power which will command and insure universal acquiescence and obedience."[22]

Warner and others favored eliminating any educational test for voting. They argued that the existence of a literacy test in Massachusetts or other northern states should not stand in the way of a federal prohibition of such tests, which could keep blacks from the polls through no fault of their own. Morton of Indiana favored barring suffrage discrimination by "nativity," and he defended "as another essential republican principle, that the right to vote and hold office should not be denied on account of religious faith or creed." Ohio Senator John Sherman, brother of the general, proposed what he termed "universal suffrage," denying the states the right to discriminate on any basis except age, residence, and sex. Sherman had first entered Congress on the wave of revulsion against the Kansas-Nebraska Act of 1854 and had been a principal architect of the Reconstruction Act of 1867, which had mandated black male suffrage in the South. Now he argued that if the proposed amendment let stand the various devices whereby some northern states limited the suffrage among white men, it would "be said this is a mere party expedient to accomplish party ends, and not a great fundamental proposition."[23]

A handful of Republicans in Congress were willing to carry the implications of such thinking beyond the last hurdle and advocate a true universal suffrage that included women. "Human nature, claiming its rights, has no sex," insisted Samuel Pomeroy; "the mind and the soul have no gender." Pomeroy rejected the contention that women were represented politically by their husbands or other male relatives. Indeed, he considered women's suffrage as part of "the distinctive character of our republican Government." Similarly, Simeon Corley reasoned that the mothers who educated their sons to a wise casting of the ballot were just as competent to cast it themselves and thereby infuse politics with "more of the moral element." Most Republicans, however, recognized limits to the nation's capacity to absorb fundamental change. "I know that woman's suffrage is not now attainable," said Willard Warner, "and I would not, as a practical legislator, jeopardize the good which is attainable by linking with it that which is impossible."[24]

Ultimately, feasibility influenced the Fifteenth Amendment's final shape. The measure required not only a two-thirds vote in each house of Congress but approval by three-quarters of the states as well. During the weeks of congressional deliberation, the proposed amendment underwent several permutations. At one point the Senate approved wording that would bar discrimination in voting or officeholding "on account of race, color, nativity, property, education, or creed." Subsequently the House passed a version that prohibited any abridgement of the right to vote or hold office "on account of race, color, nativity, property, creed, or previous condition of servitude." But as the Fortieth Congress drew to a close, party leaders recognized the need to settle on a version likeliest to win ratification in the states. Republicans could not hope to maintain two-thirds control of both houses forever, and this might be their last chance to secure any measure. As Senate sponsor William Stewart of Nevada noted, "There are no two Senators who agree as to exactly the thing which should be done. . . . [O]ne wants a t crossed this way, and another wants an i dotted that way; and thus it is that we lose time discussing little things that do not enter into the main question." Pragmatic counsel prevailed in a House-Senate conference committee, which excised provisions that might cost support in the states for one reason or another. The final version banned suffrage discrimination on the basis of race, color, or previous condition of servitude and made no mention of officeholding. Although in the end both houses accepted this conservative solution, during the course of the debate, each had witnessed arguments that limned the outer limits of the party's notions of republicanism, where the electorate would stand perfectly coterminous with the citizenry.[25]

On one point virtually all Republicans could agree—that the new amendment did no fundamental violence to the principle of federalism, as the Democrats alleged. Some denied that the amendment represented any significant shift at all in the balance of power between the national government and the states, because, except for the three specified conditions, regulation of the franchise remained with the states. Moreover, they maintained, the amendment did not increase the central government's power, for in fact, power was not given but taken away from both federal and state governments. Other Republicans did see a shift in the federal–state relationship but welcomed it as correcting the imbalance that had proven so destructive in the past. Edmund Ross argued that in reacting to the "burning wrongs" perpetrated by Great Britain, the Founders had created a government that tended "toward the other extreme and approximated that decentralization which brought anarchy upon the ancient republics." Now, said Ross, "we have practically ceased to be a confederacy, and have become essentially a nation," with an "undisputed jurisdiction on the part of the General Government over all questions involving the political status and political rights of the individual." If the past half century had taught anything, it was the dangers of unbridled "state sovereignty." After the travesty of federalism marked by the southern rebellion, said Ferry of Connecticut, it seemed absurd to criticize the Republicans' effort to enfranchise "an innocent, a law–abiding, an industrious, a peaceful portion of the citizens of the United States."[26]

Granting suffrage rights to black men would, many Republicans confidently predicted, at last settle the sectional conflict, bring peace between North and South, and provide blacks the means for self-defense. George Boutwell saw the amendment he sponsored as "a part of the great work of harmonizing the country, of pacifying all classes, of reconciling all interests." Henry Wilson declared that with Grant's administration "coming into power pledged to liberty and equality of rights, . . . before the four years pass away we shall become accustomed in all parts of the country to see all classes of our citizens peacefully exercising their rights." Some Republicans, however, sounded a cautionary note that the mere possession of the right to vote did not ensure that blacks would be able to exercise it in safety. Not everyone would regard the amendment as self-executing, and thus its second section empowered Congress to "enforce" it with appropriate legislation. Without persistent federal government scrutiny and restraints, unreconstructed southerners would, Simeon Corley warned, "threaten, overawe, and assassinate loyal men for no crime but their loyalty."[27]

By the end of March 1870, a sufficient number of states had ratified the Fifteenth Amendment to make it part of the Constitution. From the White House, Grant hailed it as "the realization of the Declaration of Independence" and as "a measure of grander importance than any other one act of the kind from the foundation of our free Government to the present day." Black Americans and Republicans generally joined in a chorus of celebration. Frederick Douglass rejoiced that black men were now "upon an equal footing with all other men" and "responsible for their own existence and their well or ill being." The Union League Club of New York City saw the amendment's adoption as "the termination of the war for the suppression of the Rebellion . . . and as the crowning glory and triumph of the Republican Party." Privately, President Grant gave a

CELEBRATION AT BALTIMORE ON MAY 19th 1870.

The Fifteenth Amendment and Its Results (Library of Congress)

sigh of relief that the suffrage question was at last "out of politics, and reconstruction completed."[28]

And yet, from the South, where black suffrage had been the law for nearly three years, came news that made such optimism appear as so much whistling in the dark. Despite some white conservatives' professions of a "new departure" in southern race relations and some wooing of the black vote by Democrats, the racial and political violence that had marred the elections of 1868 continued into 1869 and 1870. Pleas for help from southern Republicans flooded in upon members of Congress. In February 1870, for instance, as ratification of the amendment neared completion, a Texas sheriff reported to the Reconstruction Committee that blacks were being "robbed and killed by hundreds. . . . Surrounded by ruffians [and] Ku Klux Savages equal to the Comanchi Indians we need a remedy, and our only Source is from Congress." Thus, shortly after the Fifteenth Amendment was promulgated, Republicans took steps to ensure its success, beginning in late May with the passage of the first of several enforcement acts. "The best thing now," said Oliver Morton, was for Congress "to endeavor to understand the true condition of the South, and to act accordingly."[29]

Carl Schurz
(Library of Congress)

But what form should the action take? On this Republicans exhibited some disagreement as they debated enforcement bills introduced in the House and Senate. The main philosophical issue concerned how far the national government could go in regulating the conduct of elections, a matter historically the province of the states. On one end of the spectrum stood men such as Tennessee's Joseph S. Fowler, who had voted for the acquittal of Andrew Johnson and against the Fifteenth Amendment. Fowler opposed the proposed legislation on the grounds that "one of the dearly cherished features of the American system" was that "all local interests have been trusted to the control of local State institutions." House bill sponsor John A. Bingham disputed this notion. An Ohio Radical who had served as a House manager in Johnson's impeachment, Bingham frankly defended a larger federal role and scoffed at opponents' dread of "consolidation." "Consolidation to do what?" he asked. "Consolidation of the Union for the safety of the Union; consolidation to enforce the guarantied rights of the humblest citizens of this land." Bingham reminded his colleagues that in framing the Constitution, "the fathers of the Republic . . . had kept steadily in view the 'consolidation' of the Union."[30]

ambivalence among Republicans about protection of rights of blacks

The ambivalence some Republicans felt in attempting to secure the right to vote for blacks without completely breaching the traditional boundaries of federalism was best represented by the attitude of Carl Schurz, who had begun to entertain doubts about the party's approach to reconstruction. Schurz defended the proposed legislation on the philosophical grounds that legitimate constitutional changes "grow out of conditions, circumstances, events, sympathies, prevailing interests." The revolution sparked by the Civil War had "rescued" individual rights from the "arbitrary discretion" of the states and "placed them under the shield of national protection." The Fifteenth Amendment and appropriate enforcement legislation would not destroy local self-government but instead would establish everywhere a true local self-government in which "the whole people" could "cooperate in the management of their common affairs." And yet Schurz also warned against "undue centralization" and embraced states rights "as the embodiment of true and general self-government." He denied that the Constitution's clause guaranteeing to the states a republican form of government authorized "us to use the arm of the national authority for the purpose of realizing by force what conception each of us may entertain of the 'ideal republic.'" Still, oppression and disorder in the South were undeniable, and Schurz justified a federal response on the grounds that "the institution of general self-government under national protection" was "now established in the Constitution."[31]

But did the Constitution, especially the new amendments, empower Congress to pass laws that would directly regulate the behavior of individuals as opposed to states? Yes, as the enforcement bill's final form showed, most Republicans did so believe. No one stated the position more clearly than scalawag Senator John Pool, whose own state of North Carolina was plagued by Ku Klux Klan violence. Pool argued that if the states failed to provide protection to the citizens' right of suffrage, then it was "the duty of the United States Government to supply that omission, and by its own laws and by its own courts to go into the States for the purpose of giving the amendment vitality." John Sherman saw an "absolute necessity" to pass legislation "that if any man in any community in the United States should violate the personal rights of any citizen in the United States in the most sacred of rights, the right to vote, he should be punished by a sure, swift, and severe remedy."[32]

As finally passed, the Enforcement Act of May 31, 1870, did a number of things. For all elections, local as well as national, it enacted criminal sanctions for violating the Fifteenth Amendment's ban against discrimination in voting based on race, color, or previous condition of servitude, and it broadened that ban to cover the administration of any requirements or prerequisites for voting. It outlawed interference with voting by force, bribery, intimidation, or economic sanctions such as threatened loss of employment or eviction. The law granted exclusive jurisdiction over its provisions to the federal courts and authorized the president to employ the armed forces in its enforcement. As proposed by Sherman, the act also included several sections outlawing fraudulent voting practices, principally abuses in northern cities dominated by political machines usually in the interest of the Democrats. In addition, the law reenacted the Civil Rights Act of 1866 and included provisions to undergird the Fourteenth Amendment. It outlawed conspiracy to deprive any citizen of "any right or privilege granted or secured to him by the Constitution or laws of the Constitution" and mandated the same treatment for all persons as was given to whites in such areas as court proceedings, punishments, taxes, and license fees.[33]

The Enforcement Act obviously reflected Republicans' doubts that they could trust southern white conservatives to do the right thing. Not surprisingly, efforts to accompany this legislation with general amnesty for former Confederates got nowhere. Indeed, the act included two provisions that specifically reinforced the political disabilities of former Confederate leaders as outlined in the Fourteenth Amendment. A few Republicans in Congress considered this a mistake, making the former Confederate leaders "*quasi* martyrs." Some argued that the "fragmentary minority" of people who had been loyal during the war was simply too small to carry on the government in the former seceded states. Others, moreover, said that political disabilities violated the vital American principle of local self-government.[34]

But these proamnesty sentiments remained a minority view among Republicans in 1870. Although Congress regularly passed acts relieving individuals of their disabilities, most Republicans were still unwilling to take the more significant symbolic step toward reconciliation of granting general amnesty. Pennsylvania Senator Simon Cameron, who as secretary of war had advocated the enlistment of slaves two years before Lincoln's Emancipation Proclamation, reported that on a recent trip to the South everyone treated him with kindness and courtesy, but at heart the "rebels of the war were rebels still." Morton protested that a growing tendency to portray the rebellion as "a mere political movement, an honest difference of opinion" was "teaching the rising generation that rebellion was no crime." If nothing else, the continued political violence in the South revealed the former Confederates as unworthy of any policy of absolution. "As well attempt to conciliate a den of rattlesnakes," Morton declared.[35]

The question of race obviously underlay the adoption of the 1870 Enforcement Act, although congressional debate exhibited less discussion of the issue than had the deliberations concerning the Fifteenth Amendment itself. A few months later, however, it took center stage again in debate over a bill to institute closer federal supervision of the naturalization of aliens in large cities. This legislation, sponsored by New Yorkers Noah Davis and Roscoe Conkling, aimed at regulating the hasty and often fraudulent naturalization of immigrants, who largely supported the Democrats. In addition, with New York City in mind, Conkling added provisions for closer regulation of congressional elections in cities with more than 20,000 inhabitants. President Grant thought the legislation would "go far to prevent the fraudulent 'repeating' &c. in N.Y.," and behind the scenes he exerted pressure for its passage. In the course of debate, however, Charles Sumner proposed to amend the bill to strike the word *white* from all existing naturalization laws "so that in naturalization there shall be no distinction of race or color." His purpose was to "bring our system in harmony" with the Declaration of Independence and the Constitution, the "two great title-deeds of this Republic." But the proposition sparked a heated exchange that laid bare Republicans' uncertainties and divisions regarding the complex mix of race, citizenship, and suffrage.[36]

The chief objection came from West Coast Republicans who opposed the enfranchisement of Chinese immigrants that would follow their naturalization. During the debates over the Fifteenth Amendment, these Republicans had raised the specter of Chinese voting, but other party members had assured them that because the amendment referred to citizens, the Chinese could be excluded by denying them naturalization. Sumner's proposal threatened to nullify that exclusion. Pacific Slope representatives warned that its passage would spark violence against Chinese in their states, but in part, their opposition in debate reflected the racism of their constituents. Oregon Senator George Williams warned against "this mighty tide of ignorance and pollution" from Asia that could not "coalesce" with other elements in the population and was thus "dangerous to the peace and integrity of this nation." Sumner and others rejected these racial arguments and instead underscored the Declaration's vision of equality. "A man is a man," said Wisconsin's Matthew Carpenter, "no matter where he was born, no matter what may be the color of his skin." "It is 'all men,'" said Sumner, "and not a race or color that are placed under protection of the Declaration; and such was the voice of our fathers on the 4th day of July, 1776."[37]

The notion that the Chinese were ill-suited for participation in American republican government received its fullest elaboration from Nevada's William Stewart, who had sponsored the Fifteenth Amendment in the Senate. In the first place, he said, the Chinese did not "value the privileges of citizenship" because their religion demanded "devotion to pagan despotism" and was thus "hostile to free institutions." Some Republicans charged that Stewart seemed to favor an unconstitutional religious test for citizenship, but he stood by his notion that the unfree mind of the Chinese made them unsafe citizens in a republic. The Chinese were unfree in another sense, Stewart alleged, in that most of them immigrated under labor contracts and lived practically as slaves, who, under the control of their masters, could "be driven up and naturalized, and their votes disposed of as their labor is disposed of." Stewart and virtually all his colleagues favored the abolition of contract labor, but until that reform was enacted and Chinese sought citizenship of their own volition, the Republic had no room for men so lacking in independence and control over their own destinies. Former German immigrant Carl Schurz thought Stewart exaggerated the "coolie" problem, but he too wanted no right to vote granted to temporary contract laborers who could be "made a political machinery to be worked in the hands of unscrupulous employers."[38]

As Republicans agonized once again over the character of their Republic and who was fit to become a citizen, they remained mindful of the fragility of republicanism, whose eventual collapse old world despots still predicted. "We are charged with the duty of preserving these liberties for mankind," Stewart said. "America is the palladium of free institutions, and we are but the trustees to guard those rights. We must not incorporate any foreign element which is hostile to free institutions." But Samuel Pomeroy saw a greater hazard in exclusion: "If you have a class of men among you who are not citizens, they are a dangerous class. The safety of our Government consists in making every man a citizen." Matthew Carpenter considered it infinitely better to "apply our principles" to the Chinese "than confess them to be erroneous, and thus destroy the only foundation upon which free government can rest." Similarly, Sumner solemnly avowed that "the greatest peril to the Republic is from disloyalty to its great ideas." Once again, he appealed to the definitive character of "the Declaration of Independence as paramount law, not to be set aside or questioned in any respect— sovereign, absolute, irreversible, and which we are all bound to respect."

In the end, however, Sumner's proposal to excise the word *white* from the naturalization laws failed, although Congress did approve a provision extending naturalization to persons of African birth or descent. In fact, few immigrants came from Africa; the special solicitude the Republican Party felt for the millions of former slaves in the South clearly influenced its enactment of this symbolic gesture. More significantly, the willingness of some Republicans to see a racial character in the attributes of citizenship posed an ominous portent for the durability of their republican project.[39]

The first test of the Enforcement Act and the enforcement provisions of the Naturalization Act of 1870 came in the midterm elections later that year. Some Republicans harbored the optimistic notion that the mere existence of the legislation would somehow wrap the black voter in a mantle of protection. "The negro question is substantially removed from the arena of American politics," said James A. Garfield, campaigning in Ohio for reelection to Congress. "The colored men of this country, having now equal rights before the law, must vindicate their own manhood, and prove by their own efforts the wisdom of the policy which has placed their destiny in their own hands." Although the Grant administration moved to uphold the election laws in New York City, federal judicial officials in the South took little action. *1870 election*

Republicans' hopes proved mistaken. Once again, violence or the threat of violence had a telling effect in several states, especially Georgia, Alabama, and North Carolina. In elections for the Forty-second Congress, Republicans saw their margin over the Democrats in the House fall by more than fifty seats, at least fifteen of which represented shifts from the Republican to the Democratic column in the South. In December Grant's annual message to Congress noted that comparative harmony had been restored in the South but that during the recent election, violence and intimidation had blocked "the free exercise of the franchise" in some states and that "the verdict of the people has thereby been reversed." Employing language that actually went beyond the terms of the Fifteenth Amendment, the president rededicated his administration to "securing a pure, untrammeled ballot, where every man entitled to cast a vote may do so, just once at each election, without fear of molestation or proscription on account of his faith, nativity, or color."[40]

Grant's reference to voting "just once" reflected Republicans' mounting anger over the use of "repeaters" and other fraudulent practices allegedly orchestrated by big-city machines, most notably New York's Tammany Hall. Although action by federal officials under the recently passed enforcement law had in the 1870 election curtailed these techniques, they did not disappear, and Republicans in the remaining weeks of the Forty-first Congress moved to strengthen enforcement strategy. The result was the Enforcement Act of February 28, 1871, which prescribed detailed procedures for federal supervisors, marshals, and other officials charged with overseeing congressional elections in cities with more than 20,000 people. In debate, Republicans rejected Democrats' charge that the bill was unconstitutional, citing the provision in Article One that Congress could supersede state regulations regarding the "times, places, and manner of holding" congressional elections. Confronting the raw practicalities of misconduct, Republicans were determined to prevent methods that they thought injured their own election prospects. But as on former occasions, the bill's supporters were convinced that they had republican principle on their side. At stake, said Illinois Representative Burton C. Cook, were "the very fundamental theories of our Government. The question, stripped of all gloss, is simply this: shall this country be governed by a majority of its citizens, or by the repeaters of the cities?" "If these frauds cannot be checked or arrested," said Ohio's William Lawrence, "republican government will become a failure."[41]

While Republicans took action against fraud in elections in northern cities, evidence mounted of increasing terrorism against blacks and their white Republican allies in the South. In January 1871 President Grant sent Congress military reports of disorders in North Carolina, and the Senate launched an investigation. Although testimony was contradictory, Republicans saw a pattern of escalating violence and of the reluctance or incapacity of states' judicial systems to quell it. The Forty-first Congress expired without taking action, but a few days after its successor convened, Grant alerted Speaker James G. Blaine to "a deplorable state of affairs" demanding Congress's "immediate attention." The situation gained urgency with news of violent outbreaks in South Carolina and Mississippi and the impeachment of North Carolina's Republican governor largely in reaction to his aggressive action against the Klan.

The crisis led to an unusual meeting of Grant, cabinet members, and congressional leaders at the Capitol, where Grant asked for a clarification of federal authority. In a special message written on the spot, the president cited the continuing violence that threatened life and property as well as federal functions such as mail service and tax collection. Noting that state authorities had failed to restore order and that the national executive's power to do so under existing laws was "not clear," Grant asked for legislation that would "effectually secure life, liberty, and property and the enforcement of law." The result was the Ku Klux Klan Act, passed on April 20, 1871. Unlike the previous enforcement legislation, this law rested principally on the Fourteenth rather than the Fifteenth Amendment and aimed to protect individuals' rights in a broader sense than the right to vote. Even so, Republicans recognized the clearly political character of the southern violence and the inseparability of civil rights in general and citizens' right of participation in the political process. As Pennsylvania Congressman William Kelley put it, Congress must not allow "those who planned and executed the rebellion, and those who sympathized with them and are now in political association with them, to accomplish by murder, conspiracy, and terror what they failed to do by open war—take possession of this Government."[42]

In the weeks-long debate that preceded the act, several themes emerged in Republicans' thinking about the momentous step they were proposing. In the first place, while conceding the ambiguity or unreliability of some reports from the South, Republicans rejected Democrats' charges that the violence had been grossly exaggerated if not wholly imagined. "If there are no outrages committed," asked one Republican congressman, "why such opposition to this measure?" Mississippi carpetbagger Henry W. Barry, his dangling right arm rendered useless by a Ku Klux bullet, warned his House colleagues that "to-day the lost cause is worshipped with more malignant fanaticism than ever." "The transition from slave to free labor has not yet been accepted as a finality by the old lords of the soil" who "still refuse to conform to their changed circumstances and pressing necessities."[43]

In resisting the enforcement bill, Democrats alleged that bad government by the Reconstruction regimes had sparked the disorders. A few Republicans agreed with them, but most rejected such reasoning as specious. According to John Sherman, the Klan perpetrated its outrages most often in counties evenly balanced between Republicans and Democrats, where "terror is necessary to enable them to carry the election." Left unchecked, such manifestly political assaults threatened to subvert the Republic: "Whenever there is a refusal to obey the laws made by the majority in due form, and whenever popular opinion in any community can override the laws, then there is no longer a republican Government; it is anarchy first, and despotism afterward."[44]

To suppress the lawless combinations and to protect individuals in their rights, Henry Wilson exhorted his colleagues to "go to the extreme verge of constitutional power." Where that proper constitutional boundary lay formed the central question for many Republicans as they struggled to balance the needs of the hour with the dictates of American federalism. Again, a few party members in Congress joined the Democrats in resisting what they considered an unwarranted expansion of national power. They warned that the proposed legislation amounted to a national criminal code that would obliterate state lines and produce "a consolidated and not a Federal Republic." In Senate debate, the foremost advocate of this position was Lyman Trumbull, the Illinois senator who had spearheaded the drive for the Civil Rights Act of 1866, but who, like Carl Schurz, had begun his migration away from Radicalism, which would culminate in his embrace of Liberal Republicanism in 1872. According to Trumbull, the framers of the Constitution had left the general rights of person and property to be protected by the states, because the "rights of the individual are safest among the people themselves." Most pointedly, Trumbull asserted that "the fourteenth amendment has not extended the rights and privileges of citizenship one iota."[45]

With this last assertion, John A. Bingham, principal framer of the Fourteenth Amendment, took vigorous exception. He argued that that amendment, along with the other two recently ratified, endowed Congress with "power to protect the rights of citizens against States, and individuals in States, never before granted." Bingham espoused what came to be called the doctrine of incorporation—the idea that the Fourteenth Amendment applies to the states the prohibitions on the national government outlined in the Bill of Rights. He argued that the "privileges and immunities" protected from state infringement by the Fourteenth Amendment were "chiefly defined in the first eight amendments to the Constitution." "This House," he declared, "may safely follow the example

George Hoar [handwritten annotation]

of the makers of the Constitution and the builders of the Republic, by passing laws for enforcing all the privileges and immunities of citizens of the United States, as guaranteed by the amended Constitution and expressly enumerated in the Constitution."[46]

George F. Hoar of Massachusetts went further and asserted that the responsibility of the national government to afford protection to citizens' rights inhered in the original Constitution itself. Hoar was at the beginning of his long tenure in Congress, during which he distinguished himself as a defender of blacks' rights. He avowed that "it was the great and leading purpose of the framers of our Constitution to place the fundamental civil rights of the people under the protection of the strongest and supremest power known to our laws, the power of the General Government." In a similar vein, Ohio Representative James Monroe saw a broad constitutional interpretation as "not the intrusion of new principles" but the "more extended application of old ones." One should not confound the "natural expansion" of constitutional authority with "a violation of the instrument itself." Monroe, a former theology professor at Oberlin College, insisted that "principles are from God," with "endless application to human affairs."[47]

Most Republicans rejected Democrats' cries against the evils of centralization. The real threat came from the opposite tendency, and Republicans in Congress pounced on a recent declaration from Jefferson Davis that "State sovereignty, although defeated in the late struggle, will eventually triumph." In the Senate, George Edmunds reminded his colleagues that it was the notion that the national government was not a government of the people but a confederated government of states that had led to the rebellion. Edmunds, chairman of the Judiciary Committee and one of the Senate's ablest constitutional lawyers, invoked the authority of Alexander Hamilton, Joseph Story, and John Marshall in upholding the power and propriety of the national government to act directly on citizens. Under existing criminal statutes, the national government did not "invade" the states but instead "exercised the constitutional omnipresence of sovereignty, and carried forward the beneficent sway of justice among the people, for the people, and by the people." Many Republicans reiterated the position that under the Fourteenth Amendment a state's refusal or inability to afford protection amounted to a denial of protection, opening the way for federal action. But Edmunds argued that the national government and not the states had authority in the first place. The states could "not finally or independently enforce or decline to enforce the Constitution of the United States." The Constitution belonged to "the whole people as a national body, . . . and therefore whatever rights are secured to the people under it, must be guaranteed to them

[handwritten: Most Republicans rejected Democrat Cries of centralization]

and made effectual for them at last through the instrumentality of the national Government, and through no other."[48]

With obvious irony, Edmunds and others drew a parallel between Congress's responsibility to enforce the Fourteenth Amendment and its antebellum responsibility to enforce the original Constitution's Fugitive Slave Clause, as confirmed by the Supreme Court in *Prigg v. Pennsylvania* in 1842. As Kansas Congressman David Lowe put it, if the power of the United States could "be used, as it was used, to return the fugitive from slavery, overriding State laws and constitutions and courts, is it too much to say that in the interest of human rights the same powers may be exercised under analogous provisions of the Constitution?"[49]

Among the Ku Klux bill's most controversial provisions was one empowering the president to suspend the writ of habeas corpus and institute martial law in violence-plagued regions. Grant's own reluctance to take such a step without congressional authority had prompted his original message on the Klan issue. In House debate, James A. Garfield, a leading moderate, argued that this section of the bill providing for "the suspension of all law" went far beyond any similar legislation "during the wildest days of the rebellion." Garfield quoted from Justice David Davis's opinion in *Ex parte Milligan* (1866) that such a step meant in essence that "republican government is a failure." Just such action by Great Britain was among the offenses that had led the nation's Fathers to declare independence. The bill's final version omitted the reference to martial law; the authorization to suspend the writ of habeas corpus remained but would expire at the end of the next session of Congress.[50]

In defending the Ku Klux bill, Republicans frequently went beyond constitutional disputation and addressed more transcendent notions of the meaning and purposes of government. Carpetbagger James Platt of Virginia, reducing the issue to its Lockean essentials, argued that "Governments are instituted among men principally for the purpose of protecting life, liberty, and property, and that when a Government fails to do this for its humblest citizen at home or abroad, it fails to perform its first and most important duty." Edmunds traced that duty back to Magna Carta, which, he said, obligated government to "execute justice and afford protection against all forms of wrong and oppression." Should the government fail to do so, then citizens were absolved from allegiance and "remitted to themselves to protect themselves as best they may."[51]

The bill's chief Republican critic was Carl Schurz, who now stood in the vanguard of Liberal Republican opposition to Grant and the Radicals on Reconstruction and other issues. Schurz also invoked transcendent principles but saw the greatest danger coming from "legislation which tends to pervert our system of government from its true plan and purpose." "I recognize it as a high duty to protect the citizens of the Republic in their rights, as far as the national authority can protect them; but I recognize it as a still higher duty to preserve intact the great institutions which form the main bulwark of our common rights and contain the greatest guarantees for our common future." But in the minds of many Republicans who saw themselves as still grappling with the potent and implacable remnant of the Slave Power Conspiracy, Schurz got the priorities just backward. "I reverence the Constitution," said Henry Wilson, "but man is more than constitutions. I honor the laws when in harmony with the higher laws of God, but I reverence and honor humanity more. Constitutions and laws were made for man, and should be so framed and so interpreted as to guard and protect the rights which the Creator has bestowed."[52]

Debate on the Ku Klux Klan Act represented an extraordinary moment in the history of Congress. Scores of legislators participated in the discussions, which many recognized as going to the heart of the Republic's mission. Most were unwilling to be rushed. "I have never suffered more perplexity of mind on any matter of legislation," Garfield wrote privately. "We are working on the very verge of the Constitution." For others, the situation was clear; as Michigan Representative Austin Blair, one of the party's founders, put it, Congress ought not to "indulge much in constitutional hair-splitting while citizens of the United States are denied the right to live." Of course, Republicans might benefit from bolstering their southern allies, especially in the next year's presidential election. But whatever the political result, Republicans could easily convince themselves and had ample justification for claiming that they were acting on high principle. Republicans must act, said John Sherman, "if we intend to retain a republican form of government, if we intend to hold up this Government of ours as a pattern for other nations." In the words of Charles Sumner, "The Republican party must do its work, which is nothing less than the regeneration of the Nation according to the promises of the Declaration of Independence."[53]

As finally passed, the Act to Enforce the Provisions of the Fourteenth Amendment, commonly known as the Ku Klux Klan Act, outlawed conspiracy to deprive persons of their constitutional rights or to interfere with officials protecting persons' constitutional rights, and it made violators liable to both criminal prosecution and civil action. It further stated that in cases where domestic violence or unlawful conspiracies deprived persons of their constitutional rights and states either refused or failed to afford protection, the president could employ the militia or the army and navy to do so and if necessary suspend the writ of habeas corpus. The law also barred Klan members from jury service in cases arising under the act. Taken altogether, the Enforcement Laws of 1870 and 1871 implied a revolution in the federal relationship. Even so, fearful that the peace of Appomattox was ebbing away, the majority of Republicans saw no alternative. Their aim, as Edmunds put it, was to ensure that "this war is a finality and that the constitutional results of it are to be accepted in good faith and that the rights of citizens are to be protected in every State, to give life to those whose life is threatened, to give the peaceable possession of property to those who are despoiled, to revive industry, to increase education, to promote happiness."[54]

Although leaders of the incipient Liberal Republican movement, such as Schurz and Trumbull, considered the new legislation too high a price to pay for the enforcement of rights in the South, most Republicans accepted its necessity. John Sherman told his constituents that the laws were needed to defeat "organized resistance to fair elections, and to punish crimes of the most revolting character against the commonest rights of humanity." Even Schurz confessed to a Chicago audience that "a majority of those who voted for the [Ku Klux Klan Act] had no other object than to afford protection to the persons in the South who seemed to be helplessly exposed to persecution and outrage." In a proclamation to the nation, President Grant noted his reluctance to use the extraordinary powers the act conferred upon him but vowed that he would not hesitate if necessity required. He urged citizens to employ local agencies and laws to secure citizens' rights and warned that their failure to do so would impose "upon the National Government the duty of putting forth all its energies for the protection of its citizens of every race and color and for the restoration of peace and order throughout the entire country."[55]

The burden of action fell to the Justice Department under Attorney General Amos Akerman, a New Englander by birth who had lived in Georgia since the 1840s, and Solicitor General Benjamin Bristow, a Kentucky native and Union army veteran. Although hampered by a lack of funds and personnel, federal officials launched a prosecutorial effort in several parts of the South that resulted in hundreds of indictments. In October 1871 Grant suspended the writ of habeas corpus in nine counties in South Carolina, which Akerman described as dominated by "systematic and organized depravity." Federal troops made hundreds of arrests. This marked the only time Grant suspended the writ, but the vigorous use of troops coupled with Akerman and Bristow's selective prosecution of Klan leaders demoralized the organization, and incidents of violence markedly declined, at least temporarily.[56]

During the first three years of Grant's term, the president and Republicans in Congress had worked together to create a structure of law and executive power to preserve the results of the war. They had refashioned the Republic's machinery in defense of republicanism itself. Still to be tested, however, was the degree to which the changes they had wrought reflected the will of the sovereign people—the ultimate sanction in a republic. From the beginning, Democrats throughout the nation and most white southerners rejected not only the new structure but the premises upon which it stood. Thus, in the end, the perpetuity of the experiment would depend on the will of northern Republicans to persevere. "I do believe that it is of the utmost importance," Grant wrote as he looked toward the election of 1872, "that the republican party should control so long as national issues remain as they now are. Without such control I believe we would lose, largely, the results of our victories in the field. . . . The 13th 14th & 15th amendments to the constitution would be dead letters." Nonetheless, by early 1872, doubt and dissension had begun to undermine Republican resolve.[57]

Republicanism Contested
The Election of 1872

The contention that crept into Republicans' deliberations concerning the enforcement structure in 1870 and 1871 accelerated during the election year of 1872. Perceptions of corruption and other problems in the Reconstruction governments fueled a debate among party leaders over the viability of their republican experiment in the South. Propositions for amnesty for ex-Confederates raised the issue of rehabilitating former rebel leaders for active participation in the new republican polity. At the same time, civil rights legislation proposed by Charles Sumner challenged Republicans to delineate the nation's responsibility for sustaining blacks' rights of republican citizenship. During the election campaign, the Liberal Republican revolt against Grant rested on many alleged grievances, but it particularly exposed deep disparities in Republicans' imagining of the new Republic.

As the election of 1872 approached, some Republicans feared that, despite the important victories in the fight against the Klan, the enforcement mechanisms for the Fifteenth Amendment were still inadequate. Nonetheless, attempts in the spring to add auxiliary provisions met little success. Congress refused to extend the habeas corpus provision of the Ku Klux Klan Act about to expire. In June Republicans did secure legislation to permit the appointment of election supervisors in any congressional district, not just cities with a population of 20,000 or more, but these new officials had no power of arrest and could do no more than observe election proceedings in the South.[1]

Grant, Morton, + ____ viewed the corrupt. Charge as a red herry — an exaggeration to justify Klan violence

34 Chapter Two

Republicans who favored stronger legislation faced mounting criticism of the Reconstruction regimes. As tales of corruption and malfeasance filtered northward, party leaders found themselves increasingly hard-pressed to defend the southern Republican governments. Even Radicals such as Oliver P. Morton admitted the existence of bad government in some states. But Morton and others saw the underlying cause for such problems in the initial resistance of southern white conservatives to the changes wrought by the war. Southern recalcitrance in the first place had moved congressional Republicans to grant the right to vote to blacks. The old master class had made blacks "ignorant and illiterate," Morton declared, and it must now "endure the consequences of the ignorance of these people and the condition in which they were placed." As for carpetbaggers, Morton defended the majority as being as honest as their critics. Many "found themselves ostracized" and "became full of bitterness, and often necessity and poverty drove them to do things that under other circumstances they would not have done."[2]

Morton and like-minded Republicans viewed the corruption charge as a red herring, a gross exaggeration used by Democrats and conservatives to explain and justify the Klan violence. They noted that the Klans had launched "their hellish work" before the Reconstruction governments had taken office and, moreover, focused their attacks not upon corruptionists but "upon the poor and the lowly, upon those who had no power to take care of themselves." "Even if those governments were as bad as represented," said Tennessee Congressman Horace Maynard, "tell me what excuse that would be for men high in character and position to burn the churches and school-houses of the colored people." The sad truth, said Luke Poland of Vermont, was that they "still expect and require that the negroes shall exhibit the same cringing submission in their conduct and behavior to the whites as when they were slaves." At bottom, wrote Attorney General Amos Akerman, "the southern people are still untaught in the elements of the republican creed."[3]

Still, as much as Republicans might recognize the truth in such analysis, many exhibited a growing sense of futility regarding the South. Instead of strengthening the enforcement acts in the spring of 1872, they moved to lift the political disabilities imposed by the Fourteenth Amendment from all but a few hundred ex-Confederate leaders. Since the adoption of the Amendment in the summer of 1868, Congress had passed special acts removing the disabilities for almost 5,000 former rebels—nearly everyone who requested it. In April 1871 such a general amnesty bill garnered the necessary two-thirds vote in the House of Representatives. By that time all ex-Confederates could vote, and the disabilities in question related only to officeholding.

Because amnesty would affect a relatively small number of individuals, the

Charges of corruption by Negro office holders a red herring

issue was largely symbolic, but Republicans on both sides saw the symbolism as important. Black Congressman Robert B. Elliott of South Carolina said that the measure implied that "Congress desires to hand over the loyal men of the South to the tender mercies of the rebels who to-day are murdering and scourging the loyal men of the southern States." On the other side, Poland, who favored extending the Ku Klux Klan Act, supported removal of disabilities, which served only "to irritate and annoy and to keep up these very disturbances of which we complain." More than 40 percent of the House Republicans, including three of Elliott's black colleagues, agreed with Poland and voted with the Democrats in support of the bill. Although the Senate failed to act on amnesty before the close of the first session of the Forty-second Congress, the drift of opinion was clear.[4]

When the second session convened in December 1871, Grant lent his endorsement, although he suggested that Congress might wish to continue the disability of the rebellion's "great criminals." A few weeks later the Senate took up the House bill, which called for amnesty for all ex-Confederates except former members of the U.S. Congress and army and navy officers who had resigned their positions to aid the rebellion, and members of southern state conventions who had voted for secession. Variants of this proposition occupied the Senate on and off for the next several months.[5]

By this time amnesty enjoyed wide support among Republicans, but as the 1872 election loomed, the issue became entangled in presidential politics. Both regular Republicans who favored Grant's reelection and Liberal Republicans who opposed the president saw amnesty as a way to appeal for white southern support. Liberals, stressing reconciliation over recrimination, invoked the issue to condemn what they considered Grant's failed and wrong-headed southern policy. Senator Lyman Trumbull, a leading contender for the Liberal Republican presidential nomination, said that removing disabilities would do more than any other action "to restore harmony throughout the country." Carl Schurz once again rang the changes on the "rascality and ignorance" allegedly plaguing the reconstruction governments and welcomed amnesty as restoring influence to "the more intelligent classes of southern society [who had] almost universally identified themselves with the rebellion." After a rebellion, Schurz argued, punishment was more a matter of policy than of justice. Rebellion was more pardonable than a regular crime because political opinion, rather than "moral depravity," was its "principal ingredient." Because "even the most disastrous political conflicts may be composed for the common good by a conciliatory process," amnesty was not only generous but wise.[6]

Such reasoning infuriated party regulars like Morton, who recoiled at the idea that the rebellion was "a mere difference between parties, which unfortunately came to blows." In Morton's view, its leaders had committed a crime whose consequences were "more terrible" than those of all the other crimes committed since the founding of the government. A half million deaths and three or four billion dollars could not be conciliated away, and universal amnesty would be inhumane and immoral. Yet even Morton was willing to vote for the pending legislation, because it excluded from amnesty "the principal authors of the rebellion."[7]

Although many of the Grant Republicans continued to believe that the rebel leaders had gotten off easily, they conceded that expediency favored amnesty. Political disabilities had been a festering source of irritation to many leading southerners who exploited their status to incite hatred of the national government, the Reconstruction regimes, and the Republican Party. Nor had the policy assured protection to the loyal element in the South or prevented anyone from joining the Ku Klux Klan. Moreover, some former Confederates might make good public officials. Frederick Sawyer of South Carolina owed his Senate seat largely to black voters but told his colleagues that amnesty was "a means for quieting the South, and so benefiting the whole country." In sum, although Republicans saw political advantage in amnesty, they also deemed it vital to foster harmony, not only within the South but also among the sections and varied interests in the nation as a whole. Only by stimulating such harmony could they hope to restore the Republic to its accustomed proper workings.[8]

The removal of political disabilities might have sailed through Congress but for the steadfast attempt by Charles Sumner to tack onto it his Supplementary Civil Rights bill. The prolonged debate on amnesty dealt as much with this proposal as with amnesty itself. Designed to build on the Civil Rights Act of 1866, Sumner's amendment proposed to outlaw discrimination by railroads and other carriers, hotels and other public accommodations, public schools, and places of public amusement such as theaters, as well as churches, cemeteries, and benevolent institutions incorporated by law. It also banned discrimination in jury selection. "Now is the time," Sumner wrote George William Curtis, "to secure this immense boon, which is the final fulfillment of the promises of the Declaration of Indep[endence]." Although many Republicans supported the proposal in principle, some charged that Sumner's chief aim was to kill the amnesty bill, which required a two-thirds vote, by attaching sections unacceptable to the Democrats. Sumner denied the charge, noting that when he had introduced his civil rights proposal as a freestanding bill requiring only a majority vote, it had received little attention. Attaching it to amnesty would force a debate.[9]

More important, Sumner argued, there was justice in linking the two. Legislation on civil rights would remove burdensome "disabilities" from the former slaves, just as amnesty would remove political disabilities from former Confed-

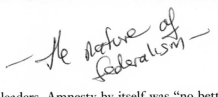 — the nature of federalism —

erate leaders. Amnesty by itself was "no better than the half of a pair of scissors." Amnesty and equal rights together formed "a measure of reconciliation, intended to close the issues of the war." Because equality was "the great issue" of the Civil War, the Union victory would be "vain without the grander victory" of enacting the "self-evident truth declared by our fathers" in 1776. For Sumner, equality of rights was "the soul of republican institutions, without which a Republic is a failure, a mere name and nothing more. Call it a Republic if you will, but it is in reality a soulless mockery."[10]

Leading the fight against Sumner's amendment was Liberal Republican Lyman Trumbull. Although the Illinois senator had been the principal author of the Civil Rights Act of 1866, he now took the position that "perfect equality" prevailed, that the rights of whites and blacks "are now the same in all these respects," and that under the common law, blacks complaining of discrimination could seek redress in the courts. In response, George Edmunds reminded Trumbull that Andrew Johnson had met his civil rights bill six years earlier with the same arguments about rights already grounded in the common law and that Trumbull had then asserted that "an act declaring what the law is is one of the most common acts passed by legislative bodies." John Sherman noted that Trumbull's earlier act had dealt with the right to make contracts, sue, deal in real estate, and the like. "How," he asked, "can you say it is a civil right to make a lease and not a civil right to travel in a public conveyance?"[11]

For many Republicans, Sumner's proposal once more raised serious questions as to the nature of federalism. Although in the debate over the Fifteenth Amendment Connecticut's Orris Ferry had denounced notions of state sovereignty as the great danger to the Republic, he now complained that Sumner's bill left "absolutely nothing" to the states. Insisting that "local self-government" had always been the "great security" for life, liberty, and property, Ferry waxed poetic about the "beneficent effects and influences" of such government as practiced in the New England town meeting. Similarly, with a states-rights strict constructionist view of the Constitution worthy of the Democrats, Maine Senator Lot Morrill asserted that the matters treated in Sumner's bill "all belong exclusively to the State." Moreover, the Fourteenth Amendment merely limited state action and in no way expanded the authority of the federal government. Neither was the Declaration of Independence "a grant of power" or "in any sense a warrant for legislative action." "An appeal to the moral forces of the age," said Morrill, "should not be sufficient to justify the action of a Senator when action under the Constitution is in question."[12]

Defenders of Sumner's amendment conceded the need for a balanced federal relationship but insisted that the measure would not disturb "the harmony of the system." For his part, Sumner was less interested in constitutional hairsplit-

[handwritten margin notes: "M tones that anticipated (use in Epilogue)"]

ting than in asserting the supremacy of the Declaration: "It is earlier in time; it is loftier, more majestic, more sublime in character and principle."[13]

As was later true in the twentieth-century struggle over civil rights, the most controversial portion of Sumner's amendment was its ban on separation of the races in the public common schools. Senators Arthur Boreman of West Virginia and James Alcorn of Mississippi, both former governors who had launched public school systems in their states, stoutly defended what later came to be known as the doctrine of "separate but equal." Boreman claimed that the school laws of his state "apply precisely to the one as they do to the other." Alcorn, elected to the Senate by both blacks and whites in the state legislature, declared that both races opposed mixed schools. Ferry noted that mixed schools prevailed in his hometown of Norwalk, Connecticut, but he would not "judge other communities by that community." Most important, he warned, any attempt to use federal legislation to dictate the management of local schools would be "fatal to the school system of the country." Lyman Trumbull stated flatly, "The right to go to school is not a civil right and never was."[14]

Sumner and his allies defended the school provision in tones that anticipated the stirring call to racial justice of *Brown v. Board of Education.* "It is not enough that all should be taught alike," said Sumner; "they must all be taught together." Otherwise, the black child "is pinched and dwarfed while the stigma of color is stamped upon him." Henry Wilson avowed that "equality in the primary schools" would "educate the rising generation of the country to forget caste and believe in the equality of our common humanity." The usually stolid John Sherman drew pictures of white and black children playing together and sitting on the same benches in the mixed schools of Ohio, where, despite fears of social equality, "all difficulty has entirely disappeared." "Boys and girls," he said, "are much more sensible, and much more logical, and much more tolerant than men and women." Therein lay hope for the future, but for now, Sherman insisted, "when we have made them voters we cannot by our laws stamp them with a stain of degradation." Sumner likewise drew the connection between political rights and civil rights: "How can you expect the colored child or the white child to grow up to those relations which they are to have together at the ballot-box if you begin by degrading the colored child at the school and by exalting the white child at the school?" Instead, "the common school [should be] the benign example of republican institutions where merit is the only ground of favor."[15]

In addition to their caution on the school issue, some Republicans hesitated to apply federal law to churches, cemeteries, and state juries. Reservations were strong enough that Sumner succeeded in attaching his amendment to the amnesty bill only with a tie-breaking vote of Vice President Schuyler Colfax. With civil rights added to amnesty, no Democrat would vote for it. On the same day,

February 9, the bill fell short of the necessary two-thirds, with thirty-three Republicans voting in favor and eight Republicans plus eleven Democrats against.[16]

The issue of amnesty lay dormant in Congress until early May, when the Liberal Republican national convention meeting in Cincinnati endorsed the "immediate and absolute removal of all disabilities." Liberals hoped to strengthen their cause by attracting white southerners to link arms with northern Republicans disenchanted with Grant. Scarcely was the ink on the platform dry when Senate Republicans moved to consider another amnesty bill passed by the House in January. Again Sumner sought to attach his civil rights bill, again Colfax broke a tie vote to do so, and again the amended bill failed to receive a two-thirds majority.[17]

Unwilling to let Congress adjourn without some amnesty legislation, Republicans in the House sponsored and passed yet another bill, this one excluding ex-Confederates who had previously served as members of the Thirty-sixth and Thirty-seventh Congresses; judicial, military, and naval officers; heads of departments; or foreign ministers of the United States. The measure had broad support in the Senate, but a majority of Republicans still hesitated to endorse amnesty without going on record for civil rights as well. In an all-night session, they forced consideration of a freestanding civil rights bill, considerably narrower than Sumner's, that outlawed discrimination in public accommodations, places of amusement, and common carriers. With more than two-fifths of the senators, including Sumner, absent, this bill passed. When the Senate proceeded to take up amnesty, Sumner arrived and again moved to add his civil rights bill. This time he failed, and the Senate passed the amnesty bill; Sumner was one of only two Republicans to vote against it. When Sumner tried to get the vote on the weakened civil rights bill reconsidered, the Senate refused. Thus defeated, Sumner lashed out at his Republican colleagues, accusing them of having "paltered with" blacks' rights. This was too much for men such as Frederick Sawyer of South Carolina, who said Sumner had "no right to crack the whip of his arrogance" over senators who could not be considered "false to the colored people" because they were "willing to take for them all that this Congress will give." In the end, the House failed to pass the watered-down civil rights bill.[18]

As the heated exchange between Sumner and Sawyer suggested, the questions of section and race would figure largely in the 1872 election campaign. Just seven years after Appomattox, the key issue that had united the diverse elements of the Republican coalition in the 1850s and 1860s now acted as a wedge driving it apart. Although the contest between Grant and Horace Greeley has often been portrayed as a campaign of personalities, the struggle that year also represented an important moment of self-definition for the Republican Party. The call for the Liberal Republicans' national convention invited all Republicans to engage in the work of reform based on "the vital principles of true Republicanism." For their part, regular Republicans deplored the Liberal revolt as fundamentally dangerous to the party's ideals. As the platform of the Illinois state convention argued, for the preservation of Republicanism "the past acts of the Republican party are a better guarantee than the mere resolutions of the new party." At the center of the debate were two opposing notions regarding the national Republic that had emerged from the Civil War. The Liberals, seeking to lay sectional animosities to rest, hoped to rekindle the sentimental nationalism of the antebellum period, with northerners and southerners accepting a common destiny borne of fellow feeling rather than coercion. Regular Republicans, on the other hand, embraced a nationalism that reflected a new federal relationship wrought by the war, whereby the national government would play a more activist role in charting the nation's destiny and protecting the individual's rights.[19]

Men joined the Liberal Republican movement for a variety of reasons, including factionalism within their own state parties, disgruntlement with Grant over patronage slights, and disenchantment with administration policies on issues ranging from the tariff and the currency to civil service reform and Grant's attempt to annex Santo Domingo. The roots of an antiadministration organization first took hold in the 1870 elections in Missouri, where Carl Schurz led a group of Republican defectors into a coalition with Democrats on the basis of shared opposition to a state-based disfranchisement of former Confederates. When the movement quickly won adherents in other parts of the nation, support for amnesty and opposition to Grant's Reconstruction policy in general formed one of its chief ingredients. At their national convention in Cincinnati, Liberal Republicans argued that the issues lingering after the war had been settled by the Thirteenth, Fourteenth, and Fifteenth Amendments. Insisting that "universal amnesty will result in complete pacification in all sections of the country," they praised local self-government over "centralized power" and called for "a return to the methods of peace and the constitutional limitations of power." The anomalous nomination of Horace Greeley, who vehemently opposed freer trade and was lukewarm to civil service reform, ensured that these issues would count for little in the reform party's campaign. Grant's approval of a 10 percent reduction in tariff rates and of new rules framed by the Civil Service Commission further undercut these issues for the Liberals. Hence, Greeley focused his appeal on the sectional issue, and "reconciliation" became the byword of his election bid.[20]

For this work Greeley was well suited. As editor of the *New York Tribune* he had long advocated amnesty, and he had won the affection of many south-

"Let Us Clasp Hands Over the Bloody Chasm." —Horace Greeley. *Harper's Weekly,*
September 21, 1872.

erners by signing on Jefferson Davis's bail bond. It was time, he said, "to clasp
hands across the bloody chasm." Although he had spent most of his career as
an unrelenting critic of the Democrats, by the time their national convention
met at Baltimore, they saw no alternative but to give him the party's presidential nomination. The Democrats also accepted the Liberal Republican platform,
thus endorsing such wonted Republican tenets as "the equality of all men before
the law" and the legitimacy of the Reconstruction amendments. Such was the
fluidity of party lines in 1872 and the Democrats' desperation to dethrone Grant
and the Republicans.

In accepting the Democrats' nomination, Greeley hailed the identical platforms as signaling "a genuine new departure from outworn feuds." But he laid
greatest stress on amnesty. Even though a scant few hundred men remained
outside the pale, he said, their political disabilities denied millions in the South
"the right to be ruled and represented by the men of their unfettered choice."
If by blocking amnesty other sections of the country could dictate the choice of
elected officials "for states remote from and unlike their own . . . then Republican institutions were unfit and aristocracy the only true political system."[21]

Breaking with tradition, Greeley took an extended campaign tour, reiterating the theme of national reconciliation at virtually every stop. With little more

to offer, he stressed the symbolic importance of universal amnesty. As long as any Confederate leaders suffered under disabilities, he said, "no part of that great people" of the South "will feel that they are entirely pardoned and restored to citizenship." Only universal amnesty could revive "fraternity South and North." At times Greeley seemed to rewrite history. For most southerners, he claimed, the "secession movement [had] meant nothing" more than a ploy to get the North to agree to the expansion of slavery. During the war, "prisoners were not unjustly treated; but . . . the people on both sides meant to treat them with humanity so far as they could do so." Since the war, the South had "fully complied" with "every single demand made on the part of the loyal States." In Ohio's Western Reserve, a hotbed of abolitionism before the war, he confidently proclaimed that "the Democratic Party has abandoned all hostility to equal rights for men of every color" and, hence, "there will never again be a serious question as to the equal rights of all citizens." In short, Greeley urged all Americans to take heart that a "renovated Republic" had been "founded on the overthrow of the Confederacy"—a new Republic with "new circumstances, new conditions, new duties" that southerners were willing to fulfill.[22]

Greeley's appeal for accommodation of sectional differences had a paradoxical impact on the thinking and the electoral strategy of regular Republicans. On the one hand, embracing reconciliation, they gave overwhelming support to the general (not universal) amnesty law passed in May, and Grant quickly issued a proclamation giving it effect. The party's national convention "heartily approve[d]" the legislation and welcomed the growth of "fraternal feeling in the land." In his letter accepting renomination, the president expressed his "desire to see a speedy healing of all bitterness of feeling between sections, parties, or races of citizens." Yet the Liberals' eagerness to abandon Reconstruction, their coalition with the Democratic party still dominated by southerners, and Greeley's pressing the American people to a kind of sectional amnesia, all combined to deepen Republicans' conviction that maintaining the war's results depended on Republican victory. "Can it be," wrote Secretary of State Hamilton Fish, "that the people of this country are so soon to recommit the destinies of the Nation to the control of those who so recently attempted its overthrow[?]" American Minister to France Elihu Washburne found it "monstrous to think of the possibility of our defeat and the consequent loss of all we fought for in the suppression of the rebellion." A similar dread hung about the Republican National Committee rooms in New York. Party secretary William E. Chandler wrote Washburne, "As I see the issues that are before us, and the efforts made under the disguise of Greeleyism, aided by murder at the South, to put Copperheads and rebels in supreme power in this country, I feel that I would rather lose my right arm than fail to do everything possible to continue in control the Republican party."[23] *Stalkg horse*

With such fears powerfully augmenting the natural partisan imperative to retain power, Republicans moved on the attack, waging what their opponents and later historians would disparage as an aggressive "bloody shirt" campaign. Grant did no speaking, but other party leaders hammered away at Greeley's brand of "reconciliation" as a stalking-horse for surrender to dangerous Democratic doctrines. At Cooper Institute, Roscoe Conkling told his audience that amnesty was a dead issue. Of far greater importance was the "real danger" posed by "State Rights in the old pestilent sense," which had "ushered in rebellion" *Conkling* and still threatened "a brood of dire heresies." Instead, Americans must embrace the Republicans' beneficent "centralism" and "strong and stable Government, under which the nation prospers, with safety to property, labor, liberty and life." Whereas Greeley urged Americans to clasp hands across "the bloody chasm," New Yorker Edwards Pierrepont reminded them who had "dug the chasm and filled it up with blood." It was time "to stop this senseless cant about the way the South have been treated." As long as southerners "*allow* scourgings and torture, and murder of innocent men, for opinion['s] sake," said Pierrepont, "they cannot expect peace, influx of capital and new population, or any great prosperity."[24]

As Secretary of the Treasury George S. Boutwell cast the sectional issue, it was less about the South's past behavior than the Democrats' future behavior. He told an audience in Greensboro, North Carolina, that the feelings of hostility generated by the war were "passing away." But Greeley's talk about clasping hands was simply a cover for "the old and dangerous advice of the Democratic party," which would "commit to the States exclusively the business of protecting the citizen." "If you are wise," he cautioned, "you will never trust your liberties and immunities to a party that denies their justness." The venerable abolitionist Gerrit Smith warned northern voters against believing that alliance with the Liberals would somehow rework the Democratic party, which had "sinned too long and too deeply to be capable of repentance." Greeley's election would "turn him into a Democrat," said Smith. "Sad day would it be for the negro if the impenitent, unchanged, and unchangeable Democratic party should come again into the ascendant."[25]

The question of race played a central role in the campaign. Democrats who were past masters at racist invective now affected to espouse a "new departure," dropping terms such as *nigger* from their partisan rhetoric. But Greeley, though denouncing Klan "lawlessness and violence," nonetheless sought to play upon racial prejudice. As early as 1870 he had described blacks as "an easy, worthless race, taking no thought of the morrow." Now during his campaign, he complained that "ignorant" blacks were "misapprehending and misrepresenting" him. In tones foreshadowing twentieth-century arguments about "reverse discrimination," Greeley claimed that with the recent constitutional amendments, "there is no longer reason for contention concerning the rights of black men" and people were now demanding that "the white man of this country shall have equal rights with the black men."

Greeley's vice presidential running mate, Benjamin Gratz Brown, was even more brazen, telling an Indianapolis crowd that in the South "the passions of the blacks have been persistently incited to hostility against the whites." "Would it be peace to-day in Indiana," he asked, "if a negro population, largely ignorant of the laws of wealth, of society, of civil government, were upheld *in organizing as a race to rule over you in subserviance [sic] to some political aggrandizement?*" Greeley was careful to connect such rhetoric to his arguments for reenfranchising ex-Confederates through amnesty, but few listeners could mistake the racial message. As New York Democrat and 1868 presidential nominee Horatio Seymour confided to Samuel J. Tilden, Greeley might be hard to swallow as their party's nominee, but at least "he can be made of use in driving negroes out of office."[26]

For no Republican was the 1872 campaign and especially the race issue more troubling than for Charles Sumner. Impelled by an almost pathological hatred for Grant, Sumner had delivered a blistering attack on the eve of the Republican national convention in the vain hope of thwarting his renomination. On the Senate floor he arraigned Grant for a host of alleged offenses including nepotism, gift-taking, quarrelsomeness, and incompetence as well as a "Caesarism, or *personalism,* abhorrent to republican institutions." Sumner strained to find some deficiency in Grant's attitude toward blacks and repeated his earlier fierce opposition to the administration's attempt to annex Santo Domingo. Grant saw Santo Domingo as a potential haven for American blacks who could employ the threat of emigration to gain better treatment in the South, but Sumner accused him of seizing the nation's war power to menace Santo Domingo's neighbor, the "Black Republic" of Haiti, thereby "treading under foot" one of the Constitution's "most distinctive republican principles." Sumner arraigned Grant for slighting Frederick Douglass, who was involved in the Dominican negotiations, a charge Douglass dismissed as "ridiculous." In early May, at a critical moment in Sumner's fight for his supplementary civil rights bill, the president had issued a public letter strongly endorsing "any effort to secure for all our people, of whatever race, nativity or color, the exercise of those rights to which every citizen should be entitled." Now, in his Senate indictment, Sumner perversely dismissed Grant's endorsement as a "meaningless juggle of words, entirely worthy of the days of slavery." Whereas most of the Liberal Republicans saw overzealous execution of the Enforcement Acts as one of Grant's chief abuses, Sumner charged that he had exhibited "little efficiency" in pursuit of the Ku Klux Klan and had never "exhibited to the colored people any true sympathy."[27]

Despite all Grant's faults, however, Sumner did not rush to endorse Greeley, whom he considered far from the ideal replacement. Finally, prompted by a group of black leaders eager for his advice, he endorsed Greeley in a public letter that covered much of the same ground as his Senate speech. In addition, he reminded blacks that before the war Greeley had been a "foremost" abolitionist, whereas Grant, as a Buchanan Democrat, had "fortified by his vote all the pretensions of slavery." Sumner denied that under Greeley blacks would "in any way suffer in their equal rights." Grant, on the other hand, deserved impeachment rather than renomination, if for nothing else for his imperialist policies and "his indignity to the Black Republic" of Haiti. Echoing the Liberal Republican nominee, the senator called for "peace and harmony instead of discord." Previously, Sumner had typically censured any violation of his own notion of civil rights as the persistence of "slavery." Now he avowed, "I am against fanning ancient flames into continued life." He called for "reconciliation, not only between the North and South, but between the two races, so that . . . instead of *irritating antagonism* without end, there shall be *sympathetic cooperation*."[28]

With this letter Sumner relinquished much of his claim to the captaincy of the movement for black rights. House Speaker James G. Blaine dashed off a public response telling the senator that when blacks "read your letter they will know that at a great crisis in their fate you deserted them." Frederick Douglass issued a call to black voters to reject "the insidious and dangerous advice and counsel of Mr. Sumner." "With Grant, our security is unquestionable," said Douglass. "With Greeley, we would enter upon a sea of trouble . . . and the great work of the Republican Party [would] prove an abortion." Republican Party leaders remained justifiably confident that, as New Yorker John Jay put it, blacks would "stand by the party to whom they owe their emancipation." The central issue, said Blaine, was whether "the rights of the colored men are [to be] absolutely sacrificed so far as those rights depend on Federal legislation."[29]

Grant won a smashing victory over Greeley, taking 56 percent of the popular vote and posting a four-to-one margin in the electoral college. Greeley won only six states, all in the South. Clearly the president still enjoyed widespread popularity, and the New York editor had proved an ineffectual challenger. But the very ineffectuality of the Greeley campaign and the candidate's repulsiveness to many Democrats tempered the Republicans' jubilation. Several states posted substantial declines in the Democratic vote from 1868, but in Blaine's estimate, Grant's "great majorities were not normal, and did not indicate the real strength

Grant - Widespread popularity

[handwritten top margin: Liberal Republicans called for sectional reconciliation but seemingly at the expense of black rights]

of parties." The Democrats were hardly on the road to extinction. Moreover, although Liberal Republicanism collapsed as a freestanding party, its demise did not herald a happy restoration of Republican unity. Some Midwestern Liberal leaders such as Lyman Trumbull and George W. Julian cast their lot with the Democrats, as did Carl Schurz eventually, after many years of carping at opponents from inside the party. Northeasterners tended to drift back into the Republican fold, but they formed the core of an emerging "independent" wing often at odds with regular party leaders.[30]

But the Liberal Republicans' fervent call for sectional reconciliation seemingly at the expense of blacks' rights did serve to solidify blacks' support for the regular Republicans. A few weeks after the election Grant received a delegation of African American leaders who declared that because he was "the first President of the United States elected by the whole people," he stood as "the practical embodiment of our republican theories." In response, Grant endorsed their "desire to obtain all the rights of citizens" and avowed his "wish that every voter of the United States should stand in all respects alike."[31]

In the end, however, the anomalous character of the contest between Grant and Greeley left in doubt the question of how long white Republicans would be willing or able to mobilize federal authority to uphold blacks' rights. Republicans had retained national power in 1872, but their triumph had brought them no closer to a satisfactory solution to the southern question—a solution that met the requirements of republicanism and that also had any prospect for permanence. Despite the failure of the Liberals' electoral challenge, their revolt augured a persistent critique of an interventionist southern policy. In the ensuing years, Republicans would find it increasingly difficult to mount a united defense of their republican project.

[handwritten bottom margin: Even though Grant & the Republicans won a smashing victory, the dark clouds hovered on the horizon.]

The Republican Project under Siege

The Grant Administration and the
Trial of Enforcement

[handwritten notes:]
— Grant tried Conciliation
pardon for Klansmen
+ others Convicted under Enforcement Act
— won few friends among southern conservatives
— Democrats moved away for their "New
Departure" of 1870 and reverted
— after yielding meager results with their
alliance with Liberal Republicans, Democrats
reverted to racist political & social
Strategy

When Ulysses Grant launched his second term in the White House, he and his Republican allies still hoped to maintain a permanent shield for the republican results of the war. As the term unfolded, however, circumstances rendered the pursuit of that goal with any degree of consistency all the more difficult. Carrying forward the election-year theme of conciliation, Grant adopted a liberal policy of pardon for Klansmen and others convicted under the Enforcement Acts, hoping that such clemency would "tranquilize the public mind." In addition, the Justice Department cut enforcement efforts and by mid-1873 had abandoned prosecution in all but the most egregious cases of violence. But these gestures won few friends among southern conservatives. Democrats saw little use in continuing their lip service to the new departure in racial and sectional relations that their campaign alliance with the Liberal Republicans had dictated. After reaping meager results by that approach, white southerners reverted to racist political and social strategies. Delaware Senator Eli Saulsbury unabashedly told his colleagues, when the Democratic Party "again proclaims the superiority of the white race over the colored race, then will the banner of Democracy once more float triumphantly in the breeze." Within the South, in places where Republicans still held control, conservatives took that lesson to heart and conciliation gave way to intense challenges for power. The result was a steady erosion of the republican project in the South and a growing realiza-

[handwritten notes:]
a steady erosion of Republican power
erosion [the___]   in the South

[handwritten: limits to Republican idea + strategy]

tion by Grant and other Republicans of the limits to the national government's capacity to preserve it.[1] *[handwritten: LOUISIANA]*

Nowhere was the battle for power bloodier or more consequential than in Louisiana, whose tangled politics epitomized the supreme difficulty of managing Reconstruction from Washington. Factional struggles had long plagued Louisiana politics, and in 1872 both major contending parties claimed victory in the gubernatorial and legislative elections. The regular or Grant Republicans stood by their nominee for governor, William Kellogg, against John McEnery, a fusion candidate backed by Democrats and a Republican faction led by outgoing carpetbag governor, Henry Warmoth. Charges and countercharges of fraud, as well as complex legal maneuvering, cast a pall of obscurity over which side had actually won. Nonetheless, the Kellogg forces secured court orders from federal Judge E. H. Durell sustaining their position. In effect recognizing the Kellogg camp, the Grant administration ordered the U.S. marshal to enforce Judge Durell's orders, employing U.S. troops as needed. Nonetheless, the McEnery forces erected a rival government. In mid-January 1873, both Kellogg and McEnery were inaugurated as governor. Their forces organized two separate legislatures, and across the state the factions established competing parish governments.[2]

The anomalous situation inevitably drew the attention of Congress, and Republicans found their party as fragmented as it had been over amnesty and civil rights during the previous session. Whether Congress ought to do anything at all, because at issue was a state election, was an important question. Those who saw a congressional role relied on the Constitution's stipulation in Article Four that the federal government should guarantee to every state a republican form of government. Because the election had been indeterminate, Massachusetts Radical Ben Butler, a vehement exponent of intervention in the South, argued for new, federally supervised balloting in Louisiana, "to take care she has a republican government in fact representing the wishes of the people." Other House Republicans argued that the state's courts constituted the appropriate tribunal to determine the election outcome. In the end, the House simply directed its Judiciary Committee to study whether any action was necessary.[3]

Senate Republicans showed scarcely more agreement. Some were inclined to leave the matter to the courts, but the majority instructed the Senate's own Committee on Privileges and Elections to investigate and determine whether Louisiana had a legal government. After a month of testimony, the committee's report hardly clarified the issue. All its members agreed that the grossest sort of fraud had marred the election, but they differed widely as to a response. Speaking for the committee majority, Matthew Carpenter of Wisconsin presented a bill mandating a new election under federal supervision. The committee chairman, Oliver P. Morton, filed a separate report that declared that if the election had been honest, with no hindrance to black voting, Kellogg would have won, and he thus held a just claim as governor. Liberal Republican Lyman Trumbull accused Kellogg of usurpation and considered McEnery the rightful governor. Rhode Island's Henry Anthony hesitated to endorse Carpenter's bill and vaguely hoped for some "better remedy."[4]

Amid this confusion and with less than a week remaining before the Forty-second Congress would expire and before Grant's second inauguration, the president urged Congress to find some "practical way of removing these difficulties by legislation." "I am extremely anxious to avoid any appearance of undue interference in State affairs," he said, but unless Congress decided otherwise, he would continue to support the government "upheld by the courts"—that is, the Kellogg regime.[5]

Much of the Senate discussion rehashed the conflicting evidence from the committee's investigation, but important themes also emerged. Morton invoked the limitations of federalism against Carpenter's bill mandating a new election, but for Carpenter, the overriding principle was the Constitution's guarantee clause. A state's government, he said, "on paper may be republican and yet it may be so administered as to be anti-republican." The real test was "whether it rests upon the consent of the people. If it does not, it is not republican." In Carpenter's view, the Kellogg government failed that test. From the Liberal Republican perspective, Carl Schurz claimed that the McEnery regime was in fact "the rightful republican government"; the federal government need only withdraw its support from the Kellogg faction, and McEnery would properly gain power. But Carpenter argued that pulling out altogether would abandon Louisiana blacks "to be slaughtered like sheep on the streets." Republicans, he declared, were "answerable to the people of this country for the conduct of this business, and we are answerable to our constituents, to our consciences, and to our God for our part in it." In the end Morton held sway, and by a narrow vote the Senate rejected Carpenter's bill calling for new elections. Still, the intractability of the Louisiana case and Republicans' deep divisions augured further troubles. Having forsaken their initial rigor in Reconstruction, said Texas scalawag Senator James Flanagan, Republicans were now "at sea without compass or rudder," moving into "a maelstrom of destruction."[6]

Nonetheless, the administration was encouraged by deceptive reports from Kellogg regarding his strength. Grant and Attorney General George Williams hoped that by taking no action against the McEnery forces the administration would deny them the status of martyrs and they would gradually lose strength. The president drew on this spirit in preparing his second inaugural. He carried forward a theme implicit in the Republicans' 1872 campaign: sectional harmony and defense of the freedmen's rights were not necessarily incompatible. He pledged to direct his efforts "to the restoration of good feeling between the different sections of our common country." But he also stated that blacks did not yet enjoy "the civil rights which citizenship should carry with it," and he promised to work to correct that wrong "so far as Executive influence can avail." He denied that legislation could effect "social equality" but thought that Americans should accord the new black citizen "a fair chance to develop what there is good in him, give him access to the schools, and when he travels let him feel assured that his conduct will regulate the treatment and fare he will receive." Perhaps with his fingers crossed—at least regarding Louisiana—Grant claimed that the former Confederate states were "now happily rehabilitated" and suffered no "Executive control" that would not be used in other states "under like circumstances." The president voiced his "firm conviction that the civilized world is tending toward republicanism, or government by the people through their chosen representatives, and that our own great Republic is destined to be the guiding star to all others."[7] WISHFUL THINKING

As Grant no doubt realized, his sanguine view of republicanism's prospects, which befitted the inaugural ritual, partook more of wishful thinking than sound analysis. Indeed, the next day in New Orleans, McEnery's militia and a mob of 600 armed men assaulted a police station, requiring the intervention of U.S. troops for their dispersal. A month later, rural Grant Parish witnessed the worst racial violence during all of Reconstruction. The incident at the new parish's county seat at Colfax began when rumors of impending white violence impelled scores of black Republicans to take refuge in a stable that served as the improvised courthouse. On Easter Sunday, April 13, 1873, a small army of whites headed by McEnery Democrats opened fire, then set the stable ablaze and systematically shot blacks as they fled. The whites captured and shot three to four dozen other blacks. According to an investigation, 105 blacks and 3 whites died. After a week, federal troops reached the town and began arresting perpetrators of the massacre, thereby inaugurating a federal court case, *U.S. v. Cruikshank*, that profoundly affected the course of Reconstruction.[8]

Although violence never again reached the scale at Colfax, the McEnery forces continued to purge Republican parish officials. On May 22, Grant issued a proclamation commanding the insurgents to disperse and authorizing the use of troops against them. Afterward, the direct challenge to Kellogg's position as governor subsided somewhat, but guerrilla warfare against his adherents continued in rural areas. The chaos in Louisiana illustrated the ultimate futility of the Republican program of Reconstruction as a whole. White conservatives remained determined to do whatever was necessary to reverse the results of the war to the greatest extent possible short of reinstating legal slavery. They had already gained control in several southern states and were prepared for a protracted struggle to overcome northern and federal government efforts to prevent their taking the rest. In the face of that determination, some Republicans began to doubt the capacity of southern blacks to meet the challenge. James A. Garfield lamented a "want of 'set' in the Negro character." As "untempered mortar in the national temple," the former slaves seemed weak material for the work of rebuilding the Republic. Hence, northerners must still rally to the cause. Representative Henry Dawes told an audience at Greenfield, Massachusetts, "There should be no more peace nor rest in the Executive Department of this government till that security which peace alone can bring shall be carried to the door of the humblest hut in Louisiana."[9]

That task grew more difficult, however, in the wake of a Supreme Court decision issued the day after the Colfax massacre. In the famous *Slaughter-House Cases* (1873), butchers in New Orleans challenged a state health law that confined livestock slaughtering to a certain section of the city in the facilities of a single state-chartered corporation. Although the statute allowed any butcher admission to the facilities for a fee, the complaining butchers alleged that it created a monopoly. They based their claim for relief on the Thirteenth and Fourteenth Amendments. The court rejected their assertion in an opinion by Associate Justice Samuel Miller, an antislavery Republican appointed by Abraham Lincoln in 1862.

Miller denied the applicability of the Thirteenth Amendment because the statute had not interfered with the butchers' right to labor in their occupation. More important, he also ruled the privileges and immunities clause of the Fourteenth Amendment inapplicable. Miller's narrow reading of the amendment differentiated between privileges protected by U.S. citizenship and those protected by state citizenship. Without presenting an exhaustive list of the former, he offered a few examples such as the right of protection on the high seas, the right to use the country's navigable waters, and rights secured by treaties. Under federalism, most other privileges and immunities, including those the butchers claimed, remained under the jurisdiction of the state governments and were not "placed under the special care of the Federal government" by the Fourteenth Amendment. Two years earlier, John A. Bingham, the principal framer of the amendment, had reminded his House colleagues that its adoption had instituted restrictions on state action "which were not limitations on the power of the States before the fourteenth amendment made them limitations." Miller disagreed, arguing that the amendment was never "intended to bring within the power of Congress the entire domain of civil rights heretofore belonging exclusively to the States." Such an erroneous interpretation, he asserted, would make the Supreme Court "a perpetual censor upon all legislation of the states" and would "fetter and degrade the state governments by subjecting them to the control of Congress."[10]

Although the case bore no direct relation to the civil rights of blacks in the South, Republicans who looked to the Fourteenth Amendment as the chief bulwark of those rights took alarm from Miller's conclusions. Anticipating such a reaction, the Justice strongly reiterated the original aims of the three Reconstruction amendments. "The one pervading purpose found in them all," he said, was the securing of freedom "and the protection of the newly-made freeman and citizen from the oppressions of those who had formerly exercised unlimited dominion over him." But achieving a practical fulfillment of that purpose was scarcely possible without a reordering of the nature of American federalism, and such a reordering Miller was unwilling to concede. Despite the pressures growing out of the war, he declared, "our statesmen have still believed that the existence of the States with powers for domestic and local government, including the regulation of civil rights—the rights of person and of property—was essential to the perfect working of our complex form of government."

Republican reaction was swift. George S. Boutwell, who had helped write the Fourteenth Amendment, considered Miller's interpretation "a great mistake." When Chief Justice Salmon P. Chase, who also disagreed with Miller, died a few weeks later, Boutwell urged the administration to replace him with "a thorough and tried Republican" who would uphold civil rights. "If we believe in our principles we should see to it that they are sustained by the courts rather than the principles of our enemies." Benjamin Bristow, who had prosecuted civil rights cases as a federal district attorney in Kentucky and as Grant's solicitor general, warned that "under the license of this opinion it is difficult to perceive what invasion of individual rights a state legislature may not authorize." Bristow regarded section one of the Fourteenth Amendment as "the crowning glory" of the Constitution, but, he wrote, "if we have not made it so explicit that it cannot be frittered away by judicial construction, it seems to me we ought to go over the work again. The Republican party can not afford to leave its work half done or to have the fruits of victory turn to ashes on its lips."[11]

When Congress reconvened in the late fall of 1873, Grant urged it to pass "a law to better secure the civil rights which freedom should secure, but has not effectually secured, to the enfranchised slave." The same day Charles Sumner again introduced his supplementary civil rights bill in the Senate, and a few days later an identical measure was introduced in the House. Democrats did not hesitate to invoke Miller's *Slaughterhouse* opinion against it. The former vice president of the Confederacy, Alexander H. Stephens, back in Washington as a representative from Georgia, told his colleagues that Miller's "soul-inspiring words" made clear that "all the essential features of our original complex federal system are still preserved." The Reconstruction amendments did "not change the nature and character of the Government," and hence Sumner's bill was unconstitutional.

The irony of Stephens's appearance in the House was not lost on black Congressman Robert B. Elliott of South Carolina. As Elliott put it, Stephens offered the government "a very poor return for its magnanimous treatment" to "come here and seek to continue, by the assertion of doctrines obnoxious to the true principles of our Government, the burdens and oppressions which rest upon five millions of his countrymen." The "leading and comprehensive purpose" of the amendments, Elliott said, was "to secure the complete freedom of the race, which, by the events of the war, had been wrested from the unwilling grasp of their owners." He denied that Miller's notion of dual citizenship invalidated the civil rights bill, whose constitutionality rested on the Fourteenth Amendment's equal protection clause. Thus, Elliott concluded, it "is as shocking to the legal mind as it is offensive to the heart" for Stephens to "assert that the decision of the Supreme Court in these cases was a denial to Congress of the power to legislate against discriminations on account of race, color, or previous condition of servitude."[12]

Ben Butler

Elliott's eloquent speech won high praise from other Republicans, and the well-educated Elliott served as the perfect embodiment of the party's ideal of equality. The Republican doctrine of equality, said Ben Butler, the House sponsor of the civil rights bill, was "not that all men are equal, *but that every man has the right to be the equal of every other man if he can.*" Butler insisted that Republicans aimed not to confer absolute equality of condition but "to give every man who is a citizen of the United States all the rights that every other man has." As for the *Slaughterhouse* decision, Ohio's William Lawrence, who had voted for the Fourteenth Amendment in the Thirty-ninth Congress, flatly stated that its legislative history "proves that the design of the fourteenth amendment was to confer upon Congress the power to enforce civil rights."[13]

Sumner's death in March 1874 gave a poignant urgency to his bill in the Senate. As in the House, Republicans in the upper chamber sought to come to grips with the *Slaughterhouse* decision. According to New Jersey's Frederick T. Frelinghuysen, who assumed sponsorship of the bill after Sumner died, the Reconstruction amendments had been passed, "as the reasoning of the court admits, to destroy all discrimination in the law among citizens of the United States." Furthermore, because the United States could not act directly on a state "to compel proper legislation and its enforcement[,] we can only deal with the offenders who violate the privileges and immunities of citizens of the United States." Thus, Frelinghuysen and other Republicans argued for an expansion of citizens' rights under the Fourteenth Amendment, which, in concert with the original Constitution, sanctioned protection through direct action by the national government. As Wisconsin Senator Timothy Howe put it, the "very fundamental defect" of the Articles of Confederation had been that the general government could issue commands only to the states. Under the Constitution, "all the commands of your law, almost without exception, are now issued to the citizen. You tell him to do his duty, and if he does not do his duty, you visit your penalties upon his head, and you do it in spite of the State."[14]

As in previous debates on Sumner's bill, the issue of mixing the races in the common schools aroused the greatest controversy. George Boutwell argued that "as a matter of public policy," permitting separate schools was wrong because it would impede the most important educative function of the schools. "In the public school," he said, "where children of all classes and conditions are brought together, this doctrine of human equality can be taught, and it is the chief means of securing the perpetuity of republican institutions." Other Republicans doubted the feasibility of such social engineering and argued that a mandate of mixed schools might drive southern states to cut off aid to public education altogether.[15]

Ultimately, whatever their disagreements over schools, Senate Republicans had come to embrace the idea that some action was necessary to ensure the legal equality of blacks in the public sphere. Morton's Indiana colleague, Daniel Pratt, reminded his colleagues that "our fathers who laid the foundations of our political edifice taught that all men are created equal." African Americans "differ in nothing but their color and lineage from the white race, except in so far as their natures have been dwarfed by slavery." This slavery-induced "inequality has existed too long," said Howe. The Republicans asked no special help for blacks, but only "to remove the last obstruction from the pathway to equal fortune" and "let the oppressed of centuries stagger to their feet if they can." After a continuous session of twenty hours, the Senate in the early hours of May 23, 1874, passed the bill by a partisan vote, with only three Republicans in dissent.[16]

Little time remained to secure passage in the House before the scheduled adjournment of the session. Again, the school provision drew opposition, and the Republicans could not muster the necessary two-thirds to suspend the rules either to refer the bill to committee for revision or to pass it. Voting against the measure were about a dozen Republican defectors, mostly scalawags from the upper South, motivated, said Louisiana carpetbagger C. B. Darrall, by "the senseless and unreasoning prejudice that has at all times controlled the white people of the South." Although one Democrat pronounced the bill "the deadest corpse you ever saw," Speaker Blaine promised that it would be among the first bills considered when Congress reconvened in the fall.[17]

While the civil rights bill was pending, Carpenter revived his bill to mandate a new election in Louisiana. He again clashed with Morton, and their debate turned on what constituted a republican government as guaranteed by the Constitution. Arguing that the essence of republicanism was government by leaders actually chosen by the people, Carpenter asserted that to "construe the Constitution so as to hold that as long as a State government observes the form it may depart from the reality of republican government, is to render the guarantee clause utterly worthless." Morton argued that to set aside a state government merely because fraud had marred an election would "place every State government at the mercy of the Federal Government, for all time to come." "The power to preserve republican forms of government in the States should not be converted into a power to destroy them."[18]

Meanwhile, rumors circulated through Washington that Grant would endorse Carpenter's bill. But in January 1874 he told a group of Republican leaders at the White House that the party should "unload" some of its "dead weight." "I am tired of this nonsense. Let Louisiana take care of herself." From New Orleans, Kellogg argued that this was precisely what his government was trying to do. Claiming the support of planters and businessmen, he raised the specter of economic and social turmoil and warned Morton that a new election would "disturb the tolerably friendly relations existing between the planters and the laborers." Kellogg and his Washington allies also urged Grant to stand by the status quo. In the end, Carpenter's bill failed again.[19]

Among the most important results of the exasperating Louisiana imbroglio was to feed Grant's growing inclination to pull back from intervention. A year earlier, during contention over the makeup of the Alabama legislature, the president had endorsed a compromise devised by Attorney General George Williams, whereby the Republicans controlled the House of Representatives and their opponents, the Senate. Now, however, Grant warned Republican leaders that "this nursing of monstrosities has nearly exhausted the life of the party." He disputed the notion "that the republican party was strong enough to uphold any burden. . . . I am done with them, and they will have to take care of themselves." When the Republican governor of Texas went to court to invalidate a Democratic victory in the 1873 elections on a technicality, Grant regarded the Republican case as "so doubtful" that he refused to lend his help. Less inclined to uphold Republicans at the expense of republicanism, the president told the governor that it would be "prudent, as well as right, to yield to the verdict of the people as expressed by their ballots."[20]

Also in the spring of 1874 the administration resisted becoming enmeshed in the tangled political situation in Arkansas, whose complexity equaled that in Louisiana. The so-called Brooks-Baxter War pitted James Brooks against

Elisha Baxter, whose rival claims to the governorship dated back to the disputed outcome of the 1872 election. Baxter had run as a regular Republican, while the Liberal Republican Brooks had enjoyed the endorsement of Arkansas's Democrats. Amid the usual barrage of charges and countercharges of fraud, Baxter had achieved an apparent victory, confirmed by the legislature early in 1873. Over the next several months, the new governor favored lifting state disfranchisement from ex-Confederates, opposed state aid to railroads, and took other positions that offended his erstwhile Republican backers, many of whom switched their allegiance to Brooks. Many Liberals and Democrats agreed with Baxter's policies and swung their support to him. Despite these shifts, however, in September 1873 Baxter had received Grant's promise of protection against a forced ouster by his opponents.[21]

Matters reached a head in April and May 1874, when, armed with a state court order declaring Brooks the rightful governor, regular Republican forces staged an armed coup to overthrow Baxter. Baxter asked Grant's help, but the president refused and merely ordered federal forces on the scene to remain neutral and preserve peace between the two armed camps. Arkansas's two senators and others from the state met with the cabinet to push for action in support of Brooks, but Grant again refused to tilt either way. After receiving reports from the army commander on the scene that the two sides were about to reach an agreement, he sent word that he would "heartily approve any adjustment peaceably" attained, and he urged both sides to disband their military forces. But no agreement emerged, and after several weeks of a tense standoff and sporadic violence, the administration decided to act.

Determined to take a strictly legalistic approach, Grant turned to Attorney General Williams for an opinion. Both Grant and Williams believed that Brooks had probably polled more votes than Baxter, but they regarded as conclusive the state constitutional provision that the legislature held exclusive power to determine the outcome of elections. The General Assembly had decided in Baxter's favor more than a year previously. Although Grant would have preferred another statement from the legislature, he nonetheless moved to prepare a proclamation under the U.S. Constitution's guarantee clause. Citing that clause and calls for assistance from both Baxter and from the legislature "to protect the State against domestic violence," Grant issued a proclamation recognizing Baxter as the legally elected governor and commanding "all turbulent and disorderly persons to disperse." Brooks and his Republican followers promptly relinquished the statehouse to Baxter.[22]

Although the administration had achieved a peaceful outcome of the Brooks-Baxter War, the prospects for tranquility wherever Republicans held power remained dim. Indeed, Grant's reluctance to intervene in Texas and Arkansas may have nourished the determination of white conservatives to regain control by whatever means they could. While Carpenter's Louisiana election bill stalled in Congress in the spring of 1874, conservatives in that state took matters into their own hands, forming so-called White Leagues with the aim of forcing Republicans from power in the parish governments. Eschewing the secrecy of the Klan, the Leaguers avowed their purpose to restore white supremacy and Democratic Party rule.

The movement got a boost from an opinion by Associate Justice Joseph P. Bradley sitting at New Orleans with a federal district judge as a circuit court of appeal in the Colfax Massacre prosecution. Three men convicted under the Enforcement Acts appealed to the circuit court, and Bradley upheld their appeal. In a convoluted opinion, Bradley concluded that the Fourteenth Amendment authorized Congress to legislate regarding state action but not action by individuals, thus invalidating portions of the Enforcement Acts. The district judge disagreed with Bradley, thereby sending the case to the Supreme Court. In the meantime, however, white Louisianians took heart that the justice's opinion augured the curtailment of federal prosecutions against racial and political violence. Governor Kellogg told Attorney General George Williams that Bradley's opinion and the administration's recent forbearance had encouraged the White Leagues and produced "a very bad effect."[23]

Nor was that effect limited to Louisiana, as White Leagues and similar organizations formed in other southern states. Some northern Republicans reacted skeptically to reports of threatened violence, which the *New York Tribune* labeled "a bogy conjured up by evil imagination" and "exaggerated for political effect." But in late August, Senator Morton, who was partially paralyzed, traveled to Arkansas to take the waters at Hot Springs, and concluded that southern attitudes were truly ominous. In a letter to Vice President Henry Wilson, he reported "an avowed antagonism of race, the whites against the blacks, not because the blacks are Republicans, but because they are blacks. The 'white man[']s party' is generally known as the Democratic Party yet, but it asserts no Democratic principle except opposition to the civil and political rights of the [blacks] and the social and business ostracism of every white man who will act in any political organization with the negro." Morton warned of the rapid development of "a most formidable, aggressive, and hostile movement against the colored people and white Republicans." Similarly, from Louisville, Secretary of the Treasury Benjamin Bristow's former law partner, John Marshall Harlan, wrote that the "recent slaughter" of blacks in Tennessee would likely recur and warned that the "north must buckle up and exhibit earnestness in the protection of the colored people, otherwise, we will drift into a state of utter helplessness and anarchy." A few days later at Coushatta, Louisiana, a White League mob murdered six white Republican parish officials and killed at least three blacks as well. By September, similar, if less bloody, tactics had routed Republican regimes in eight of the state's parishes. The violence was timed, moreover, to coincide with the beginning of voter registration for the fall elections.[24]

These developments worked to reverse Grant's drift toward nonintervention. Believing that the "recent atrocities" in Louisiana and elsewhere showed "a disregard for law, civil rights and personal protection that ought not to be tolerated in any civilized government," the president ordered the War Department to position troops "to be available in case of necessity." He was careful to note, however, that the protective policy would be directed by "the Law Department of the Government" in accordance with the Enforcement Acts, and no orders would go to the troops except on advice of the attorney general. But in mid–September the emboldened White Leaguers in Louisiana went after the big prize, staging a coup in New Orleans to oust Kellogg and other Republican state officials. In a pitched battle the insurgents triumphed, and more than thirty men lay dead in the streets. Invoking the Constitution's guarantee clause, Governor Kellogg asked Grant to "take measures to put down the domestic violence and insurrection," and the president responded with a proclamation ordering the "turbulent and disorderly persons" to return to their homes in five days.[25]

Awaiting the outcome, Grant and his cabinet debated further measures, and their discussions reflected the central frustrations thwarting Republicans' Reconstruction efforts: how to direct a policy from Washington to reintegrate the southern states into the national polity when the instruments within those states were so ill-suited to the task. Postmaster General Marshall Jewell noted that Grant "means business in this thing," but the problem was how "to back the Government without backing these worthless reprobates." As Jewell expressed it, Kellogg "is a first-class cuss, but there's no getting rid of him." Likewise, Grant decried the governor's "weakness and imbecility" but vowed that he would "never make it up as long as there's an insurgent pretender in the chair" and would "not hesitate to call out all the force of the United States." Grant raised the question of calling Congress into special session, but decided against it because the fall congressional election campaign was under way. Jewell and Bristow noted that the insurgents actually enjoyed considerable support among prominent men in New Orleans as well as some of the U.S. troops, and Bristow even suggested the possibility of Grant's withdrawing his proclamation. But Secretary of State Hamilton Fish argued that any tilt toward the insurgent government would lend "encouragement to lawlessness and usurpation." This view prevailed. Grant, hoping that simply the threat of force might prove sufficient, issued orders to the military commanders in Louisiana affirming that the administration would recognize the insurgents under no circumstances and "intimating military orders at the expiration of the five days." The tactic worked; after three days the insurgents withdrew and Kellogg resumed power.[26]

This fortunate outcome bought the Republicans some time as the national elections approached, but it provided no permanent solution to Louisiana's internecine struggles. Indeed, Grant's disillusionment with southern "monstrosities" in general reflected the futility inherent in Reconstruction policy. The more time that elapsed, the less patience national leaders could muster, the less willing the northern public was to endorse intervention, and the more determined white conservatives in the remaining Republican states were to achieve the "redemption" their counterparts enjoyed in other states. Republicans' chances in the midterm elections were already ebbing because of the depression following the Panic of 1873, as well as voter disgust over scandals such as the Crédit Mobilier scheme and Congress's so-called Salary Grab. The mounting frustrations over southern events had the potential to damage the party even further.

In the campaign of 1874, Republicans highlighted a variety of issues including the currency, tariff, and civil service, but they could not ignore the southern question, especially when Democrats arraigned the Senate-passed civil rights bill as a mandate for social equality. Some antiadministration Republicans such as Carl Schurz refused to defend the bill, saying that now that blacks possessed the vote, it was "much wiser and safer" to "leave all else to the gradual progress of public opinion." Other party leaders, however, staunchly defended the legislation. "I voted for the civil rights bill," declared John Sherman, "not only because I thought it was right, but because I felt bound, in honor, to stand by and enforce the great amendments to the Constitution—the pride and boast of the Republican Party, and the connecting link by which the immortal Declaration of Independence was made a part of our frame of Government." Henry Dawes told Massachusetts voters that they should elect no Democrat to Congress because "Massachusetts has a sacred legacy in the Civil Rights Bill which she cannot barter away nor entrust to any unfriendly keeping." Speaking for Republicans in general, the party's congressional campaign committee issued an address asserting that the "fourteenth amendment is not yet enforced by 'appropriate legislation'" and that "the Republican party alone can do it."[27]

Such rhetoric won Republicans few friends among white southerners, and nationwide it failed to overcome the damage Republicans suffered from hard times and scandal. Voters elected a Democratic House for the first time since before the Civil War. The result confirmed the emerging dominance of the Democrats in the South where their party won more than half its seats, eighty-nine representatives to the Republicans' seventeen. Fourteen years would pass before Republicans would again win the presidency and both houses of Congress, a fact that stymied any forward thrust of Reconstruction.

But in late 1874 Republicans considered their defeat a Bull Run rather than a Waterloo, as one editor put it. Indeed, said the *Chicago Tribune's* Joseph Medill, this "merited chastisement" might save the party "from a worse disaster in 1876." Some Republicans read the result as a rejection of the party's southern policy, especially the civil rights bill, which Postmaster General Marshall Jewell called "a Pandora's box left us by Sumner." Others, such as Treasury Secretary Bristow, blamed the loss on "hard times and financial revulsions. . . . For myself, I cannot believe that the patriotic people of this country mean to restore to power the old pro-slavery Democratic party." Indeed, the old abolitionist leader Gerrit Smith told Vice President Henry Wilson that the short session of Congress presented the Republican Party "a precious opportunity . . . to redeem itself. . . . If, in stern defiance of the enemies of God & man, it shall pass the Civil Rights Bill, it will, by force of such justice & bravery, be stronger than ever." Some party strategists such as Philadelphia editor John W. Forney thought that "the follies of the Democrats" would hasten Republican recovery: "Their victory will make them insane, *and there is our real hope.* Already they talk of repealing the [constitutional] amendments and remanding the colored people back to slavery, and even of adding the rebel debt to our own. God speed them! Anything to save the nation from the rebels and put good Republicans in power."[28]

Grant was not so certain the Democrats would self-destruct, nor did he read the election as a call for a radical reversal of his policy. Continued violence in the South during the campaign had sparked his anger, which he vented in several fiery passages in the draft of his annual message to Congress. When he read the draft to the cabinet, Fish considered these points "very strong & very just" but better suited for "a heated Congressional debate or a rough newspaper article" and "wholly beneath the dignity of his official position." After considerable criticism and discussion, Grant moderated his remarks, but they nonetheless retained a striking candor regarding the frustrations of Reconstruction.[29]

In his message the president admitted that southerners in some states "have had most trying governments to live under," but he asked, "do they do right in ignoring the existence of violence and bloodshed in resistance to constituted authority?" During the recent election, he said, "murders enough were committed to spread terror among those whose political action was to be oppressed." Citing the Fifteenth Amendment, the Enforcement Act, and his own constitutional charge to "take care that the laws be faithfully executed," he justified his use of troops as his bounden duty. Denial of his authority to respond would deprive the amendment and the act of all "meaning, force, or effect" and render "the whole scheme of colored enfranchisement . . . worse than mockery and little better than a crime." He warned southerners that the "theory" that there

"Shall We Call Home Our Troops?" *Harper's Weekly*, January 9, 1875.

would be no further federal government "interference" was "a great mistake." He vowed to enforce "with rigor" all "the laws of Congress and the provisions of the Constitution, including the recent amendments added thereto." As for a permanent solution, he concluded, "Treat the negro as a citizen and a voter, as he is and must remain, and soon parties will be divided, not on the color line, but on principle. Then we shall have no complaint of sectional interference." As the *New York Times* observed, the president had given the people of the South "some very plain advice in a spirit of frankness and kindness." Events would shortly show the pertinence of the advice as well as its futility.[30]

On the same day Congress received Grant's message, a thousand miles away in Vicksburg, Mississippi, racial violence left a dozen blacks dead, and later that night, white raiders killed untold numbers more in their homes. At the call of the state legislature, Grant issued a proclamation against the Mississippi "insurgents," preparatory to sending additional U.S. troops into the state. He also ordered General Philip Sheridan to travel to Vicksburg and to New Orleans to "ascertain the true condition of affairs." As matters turned out, Sheridan would be on hand in New Orleans for an incident that had a devastating impact on the already ebbing northern will to continue intervention.[31]

The Louisiana elections of 1874 had followed a familiar pattern. Conservatives intimidated blacks and their allies, and Kellogg's Republicans in control of the Returning Board overturned results allegedly achieved by such intimidation. In the weeks after the balloting, the Returning Board had reduced a considerable Democratic majority in the next state House of Representatives to a tie, leaving five contested seats to be determined by the House itself. As the end of the year approached, the administration in Washington received indications that the Democratic Conservatives would insist on filling the offices they considered rightfully theirs. Grant contemplated putting the state under martial law "in case of trouble," but Attorney General Williams expressed doubt as to his authority to do so. While the cabinet deliberated, congressional Republicans also surveyed options. Ohio Senator John Sherman privately mused that "nothing but a firm and just military government" erected under the Constitution's guarantee clause would "secure order in Louisiana." But the assertion of such power would represent "a dangerous precedent," likely "to be hereafter greatly abused and almost the beginning of the end of our institutions. No wonder that Congress hesitates."[32]

Matters reached a head on January 4, 1875, when, as the lower house of the General Assembly was organizing, the Democrats seized control. Under the rules, the clerk of the previous session called the roll with fifty-two Republicans and fifty Democrats answering. Immediately a Democrat nominated Louis Wiltz for speaker and conducted a voice vote unrecognized by the clerk. Wiltz then seized the gavel and organized the body in the Democrats' interest, including the election of a clerk and the appointment of sergeants-at-arms prepared to enforce his rulings. Many Republicans bolted, and when several in the rear of the hall and the lobby loudly protested the proceedings, Wiltz invited Colonel Philippe Regis De Trobriand, the local commander of U.S. troops, to restore order, which he did with a few words to the crowd. The Democrats then awarded the five contested seats to their colleagues, thereby claiming a majority. Republican members sought help from Governor Kellogg, who asked De Trobriand to return to the House and remove "all persons not returned as legal members." With a squad of troops, the colonel escorted the five men out. When most of the legally elected Democrats also left in protest, the Republicans organized the House.[33]

Sheridan arrived in New Orleans later that night and soon reported the proceedings to Secretary of War William Belknap. In a series of dispatches, he observed that "defiance to the laws and the murder of individuals seems [*sic*] to be looked upon by the community here from a standpoint which gives impunity to all who choose to indulge in either." Citing the terrorism practiced by the White League and similar groups, Sheridan called for legislation or a presidential proclamation declaring them "banditti" to be "tried by a military commission." Without explicitly endorsing this proposal, Belknap replied generally that the "president and all of us have full confidence and thoroughly approve your course." In an effort to clarify the confused reports coming out of New Orleans, the administration gave these dispatches to the press.[34]

The events in New Orleans and the publication of Sheridan's exchange with Belknap startled the nation and sent shock waves through the Republican Party. In the view of many, the reported intrusion of the military into a legislature posed the gravest threat to republican institutions. Protest meetings convened in several major cities. In New York, the *Tribune*'s Whitelaw Reid, William M. Evarts, and other prominent Republicans joined Democrats in a call for a meeting at Cooper Institute to "give expression to the outraged feelings which every citizen of a free commonwealth must experience at a crime, happily in this country so unparalleled, against the underlying principles of our Government." "I have never given wholly away to despondency," Garfield wrote a friend, "but I say to you now that this is the darkest day for the future of the Republican party I have ever seen. The Louisiana question . . . has been so terribly botched by the President and General Sheridan during the last four days as to place the great burden of trouble upon us." Henry Dawes reported to *Springfield Republican* editor Samuel Bowles that congressional Republicans were "amazed and dumbfounded" at the administration's political "stupidity and blindness" in publishing and publicly approving the general's "banditti" dispatch. "I cannot account for it in any way except in the fact that suicide is sometimes epidemic." Belknap had, in fact, not consulted other cabinet secretaries before responding to Sheridan, and several pointedly rebuked him for his "all of us" dispatch.[35]

While Grant and the cabinet weighed alternatives, both parties in Congress demanded more information. Debate had already begun regarding the details of the incident and its broader significance for the safety of the nation's republican institutions. Among the administration's severest critics was its old Liberal Republican nemesis, Carl Schurz, who fired a fusillade of anti–Grant rhetoric hardly less frenzied than the most violent bloody-shirt oratory. The "most essential safeguard of representative institutions," said Schurz, "is the absolute freedom of legislative bodies from interference on the part of executive power, especially by force. . . . How long before a soldier may stalk into the national House of Representatives, and, pointing to the Speaker's mace, say, 'Take away that bauble?'" The American people held "sacred as the life element of their republican freedom" the right of "that self-government which lives and has its being in the organism of the States," and unless the power of national government

Which is the problem? lawlessness of the mob or power?

interference was "most scrupulously limited, . . . we shall surely have reason to say that our system of republican government is in danger." Sneering at "the blood and murder cry" and at arguments that government's first task was protection of citizens, Schurz argued that "the lawlessness of power is becoming far more dangerous to all than the lawlessness of the mob." Perhaps some violence had occurred in the South, but, he said, "Who does not know that republics will be sometimes the theatre of confusion, disturbance, and violent transgressions[?] . . . The citizens of a republic have to pay some price for the great boon of their common liberty."[36]

For the president's backers, that price was too high. "I fail to see any excellence in that kind of self-government," said Mississippi carpetbag Senator Henry Pease, "where a minority, by means of the pistol and the bowie-knife, riot, murder, and assassination, subverts the will of the majority." "Government for the people and by the people," said Morton, must "mean all the people." The question, according to George Edmunds, was whether "the people of this country, who love law and order and liberty combined, are going to sit down and see thousands and tens of thousands of their fellow-citizens in any part of this country made the victims of oppression and assassination." Although few Republicans felt comfortable defending the military's incursion into the legislature, Timothy Howe argued that De Trobriand had come to the rescue of republicanism: the five ejected Democrats, who "had no business there," had "held that Legislature by the throat and thus strangled for the time being the voice of Louisiana."[37]

Whatever the incident's immediate consequences in New Orleans, it underscored the ultimate intractability of Reconstruction. As Morton put it, until "the colored people of these States are a part of the people of the United States, entitled to take part in the government, I am sure there will be no peace." But the actions of southern conservatives made clear that there would be no peace until the national government stopped interceding in behalf of blacks. "Why, sir," said California's Aaron Sargent, "we have been holding for years past a wolf by the ears in the South; we have been trying to hold men still who were in armed rebellion against the Government, with their passions and hatreds excited against us; and we have pursued a course of peaceable reconstruction measures, . . . but we have been continually confronted by men acting with nefarious purposes, who would not extend to others the mercy which we so willingly extended to them." For John A. Logan, the impasse was simple, if no less maddening: "Give the democracy control and you will have peace, but if they cannot have control they will not let us have peace!"[38]

In the present crisis, all eyes turned to the president, who held marathon sessions with his cabinet trying to devise a response. Williams favored justifying the intrusion in the legislature by "treating the Military as a 'Posse comitatus' called in to maintain the peace." Fish thought that that course would simply compound the wrong and proposed instead that the administration "disclaim and denounce the action of Genl. de Trob[r]iand." Grant snapped back that he "would certainly not denounce it" or censure Sheridan. After several hours of discussion, however, Fish believed that the president had begun to feel some "doubt as to the entire correctness of what had been done."

Bristow also disapproved the military action, not the least because of the deplorable dilemma it presented the administration. "It is impossible to condemn the act," he told John Marshall Harlan, "without giving more or less encouragement and countenance to the infamous White Leaguers." Although the Treasury secretary would not endorse Sheridan's "wild and injudicious suggestions," he was willing to "go to the very verge of Constitutional power" to fight the South's white supremacist groups. As the cabinet's sole southerner, Bristow believed he had a special understanding of "the character & feelings of the people in those states." He was convinced that the purpose of the White League and similar groups was "to overthrow the late amendments to the Constitution, and reduce the colored people to actual, if not nominal, slavery; that is to say, they mean to reduce them to the condition of subordination to the will of the white man wherein they shall be left no choice but to vote the Democratic ticket, and to perform the labor of the white man on such terms and for such compensation as he may dictate." "Entertaining these views," Bristow said, "I cannot fail to favor the most vigorous measures for the suppression of the organization and the punishment of its leaders and participants."[39]

The cabinet's dilemma grew even more perplexing when rumors surfaced regarding the expected report of a House investigative subcommittee just back from New Orleans. A portion of a larger select Committee on the Condition of the South, the subcommittee comprised Democrat Clarkson Potter and two Republicans, Charles Foster and William Walter Phelps, neither of whom held the administration in high regard. The group happened to be present in the Louisiana legislature when the Democrats were expelled, and they confirmed Sheridan's version of the events. But the subcommittee had gone to Louisiana originally to investigate the 1874 elections, and they were now prepared to report that virtually no intimidation had occurred and that the Republican Returning Board had counted in Republicans from many legislative districts where Democrats had been elected. Although their report was not yet public, Schurz hailed the subcommittee's "conscientious investigation," which he said proved that the will of the people of Louisiana had been "crushed out under the heel of a lawless military invasion." Bristow concluded that the committee was going to "whitewash the White League and the rebels of Louisiana

At the Door. U.S.G.: "If I hammer long enough, perhaps they'll wake up." *Harper's Weekly,* January 30, 1875. (Image courtesy of HarpWeek, LLC).

generally." Nonetheless, although the unanimity of the bipartisan committee lent the report an air of indisputability, Grant remained "determined under no circumstance to apologize for anything that had been done" by the forces at New Orleans. The president set to work on a special message, and, consulting with Morton, Edmunds, and other leading Republican senators, he laid the groundwork for an endorsement by Congress.[40]

Not unexpectedly, Grant's January 13 message on the incident in the legislature placed great stress on the endemic violence in Louisiana. In gruesome detail, he recounted the "lawlessness, turbulence, and bloodshed" that had long characterized the state's politics. Tracing the current crisis to the uncertain outcome of the 1872 election, he concluded that Kellogg probably had "more right" to the governorship than McEnery. But more important, with a biting irony, he noted that while "fierce denunciations ring through the country about office holding and election matters, . . . every one of the Colfax miscreants goes unwhipped of justice, and no way can be found in this boasted land of civilization and Christianity to punish the perpetrators of this bloody and monstrous crime." As for the 1874 elections, he cited specific evidence of intimidation and of the Democrats' avowed determination to defeat the Republicans "at all hazards, which very naturally greatly alarmed the colored voters." He upheld the Returning Board's proceedings as being "in accordance with the law under which they acted."

Regarding the military interference in the legislature, the president noted that both parties had relied on the troops to preserve peace. The imbroglio arose when "the Democratic minority of the house undertook to seize its organization by fraud and violence." Kellogg's call on the troops to remove the five Democrats was "debatable," but "nobody was disturbed by the military who had a legal right at that time to occupy a seat." Grant affirmed that military intervention in the organization of a legislature was "repugnant to our ideas of government," but he made no apology for De Trobriand or Sheridan. When Sheridan sent his "banditti" dispatch, he may have been thinking less of "proper" proceedings in time of peace than of the "utterly lawless condition of society surrounding him at the time." But even at that, the general had "never proposed to do an illegal act." The president earnestly avowed that "nothing would give me greater pleasure than to see reconciliation and tranquility everywhere prevail, and thereby remove all necessity for the presence of troops." But, he warned, "neither Kuklux Klans, White Leagues, nor any other association using arms and violence to execute their unlawful purposes can be permitted in that way to govern any part of this country."[41]

The message gave a powerful jolt to Republican morale. Blaine assured Grant that it "will exercise an immense influence on the public mind and will bring the People face to face with the real question." From North Carolina, ex-Governor William Holden congratulated the president on the "triumphant vindication of your whole course," and he avowed that "your friends in these Southern States, that can do but little, will never desert you."[42] The *New York Times* printed a lengthy letter from a prominent New York lawyer, Edwin W. Stoughton, defending the administration. Stoughton offered a careful analysis of the New Orleans incident to show that the usurping House Democrats had violated the precept "that members lawfully returned, and they only, can participate in the organization of a legislative body." In standing by the result of De Trobriand's action, Grant was upholding an "inflexible rule" that was "indispensable to the existence of every representative assembly, and, indeed, to representative governments." That the *Times* misidentified Stoughton as a Democrat gave the overall reaction to Grant's message a bipartisan aura that was perhaps unwarranted, but no less powerful. From within the cabinet, Bristow told the New Yorker that his letter "affords much pleasure to the President and his friends."[43]

But could Republicans sustain this sense of triumph? The publication two days later of the House subcommittee's report robbed Grant's message of some of its glow. More important, despite the power of the president's rhetoric, his message had settled nothing. Indeed, he had "earnestly" asked Congress to take such action "as to leave my duties perfectly clear in dealing with the affairs of Louisiana." To Republican skeptics such as New Yorker Edwin Merritt, the whole controversy revealed "a weakening of party ties" that "will be increased or diminished as Congress shall act wisely or unwisely on the subject."[44]

In the Senate, men of both parties exhibited an almost limitless capacity to dissect the events of January 4 in New Orleans. In laying blame on the Louisiana House Democrats, New Jersey Republican Senator Frederick Frelinghuysen reminded his colleagues that "a republican government is not only one in which the representatives elected by the people govern, but is one in which the succession or continuance of organized authority shall be in accordance with the law of the land." Frelinghuysen and other Republicans stoutly defended the administration's handling of the situation, but they appeared to be at a loss to propose any concrete action. Again, the Louisiana mess symbolized Republicans' growing sense of futility at losing what amounted to a guerilla war. It was clear, said Henry Pease of Mississippi, that southern conservatives were determined to "destroy this Government by anarchy; and to-day the seeds of anarchy have already germinated and are ready almost to blossom in fifteen of these States." It was possible, said John Sherman, that southerners "may submit to the democratic party and produce a kind of peace." But that "is not the peace of equality of rights; it is not the peace that your Constitution guarantees to every man; it is the peace of despotism." Barring that, "the struggle will go on . . . to reconstruct our republican institutions upon the broad basis of equality before the law." But moving from general principle to the specific situation in Louisiana, Sherman simply said, "I will not now dwell upon the remedy." Vermont's Justin Morrill was "confident very little legislation would be required" if white southerners would observe the Thirteenth, Fourteenth, and Fifteenth Amendments as well as the Sixth Commandment, "Thou shall not kill"—a position whose very utterance bespoke its futility.[45]

Never far from Republicans' minds was the impact that any "remedy" would have on their own political prospects, especially in the wake of their devastating loss in 1874. Liberal Republican Thomas Tipton of Nebraska chided his erstwhile party colleagues in the Senate, reminding them that after the wreckage of the Panic of 1873 voters who "were scarcely able to live for want of bread" had rejected "a party that proposed to live on blood." No less a party figure than Vice President Henry Wilson called for a change of course. Author of *The Rise and Fall of the Slave Power in America* and a Radical of unquestioned bona fides, Wilson sent an open letter to the *Springfield Republican* advocating a "broad, wise, and magnanimous policy" for the South to detach old-line Whigs and other men of "experience, ability, and character" from the white supremacist conservative party. Only thus could Republicans achieve "peace in the South, the blotting out of divisions on the line of race, the advancement of real reconstruction, permanent Southern prosperity, and the success of the Republican Party." Wilson's letter was widely reprinted and struck a responsive chord among Republicans who favored a more conciliatory policy.[46]

In the House of Representatives, Republicans sought to defuse the embarrassment by dispatching to New Orleans the Committee on the Condition of the South, the parent committee of the Foster Subcommittee. The ostensible object was a fuller investigation than time had allowed the subcommittee, but the committee's Republican leaders, George F. Hoar and William A. Wheeler, also hoped to reach some accommodation that all parties in Louisiana could accept and that would relieve the Republican Party of the Louisiana curse. Within the cabinet, Fish expressed the hope that "this Louisiana nuisance may not only be abated, but its past unsavoriness be removed from nostrils in which it has become a stench."[47]

While the committee pursued its investigation in New Orleans, more radical House Republicans concluded that the situation in Louisiana and the South generally warranted further legislation—laws to strengthen enforcement of voting rights and secure protection for civil rights. Led by Benjamin F. Butler, these men decided to concentrate first on civil rights, believing that on that issue they could more readily achieve party unity which they hoped then to swing behind new election enforcement legislation. Sumner's bill had passed the Senate the previous spring, and Butler now calculated that House Republicans would come together to pass the measure in some form to complete the memorial to the patron saint of equal rights. But in the winter of 1875, little time remained in the short session of the Forty-third Congress, after which the Republicans would relinquish control to the Democrats. Success turned on overcoming Democrats' determined obstructionism. On January 27, when Butler attempted to call up a House version of the bill, men across the aisle launched a series of dilatory motions that led to seventy-five roll calls, each occupying forty minutes. Undaunted, Republicans ate at their desks and napped on committee room tables to match their opponents' stamina through a continuous session of forty-six hours. The Democrats' tactics backfired, for the Republicans concluded to change the rules to limit debate and expedite business. "Party intensity runs higher than at any time since the war," Henry Dawes reported.[48]

After the rules fight, debate on the civil rights bill proceeded, largely over familiar ground. Particularly affecting were speeches by several black representatives, who spoke not only to their colleagues but also to the galleries filled with "fifteenth amendmenters," as one Democrat derisively called newly enfranchised freedmen. Mississippian John R. Lynch told how during his trips by train to Washington he was "treated, not as an American citizen, but as a brute," forced "to occupy a filthy smoking-car both night and day, with drunkards, gamblers, and criminals." What blacks asked, Lynch said, was not social equality but "protection in the enjoyment of *public* rights." Any discrimination based on race or religion amounted to "a violation of the principles of republicanism." "The time is at hand when you must cease to take us for cringing slaves," said Joseph Rainey of South Carolina. "Either I am a man or I am not a man," declared James Rapier of Alabama. "If I am a man, I am entitled to all the right[s] and privileges and immunities that any other American citizen is entitled to."[49]

Many white Republicans echoed these sentiments, including Butler, who condemned southern whites' prejudices as "illogical, unjust, ungentlemanly, and foolish." When Democrats argued that blacks in the South already enjoyed their rights, New Yorker Ellis Roberts asked scornfully why then they opposed the bill. But some Republicans, especially white southerners, were skeptical. Citing the *Slaughterhouse* case, Virginia scalawag J. Ambler Smith argued that despite the Fourteenth Amendment, police power remained with the states. Moreover, Ambler spoke of property as "one of the great elements of society" and asked "what becomes of its sanctity, if any human power, even that of my own State, can prescribe to me whom I shall admit to my hotel and whom I shall exclude?" Independent Republican Simeon Chittenden of Brooklyn argued that although the measure might be just, "the dominant race" would view it as "an offense and menace," and it was "impolitic unnecessarily to vex white men, North and South."[50]

Nonetheless, most Republicans believed that some civil rights bill would pass before the Republicans lost control of the House in March. In some ways Butler may have been a less than ideal instrument to further this goal. Even some Republicans were embarrassed by his somewhat unsavory record as a spoils politician.[51] During the debate, Butler spent as much time tweaking the Democrats as he did arguing the bill's merits. He infuriated his opponents, one of whom responded so caustically as to be censured by the House. And yet the intense exchange of personal barbs may have served to energize the Republicans, for many shared Butler's determination that some form of the bill should pass.[52]

Benjamin F. Butler
(Library of Congress)

Few party members could ignore the civil rights bill's potential political consequences. New Jersey's William Walter Phelps, who had served on the subcommittee that had "whitewashed" the Louisiana election, called Sumner's bill "an unmitigated evil" whose passage would "defy the opinion of the people of these United States recently and emphatically declared" in the fall elections. Moreover, Phelps argued, white southerners would close the public schools rather than grant equality of treatment to blacks. Thus, realistically affecting only hotels, trains, and amusements, the bill would secure to the ex-slave only "sentimental advantages, which he will never use." Butler denied Phelps's political analysis. So few Republicans had won reelection, he said, "because we did not pass this bill a year ago. The people turned from us because we were a do-nothing party, afraid of our shadows."

Similarly, from the moderate wing of the party, Garfield made a speech "answering the fears of some of our timid members that we are injuring the party by doing justice to the Negro." He reminded Phelps that the first charge made against the antislavery movement had been that it was "a sentimental abstraction rather than a measure of practical legislation." He denied that the party's "recent disasters" had "sprung from any of the brave acts done in the effort to do justice to the negro." Urging his comrades to reject the "cowardice which shrinks from the assertion of great principles," Garfield insisted that "it is safest for a nation, a political party, or an individual man to dare to do right, and let consequences take care of themselves."[53]

Butler in effect presented four versions of the civil rights bill to the House, "in order that all shades of republican opinion may be voted upon." One was the bill the Senate had passed earlier, calling for equality in public accommodations, transportation, amusements, juries, and schools. An alternative proposed by Alabama scalawag Alexander White would allow the facilities and institutions covered by the bill to be separate as long as they were equal. A third, the House Judiciary Committee's bill, would mandate equality and apply the "separate but equal" formula only to schools. And a fourth version, the committee bill amended, eliminated all mention of schools.

Among House Republicans, enough moderates and conservatives opposed Sumner's Senate bill to defeat it, while Radicals resisted giving congressional sanction to the "separate but equal" doctrine. Thus, party leaders could muster enough votes to pass only the last version, and even then twelve regular Republicans, almost all from the upper South, voted no. Of one thing, however, all Republicans appeared certain: the Democrats' fierce obstructionism had given the lie to their earlier professions of a New Departure in race relations. As Michigan's Julius Burrows put it, their opponents' behavior had shown "beyond all controversy . . . that the struggle for the equal rights of all American citizens before the law is not yet ended." To underscore the point, Republicans inserted as a preamble to their civil rights bill the 1872 Democratic and Liberal Republican platform plank recognizing "the equality of all men before the law" and the duty of government "to mete out equal and exact justice to all." Because the House bill differed from the Senate's, it required consideration and approval by the upper house, which would take two more weeks.[54]

The House struggle over civil rights, like Grant's Louisiana message, galvanized the Republicans anew. Dawes wrote Samuel Bowles that "both parties have resolved to stand or die in the old attitude toward the south." But alas, within days the Brooks–Baxter War flared up again in Arkansas, and Grant's handling of events in the Ozark state undercut much of the administration's new-found credibility. The previous spring, before the administration's recognition of Baxter as governor over rival claimant Brooks, Baxter and the Democratic legislature had moved to secure Democratic control of the state by calling a convention to frame a new state constitution. In the fall 1874 elections, held under the supervision of the Baxter government, a substantial majority approved the new constitution and elected a new governor, Democrat Augustus

H. Garland. Baxter handed his office to Garland, but Republicans in the state cried foul. Now claiming that fraud in the 1872 election had cheated Brooks out of the governorship, Republicans charged that Baxter, as only an illegitimate claimant to the office, had had no authority to convene the special session of the legislature that had called the constitutional convention. Hence, the constitution itself, as well as the election of new officers in 1874, was fraudulent. For several months affairs in Arkansas had been under scrutiny by a congressional committee headed by Luke Poland of Vermont. Now, in the winter of 1875, just as Louisiana bedeviled Republicans in Washington, the Poland Committee prepared to make its report.[55]

Grant had followed the events in Arkansas with great skepticism. Garland's promise that he would pass "the most stringent laws" against the White Leagues, whose existence in Arkansas he denied, hardly reassured the president. Nor did a meeting with the Poland Committee at the Capitol allay Grant's suspicions. In early February the committee issued its report upholding the new constitution and Garland's election under it. The committee declared itself "satisfied" that the new document was "republican in form, and in many respects an improvement upon that of 1868." Although its creation deviated somewhat from the method of amendment outlined in the previous constitution, the new instrument had won wide approval in the election. "The people of every State have the right to make their own Constitution to suit themselves, provided it be republican in form," the majority concluded, and the "committee cannot find any solid ground on which to stand to say the General Government can or ought to interfere." On February 6, the day after the House passed the civil rights bill, Poland took his report to the House.[56]

Two days later, Grant responded in a brief but passionate message. The evidence now available, he maintained, showed that Brooks had been elected governor in 1872 and had been illegally deprived of the office ever since. The new constitution had come into effect through "violence, intimidation, and revolutionary proceedings" that "practically ignore all rights of minorities." Looking beyond the issue at hand, the president asked "whether a precedent so dangerous to the stability of State government, if not of the National Government also, should be recognized by Congress." He earnestly implored Congress to "take definite action in this matter to relieve the Executive from acting upon questions which should be decided by the legislative branch of the Government."[57]

Many of Grant's fellow Republicans found his Arkansas message one of his most indefensible, if not incomprehensible, acts in relation to Reconstruction. Secretary of State Fish thought the message "inconclusive in its argument" and "dangerous in its tendencies." With no consultation with his cabinet, the president had reversed his position on the Brooks-Baxter fight and had summarily rejected the House committee's acceptance of the new constitution and the apparently peaceful government. Because the message offered no real explanation of either move, many observers suspected the worst sort of motives. Fish speculated that Arkansas's Republican senators and their cronies had "induced" Grant to send the message. Bristow's Kentucky friend, John Marshal Harlan, said that Grant's "astonishing" message "should alarm every lover of peace," and he warned that if "the President should overturn the Arkansas government by force, the Republican party will go under never to rise again."[58]

But Grant had, in fact, raised an important question regarding the undermining of Reconstruction by constitutional means. "What is there," he asked, "to prevent each of the States recently admitted to Federal relations on certain conditions changing their constitutions and violating their pledges if this action in Arkansas is acquiesced in?" As it turned out, most Republicans believed nothing could prevent such changes. As Fish put it, "Too many of the states have changed their constitutions by proceedings similar to those under which the new constitution of Arkansas has been adopted to question the rightfulness of the proceedings." Grant himself soon began to beat a retreat, telling Bristow that he had issued his message not with "any intent of definite action" but "to urge Congress to make some expression of opinion."

The message sparked a brief but sharp debate in the House. J. D. Ward, the lone dissenter on the Poland Committee, asserted that Garland's government was "upheld by fraud and violence" and not "a government republican in form." On the other hand, Henry J. Scudder, Poland's Republican ally on the committee, hailed the new constitution as "far superior" to those of many other states "in the essential characteristics of republicanism," especially in making elective some two thousand officers previously appointed by the governor. "If 'republican form of government' has any correct definition," said Scudder, "it lies right in the line of the present state of things in the State of Arkansas." Whether most Republicans agreed with that extravagant assessment is doubtful, but the opinion did prevail that the national government could not freeze indefinitely the state constitutions formed during congressional Reconstruction. By a margin of 150 to 81, with sixty-five Republicans in the affirmative, the House voted to accept the Poland committee's position and to reject the president's call for action. This vote, sighed Fish, removed "a threatening difficulty" and gave "confidence & hope to a great many." A week later Grant recognized Garland as governor.[59]

The Arkansas flap made a quick and popular settlement of the Louisiana issue all the more imperative. After his committee had completed its investigation in New Orleans, Hoar presented a report that exonerated few of the players in Louisiana politics. It recounted the state's long history of violence and, contrary to the subcommittee's previous report, found substantial intimidation in the

1874 elections. The report also stated, however, that the Returning Board had exceeded its statutory authority in throwing out allegedly fraudulent returns, thereby declaring Republicans winners in several of the state legislative races. But, on the other hand, Hoar concluded that the Democrats had used a "totally objectionable" method to redress this wrong in their usurpation of control of the house of representatives. The committee passed no judgment on the "lawfulness" of De Trobriand's intervention in the legislature but did credit it with preventing bloodshed. Such intervention, however, had little prospect of working fundamental change. In a telling passage, Hoar reflected the growing sense of resignation among Republicans that they had lost the peace in the South:

> This great movement of the public mind in great States is not to be dealt with as if it were a street riot. You cannot change great currents of public sentiment or the habits of thought and feeling of great bodies of men by act of Congress. In a republic you cannot long or permanently check their manifestation by the exercise of national power. Until the great body of the white people of Louisiana shall learn to obey the law, to submit to the Constitution, to respect labor, to base their institutions on liberty, equality, and justice, they can enjoy neither prosperity nor peace.

For the long term, the committee advocated financial aid for education in the state. In the short term, it rejected the idea of a new election. Instead, it proposed resolutions recognizing Kellogg as governor and urging the Louisiana house to place members rightfully entitled in their seats. In a strictly partisan vote, Republicans in the national House overwhelmingly approved Hoar's resolutions. While his committee was in New Orleans, William A. Wheeler had begun negotiations with both sides to agree to a settlement. With the imprimatur of the House vote, this effort proceeded, resulting in the so-called Wheeler Adjustment. By its terms, both parties in Louisiana would accept Kellogg as governor, and the house would seat enough Democrats to give their party control. This "compromise of 1875" was widely applauded. Among Republicans, most could heartily endorse James A. Garfield's fervent hope that this "substantially settles the relations of the Federal Government to the recent troubles in that state."[60]

In ridding themselves of the twin incubi of Louisiana and Arkansas, Republicans in Washington showed a distinct inclination to draw back from direct intervention in the South. Not surprisingly, efforts in the waning days of the Forty-third Congress to strengthen general enforcement legislation failed. In early February Grant's allies in the House formulated a bill to reinstate the president's power to suspend the writ of habeas corpus and otherwise strengthen federal election supervision especially in the rural areas of the South. But they soon found that they could not transfer the solidarity forged for civil rights to this bill. In the Republican caucus, the measure met stiff opposition from Speaker Blaine, Garfield, and other party leaders. Describing its advocates as "extremists," Garfield reported to a friend that "those of us who believed in a government of law, and not of the bayonet, were compelled to take grounds against our associates." Nonetheless, the measure cleared the caucus, and with only two weeks remaining before control would pass to the Democrats in the new Forty-fourth Congress, Indiana Republican John Coburn introduced the bill in the House.[61]

To men of Coburn's thinking, recent events in the South had underscored the need for such additional legislation. "Of what value is the writ of *habeas corpus* in Arkansas or Louisiana to the citizen when other more important and vital rights are utterly disregarded and unprotected?" Coburn asked. If the government could not restrain "restless and ambitious leaders in political strife," then "the sun of republican government is sinking already beneath the horizon." Like many House Republicans, Pennsylvania's Charles Albright agreed that republicanism was at the center of the issue. "The safety and perpetuity of our institutions depend more upon free and fair elections than on anything else," he said. "If this guarantee is not sacredly maintained our free institutions cannot be continued, because 'the consent of the governed,' when thus outraged, will be wanting." As Charles Williams of Wisconsin put it, "Any schemer can draft a constitution republican in form, but until the will of the people has breathed upon it, there is no life in it; and to give it vital force, that will must be free, not expressed under intimidation, force, or fraud."[62]

Thus, the need for further legislation was clear to men who saw the victory at Appomattox steadily eroding under the pressure of continued guerrilla war. In the words of Michigan's Julius Burrows, the white conservatives of the South had "sheathed the bloody sword of open revolt only to draw the bloodier dagger of the assassin." Although they had accepted the emancipation of blacks, conservatives had moved to create a legal structure that would "consign that people to a servitude no less terrible than slavery itself." And the strategy was working. "Our want of nerve and firmness," said Thomas J. Cason of Indiana, "our disregard of the security of the rights of American citizens has permitted the confederate element to a great extent to consummate in violation of law that which they failed to gain by arms." "The question has resolved itself into this," said Alabama scalawag Charles Hays, "Is this a 'government of the people, for the people, and by the people,' or is it a government of a country which proposes to control all votes of the people by intimidation and violence?"[63]

Although a majority of House Republicans favored the new enforcement bill, a substantial minority did not. Henry L. Pierce of Massachusetts, a longtime ally of Charles Sumner, claimed that the bill was "worse than useless," for its suspension of the writ would present a threat to republicanism far graver than the evils it was supposed to cure: "Better far that we endure a few calamities, a few hardships, than imperil the nation." Michigan Representative George Willard argued that increasing the president's power "would inevitably inflame the communities suspected and invite them to further discontent and even open hostility." Citing the Tenth Amendment, Willard said that the national government should use "every incentive we can offer" to foster "home or local government, which serves as the indispensable basis of republican liberty."[64]

Amid a swirl of allegations that Grant was angling for southern electoral votes for a third term, Pierce charged that the bill's proponents aimed "simply and solely for the continuance of political party supremacy." But the politics of the issue cut both ways, and Pierce himself declared "it is not in the interest of the republican party that this should be done." With the uproar over the "banditti" incident in New Orleans still ringing in their ears, many northern Republicans shrank from endorsing anything that smacked of further military interference. Garfield saw De Trobriand's action in the Louisiana legislature as "a rash and indefensible act which makes it all the more difficult for us to handle the Southern Question wisely." The *Chicago Tribune*'s Joseph Medill had complained that "the Louisiana row has done us considerable harm" and now he warned Speaker Blaine that a new force bill would "arm the Democrats with a club to knock out our brains." Connecticut Congressman Joseph R. Hawley heard from an irate constituent, "I am so indignant that if an election should take place tomorrow I would only ask, How can I best rebuke this outrage of Sheridan at New Orleans?"[65]

In fact, Connecticut's congressional elections would take place shortly after Congress adjourned, and Hawley's agonized response to Coburn's enforcement bill reflected the anxiety of many party leaders in the face of flagging northern will. Describing himself as "a radical abolitionist from my earliest days" who had "worked with the republican party for its most radical measures," Hawley now felt "compelled in a measure to part company" with his radical associates, because he could "not agree to put any further or greater powers into the hands of any President of the United States." The federal government, "an imperfect government" with only "defined and limited powers," had been founded on the premise that "the personal rights of the citizen would be best protected by this limited local State sovereignty around him." Hawley did not deny that "great wrongs" still occurred in the South, but northerners "did not believe it" and could not "be convinced until things were let to run there to such an extent that hell would reign in the South." More important, if northern attitudes could not be changed by argument, even less could one expect legislation to change southern attitudes, the product of centuries of relations between the races: "There is a social, and educational, and moral reconstruction of the South needed that will never come from any legislative halls, State or national; it must be the growth of time, of education, and of Christianity. . . . We cannot put justice, liberty, and equality into the hearts of a people by statutes alone."[66]

Eventually the bill's proponents agreed to limit the application of the habeas corpus section to Louisiana, Arkansas, Mississippi, and Alabama and to limit it to two years. In this form the bill passed the House at midnight on Saturday, February 27, by a vote of 135 to 114, with thirty-two Republicans voting against it. In Garfield's analysis, a "great many Republicans in the House felt deeply indignant at the conduct of the White Leaguers at the south, and felt the necessity [of] getting a strong hold upon them." And yet, he noted, "the bill might have been prevented if Blaine, Dawes, myself and others of some standing in the House had taken the floor and made speeches against it." With just a few days remaining in the session, Garfield and others knew "the bill would not pass the Senate and less resistance was made on that account."[67]

Garfield's prediction was correct. The enforcement bill did not go beyond a second reading in the Senate. That body did, however, pass the civil rights bill. Democrats tried to attach amendments that would necessitate further House action and thus kill the legislation, but Republicans beat back these efforts. In closing arguments, George Edmunds defended the bill as protecting citizens' rights "in some measure." That the bill did not do more, said Edmunds, was due mostly to the "very extraordinary consistency of attitude" that the Democrats had maintained since at least 1860. Although not generally given to wild waving of the bloody shirt, Edmunds echoed the dismay of many of his colleagues that "the contest from 1860 to 1865 is not ended." Southerners may have lost the institution of slavery, but through contract and vagrancy laws and other measures they were persistently taking steps "to provide for controlling labor, as they call it." Their intention was that "the old system of planting or a baronial system may be restored, and that those who own the lands, as in some other countries it is unhappily true, control with a rule that is as real and effectual as any slavery the operations and the liberties of the people who live upon their estates." The ultimate aim reflected in the Democrats' attitude, Edmunds told his colleagues, was that "either by absence of legislation or in some other way there shall be no effectual life in any of these three [constitutional] amendments." The Senate Republicans passed the civil rights bill with only a handful of defections from their ranks. Without fanfare, President Grant signed it on March 1.[68]

With the exception of a few Republican newspapers, press reaction to the Civil Rights Act of 1875 was lukewarm. Radical papers in the abolitionist tradition considered it fatally weak. Democratic papers raised mock cries of tyranny, but the *Chicago Tribune* was closer to the mark in labeling the law "harmless."

The Washington *National Republican*, widely seen as an administration mouthpiece, belittled the act as a "piece of legislative sentimentalism, the passage of which would not change the condition of affairs in the slightest."[69] Within three weeks the judicial emasculation of the act had begun when a federal judge at Memphis instructed a jury that the law represented an "almost grotesque exercise of national authority" over "matters not only not granted to the general government, but in the constitution itself expressly reserved to the States." The *New York Tribune* hailed the judge's interpretation as helping "to quiet the inordinate hopes of the more ignorant negroes as well as the foolish fears of the ignorant whites."[70]

When the Forty-third Congress was gaveled to a close sine die on March 3, 1875, most Republicans no doubt looked back on the traumas of the previous three months with a profound resignation. But mingled with that resignation was a maturing sense of the limits their countrymen had imposed on them—limits borne of the human heart and human psyche that political institutions proved powerless to surmount. Time and the sinking of generations and their replacement by new ones would be necessary if they were to redefine what was possible in order truly to reinvent the Republic. In the interim, Republicans had reconfigured some boundaries—slavery abolished and citizenship broadened—but fundamental change in the polity, it seemed, awaited another day. "The temper of the nation is now *conservative* and desires peace, union and active enterprise and industry all over the country," Edwards Pierrepont told Fish. "Party has but feeble hold upon the great mass of people."[71]

After the close of Congress in early March 1875, Republicans watched the spring elections in various states for some indication of the reaction to their course during the previous several months. The most important northern bellwether was Connecticut, which held elections for the next Congress. Blaine, Garfield, and other party leaders spent several days campaigning for Hawley and other Republicans. More was at stake than Connecticut, and Blaine and others tested new themes for elections in the fall and 1876. With the Democrats already having won control of the House, Republicans shifted from advocating new measures to securing what they had already done. Hawley told his constituents that he had voted against the force bill because existing laws were sufficient and the extraordinary powers it would give the president were unnecessary in time of peace.

Blaine warned a New Haven audience that rule by the Democrats threatened "a counter-revolution" that would overturn "many of the now accepted and most important points of public policy." Hence, the Speaker cautioned Connecticut voters against entering into any "unholy alliance" with the white conservative South that would place the Democrats in control of the national government. Yet he avoided extreme sectionalist rhetoric and instead acknowledged that most Americans desired "peace, cordiality, and kind feeling between the North and the South." Counseling against further interference in the South except in case of dire need, Blaine suggested instead that if "Northern firmness be as conspicuous and as enduring in peace as it was in war, . . . the South will weary of the contest and divide on other issues." Northerners could best show their firmness by voting Republican: "What is wanted is not more law, but a better public opinion, and the only way to bring that about is for the Northern States to hold the political power of the country tenaciously and unwaveringly in the hands of those who held the country together in its hour of extreme peril." Such a strategy had little prospect for success, however, for in truth white conservatives in the South had implicitly vowed never to relax their aggressive efforts until northern fatigue allowed them to take control of the whole region.[72]

Blaine and Hawley had adopted their low-key approach in hopes of assuaging northern anxieties about Republican southern policies, but the strategy failed to salvage the party's prospects in Connecticut. Hawley lost, as did two other Republicans, and the state's congressional delegation went from being 3–1 Republican to 3–1 Democratic. In the largest vote ever cast in a spring election, Connecticut voters reelected their Democratic governor with 53 percent of the vote, and the Democrats retained control of the legislature. Republican leaders cited a range of causes. Postmaster General Marshall Jewell, himself a Connecticut Republican, blamed "a growing feeling of distrust of our Administration" as well as a "general cussedness and a desire for change." Uppermost in voters' minds was the economy, still reeling from the Panic of 1873. "Labor is depressed, and men are out of employment, and capital is idle. Everything is at a standstill. These are the reasons." Whatever led to the Connecticut loss, however, few party leaders would argue that the southern question had benefitted the party.[73]

Jewell also noted that fears that Grant desired a "third term had something to do with" the Connecticut loss. For months, rumors that the president hoped to stay another four years had generated anxiety among party leaders. Even Vice President Wilson had whispered to Garfield that Grant's "struggling for a third term" was a "mill-stone around the neck of our party that would sink it out of sight." On one level, worried Republicans could wrap their opposition in the sanctity of the two-term tradition in the nation's republican institutions. But beyond the argument from principle, Republican strategists sought to distance the party from the administration's corrupt image as well as some of its unpopular actions, including the southern policy. Republicans must remember, said Daniel Sickles, that "the party is greater than the President." "The *Administration* was struck dead" in the 1874 elections, "and the corpse may infect & kill the party if not buried." Grant initially thought it "beneath the dignity" of his office to take notice of mere rumors about his intentions, but when nervous state party leaders pressed him in May, he declared that he was not a candidate for renomination. As a result, party campaigners in 1875 felt less obligated to defend the administration's course in the South. On the other hand, the decision troubled supporters such as Frederick Douglass, who considered Grant "the shelter and savior of my people in the hour of supreme danger."[74]

After the Connecticut election, attention turned to contests pending in the fall, and the shift in emphasis was readily apparent. Even New York Republicans, whose leader Roscoe Conkling was an administration ally, declared that "the welfare of the country requires a just, generous, and forbearing national policy in the Southern States." The most important of the northern state elections would occur in Ohio, which, like Connecticut, was a swing state politically, but one that would cast nearly four times as many electoral votes in 1876. Ohio Republicans nominated their popular former governor, Rutherford B. Hayes, and waged a campaign emphasizing the currency question and the state issue of guarding public schools from alleged Catholic encroachment. Garfield told one audience that sectional issues, "which were so lately tossed in the arena of fierce debate, have ceased to be contested." He and Senator John Sherman crisscrossed the state defending the Specie Resumption Act passed in January but making little mention of the South or race relations. Sherman, who chaired the Senate's Finance Committee, opened the campaign with a speech devoted almost exclusively to the currency; on the sectional front, he said merely that the "prayers of four millions of freedmen rise perpetually to Almighty God for the Republican party."[75]

Sherman regarded the money question as the "chief subject of controversy," but to fire Buckeye emotions, Republicans turned from sectionalism to the school question. At issue was the movement in this period by the Catholic Church to secure a portion of public school funds for its parochial schools. The issue took on great significance in Ohio in 1875 after the Democratic legislature had passed the Geghan law. Sponsored by a Roman Catholic Democrat, this legislation stipulated that state prison inmates and patients in state hospitals were entitled to receive religious instruction in their own faiths and required "ample and equal facilities" for such instruction. The law alarmed many Protestants, who saw it as the entering wedge for a division of the common-school fund. The state's Republicans pounced on the issue. "Under our republican system of Government," said the state party platform, "there should be no connection direct or indirect, between Church and State, and we oppose all legislation in the interest of any particular sect."[76]

In opposing public funding of sectarian education, Republicans cast themselves as defending a bedrock American institution. "The common schools of the United States," Garfield told Ohio voters, "are a part of the secular machinery of our State governments, believed to be absolutely essential to the safety of our Republican institutions." Quoting from a recently published book by a Catholic priest that characterized the common schools as purveyors of "infidelity and immorality," Garfield denied that the Republicans were attacking the Catholic Church. Rather, he said, "the church is the attacking party. In the name of religion they have attacked a cherished institution, a vital principle of our political system." Nor was such talk mere campaign fustian. Privately, Garfield worried "that the Catholic Church is moving along the whole line of its front against modern civilization and our fight in Ohio is only a small portion of the battle field." For his part, gubernatorial candidate Hayes saw immense political advantage in rebuking the Democrats "for subserviency to Roman Catholic demands." "As to Southern affairs," he said, "'the let-alone policy' seems now to be the true course."[77]

Not all Republicans agreed. Oliver P. Morton stumped Ohio for Hayes but refused to bury the southern question. "We are told that the issues of the war are settled," he told an audience at Urbana, Ohio. But "the restoration, as far as possible, to things *ante-bellum*" remained "the cardinal, all-absorbing, over-ruling purposes of the Southern Democracy, compared to which questions of currency, tariffs and banks are but as dust in the balance." For the moment the White Leagues might forbear "to cut throats, burn, whip, and drive out," and southerners might "do everything in their power to lull the apprehensions of the people of the North." But, warned Morton, southern Democrats "with few exceptions look upon the colored people as a race that ought still to be enslaved, who were made free wrongfully by the accident of war, and deeply resent their elevation to civil and political rights and equality." True reconstruction, he said, could occur only when southerners conceded "to people of all colors and opinions equal protection, justice and the full enjoyment of their rights under the Constitution and Laws of the United States, and of the States in which they live. When that time comes, the great result for which I have been laboring will be accomplished, and I shall know that the war is over."[78]

Morton's widely circulated speech sparked considerable comment among Republicans about their party's direction. *Harper's Weekly* agreed with the senator that "those who assert that there is no Southern question, because 'the South' is at peace, carefully conceal the fact that it is at peace chiefly because the national government is in Republican hands. . . . The gushing eagerness to shake hands over the bloody chasm is very likely to lead us to forget the eternal gulf that separates 'the lost cause' of slavery from the sacred cause of liberty and

Oliver P. Morton
(Library of Congress)

justice." The *New York Tribune,* on the other hand, decried Morton's rhetoric as "not merely childish" but "mischievous in the extreme," for it tended "to create distrust and doubt between two sections of the country that should be cultivating mutual confidence and esteem." The predicament that shifting northern attitudes posed for Republicans was best captured by Benjamin Bristow, who wrote John Harlan, "The fact is, it is impossible to impress the people of the North with the true state of affairs in the South. There is a general disinclination to turn to that subject, and even our best friends in the North regard Morton's efforts in that direction as mere political claptrap, calculated to do more harm than good." "We must take the public mind as we find it," Bristow wrote. "My own judgment is that not much is to be made out of the discussion of anything else than the financial and school questions in Ohio."[79]

As the campaign progressed, Bristow's chief, the president, grew more nervous about the party's prospects. Less than two weeks before the Ohio balloting, Grant made a rare public speech to help tip the balance. The occasion was the annual reunion of the Army of the Tennessee, in Des Moines, Iowa, an event that permitted him to be both firm and statesmanlike on the southern issue. Union soldiers, he told the veterans, would not "apologise for the part we took in the war," but neither would they deny to their former enemies "any privilege under the government which we claim for ourselves." Now the nation confronted new dangers that the former antagonists should face together, united "as brothers" with "a common heritage." Citing the need to guard "against every enemy threatening the perpetuity of free republican institutions," Grant adroitly shifted ground to the school issue.

> In a republic like ours where the citizen is the sov[e]reign and the official the servant, where no power is exercised except by the will of the people, it is important that the sov[e]reign—the people—should possess intelligence. The free school is the promoter of that intelligence which is to preserve us as a free nation. If we are to have another contest in the near future of our national existence, I predict that the dividing line will not be Mason & Dixon[']s, but between patriotism & intelligence on the one side & superstition, ambition & ignorance on the other. . . . Encourage free schools and resolve that not one dollar of money appropriated to their support no matter how raised, shall be appropriated to the support of any sectarian schools.

Identifying republicanism as the crucial American value, the president applauded the veterans for having sustained it against armed rebellion. Now all patriotic Americans must defend republicanism again from dangers posed by an unenlightened, benighted citizenry. Although Grant's political intent was clear, philanthropist Peter Cooper wrote the president to thank him "for the patriotism and intelligence which dictated your whole speech."[80]

Anxiety over the election in Ohio influenced the Republicans' approach to renewed calls for intervention in the South. Reluctant to offend northern voters tired of the southern issue, the administration responded warily to calls for action in Mississippi, which was also holding elections. As the balloting approached, Democrats had determined, according to one observer, "to carry the election peaceably if they could, forcibly if they must." Conservatives joined White Line paramilitary units, determined to use terrorism if necessary to control the state. In the face of such threats, Republican Governor Adelbert Ames, a carpetbagger and son-in-law of Ben Butler, had little success in organizing state militia units among blacks and their white allies. In early September, racial violence at Yazoo City and Clinton left more than thirty dead. Powerless to maintain peace, Ames asked Grant to intervene under the Constitution's guarantee clause. The president immediately put the small band of U.S. troops in Mississippi on alert but would take no overt action without a presidential proclamation, as in past interventions. Being away from the capital, Grant counted heavily on Attorney General Edwards Pierrepont to coordinate the administration's handling of the situation, including the preparation of the proclamation.[81]

Pierrepont, a New Yorker and a Democrat until 1868, had served on the Committee of Seventy that helped overthrow Boss William M. Tweed earlier in the decade. His appointment to head the Justice Department provided the scandal-tainted administration a modicum of reform cachet. On the southern question, however, he was distinctly conservative and inclined against intervention. Grant's reliance on the attorney general limited the president's alternatives. Pierrepont had taken office in the spring, and after the political repercussions of the interventions in Louisiana and Arkansas, he worked to prevent the administration from incurring further damage. Early in the summer he had tried to impress upon Grant the need to retain support in the North, especially the "great importance of carrying Ohio." Now, on the president's orders, Pierrepont got the State Department to prepare the appropriate proclamation for Mississippi, but he also labored to ensure that it would never be emitted. He leaked to the press his opinion that "a proclamation will not be issued and no Federal troops ordered to Mississippi." To justify this conclusion, Pierrepont permitted reporters to copy and publish telegrams from officials and politicians in Mississippi alleging that all was quiet in the state.

The attorney general urged Governor Ames to take steps himself to suppress any insurrection, but Ames replied that any attempt to organize blacks into a militia force would spark "a war of races" that would "extend beyond the borders of this State." In essence, the governor argued that the guarantee clause left the president no discretion in such cases: "As the Governor of a State, I made a demand which cannot well be refused." Willing to take the political heat himself, Ames noted that "the odium of such interference shall not attach to President Grant or the Republican party." But Pierrepont insisted on prior state action, telling Grant that he did not think the constitutional guarantee applied in a case "where the State Government was not found inadequate to the emergency after some effort to quell the riot." When the attorney general sent his report to Grant, he recommended no specific action but enclosed additional Mississippi dispatches claiming that the state was peaceful.[82]

The appearance of such reports and Pierrepont's conclusions in the press before the attorney general made his official recommendation to the president imposed narrow political limits on Grant's options. The president frankly told Pierrepont that his report left him "somewhat perplexed to know what directions to give in the matter." On the one hand, in an oft-quoted passage, he conceded that the "whole public are tired out with these annual, autumnal outbreaks in the

Pierrepont imposed narrow limits on Grant

South, and there is so much unwholesome lying done by the press and people in regard to the cause & extent of these breaches of the peace that the great majority are ready now to condemn any interference on the part of the Government." But Grant also seemed to agree with Ames regarding the lack of presidential discretion: "I do not see how we are to evade the call of the Governor, if made strictly within the Constitution and Acts of Congress thereunder." If the president were "to be the judge when such insurrection or invasion exists as to warrant federal interference," then the guarantee clause might "become a dead letter." That being the case, he added, perhaps with Pierrepont's leaks in mind, "The so-called liberal and opposition press would then become the power to determine when, or whether, troops should be used for the maintenance of a republican form of Government." Under the present circumstances, Grant concluded that Ames could best strengthen his constitutional and political position "by exhausting his own resources in restoring order before he receives Govt. aid." In the meantime, the proclamation could be held in abeyance. But if "peace and good order" could not be restored, Grant told Pierrepont, "the proclamation must be issued; and if it is I shall instruct the Commander of the forces to have no child's play. If there is a necessity for military interference, there is justice in such interference as to deter evil doers."[83]

In relaying the president's position to Ames, Pierrepont quoted selectively to give primacy to Grant's recognition of flagging northern will, and he underscored the call for prior state effort. "I suggest," he wrote the governor, "that you take all lawful means and all needed measures to preserve the peace by the forces in your own State, and let the country see that the citizens of Mississippi, who are largely favorable to good order, and who are largely Republican, have the courage and the manhood to *fight* for their rights." He added, however, that if Ames could not suppress resistance "by all the means at your command," the Administration would "swiftly aid you in crushing these lawless traitors to human rights." Pierrepont's apparent hope was that this last, strongly worded promise would suffice to deter the Mississippi White Liners and thus obviate actual military intervention. In this belief he was seconded by a delegation of Mississippi Republicans who, along with cabinet members Bristow and Jewell, urged Pierrepont to publish his letter to Ames. Asking permission to do so, the attorney general assured Grant, "They all say it will produce quiet." Significantly, Pierrepont added, "No proclamation needed." Pierrepont's telegram reached Grant traveling in New York state, where just a few days earlier the Republican convention had issued a platform with a general plank calling for "a firm refusal to use military power, except for purposes clearly defined in the Constitution."[84]

Grant issued no proclamation —

Ames left to his own devices —

Grant issued no proclamation, Pierrepont published his letter, and Ames was left to his own devices. The governor moved to organize militia units, composed of both blacks and whites, but met with meager success because, Ames said, "the Republicans are paralyzed through fear." The White Liners continued their terrorist tactics but refrained from overt violence against the few units Ames created, because open violence would likely lead to federal intervention. But the peace was deceptive, and Ames predicted that the White Liners would "open fire along the whole line about election time, when the time will be too short for the President to issue his proclamation for them to disperse—a proclamation which gives at least five days grace." "The nation should have acted," the frustrated governor wrote to his wife, "but it was 'tired of the annual autumnal outbreaks in the South.' . . . The political death of the negro will forever release the nation from the weariness from such 'political outbreaks.'"[85]

Despite Ames's pessimism, however, Pierrepont monitored the continued volatility of the situation. He dispatched a representative, George Chase, to observe events and broker an accommodation. Meeting with the governor and leaders of both parties, Chase secured an agreement whereby the Democrats promised a peaceful election and Ames disbanded the two militia units he had raised. With his mood now almost giddy, Ames dashed off a letter to Pierrepont lavishing praise on Chase and asserting that the state would have "peace, order, and a fair election." Pierrepont read Ames's letter to the cabinet and thereby cut off any prospect for federal action. "Judge Pierrepont alone," Chase later said, "prevented Federal interference in Mississippi." Meanwhile, the attorney general's "northern strategy" had worked. Ohioans had voted in mid–October and narrowly elected Hayes governor. "I think," Chase reported to Pierrepont, Hayes "is convinced that you did him great good." Over a year later in the White House, Hayes told Chase that "had troops been sent to Mississippi in 1875, [his opponent] Old Bill Allen would have been Governor of Ohio and probably now President of [the] US."[86]

The denouement in Mississippi was less cheering. As Ames had predicted, on the eve of the November election, too late for federal intervention, the Democrats carried out a reign of terror. Violence earlier had left so many dead that now little actual killing was required to intimidate Republicans. Moreover, whenever Republicans complained of an incident of violence, the Democrats produced an avalanche of counterstatements denying the occurrence or attributing it to personal rather than political causes. So effective was the work that even Chase wired Pierrepont that it was "impossible to have a fair election November 2nd without the aid of U.S. troops." But it was too late. Blacks stayed away from the polls in droves, and the Republicans lost by a landslide. They were reduced to a

too late

for the first time one before the war Grant sent an annual message to Congress [December 1875] that

tiny minority in the legislature and lost all but one of the six congressional seats. The "Mississippi plan" had "redeemed" the state for the Democrats.[87]

Across the North, however, the Republicans won large victories in several states, reaping what Garfield described as "a great reaction against the Democracy" on the money question. A delighted Edwards Pierrepont wrote Elihu Washburne, "The elections yesterday *insure* a Republican success in 1876 so far as human foresight can look. I *rejoice* with you." But there was little reason to rejoice for southern Republicans and others who saw the Mississippi loss as one more indication that the party was losing the guerrilla war that had plagued the South since Appomattox. From his diplomatic post in Turkey, Tennessean Horace Maynard wrote Hamilton Fish, "Ever since the close of flagrant war, [southern Republicans] have fought the rebellion singlehanded, with very little sympathy or material support from without. . . . Betrayed by self-seekers & distracted by disorganizers, they have gone down in one state after another." Thus, as 1875 wound down, Republican hopes of reinventing the Republic through a genuine reconstruction of the South seemed ever more remote. "War issues cannot be much longer kept alive," wrote Benjamin Bristow. With the Democrats about to control the House of Representatives for the first time since before the war, President Grant prepared to send Congress an annual message that made no mention of the South.[88]

As Republicans looked ahead, the relative weight they would give the southern question as compared with other issues was inextricably entangled with the presidential politics of the coming year. Potential candidates and other leaders explored new directions and weighed alternative strategies both for securing support for the presidential nomination and for defeating the Democrats. Most prominent among the contenders was James G. Blaine, who had talked about southern problems in the campaign of 1875 but who had also stressed the importance of other issues. When he invited Oliver Morton to campaign in Maine, for instance, Blaine told the Radical senator, "Your views on the southern question are popular here, but I want you to be very explicit on the finances—& especially to sail into the Ohio Rag money humbug." Blaine had also closely followed the school issue, which, he told the Ohio Republican chairman, "though more local in its character, may yet have far-reaching consequences."[89]

In the wake of the general Republican success in November, Blaine decided to "elicit a fair discussion" of the school question by proposing a constitutional amendment to ban the use of public money for sectarian schools. President Grant also considered the time propitious and used his December 1875 annual message to propose his own version of a new amendment. Grant called for a ban against the teaching of "religious, atheistic, or pagan tenets" in the common schools as well as a prohibition against the granting of public school funds

Made no mention of the South

to "any religious sect or denomination." Moreover, the president's amendment would require the states to "establish and forever maintain free public schools adequate to the education of all the children in the rudimentary branches." Grant otherwise said nothing in his message about the South, but he did call for a guarantee of free access to schools by all children "irrespective of sex, color, birthplace, or religions." He thus lent the prestige of his office to the movement in several southern states to sustain the newly launched public education systems for both races. Pressing the theme of republican civic instruction, Grant advocated making education "compulsory" and barring "all persons who can not read and write from becoming voters after the year 1890."[90]

The House referred Blaine's amendment to the Judiciary Committee, where the Democratic majority held it under consideration for more than half a year, until well after the two parties' presidential nominating conventions. If Blaine had intended to use the schools question to differentiate himself from the pack of Republican presidential contenders, it proved a poor instrument for doing so. At best, Grant had forced him to share leadership on the amendment, which, despite fairly wide support, eventually failed. As matters turned out, the southern question, rather than the schools issue, sparked virulently partisan debate early in 1876 and played a pivotal role in that year's momentous election.[91]

The Southern Question Revived

The Campaign of 1876

[handwritten annotation: × twin issues of ① race & ② section unreconstructed]

Republicans' ideas regarding the twin issues of race and section had been evolving since Appomattox, and in considerable measure their actions during the election year of 1876 and the subsequent electoral crisis simply carried that evolution forward. By 1876 their notions about how to sustain the republican project of Reconstruction no longer rested primarily on upholding individual state regimes against the implacable opposition of southern white conservatives. Events in Louisiana and Arkansas in early 1875 had demonstrated that continued aggressive intervention to prop up unpopular governments was futile and impolitic. Although the success of the Democrats' "Mississippi plan" in 1875 had revealed the devastating consequences of a hands-off approach in the states, Republicans in 1876 hesitated to revive military intervention as the centerpiece of their southern policy.

Instead, even before the electoral crisis, Republicans had come to emphasize that the key to sustaining the peace of Appomattox as well as the constitutional amendments and enforcement legislation was to prevent the Democrats from regaining control of the national government. Republicans knew that under any Democrat in the White House, southern conservatives would have no fear of national government intervention, no matter what their behavior. Although a growing number of Republicans accepted the idea of rule by the conservative "better element" in the South, most still bristled at the continuing risk of racial and political violence posed by the unreconstructed vicious. Thus, even though Republicans were moving away from a policy of intervention, they still embraced the threat of intervention by a Republican administration as a kind of latent power that could force southerners into moderately good behavior. Even more important, Republicans feared that if the Democrats should ever gain control of both houses of Congress as well as the presidency, they would wipe out Reconstruction legislation wholesale (as in fact they did when they had the power in 1894).

Republicans got a taste of Democratic dominance when the first session of the Forty-fourth Congress convened in December 1875. Ever since losing the congressional elections the previous year, Republicans had pondered how the Democrats, including sixty-one former Confederate officers, might use their new majority in the House. "Like the Trojan horse," wrote Representative Henry L. Dawes, "rebeldom" had come "into our midst and now constitutes the controlling power." When the new House organized, the chairmen of twenty-one of the thirty-four most important committees came from the former slave states. "This," James A. Garfield confided to his diary, "is the old Southern Rule returning again with a vengeance."[1]

Early in the session, James G. Blaine, who had served as Speaker of the House during the previous six years, seized an opportunity to dramatize the lingering southern domination of the Democratic party. Democratic leader Samuel Randall of Pennsylvania introduced a bill to remove all disabilities remaining on ex-Confederates under the terms of the Fourteenth Amendment. The previous, Republican, House had passed a virtually identical measure unanimously, but when Randall's measure returned from committee in early January, Blaine startled the House and the country by proposing an amendment to exclude Jefferson Davis from its provisions. He did so not because Davis had headed the rebellion but rather because Davis "was the author, knowingly, deliberately, guiltily, and willfully, of the gigantic murders and crimes at Andersonville." Blaine cataloged the horrors Union soldiers had suffered in the wretched prison in Georgia, which was commanded by men appointed and sustained by the Confederate president. Ultimate responsibility lay with Davis, who, Blaine said, "by a wave of his hand, by a nod of his head, could have stopped the atrocity." If Blaine's charge at first seemed tenuous, Garfield followed with evidence from captured Confederate documents connecting Davis with Andersonville's management. In one damning report, the Confederate inspector general had labeled the prison "a reproach to us as a nation," but a few days later, Davis had promoted its commandant and made him commissary general of all prisons.[2]

But Blaine's purpose was not denying amnesty to Davis, who had no chance of returning to public office. Instead, as he later put it, the Maine congressman wanted "to test the real feelings of the House concerning the Southern question." "You stirred up the animals," Garfield told him as the Democrats rose to the bait. Southerners defended Davis and Confederate policy and blamed the Union prisoners' suffering on actions by the North, such as making medicines contraband and refusing to exchange prisoners. Again Garfield turned the arguments around, noting that the Union government had suspended prisoner exchanges when the Confederates had adopted a policy of returning black Union soldiers to slavery. "The decision of the Union people everywhere," said Garfield, "was that, great as was the suffering of our poor soldiers at Andersonville and elsewhere, we would never make an exchange of prisoners until the manhood and the rights of our colored soldiers were acknowledged by the belligerent power."[3]

Blaine and Garfield had the better of the argument on the details, but, more important, they had drawn the Democrats into an unseemly defense of the discredited Confederacy, a defense of broad symbolic significance. Henry Dawes confided to his diary that during the amnesty debate the "rebel element" had torn "off the mask it has been wearing" to reveal "the real sentiment of the heart and disclose the real purpose to which it is aiming. . . . Good will come of it, I am sure. The danger of trusting all branches of the government in their hands will be realized before it is too late."[4]

But would Republicans themselves realize that danger? Dawes feared that the amnesty imbroglio had "awakened hostility and antagonisms in our own ranks." Particularly worrisome was the "slow conservative sentiment" in the party which "has been making a fool of itself and has been running after rebeldom." The chief spokesman for that group, Carl Schurz, gloated that "Blaine had virtually killed himself as a candidate" for the presidency. In the House amnesty debate, Dawes's Massachusetts colleague, erstwhile Liberal Republican Nathaniel Banks, called upon his countrymen to "cease controversy upon that which is past" and to emphasize instead the sentiments of "reconciliation and peace" that suffused the nation's centennial. In the coming year, said Banks, visitors from around the world would "come to witness the achievements of republican government after the expiration of a century," and the nation's "whole people" should show them "the restoration of peace" and a concomitant "restoration of hope in the hearts of oppressed nations elsewhere." Banks's speech won wide praise, especially in the South and New England. "Let Mr. Blaine fight if he wants to," wrote Herbert Radclyffe from the Boston *Journal of Commerce;* let him "go to the South & have it out with Davis—we think he isn't worth the powder."[5]

How the amnesty debate would affect Blaine's and the party's political prospects was not immediately clear. "If Jim Blaine ever had any standing," John E.

Russell of the *Century* wrote Samuel Bowles, "he has killed it & I am glad of it. . . . Will we ever have peace?" Even the sympathetic Whitelaw Reid told Blaine that the Andersonville charge "has damaged you with the class of men whose support you most wanted in New England." "On this point, however," Reid added, "I find shrewd politicians differing with me." John Hay, for one, assured Blaine that the debate "has left you stronger than before and has strengthened the Republican party in an unexpected manner." Blaine himself told Bowles that if he would come down to Washington more often he could feel "the real throb of the people's patriotism" and "you would not blunder so egregiously about Jeff Davis." Journalist Charles Nordhoff reported to Bowles, that "B. & the Repubs generally get bushels of letters & despatches to say well done, & the Dems are gen[eral]ly demoralized." No one helped Blaine more than Davis himself, who weighed in with a public letter asserting "the justice of our cause and the rectitude of my own conduct." To this, said Reid's *New York Tribune*, "the comment of the multitude at the North will be, 'Well, Blaine knew Jeff. Davis best, after all.'" Garfield told friends that despite the "violence and extravagance" of the amnesty debate, "on the whole it has done good." Having received more than a hundred letters of congratulation, he wrote, "From all parts of the country the evidence comes in that the people are greatly aroused over the revelations of rebelism developed by the debate."[6]

The question of amnesty for Davis had about it an air of artificiality, but at its root lay genuine Republican anxieties about the return of former Rebels to power. Seasoned party journalist John W. Forney, who had previously begun to feel that "the hour for forgiveness of the rebels had come," now found that their part in the debate had "extinguished all these kindred emotions" and rekindled "the old fire in my heart." "I think the Republican party with all its rings and rascals is Heaven to the Hell of a restored Democracy," he confessed to Elihu Washburne. "How true it is that slavery gave birth to Treason, [and] that Treason is ever crying revenge!" Over two months later, in a philosophical mood, Garfield wrote a close friend that because of "the Rebel spirit manifested in Congress, and the subserviency of the Democracy to it, . . . it would not do to let the old issues wholly die out; that after the war of guns came the war of history, and unless our cause was vindicated in history, the war itself would in the long run prove a failure. Therefore I thought we should maintain in politics what we fought for in the field."[7]

Thus, as Republicans faced the coming presidential race with a wide-open convention for the first time since 1860, how they should deal with the lingering southern question would weigh heavily in their selection of a nominee. On one end of the spectrum was Indiana's Radical Senator Oliver P. Morton. Morton's claim to the nomination rested largely on his untiring advocacy of continued

— Morton + Conkling — the Grant wing of the party

federal action in the South to protect blacks and their white Republican allies. While the House debated the fate of Jeff Davis's citizenship, Morton pushed the Republican Senate to appoint a special committee to investigate the 1875 election in Mississippi. "The best way to preserve the peace is to avoid the practices which are charged to have taken place in the State of Mississippi," Morton said, "not by submitting in silence to these great wrongs." If "the republican party should become tired and so act that their enemies can say that they admit that the brief experiment of negro freedom and suffrage is a failure, it would deserve the execration of men and, I doubt not, receive the punishment of Heaven." Although few Republicans other than black Mississippian Blanche K. Bruce spoke for Morton's resolution, it carried, and the Senate committee began its work.[8]

Among those who voted for Morton's resolution was New Yorker Roscoe Conkling, one of his principal rivals for the presidential nomination. As a close friend of the president, Conkling battled Morton for convention delegates from the Grant wing of the party. Representing, however, a state where many Republicans wished to back away from the southern question, Conkling had conceded the more conspicuous leadership on that issue to the Indiana senator.[9]

While the Senate committee pursued its investigation of Mississippi, two Supreme Court decisions in late March 1876 threatened the effectiveness of future federal action to protect blacks' rights. In the first, *U.S. v. Cruikshank,* the 1873 Colfax Massacre in Louisiana came before the court, and the justices dismissed the indictment against the perpetrators on several points. Following the *Slaughterhouse* decision's differentiation between national and state citizenship, Chief Justice Morrison R. Waite, a Grant appointee, noted that the right of assembly antedated the Constitution and that the First Amendment protected it from encroachment only by Congress. Therefore, citizens who sought peaceably to assemble must look to the states, not the federal government for protection. Moreover, the Fourteenth Amendment dealt with state actions, not actions by individuals against others. As for the Fifteenth Amendment's guarantee of the right to vote, citizens did enjoy an "exemption from discrimination in the exercise of that right on account of race," but the Colfax Massacre indictment was defective because it failed to allege that the perpetrators had been motivated by racial discrimination. Under the Court's narrow interpretation, the defendants went free.[10]

On the same day, Waite issued an opinion in *U.S. v. Reese.* In this case, Kentucky election officials who had refused to receive and count the ballot of a black citizen had been convicted in federal court under Sections 3 and 4 of the Enforcement Act of May 31, 1870. The Supreme Court threw out the convictions on the grounds that Sections 3 and 4 did not specifically state that the proscribed behavior was wrongful because it derived from discrimination based

The court's restraint on federal intervention [handwritten annotation]

on race, color, or previous condition of servitude, as stipulated by the Fifteenth Amendment. Although Section 2 did specifically mention such discrimination and Sections 3 and 4 referred to such offense "aforesaid," the Court nonetheless considered the sections cited in the indictment fatally unspecific. Waite did say, however, that Congress possessed the power to pass "appropriate legislation" to enforce blacks' right to vote; it just had not done so in the 1870 Act. Taking the hint, Senator Morton immediately introduced legislation to correct the omission. The bill passed the Senate but had virtually no chance in the Democratic House. (Two years later, however, in a new edition of the *Revised Statutes* conducted by Republican George Boutwell, the sections from the Act of May 31, 1870, remained on the books.)[11]

The Court's apparent constraint on federal intervention pleased some observers, including many of the old Liberal Republicans of 1872, who now favored reform from within the party. Although corruption and civil service reform remained their chief concerns, they also pushed strenuously for a presidential nominee who, unlike Morton or Conkling, would back away from Grant's policy toward the South. A reform gathering in New York called for maintaining the "settlements of the civil war" but emphasized the need to pursue "a policy of mutual justice and conciliation" to revive "the old brotherhood of the people." For many reformers, the likeliest person to do that was Treasury Secretary Benjamin Bristow. They esteemed Bristow's reputation for probity, earned especially by his vigorous prosecution of the Whiskey Ring. On southern matters he had been a moderate voice. In the spring of 1876 his backers highlighted a speech of reconciliation he had delivered the previous Decoration Day at Louisville. Americans, Bristow said, should "bury the animosities that belong to the past." Northerners could now "look with indulgence" on the Rebellion's sympathizers and "agree to differ with them on what is rapidly becoming a mere chronicle or record, and a theory." Privately, Bristow asserted, "I cannot agree that the best interests of the country are to be subserved by keeping alive the asperities engendered by the strife."[12]

Other Republicans, however, were uncertain that the southern question could, or should, be avoided. Republicans won the spring elections in New Hampshire by a large majority, and Garfield was convinced that the outcome resulted from "the developed rebelism of the present House of Representatives." When the delegates to the national convention gathered in Cincinnati in June, a majority was determined not to evade the issue, as many Republicans had appeared willing to do in the previous year's state elections. The platform covered a range of issues, but the sectional question occupied more space than any other. Republicans promised to pursue not only a "permanent pacification" of the South but also "the complete protection of all its citizens in the free enjoyment of all their rights." The platform sincerely deprecated sectionalism but asserted that it was the Democrats' strategy of creating a solid South that threatened to "reopen sectional strife and imperil national honor and human rights." "We charge the Democratic party with being the same in character and spirit as when it sympathized with treason; with making its control of the house of representatives the triumph and opportunity of the nation's recent foes; with reasserting and applauding in the national capitol the sentiments of unrepentant rebellion."[13]

In the speeches placing the several candidates in nomination the southern question predominated, as some orators did their utmost to tap the old sectional feeling. Oliver Morton in the presidential chair would "strike terror to the hearts of those monsters in the South" and bring "a complete and final settlement of all the great questions arising out of the late unfortunate war." In the continuing fight "between barbarism and civilization," James G. Blaine had "snatched the mask of Democracy from the hideous face of rebellion." Citing Bristow's prosecutions of the Klan, even the reformer George William Curtis avowed that "the liberty, the life of every man at the South,—is safe in the hands of this man from Kentucky." But Curtis's tone was one of reassurance, not emphasis. Rather than focusing on the southern question, speeches for Bristow touted his honesty and his battles against corruptionists. Those who said the least about the southern question, or indeed any specific issues, were the speakers for Ohio's favorite son, Rutherford B. Hayes, whose backers stressed his vote-getting ability against Democrats.[14]

The strategy of the Bristow supporters worked against their candidate. Morton and Conkling were steadfast friends of the Grant administration, and raising the ethics matter was sure to irritate their backers, many of whom censured Bristow for acts they considered treacherous to his chief and his party. Nor would such tactics attract second–choice support from the friends of Blaine, whose alleged corrupt dealings with railroads had come under severe attack in the press and Congress. Ironically, the heightened sensitivity to the corruption issue nurtured by the Bristow people played directly into the hands of Hayes's friends. It proved strong enough to kill off Morton, Conkling, and even the front-runner Blaine, who entered the convention with three–quarters of the delegates needed to win. But it did little to attract delegates to Bristow, who never received more than a sixth of the convention votes cast. Edward Noyes and other Hayes speakers portrayed their man as a perfectly clean public servant, "against whom nothing can be said" and who also had "no personal enmities." The strategy worked, and on the seventh ballot Hayes squeaked past Blaine, taking the nomination with just 50.8 percent of the delegates' votes.

Rutherford B. Hayes
(Library of Congress)

Thus, circumstances had led Republicans to nominate a man whose chief claim to their consideration was his striking victory in the Ohio gubernatorial race the previous year in a campaign that had paid little attention to the southern question. Moreover, for vice president, the Republicans nominated New Yorker William A. Wheeler, chief architect of the "Wheeler Compromise," which had taken the vexatious Louisiana question out of national debate.[15]

What role would the southern question play in the fall campaign? As a congressman from 1865 to 1867, Hayes had given his support to the creation of the Republicans' Reconstruction policy. But, like many others in his party, he had with the passage of time recoiled at the mounting evidence of that policy's mistakes and failures. Corruption in the Reconstruction regimes and especially the continuing need for federal military intervention to sustain them had so vitiated the noble experiment that Hayes increasingly "doubt[ed] the ultra measures relating to the South." Thus, a year before his presidential nomination, he had come to see wisdom in "the let-alone policy." And yet Hayes also believed that any reorientation of federal policy toward the South could be pursued safely only by the Republicans, who, unlike the Democrats, remained committed to the well-being of the former slaves. As early as 1871, as the Reconstruction effort began to unravel and the Democrats had already "redeemed" some southern states, he noted that "the important question is what will the Democratic party do on the subject of the Constitutional Amendments if they obtain complete power in the Government in all its departments? If they get power in the Supreme Court, in Congress, and in the Executive Department, what will they do? Will they maintain and enforce the Amendments or will they overthrow them?"[16]

These questions still haunted Hayes's thinking as he contemplated the fall campaign in 1876. Carl Schurz advised the nominee to use his letter of acceptance to stress the civil service and currency questions over "the old war issues." Hayes might say something about maintaining "the equality of rights without distinction of color," but he should also declare that "the Constitutional rights of local self-government must be respected." Hayes was inclined to agree with Schurz, but he hesitated to use the phrase "local self-government," with its "Democratic associations." "It seems to me to smack of the bowie knife and revolver," he told Schurz. "'Local self-government' has nullified the 15th amendment in several States, and is in a fair way to nullify the 14th and 13th." Hayes believed that if the Democrats gained full control of the national government, they would complete that nullification and terminate the republican project, and for that reason Republicans must defeat them at all costs.[17]

Hayes's July 8 letter of acceptance dealt with four main issues. The first and longest section promised civil service reform, the second and third touched briefly on the currency and common schools issues, and the last dealt in a balanced fashion with the southern question. "What the South most needs is 'peace,'" he said, "and peace depends upon the supremacy of the law." If the southern states were to advance materially and achieve a "progressive recovery from the effects of the war, their first necessity is an intelligent and honest administration of the government which will protect all classes of citizens in their political and private rights." Hayes left little doubt as to which rights he meant, noting that "all parts of the Constitution are sacred and must be sacredly observed—the parts that are new no less than the parts that are old."

Hayes thus signaled his willingness to allow conservatives to exercise power in the South, but he insisted that any federal "let-alone" policy be contingent upon white southerners' adherence to the Thirteenth, Fourteenth, and Fifteenth Amendments. This stipulation was the sine qua non that Hayes maintained for the rest of the campaign and through the electoral crisis that eventually resulted in his victory. If the South exhibited "a hearty and generous recognition of the rights of all, by all," he would find it "practicable to promote, by the influence of all legitimate agencies of the General Government, the efforts of the people of those States to obtain for themselves the blessings of honest and capable local government." Hayes thus employed the phrase Schurz had recommended, and Schurz congratulated him on the letter's "excellent effect," especially in "the number of independent voters who have left the fence in consequence." Similarly, George William Curtis applauded the letter for a "tone and grasp" that showed "unmistakably that it is not the work of a politician."[18]

Curtis was wrong, however, for if Hayes's career had showed anything, it was that he was a deft politician, attuned to concerns that resonated with the electorate. In the weeks after his letter appeared, his political instincts began to tell him that on the southern question, many northern voters shared his anxiety about the dire consequences if the Democrats should capture the national government. He wrote Schurz, "I wonder if you see what I am discovering beyond all question in Ohio. A vast majority of 'the plain people' think of this as the main interest in the canvass: *A Democratic victory will bring the Rebellion to power.*"[19]

Reports from the South seemed to justify this anxiety and Hayes's insistence on the Reconstruction amendments as nonnegotiable. Former Attorney General Amos Akerman told party leaders that in the South, "Men are Republican or Democratic according as they are or are not attached to the last three amendments to the Constitution." Those who "control the Democratic party mean to keep labor in servile subjection to capital, and to keep the Confederate cause and Confederate ideas popular." Slavery "dies hard," Akerman wrote, "and most of the Southern whites have not yet been able to dismiss the ideas, the feelings, and the hatred which it bred."[20]

That hatred burst forth again in racial violence in early July, this time at Hamburg, South Carolina, which left a half dozen blacks murdered. Grant labeled the attack "cruel, bloodthirsty, wanton, [and] unprovoked," and he urged Governor Daniel Chamberlain to do all in his power to protect "the humblest as well as the proudest citizen." The president promised that if necessary he would "give every aid for which I can find law or constitutional power." For Republicans, the Hamburg violence underscored the absolute necessity of victory in 1876 to safeguard the surviving remnants of the republican project in the South. The incident reinforced their fears about federal reaction in the future should a Democrat be sitting in the White House. In Congress black Representative Joseph Rainey demanded to know "whether we are to be American citizens with all the rights and immunities of citizens or whether we are to be vassals and slaves again." In response, Mississippi Democratic Congressman L. Q. C. Lamar deplored the massacre and called for the punishment of its perpetrators, *[handwritten margin note: Grant recommend 1) southern men 2) North will]*

but he also insisted that the "corrupt and lawless" Republican state governments often invited such violence.[21]

Over the years Lamar had emerged as the leading congressional spokesman
of moderate southern Democratic views. In early August he delivered an extended oration claiming that, despite the allegations of Hayes and other Republicans, a Democratic victory in 1876 would leave the new constitutional amendments and blacks' rights secure. The return to home rule would not only "take
the question out of national politics" but also give the black man "a higher and
better life than he now leads as the misguided and deluded constituency of dishonest office-holders."[22]

Lamar's attempt to allay northern fears spurred a passionate response from
Garfield, which so effectively conveyed the Republican view that the party's national committee printed 400,000 copies as a campaign document. Garfield recognized that with the Civil War more than ten years past, the contested terrain
now was northern memory and northern will to sustain "the whole meaning of
the revolution through which we have passed and are still passing."

> After the battle of arms comes the battle of history. The cause that triumphs
> in the field does not always triumph in history. And those who carried the
> war for the union and equal and universal freedom to a victorious issue can
> never relax their vigilance until the ideas for which they fought have be-
> come embodied in the enduring forms of individual life. Has this been done?
> Not yet.

Garfield traced the origins of the different social philosophies of the North and
the South as far back as 1620 with the arrival on American shores of two "ideas
irreconcilably hostile to each other." At Plymouth Rock the *Mayflower* landed,
carrying the idea that "private judgment, in politics as well as religion, is the
right and duty of every man," while at Jamestown a Dutch brig brought slaves
and the idea that "capital should own labor." Garfield traced the history of these
notions down through the Civil War and after. Lamar had claimed that white
southerners had experienced a change of heart since the war, but Garfield cited
quotation after quotation from unreconciled southerners suggesting that such a
transformation extended at best to only "a few patriotic and philosophic minds."
Moreover, Garfield warned against entrusting the country's other "vast and important interests for the next four years" to the parochial and negative Democrats, "whose principal function has been 'to lie in cold obstruction' across the
pathway of the nation."[23]

Garfield's answer to Lamar delighted Hayes, who thought it would "do
good" in the campaign. "Our main issue must be *It is not safe to allow the Rebellion to come into power.*" That strategy seemed all the more appropriate when the

Senate committee investigating the 1875 election in Mississippi released its report. The committee's Republican majority found that the Democrats had broken their promise to Governor Ames to maintain peace and that considerable violence had marred the voting. As a result, "Mississippi is at present under the control of political organizations composed largely of armed men whose common purpose is to deprive the negroes of the free exercise of the right of suffrage and to establish and maintain the supremacy of the white-line democracy, in violation alike of the constitution of their own State and of the Constitution of the United States." By mid–August Hayes had become convinced, as he told Garfield, "The true issue in the minds of the masses is simply, Shall the late Rebels have the Government?"[24]

The common-school issue still stirred interest in some quarters, and Hayes even felt the need to deny allegations of having been a Know-Nothing. The Democratic House of Representatives passed a diluted version of the Blaine Amendment, but it died in the Senate, and Hayes was content to let the issue "be debated and considered by the country." In any event, he was satisfied that the southern question was "rapidly becoming the one topic of the press and of speakers. It *does* tell."[25]

Republicans did not ignore other issues such as the currency and civil service reform, but as the campaign unfolded, they made the southern issue their focus. Party committees issued pamphlets with titles such as *A Democratic Counter Rebellion: Conquering the Union They Failed to Destroy* and *The Rebel South Victorious*. Speakers invoked similar themes. In Indiana the gubernatorial candidate Benjamin Harrison told voters, "The great crime which has removed the Democratic party from the confidence of the people has been the crime of treason, and never until that taint is eradicated can it ever expect to enjoy that confidence." Continued violence in the South coupled with steadfast adherence to the heresy of states rights marked the Democratic party as yet unfit to take possession of the national government. Although the Democrats nominated two northerners, Samuel J. Tilden and Thomas A. Hendricks, on their national ticket, evidence from the recent session of Congress showed unmistakably that the southerners ruled the party. In the House, Blaine told a Boston audience, northern Democrats did "not know enough to sneeze until the Southern members took snuff." Democrats might accuse their opponents of waving the bloody shirt, but Republicans accepted the charge with equanimity. "We will march under the 'bloody shirt,'" Harrison declared, until the Democrats "purge their party of the leprosy of secession."[26]

One may ask how sincere Republicans were in such seemingly extravagant professions. The evidence suggests that among themselves, party leaders in fact felt deep foreboding at the thought of Democratic victory, expressed in the same dramatic language they used in public. "I shudder," Elihu Washburne confessed to a friend, "at the thought of a possibility that the country can be turned over to the tender mercies of the Southern rebels and northern Copperheads who endeavored to destroy it." Cincinnati *Commercial* editor Murat Halstead shared with Hayes his apprehension that "the Confederacy is attempting now what the idiots missed doing when they preferred war." Perhaps most telling were the fears expressed by Edwards Pierrepont, who as attorney general had designed the administration's hands–off policy in Mississippi the previous year. Possibly with pangs of remorse, Pierrepont now wrote Washburne from his post as minister to London:

> If Tilden is elected we shall have lively times. The Confederacy, as you rightly say, will be extended over New York. Of course the Negro vote will amount to nothing. There will be no Negro vote except for the Confederacy one year after Tilden is President. No matter what Tilden may want, he must do the bidding of the Confederates. I am not of a desponding temper, but the contrary; yet I say to you, in confidence, that if Tilden is elected it will be the beginning of the end, and that end will not be as far off as a hundred years. It may go on well enough for a while but the fact of the success of the Rebellion so soon, tells all that a thoughtful man needs to know.

The task that lay before Republicans, Pierrepont believed, was to convince skeptical northerners that a Democratic victory threatened disaster for their section as well as the South. He told Washburne, "If the Confederates secure the power *they will use it.* The North will have a heel upon its neck which it little dreams of." Chief among the ex-rebels' objectives was "to be paid back what they have lost. It is useless to tell our Northern people this. They turn a deaf ear, do not believe it, & do not heed it any more than they believed the South meant war in 1860. There is a strange fatuity about our Northern people in their reluctance to believe that the South would attempt when restored to power to get pay in some direct or indirect way for their slaves. God grant that the opportunity to make such attempt may not come."[27]

The greatest obstacle to Republican victory in 1876, as in 1874, was the depressed state of the economy lingering after the Panic of 1873. Hayes considered it "our deadliest foe" and urged speakers to stress "the dread of a solid South, rebel rule, etc." because it "leads people away from 'hard times.'" But the tactic was not merely diversionary. Republicans also sought to demonstrate that the pro-South Democratic party in power would pursue policies that would prolong if not deepen the nation's economic woes. As vice presidential nominee William Wheeler put it to Whitelaw Reid, "The ingrained Republicans who look upon the success of the Democratic party as threatening the loss of everything gained by the war *to the negro* need no looking after. Men engrossed in business, with whom politics is an incident but upon whom we must depend for success, are the ones to be aroused to the danger which impends." Senator George Boutwell, who chaired the Mississippi investigation, believed that with northern interest in the fate of southern blacks flagging, emphasizing the economic consequences of "rebel rule" might be the only way to overcome the influence of "those men and presses who have ridiculed the idea that the Southern question is a living question. Thank God," he wrote James Redpath, "the country can not have either political peace or security in its business and financial interests until justice, absolute political justice, is secured to the negro."[28]

Republicans tried to pin repudiation and inflation on the Democrats, but because views on the money issue cut across both party and sectional lines, it was not ideally adapted to draw a partisan distinction between Democrats and Republicans. Instead many Republicans laid more stress on what they pictured as a rebel design to raid the treasury should the Democrats attain full power in the national government. This was the so-called rebel claims issue, the effort by southerners to secure congressional legislation compensating them for property destroyed or appropriated by Union armies during the war. "The point is by all odds the best we have," Hayes told Murat Halstead. "It touches the two vital things 1st the Rebel menace 2d It reaches men's pockets—is an answer to 'hard times.'" At Hayes's urging, Halstead addressed a mass meeting on the issue in New York's Cooper Union. A Democratic victory, Halstead warned, would inaugurate "the Confederate system of finance—the issue of legal-tender paper to pay the claims, a policy that would reduce the finances, the credit, the bonds of the nation to a level with those of the Southern Confederacy—the level of hopeless bankruptcy." John Sherman, the Republicans' premier financial statesman, charged that allowing the claims would double the national debt and "endanger our whole financial system." The "Republican party alone," he told Ohio voters, "can protect you from the untold multitude and magnitude of claims for losses . . . sustained by the rebels themselves."[29]

But Sherman also framed the southern question in terms of northerners' "higher sense of duty and obligation . . . to the freedmen of the South." "Who among you believes that a Democratic administration will ever attempt to protect them in their political rights?" he asked. The question seemed all the more relevant as reports filtered northward of growing violence and intimidation in South Carolina, perpetrated in large measure by mounted rifle clubs. Numbering in excess of 10,000 men, these clubs constituted an imposing force in the interest of the Democratic party. With the state militia outnumbered and outgunned, Governor Chamberlain again turned to Washington for help. In response, Grant issued a proclamation ordering the clubs to disperse and also dispatched more federal troops to the state. With the stationing of troops at trouble spots, the violence subsided, in large part, however, because the work of intimidation had already been done.[30]

Grant intervened in South Carolina at considerable political risk for the Republicans in some parts of the North, especially in the swing state of New York. Even so, party speakers rallied around the president's move. Even Carl Schurz, anxiously working for Hayes's election, told the New York Union League Club that the Democratic party stood as "a continual threat of reaction against the results of the war." "I believe in reform, gentlemen; but I do not believe in the reform of the rifle and the revolver in the hands of a terrorist." In a speech in Brooklyn on the eve of the election, Blaine returned to the "trite and well known" assertion that "loyal men" ought to run the government. Although Appomattox had receded in public memory, the issue still came back to the preservation of the republican experiment. "The Republican Party have no proscriptive right to rule this country," Blaine said, "but they have the right to rule it until an honest majority of votes legally cast decides that they shall not rule it. It ha[s] taken centuries to educate the Anglo-Saxon race to a belief that a majority even of one, if it be honest, shall rule."[31]

Thus, the southern question played a central role in the 1876 campaign. As James A. Garfield prepared to go to bed on election eve, he confessed that "my own discussion of the issues has given me an exaggerated view of the dangers which may follow if Tilden is elected." And yet as the people cast their ballots on the next day, he still shuddered at the possibility "that the good sense and patriotism of this country can allow the destiny of the nation to pass into the control of the rebels." Hayes thought the Democrats had the better chance to win, but, he noted, "If we lose, the South will be the greatest sufferer. Their misfortune will be far greater than ours. . . . The South will drift towards chaos again."[32]

5

Rescuing the Republic
The Electoral Crisis of 1876–1877

The indeterminate outcome of the 1876 election forced a test of the nation's republican foundation second only to the Civil War itself. In the crisis of 1860–1861, southerners had resorted to war to protect their interests; sixteen years later, hotheads once again called for the arbitrament of arms to achieve their political ends. Although the chance of war in 1877 was slim, the nation struggled through an acute crisis that stretched from election day to the inauguration. The episode remains one of the most controversial in American political history.[1] The principal concern here is how the unfolding events reflected and affected the Republicans' beliefs, especially as they related to their republican project in the South.

During the campaign, Republicans had concluded that not only the country's well-being but perhaps its very existence depended on barring the rebel-dominated Democracy from retaking power. When the uncertain result of the November balloting rendered the nation's political condition even more troubled, that same cast of mind lay at the root of Republicans' maneuvers during the ensuing contest. According to Republican national chairman Zachariah Chandler, people throughout the North viewed "Southern barbarism, ostracism, & persecution" with "horror and indignation." "If our cause is lost," Edwards Pierrepont wrote Hayes in early December, "then the Confederacy rules for many years over a humiliated northern people who sacrificed three hundred thousand of their sons and countless treasures of their goods to keep a Union for Confederates to rule and revel in."[2]

Given that prospect, promising to "withdraw" the troops from Louisiana and South Carolina might seem a small price for Republicans to pay to achieve the larger goal of preventing the Democrats from advancing their dangerous power in the national government. As it happened, paying that price proved unnecessary to secure a Hayes victory, for ultimately the Democrats could marshal no realistic threat to block his taking office. The allegations of Hayes's critics notwithstanding, the policy of "removing" the troops was not extorted from Hayes as a prerequisite for his election but instead flowed more or less naturally from a movement begun in the latter years of the Grant administration. Hayes's attitude toward the South before the election had more than implied that he was prepared to take this final step regardless of the nature of his victory. His main concern was to put his definition on the conditions under which the troop withdrawal would go forward. The electoral crisis evolved through several stages; at the beginning no one could have predicted the precise course it would follow. But when the electoral count reached the point when Hayes could be confident that he would become president, he believed he was in a position to insist that the withdrawal be contingent upon a pledge by southern conservatives to uphold the constitutional rights of the blacks, the principal condition he had asserted in his letter of acceptance in July 1876. The last few days of the controversy in Washington generated a set of circumstances that allowed his associates to wring from southern spokesmen the very guarantees Hayes sought. Thus, Hayes could enter the White House satisfied not only that the Democrats had not captured the national government but also that a reordering of federal-state relations in the South could proceed with the core of the Republican policy— protection to the former slaves—still intact.

In the immediate aftermath of voting on November 7, unofficial returns indicated a victory for Tilden, who apparently had carried a solid South as well as the northern swing states of New York, Indiana, Connecticut, and New Jersey. But William E. Chandler and other Republican strategists at party headquarters in New York quickly realized that if the three southern states still under Republican governments—Louisiana, Florida, and South Carolina—plus late-reporting Oregon went to Hayes, he would take the presidency by a single electoral vote, 185 to 184. Telegrams from headquarters urged Republican officials to "hold" those states, thereby launching the months-long controversy.[3] Chandler immediately set off for the disputed southern states and from Lynchburg, Virginia, wrote Hayes, "The Negroes here are timidly anxious that the one maj[ority] may save us." What was at stake in the outcome of the contest was clear to black leaders such as John Mercer Langston, who wired Hayes, "I speak for four millions of Colored Americans lately emancipated[,] lately devoted to the Govt even unto death in the expression of congratulations upon your election to the presidency."[4]

In the three southern states the official canvassing of the popular votes lay in the hands of returning boards, which were authorized not only to count the votes but also to reject any returns they considered fraudulent. Because Republicans controlled the boards, Democrats feared the worst, and national chairman Abram Hewitt dispatched "visiting statesmen" to the state capitals to witness the panels' work. ~~President Grant~~ requested leading Republicans to go south to perform the same function. In addition, in response to rumors of threatened violence, ~~Grant put U.S. army troops on alert~~ to preserve peace and to see that the boards were "unmolested in the performance of their duties." "~~No man worthy~~ of the office of President," he declared, "~~should be willing to hold it if counted in or placed there by fraud~~." For his part, Hayes was convinced that during the election the Democrats had "endeavored to defeat the will of the lawful voters by the perpetration of crimes whose magnitude and atrocity has no parallel in our history." Hence, the evidence would "justify the throwing out of enough [returns] to secure the State to those who are lawfully entitled to it." Over the next few weeks, the board in each state rejected at least some votes as fraudulent. By early December all three had completed their labors and declared the Hayes electors victorious.[5]

On December 6 electors convened in state capitals to cast their ballots. But in Florida, Louisiana, South Carolina, and Oregon, ~~two sets of electors~~ met and prepared certificates to send to Washington. According to the Constitution (Amendment 12), "the President of the Senate shall, in the presence of the Senate and House of Representatives, open all the certificates and the votes shall then be counted." The vague passage left indeterminate who should actually count the votes. The president of the Senate, Thomas Ferry, was a Republican, and many of his party colleagues believed that the Constitution empowered him to count the vote and declare the winner. Many Democrats argued that the passage signified participation by the two houses in the count. If the two houses acted in combination, then the large Democratic majority in the House would outstrip the Republican edge in the Senate and thus tip the balance toward counting the Democratic electors from the disputed states. If the House and Senate acted separately, they would deadlock on which votes to count and thus count neither set, and Tilden would be elected with a majority of a smaller whole number of electors. Or alternatively, if the whole number of electors was not reduced, the lack of a majority would throw the election into the House, where the Democrats would proceed to elect Tilden. In years past Congress had agreed on procedures before moving to the count, but now the obvious unacceptability of each of these schemes to one of the parties seemed to prevent such an agreement—unless, that is, enough members of one party or the other in one house or the other could be persuaded to abandon their party's position.[6]

As the year drew to a close, Hayes and other Republicans received indications that some southern Democrats would be willing to do just that. Discussions proceeded at several points, but for Hayes the main concern was that any understanding be on his own terms, based on the balanced approach he had already adopted in his letter of acceptance. That document had indicated that he would not revive the policy of intervention of previous years and instead would encourage responsible home rule by reasonable leaders within the South, but that he would do so contingent upon the guarantee of blacks' rights. Thus, before the November election had occurred, Hayes had developed the central text of the position he would take, and after the election he continued to insist that his "views on the Southern question were given authoritatively and correctly in my letter of acceptance." Those views remained the essence of his approach during the months of the crisis.[7]

On December 1 Hayes granted an interview to William H. Roberts, managing editor of the New Orleans *Times,* who claimed to represent the views of Congressman L. Q. C. Lamar of Mississippi, Wade Hampton, the Democratic candidate for governor in South Carolina, and other prominent southerners. Roberts assured Hayes, "You will be President. We will not make trouble. We want peace." What southerners hoped to see under Hayes was "an Administration which will favor an honest administration and honest officers in the South." Roberts claimed that southerners wished to see "the color line abolished"—that is, that issues other than race would divide southern parties in the future. In return, he noted, "we will favor measures to secure the colored people all of their rights." Hayes responded with caution. He noted merely that his "letter of acceptance covered the whole ground" and that "it meant all it said and all that it implied." Although news reports suggested that Hayes and Roberts had struck some sort of deal, that was not the case, for Hayes closed his diary description of the meeting: "In case of my election there will be further conference, and I hope for good results."[8]

As members of Congress returned to Washington, Republicans and southern Democrats held similar discussions. Several southerners approached Ohio Congressman James Garfield, urging him to make a speech clarifying the prospective southern policy of a Hayes administration. In a letter to Hayes, Garfield reported an apparent division in the Democrats' ranks. Northerners seemed determined to "keep up the popular excitement" until House committees investigating the returning boards in the South could make such reports as would "aid them in breaking down the count in February and thus throw the election into the House." Southerners, however, as Georgia's Ben Hill told Garfield, had little taste for "this sort of reckless warfare" under the lead of northern Democrats who in times past had been "invincible in peace and invisible in war." To Garfield, the time seemed right for an overture, although what the disgruntled southerners desired from the Republicans was "not quite so clear, for they are a little vague in their expressions." Apparently they hoped for assurance that "the South is going to be treated with kind consideration" by Hayes. Old Whigs among southern leaders looked for confirmation of their assumption that in matters of internal improvements they would be "much better treated by the Republicans than they were likely to be by the Democrats."

Garfield outlined for Hayes several points that he, Garfield, might make in a speech. First was the indisputable fairness and legality of Hayes's election. Second, the Republicans would "pursue a broad national policy" to "build up the industrial interests of every section of the country, and to invite the cooperation of all men north and south who believe in the new birth of the nation." Third, Garfield would assert that southerners could "not ask a more liberal and generous policy than is set forth in your letter of acceptance; and that all who know your character and spirit will feel assured that you will carry out the programme set forth in your letter, faithfully and fearlessly." The ultimate goal of such an approach would be a South where parties "shall not be divided on the color line" and where "the constitutional rights of the negro may be as safe in the hands of one party as the other—and that thus, in the South as in the North, men may seek their party associations on the great commercial and industrial questions rather than on questions of race & color." Hayes replied that Garfield's "views are so nearly the same as mine that I need not say a word." But, he added, "I am *wholly uncommitted* on *persons* and *policies* except as my published letter and other *public* utterances show." To discount newspaper rumors that he had struck a secret deal with Roberts, he noted, *"There is nothing private."* Despite his long letter to Hayes, Garfield also questioned the efficacy of any bargain to secure southern Democrats' acceptance of the Republicans' position on the Senate president's power to count the vote. He did not make the speech the southerners had hoped for, and indeed doubted that their revolt against northern Democrats in Congress would "amount to anything in the long run."[9]

Other Republicans advising Hayes were more hopeful. The governor's good friend William Henry Smith, general agent of the Western Associated Press, worked closely with Henry Van Ness Boynton, Washington correspondent of the *Cincinnati Gazette,* and Andrew J. Kellar, editor of the Memphis *Avalanche,* to try to foster an accommodation with southerners in Congress. In mid-December Kellar argued that the way to win southern congressional support for the Republicans' position on the count was to appeal to southerners' desire for "home rule" and an end to federal support for carpetbag governance in the South. In Kellar's view, what Hayes had said in his "letter of acceptance sh[oul]d satisfy any man who thought Hayes honest." Boynton, however, thought that their strategy should focus on an appeal to the South's need for federal aid to build its infrastructure, particularly railroads. If southerners could feel confident of Hayes's support for such aid, they would be more inclined to accept his accession to the presidency. More specifically, southerners in several states hoped for federal assistance in the building of the projected Texas and Pacific Railroad. Emphasis on this project, Boynton claimed, would have the added advantage of bringing to the Republicans' cause the material assistance of Pennsylvania Railroad president Thomas A. Scott, the chief promoter of the Texas and Pacific, who supposedly had ample resources to fund a lobbying effort among southern congressmen.[10] The *Chicago Tribune* editor, Joseph Medill, gave his blessing to the scheme as a way to achieve the Republicans' higher goal: "I shall not think any price too high," he told Smith, "that will secure protection to the lives of the poor Negroes and peace to the South."[11]

But however inviting such a strategy might be to Republicans, and however much they might favor government aid to enterprise, the political climate of mid-1870s was hardly conducive to a subsidy program. Scandals such as Crédit Mobilier, defaults by previous recipients of railroad grants, and a general embrace of government frugality after the Panic of 1873 all combined to move public opinion against subsidies. In 1875 House Republicans had voted overwhelmingly with Democrats to pass a resolution against further subsidies. In 1872 and again in the election just passed, the Republican Party's platforms had pronounced against further grants to railroads. Even Boynton conceded that the plan would require "an exception to the republican policy of opposition to subsidies." Bucking the party's antisubsidy stance in a nebulous bargain had little appeal. Although Kellar and Boynton sought to reassure Garfield about southerners' good intentions, the congressman was "not sure that these men can be trusted." Just a week after Garfield had written to Hayes about southerners' desire for internal improvements, and just two days after meeting with Boynton and Kellar, Garfield worked assiduously in the Committee on Pacific Railroads to stymie consideration of Scott's Texas and Pacific bill. In early January Garfield agreed with Hayes's friend and confidant James M. Comly, editor of the *Ohio State Journal,* that backing the subsidy might further split the Democrats and help develop Republican support in the South, but he nonetheless noted that "the whole business of subsidies to railroads had been brought into disrepute" and that "the Republican party was so squarely committed against further subsidies as to prevent them from advocating the building of the Texas

Pacific R.R. by the help of Congress." Garfield persisted in his opposition to the bill, and it failed to pass.[12]

Like Garfield, Hayes was skeptical about negotiations with the southerners. Privately, he conceded that it was "so desirable to restore peace and prosperity to the South" that he would be inclined to be "exceptionally liberal" in support of "education and internal improvements of a national character." But, he pointedly told William Henry Smith, "I do not wish to be committed as to details." He resisted suggestions that he designate some single representative to speak authoritatively for him, preferring instead to rely on the Ohio men in Washington to represent his views. When South Carolinian Thomas J. Mackey dropped in on the governor in Columbus to assure him that "good results" would come from "a wise policy in the South," Hayes had to weigh these professions against reports that Mackey was "a first class fraud." "This is a specimen of the Southern complications!" he noted in his diary. When Carl Schurz asked him about the rumored southern overtures, Hayes replied that "the influence referred to is too small to control the large [Democratic] House majority. . . . I am sure nothing will come of it." "I am not a believer in the trustworthiness of the forces you hope to rally," Hayes frankly told Smith. "After we are in, I believe a wise and liberal policy can accomplish a great deal. But we must rely on our own strength to secure our rights."[13]

Hayes's conception of those rights helps explain his reluctance to place much stock in the various efforts at bargaining at the capital in December and early January. As the old year gave way to the new with no resolution in sight, he remained committed to the idea that the president of the Senate should simply count the votes and declare the winner. "There are too many cooks at Washington," he wrote a friend. "The true thing is, a firm adherence to the Constitution. The V.P. ought to be able to finish the work at one sitting." To former Congressman Samuel Shellabarger he declared, "There should be no compromise of our constitutional rights." Shellabarger, whom Hayes had tapped as an unofficial legal adviser, agreed that procedures followed during the first thirty years under the Constitution established the precedent that "the Pres[ident] of [the] Senate 'counts' as well as 'opens' votes." Another Republican operative in Washington, John D. Defrees, similarly told Hayes that "the President of the Senate has the discretion & the right to present and count whatever he may determine to be the genuine returns. . . . All talk about compromises, or concessions, but weakens our cause."[14]

Rather than bargaining with southerners in this period, Hayes was more concerned about a rumored defection of Republicans from the party's constitutional position. His fears were justified. In part, Republican unity fell victim to factionalism. New York Senator Roscoe Conkling, still smarting over his loss to Hayes in the 1876 convention, had done virtually no campaigning in his pivotal state, which Hayes had lost. Conkling explained his nonparticipation by ill health, but he could not disguise his anxiety that a Hayes administration would follow the advice of Carl Schurz, George William Curtis, and other reformers whose civil service notions would undermine Conkling's control of New York patronage. In early December emissaries from the New York Reform Club visited Hayes and alleged that Conkling had been guilty of treachery in the campaign; they then proceeded to Washington to spread the rumor that Hayes would bar regulars from the patronage. That the circumspect Hayes had even hinted at such a course was doubtful, but the insinuation was doubly dangerous. If the rumor was not refuted, it could turn Conkling and whatever Republican senators he could carry with him against the party's position on the electoral count. Moreover, President Grant might interpret Hayes's supposed patronage policy as a reproach to his own administration and withhold his support. From Washington, both Garfield and John Sherman urged Hayes to counteract that impression.[15]

At Sherman's urging, Hayes met with Albert D. Shaw, a close Conkling friend in the New York Republican organization. Shaw warned Hayes that the apprehension that he was "in the hands of the reform element" of the party could cost him "the friendship and support of enough Senators on the approaching struggle in the Senate to change the result of the Presidential election, and bring in Mr. Tilden." In response, Hayes gave no pledges but merely said that in appointments he would give "consideration to the claims of all sections of the Rep. party." Shaw, Hayes noted, "seemed to be pleased with what I told him." Shaw also conveyed the anxiety of several carpetbag senators that they would be abandoned by "the Hayes policy of conciliation." Once more Hayes said that he had "no private views or pledges to give" and that his letter of acceptance "plainly indicated what I thought desirable." The governor again underscored his letter's main stipulation, asserting that "the Southern people must obey the new amendments, and give the colored men all of their rights—that peace in that country could only be had in this way." To allay the carpetbaggers' fears, he told Shaw "that prosperity would come to the South with immigration from the North and from Europe—that to get this, people must feel as free to go to the South as they now do to go to Kansas or Nebraska." After the meeting, Hayes recorded in his diary, Shaw left "professing to think that he could overcome difficulties at Washington." Nonetheless, Shaw's New York associates remained unmoved by Hayes's vague patronage assurances. When Shaw later asked Hayes for "more than a general outline," the governor refused.[16]

As for Grant, Hayes proved more solicitous. The president had been annoyed by news reports of Hayes's interview with the southerner Roberts, which stated that Hayes had indicated that he would offer no appointments to men connected with the Grant administration. On Christmas Day, Hayes penned a personal letter to Grant to be delivered by fellow Ohioan, Attorney General Alphonso Taft. Hayes told the president that he would "never cease to regard with admiration and gratitude the course you have taken before and since the Election." Hayes and Taft were "in perfect accord" on the situation, and, Hayes wrote Grant, "I have no doubt whatever that if you and I could meet and talk over present affairs it would be found that we were equally agreed on the same topic." The effort bore fruit, for Taft soon reported that Grant was "very much gratified with your letter."[17]

Nor did Hayes's solicitude end with this letter. Avowing a purpose "to heal by compromise, not to aggravate," he authorized Sherman in Washington to "speak in pretty decided terms for me whenever it seems advisable." In addition, he dispatched his friend James Comly to Washington to convey directly to the president his assurances of goodwill for the Grant wing of the party. Significantly, whereas he had refused to send an emissary to court southern Democrats, Hayes readily appointed Comly to meet with Grant. At this point he was more concerned about striking a "compromise" with factions within his own party than with southern Democrats. At the White House in early January, Comly assured the president that Hayes would give no cabinet seat to Grant's old nemesis, Benjamin Bristow, and would otherwise "avoid anything that could seem to be a reflection upon the President or a censure of his Administration." These assurances gratified Grant, but he could offer little in return. He said nothing explicit about his own attitude about the electoral count, and he reported that "Conkling had not reached a definite conclusion as to the power of the Vice President." (Less than two weeks after the election, a Democrat from Conkling's hometown had spoken with the senator and had assured Tilden that he could rely on Conkling's *"hearty cooperation"* in the matter of the count.) In any event, Grant showed no willingness to try to influence the New York senator, although he noted that Conkling thought Hayes deserved the 185 electoral votes and that the senator "would come out all right."[18]

Grant's optimism proved unwarranted, for Conkling came out against a simple count by the president of the Senate. So did other important party leaders. For weeks Carl Schurz bombarded Hayes and others with letters advocating submitting the dispute to some tribunal such as the Supreme Court. Schurz readily conceded the "dangers and evils of the accession of the Democratic party to power." "But," he argued, "any action on the part of the Republicans looking like a *coup d'etat,* resorted to for the purpose of retaining power, would inevitably be the destruction of the party and would thus prepare the way for Democratic ascendancy under circumstances a great deal worse." Moreover, he warned that an "unscrupulous use of power" would inflict "an injury . . . on our republican institutions fraught with mischief beyond all present calculation."[19]

Some Republicans questioned the legality of a count by Senate president pro tempore Ferry, while others cited the political dangers in seeming to grab power over the futile objections of the House of Representatives. The congressional session had barely gotten under way when Republicans George McCrary in the House and George Edmunds in the Senate secured the creation of special committees to devise an alternative method. In addition, Edmunds proposed a constitutional amendment to submit the dispute to the Supreme Court. At the time the Court comprised six Republicans, two Democrats, and independent David Davis. Democrats could thus find little to commend Edmunds's amendment. But a movement for an ad hoc tribunal did gain support, especially from the congressional special committees. As Edmunds, who sat on the Senate committee, told Schurz, "No plan can pass that absolutely or even with strong probability, determines the result either way. There must be found therefore, a method that leaves the result uncertain, although the steps be clear." The two committees pooled their efforts and drafted a bill, which Edmunds introduced on January 18, calling for an electoral commission to decide which electoral ballots to count. Its fifteen members would include five elected from the Senate, five from the House, and four Supreme Court justices ostensibly chosen for geographical distribution but actually balanced between the two parties. These four would, in a manner unspecified, choose a fifth justice, who many presumed would be the independent Davis.[20]

The proposal embodied the uncertainty Edmunds thought necessary to pass both Houses, and it won general favor among Democrats. But the bill's virtue was its principal vice to a substantial group of Republicans who agreed with Garfield that it meant "a surrender of a certainty for an uncertainty."[21] Hayes likewise considered the measure "a surrender, at least, in part, of our case" as well as "a very dangerous violation of the Constitution." Not only did it subvert the power of the Senate president to conduct the count, but in creating the commission with members chosen by Congress, the bill violated the president's constitutional power to appoint government officers. Although this latter point may appear flimsy, John Sherman elaborately defended it in the Senate.[22] Moreover, Sherman objected to the indeterminate method of choosing the fifth justice, who could have the decisive say. It was absurd, Sherman argued, to disempower the president of the Senate, "the one man selected by the Constitution as the custodian of these papers and substitute an unnamed man . . .

to have all his powers and all the powers of the Senate and House combined." Such a scheme, Sherman told Hayes, reduced the election of a president to "a Gambler's chance."[23]

In the House, Hayes's strongest ally was Garfield, who also defended the power of the Senate president. He focused not on the vaguely worded constitutional power to count the electoral votes but instead on the Senate president's explicit mandate to "open all the certificates." "To open the certificate is not a physical, but an intellectual act," Garfield argued. "It is to make patent the record,—to publish it." Hence, the Constitution empowered the Senate president to make the key determination as to which certificates he should open. "When that is done, the election of President and Vice-President is published." Counting the opened votes was mere arithmetic, and even a clerk could do it.

But beyond this textual analysis of the Constitution, Garfield had broader philosophical objections to the commission. He feared that passage of the bill would work a fundamental reordering of the balance of powers in the national government and jeopardize a central bulwark of the nation's republican institutions. "I doubt if we shall ever have another Presidential Election by the people in the old sense of the term if this bill becomes a law," he worried in his diary. "It will be a Presidential Election begun by the people, but finally determined by Congress." In the House he cited Montesquieu and Locke on the separation of powers as essential to liberty, and he offered a detailed account of the debates in the Constitutional Convention regarding the method of choosing a president. Although the Framers had first called for election of the executive by Congress, they ultimately hit upon the electoral college because they realized "that it would be ruinous to the liberty of the people and to the permanence of the republic if they did not absolutely exclude the national legislature from any share in the election of the President." Even though the commission bill applied only to the present election, it would "forever destroy the constitutional plan of electing a President" and substitute one whereby "Presidents can be made and unmade at the caprice of the Senate and House." Garfield implored his colleagues to mimic the founders, so that future Americans would look back at their generation and say that "the preservation of their institutions was to them an object of greater concern than present ease or temporary prosperity."[24]

Other powerful Republicans, including Indiana's Morton, raised their voices against the bill. Morton could hardly disguise his intense partisanship in this fierce struggle for power, but the longtime defender of southern blacks and carpetbaggers also insisted that "the greatest considerations of humanity and of public and private interest" demanded that the Democrats be kept from taking control of the national government. Such arguments won Morton the gratitude of black southerners, such as one from Arkansas, who wrote that if Tilden "does become President we of the South and Especially the Colored People will Occupy a position *which will be worse* than *Slavery*. Our *Liberty* will be *entirely gone*." The core of Hayes's support in opposition to the measure was the Ohio delegation, all but one of whom voted against it.[25]

Early in the bill's consideration Hayes took heart that even should it pass, Grant's "veto ought to prevent it from becoming law." That sentiment, privately expressed, illustrated the lack of coordination among Republican leaders. For, in fact, shortly after the bill's introduction, Grant went to work lobbying for its passage. As commander in chief, he feared "anarchy and possibly bloodshed" without "some mode of settlement, and some tribunal whose decision both political parties would accept." Grant even pushed Conkling to come out for the bill. The New York senator served on the joint committee and defended its bill in a legalistic speech that denied the Senate president's power to count the votes. Determining the validity of the electoral votes was a "political" power involving "the very highest attributes of sovereignty." Conkling scoffed at the idea that "our fathers" meant for such authority to reside in "one functionary" who could be made or unmade by a simple vote of the Senate. Such "one-man power" had no place in the Republic.[26]

It is interesting to note that proponents and critics alike considered the commission bill vulnerable to the charge of being a "compromise." "A compromise like this," Garfield wrote Hayes, "is singularly attractive to that class of men who think that the truth is always half way between God and the Devil, & that not to split the difference would be partisanship." On the other side, Conkling took pains to insist that the bill "is no compromise. . . . It surrenders the rights of none, and maintains the rights of all." Similarly, Edmunds claimed that "the measure we recommend is not what is called a compromise in any sense of the term, but is a measure of justice in aid of the exercise of constitutional government."[27]

However one might label the step, the commission bill's proponents, like its critics, saw the preservation of republican institutions at stake. As Edmunds put it, throughout history, "advances in human liberty and human happiness have always been thwarted by just this decisive ordeal of the Chief Magistracy of the government. . . . Is it not wise that we should risk something in order that the great experiment of a Republic of peace and of law among men may not utterly fail?" Nevada Senator John P. Jones wrote his wife that the bill would "strengthen the cause of freedom & free governments throughout the world. It will be striking & convincing proof of the capacity of our race to govern themselves. . . . No York & Lancaster. No White and Red roses."[28]

Most Democrats thought the commission bill revived Tilden's chances, and their substantial majority in the House ensured its passage there. In the Senate some Republicans supported the bill because they feared that in the absence of such legislation, not enough of their colleagues would uphold the Senate president's right to count the votes. Others, however, believed that those fears were unwarranted and that, if the necessity arose, Ferry would proceed with the count with the blessing of a majority of the Senate. While the bill was still in committee, Ferry told Hayes's legal adviser, Samuel Shellabarger, that he, Ferry, hoped "for a rule from the two houses which will be the law for him in the counting, & that if none shall be adopted *he* will count the vote." William Chandler, who regularly reported to Hayes, wrote that in the event that the bill failed, then, except for Conkling, "I think nearly all the other Rep[ublica]n Senators who now doubt the right of the President of the Senate to count the vote would still fall back on that plan *ex necessitate*." Indeed, many Democrats agreed that, as one Pennsylvanian put it, if Democrats blocked the bill, "Conkling and those acting with him . . . will be driven back into the folds of their party." Although some Democrats thought that a continued stalemate would justify the House in acting alone to elect Tilden, others warned of the political dangers of such a move and recognized the Republicans' superior tactical position. As former Maryland Senator George Vickers wrote House Speaker Samuel J. Randall early in the session, if "the Pres[iden]t of the Senate undertakes to open & announce the votes, what could you do? He would have his Sergeant at Arms & other officers at his side to preserve order, and if they could not do it, the military would be at hand to enforce the order of the Senate!" Until the very climax of the whole electoral crisis in early March, the prospect of a count by Ferry remained the Republicans' ace in the hole. Republican acceptance of the commission bill received an unexpected boost when the Illinois legislature elected Justice Davis to the Senate, thus apparently removing him as the putative swing vote on the commission and leaving only Republicans to fill the fifth Supreme Court slot. "There is," Sherman reported to Hayes, "a growing feeling that the passage of the bill will result in your inauguration."[29]

The exertions of Kellar, Boynton, and Scott had virtually no impact on congressional action on the bill. Kellar arrived in Washington just hours before final passage in the House and confessed that he had "not seen enough to know the situation here." His subsequent speculation that "perhaps the movement in favor of public works in the Southwest" had "so alarmed" Tilden that he had accepted the commission plan as "a necessity," was just that—speculation, for Boynton, too, had made scant headway. He had never even met the railway magnate Scott before and did not do so until less than two weeks before the bill passed. After the meeting Boynton confidently reported to Smith that "Scott is for Ferry's declaring the result without flinching"—that is, Scott *opposed* the commission bill. According to Boynton, Scott agreed that Hayes's willingness to help southerners "in their material interests can be so used here among prominent southern democrats as to effectually kill all measures looking toward revolution. . . . Scott's whole powerful machinery will be set in motion at once & I am sure you will be able to detect the influence of it in *votes* within ten days." But Boynton's strategy to force a count by Ferry by securing southern help in defeating the commission bill was a miserable failure. No southern Democratic senator and only thirteen southern Democratic representatives voted against the bill. When the legislative outcome was clear, Boynton himself admitted the inefficacy of his behind-the-scenes maneuvering: "If the knowledge which a few of us possessed could have been imparted to all republicans," he wrote James Comly, "I think we could still have held them up to a count by Ferry, & could have put it through without violence from the democrats. But the matters to which I refer & of which you know were not such as could be trusted outside a narrow circle." In any event, as Congress completed passage of the bill, Boynton conceded that "after giving up a certainty," the commission plan was "probably the best *uncertainty* which could be obtained." With the need to woo southern Democrats apparently passed, the task now for Republicans, Boynton believed, was to keep anti-Hayes Republicans such as Conkling off the commission and to secure the selection of an acceptable Republican fifth justice.[30]

The Electoral Commission Bill passed the Senate by a vote of 47 to 17, with the Republicans split 21 to 16 in favor. In the House the tally was 191 to 86, with 33 Republicans for and 68 against. Ninety percent of the Democrats voted "yea," believing, as a Tilden adviser put it, that the bill "afforded the only possible escape from the announce[men]t of Gov. Hayes as President" by Ferry. Among all the Republicans who voted in both houses, fewer than two-fifths voted for it.[31] Nonetheless, President Grant was delighted and hailed the result in a special message. "Far from being a compromise of right," the measure represented "an enforcement of right and an execution of powers conferred by the Constitution on Congress." "In all periods of history," Grant lectured his countrymen, "controversies have arisen as to the succession or choice of the chiefs of states, and no party or citizens loving their country and its free institutions can sacrifice too much of mere feeling in preserving through the upright course of law their country from the smallest danger to its peace on such an occasion." With a greater sense of resignation than enthusiasm, Hayes rationalized that the bill's passage was "a great relief to me," for "after a full and public hearing" defeat "is not mortifying in any degree, and success will be in all respects more satisfactory."[32]

The Electoral Commission included three Republican senators, two Democratic senators, two Republican representatives, three Democratic representatives, and two Republicans and two Democrats from the Supreme Court. After

Davis disqualified himself, Justice Joseph Bradley took the fifteenth seat, making the commission's political composition eight Republicans and seven Democrats. This turn of events, along with the appointment of Morton and Garfield, did much to appease Republican skeptics. "We all feel hopeful that the grand commission will find that you have been duly elected President," Sherman wrote Hayes. "If so, this contrivance will make your entry into the office easy." Democrats who had seen the commission as Tilden's best hope were profoundly disappointed by Bradley's appointment, although it remained true that Tilden needed only one disputed vote for victory whereas Hayes needed all twenty.[33]

Setting to work immediately, the commission awarded Florida's vote to Hayes on February 9 by a vote of 8 to 7. Republicans were overjoyed, for as James G. Blaine wrote Hayes, "The Florida decision is regarded here as so hopeful & promising in its bearings as virtually to settle the impending contest." William Chandler felt "a sense of infinite relief and thankfulness," but he also reminded Hayes of the larger issue at stake: "I should hate to think that this work we have been doing before and since [the] election has been only keeping a political party in power. I must believe that it has a higher purpose—that of protecting the colored man and saving the nation from great peril." Murat Halstead thought Hayes could start working on his inaugural address, but, like Chandler, he argued that "the importance of the pacification of the South—by the complete protection of the laboring classes—blacks—is too great to be overlooked" in the speech.[34]

The Florida decision ushered in a new phase in the election controversy, making Republicans wary that the Democrats might adopt obstructionist tactics. Still, they remained essentially optimistic. The law stipulated that the commission's decisions would stand unless rejected by both the House and the Senate voting separately. On Saturday, February 10, the Republican Senate promptly accepted the Florida judgment, but in the House, the majority Democrats thwarted a vote by taking a recess till the following Monday. After the Senate action, which ensured Florida's vote for Hayes, a confident Sherman assured the governor, "I can see no way in which your inauguration can be prevented except by the House nullifying the law by delays. This is Revolutionary and I do not believe the House will resort to it." Later that evening a Democratic caucus rejected further obstruction, thereby bolstering Sherman's optimism. As Stanley Matthews, one of Hayes's lawyers before the commission, reported, "The Democrats have given up the idea of defeating the election by delays. It was discussed Saturday night, urged and abandoned."[35]

This was less than cheering to Henry Van Ness Boynton, who saw the Democrats' potential reaction to the Florida decision as a way to rekindle his president-making efforts. Boynton sought to portray himself as breaking a House logjam and thus brokering a bargain between the Hayes interest and southern Democrats, especially through the influence of Tom Scott's lobbying effort. On Sunday, February 11, Boynton wrote to the Hayes people in Ohio, "It does not clearly appear this morning what the outlook for filibustering may be tomorrow. I hope it will take a strong start, but fear it will not. My wish to have it begun by the democrats rests upon a confidence that the plan we were at work upon before the compromise bill was passed will work beautifully & effectively in in [*sic*] case the hot-headed democrats attempt to defeat Hayes by delay."[36] In a letter on the same day to William Henry Smith, Boynton sought again to magnify his influence: "At the most opportune time the good seed we planted brings pleasant fruit. Enough Southern men stand in the way of filibustering to make it certain in my mind that the democrats cannot beat Gov. Hayes by delay, even if they attempt it."[37]

But in fact southern Democrats' action in the House belied Boynton's claims. In the previous day's vote for a recess, every Democrat from the old Confederacy who voted, voted for recess and hence for delay. Only one Democrat who could be classed even remotely as a southerner, Missouri's Charles H. Morgan, voted against recess and against delay. Moreover, when the House met on Monday, February 12, it was a leading southerner, J. Proctor Knott of Kentucky, who sought to engineer another delay by moving to send the Florida question back to the Electoral Commission. Speaker Randall, a Pennsylvanian, ruled Knott's motion out of order, and the House proceeded to act on the commission's Florida report. Its rejection of the report meant nothing, of course, in light of the Senate's acceptance. Thus, Postmaster General James Tyner, who witnessed these proceedings in the House, could confidently report to Comly that the "revolutionary fever is over." The Democrats would merely "wriggle their tails like the snake, occasionally attempting to strike us with their fangs, until sun-down, when they will die."[38]

Democrats had not, however, completely lost heart after the Florida decision. Many believed that their strongest case was Louisiana, where the actions of the Republican returning board were most suspect. But on February 16, Justice Bradley joined the other Republicans on the commission in awarding Louisiana to Hayes. This decision, wrote Senator Jones of Nevada, "practically settles the presidential contest in favor of Hayes. The Republicans are of course jubilant & the Democrats to an equal degree despondent." Hayes himself breathed a sigh of relief, noting that there was "still some doubt, but apparently very little, of the result."[39]

Events the next day, Saturday, February 17, seemed to justify his confidence, despite some Democrats' hopes for obstructionist maneuvers. Before the House convened, Democrats gathered for a strategy session. A small number favored going forward that day with the count procedures, but a somewhat larger group favored exploiting all available parliamentary tactics to frustrate the count. Between these two groups, a much larger contingent fashioned a middle way: The House would refuse to go into joint session with the Senate on Saturday to receive the commission's Louisiana report, but it would set a specific time, 11:00, to do so the next Monday. A resolution to this effect passed the House by a vote of 152 to 111, largely along party lines. This was a limited victory for obstructionism, and once again every Democrat from the old Confederacy who voted, voted for the postponement. But according to news reports, southern Democrats were also prominent in reconciling the extreme groups. Garfield thought that the Democrats showed "every disposition to prevent the completion of the count by delay, though some of the better men among them say that they wish to gain time to cool down the fiery spirits of their extreme men." The cooler heads prevailed in a Democratic caucus that night. In that stormy meeting, some angry Democrats argued for filibustering and other extreme tactics to block the count. But others maintained that the party's earlier support for the creation of the commission now compelled acceptance of its decision. In the end the caucus decided, by a vote of 69 to 40, that "the count of the electoral vote shall proceed without dilatory opposition." The import of the vote was clear to rank-and-file Democrats. The action of the caucus, one constituent wrote Randall, deserved "the curses and condemnation of an outraged Democracy," but Philadelphia lawyer George M. Dallas assured the Speaker that the Democrats' best course was "clearly not futile contention" against the commission's decision. Rather, they should "accept the result but . . . resent the manner of its accomplishment." On the Republican side, Sherman assured Hayes that the "action of the Demo[cratic] Caucus last night makes it certain that the result will be announced without very much delay."[40]

Once again, Boynton sought to ascribe Democratic capitulation to the lobbying effort among southerners. But even he admitted that it was "difficult to distinguish between the comparative effects produced by the two elements—the purely political & the Scott forces." Moreover, he conceded, "other forces than ours worked & contributed much." Ultimately, whatever the validity of Boynton's rhapsodic claims, the caucus decision on February 17 marked a recognition by both northern and southern Democrats that in light of the commission's pro-Hayes decisions, nothing they could do now would secure a victory for Tilden. Republicans controlled the White House and the army, the Senate, and the Supreme Court. If at any time the Democratic House should seem to go back on the Electoral Commission Act, the Republican president of the Senate could count the electoral votes and declare a winner. With little in their quiver, Democrats realized that obstruction till the fourth of March meant chaos, not triumph. As the *New York Herald* reported, "The democratic leaders prefer the peace and quiet of the country to any measures, however advantageous they might seem to their party ends, which by delaying the count of the vote would continue the uneasiness of the country." "We all think the case virtually decided," Samuel Shellabarger wrote Hayes from Washington, "& that the Democracy will make little further fight." State party leader James Robinson wrote Sherman from Ohio, "Our Republicans are feeling very jubilant."[41]

Hayes shared the confidence. After the Democrats' caucus, he wrote that "the affair now looks extremely well," and he proceeded in earnest to prepare his inaugural and select a cabinet. In planning to assume power, Hayes made the southern question one of his chief concerns, as he contemplated ways to gain "support from good men of the South, late Rebels" for his administration.[42] For weeks fellow Republicans had been offering him abundant advice on the issue. Particularly cogent was a long letter from fellow Ohioan Jacob D. Cox, former secretary of the interior who had just won election to Congress. Cox argued that the best protection for southern blacks lay in a reorientation in southern politics whereby both parties would esteem and bid for their support. "Their safety," wrote Cox, "the very existence of the political rights already given them must depend upon our getting rid of the division of parties according to race and color."

> We ought not to have great difficulty in finding means to rally to the support of a Republican administration, a strong body of the best men representing the capital, the intelligence, the virtue & the revived patriotism of the old population of the South, willing to co-operate in the good work of bringing in an era of real peace, prosperity, & good brotherhood. To accomplish this, we must pledge for the Republican party & its administration a sincere promise to scrutinize all appointments with care, & to choose men for federal office whose reputations shall command the confidence of all classes, to moderate the new kindled ambition of the colored people to fill places which neither their experience nor their knowledge of business or of the laws fit[s] them for; and to mingle sympathy for the millions who are rising from the degradations of centuries of slavery, with the recognition of the absolute necessity for honest, stable & sagacious government, without which there can be no continuance of political freedom for either race on this Continent.

But the premise of Cox's advice was that such a new policy should proceed "upon the basis of a hearty & earnest avowal on the part of Southern white men that they will in honorable good faith accept & defend the present constitutional rights of the freedmen."[43] On February 2, Hayes replied, "On the Southern question your views and mine are so precisely the same that if called on to write down a policy I could adopt your language." On the question of use of the military in the South, Hayes told Carl Schurz two days later that he had concluded that "there is to be an end of all that, except in emergencies which I do not think of as possible again."[44]

Thus, well before the commission's Florida and Louisiana decisions, Hayes had determined upon a new departure in southern policy whose outlines he had sketched in his letter of acceptance. Now, after the Louisiana decision and with his assumption of the presidency a virtual certainty, he realized that "how to do it is the question." Hayes met with black leader Frederick Douglass and frankly informed him of his decision "to recognize all Southern people, without regard to past political conduct." He insisted, however, that his policy would also emphasize "a firm assertion and maintenance of the rights of the colored people of the South according to the Thirteenth, Fourteenth, and Fifteenth Amendments." Douglass expressed his approval and offered "many useful hints about the whole subject."[45]

But the central question remained: How could Hayes plan his administration and develop his policy with any sense of assurance that "the South" would respond in the proper vein? How could he ensure that white southerners would accept his stipulations regarding the "rights of the colored people," which he regarded as essential to preserve the republican experiment in the South? The former Confederate states exhibited great diversity in their political arrangements and otherwise, and although everyone might recognize an abstraction known as "the South," it had no identifiable, corporeal being, with a single voice to present its interests and offer its bond. How could Hayes get the "hearty & earnest avowal on the part of Southern white men" that he and Cox agreed was necessary in exchange for home rule? To launch an administration with a new departure in policy whose success turned on the promise of good behavior from an entity so amorphous as "the South" was, to say the least, problematic. As fate would have it, the anomalous political condition of Louisiana and South Carolina sparked a sequence of events that yielded as a byproduct the "avowal" Hayes sought.

Louisiana and South Carolina were the last southern states remaining in Republican hands, and, like the presidential contest, the 1876 state elections resulted in claims of victory by both parties in each state.[46] Whatever the outcome of the national dispute, the overriding goal of the Democrats in both states was to achieve "home rule." In the maneuvers to gain that end, attention focused on the Louisiana Democrats' abler representatives in Washington, although South Carolina stood to gain from Louisiana's success. The mastermind of the Louisiana Democrats' efforts in behalf of their gubernatorial candidate, Francis T. Nicholls, was Edward A. Burke, a political adventurer of obscure background.

During the 1876 campaign in Louisiana, Burke had served as chairman of the Democrats' Committee on Registration and Election, a party group that monitored registration, voting procedures, and the compilation of the result.[47] Burke and his allies knew that should the Republican gubernatorial candidate, Stephen B. Packard, fail to secure support from the national administration, the weaker Packard forces would have to yield control of the state to Nicholls and the Democrats. In Washington, Burke's principal aim was to prevent support of Packard either by the Grant administration or by the putative Hayes administration. It was these efforts by Burke and his allies that eventually resulted in an arrangement that included the assurances of southern good behavior that Hayes required.

As for the outgoing administration, Grant had no intention of reversing the scaling back of intervention he had begun two years earlier in the wake of the Louisiana fiasco of 1875. On January 7, he refused a Republican request for troops to support Packard's inauguration, and the next day both gubernatorial claimants took the oath of office. Grant was determined to remain neutral, despite pleas from John Sherman and other Republicans to take "extreme measures." The president had long been contemptuous of the Louisiana carpetbaggers who, he said "had no interests there, but had simply gone there to hold office and so soon as they should lose it, intended to come away." Thus, before Burke ever met the president, Grant had become convinced of the "extreme incapacity" of Packard and his allies, although he was unwilling to saddle his successor with any policy he might not want. Burke found the president "favorably disposed," but Grant also made clear that he was officially neutral between the two claimants and would remain so until the count was settled. He would not use troops in the state unless, he warned Burke, violence arose requiring military intervention. Burke took the hint and admonished his Louisiana allies to avoid any disorder that would provoke such interference.[48]

At the beginning of the Electoral Commission's deliberations, Burke harbored some hope that a decision for Tilden might produce "home rule" in Louisiana. But the commission's Louisiana decision made clear that Louisiana's fate would lie in Hayes's hands, not Tilden's, thereby necessitating an accommodation with the incoming president. A few weeks earlier, Hayes's counsel before the commission, Stanley Matthews, had casually offered to discuss with Burke Hayes's attitude toward the South, but Burke had declined, still hopeful of a decision for Tilden. Now at the close of the commission session on Louisiana, the two men agreed to a talk that evening. Burke opened with a bit of bluster, asserting that "under no circumstances" would Louisiana's people submit to the Packard government. Disclaiming any authority to negotiate, Matthews replied that his long acquaintance with Hayes and his views permitted him to say that the new president "would not aid in the perpetuation of carpet-bag rule in Louisiana." But Matthews also noted the need for Louisiana Democrats to provide assurances to dispel "the belief in the minds of Republicans that the political rights of the colored people would be put in jeopardy if a Democratic gov'm't should prevail." The two settled nothing but agreed to meet again.[49]

In negotiating with Hayes's people, the only leverage that Burke and his Louisiana allies held was a threat to disrupt the electoral count by the Democratic House. Hence, Burke was greatly disturbed when, the day after his talk with Matthews, the Democratic caucus decided to proceed with the count without obstruction. The Democrats in Congress "should have used their power [to] secure Louisiana and [South] Carolina as a condition at least," he wired Nicholls. "Now [we] will [have to] save ourselves." The morning after the caucus, Burke laid his complaints before Democratic national chairman Abram Hewitt, who represented a New York district in the House. Hewitt denied that the national party had abandoned Louisiana, but he told Burke that Democrats could "not afford to take the responsibility for plunging this country into anarchy and strife, upsetting values and disturbing trade." Instead of blocking the count and incurring the nation's wrath, the Democrats would put "this great fraud fairly and squarely upon the shoulders of the Republican party, and go before the people four years hence." But, replied Burke, that would not help Louisiana and South Carolina, where the continued carpetbag rule would produce the "anarchy and strife" Hewitt hoped to avoid. Hewitt insisted that his support for the commission bill prevented his taking a leadership role in blocking the count, but he promised Burke to present his views to other House Democrats. Burke and his Louisiana associates also spoke with other congressmen, many of whom cited constituent pressure to proceed with the count but who also were willing to delay the count as a way of "forcing the Republican leaders to give . . . guarantees" regarding Louisiana and South Carolina.[50]

With at best lukewarm expressions of support from Hewitt and other House Democrats, Burke met with Matthews later the same day, Sunday, February 18. To allay Republican anxieties about the treatment of blacks, he gave Matthews a memorandum containing assurances that a Nicholls government would accept "the civil and political equality of all men, and agree not to attempt to deprive the colored people of any political or civil right." The government would enforce the laws "rigidly and impartially" to afford blacks as well as whites "full protection of law in person and property," and it would also support "equal advantages" in education for black and white children. In addition, Louisiana Republicans would suffer no "persecution" for "past political conduct." Burke conceded that he believed Hayes was inclined to end intervention in Louisiana, but he and other Louisiana Democrats feared that Hayes would have trouble pursuing such a policy over the objection of Republican leaders such as Garfield, Sherman, and Morton. Burke hoped the memorandum would assist Matthews in bringing these leaders around, but Matthews flatly stated that he could not speak for them. At this, Burke said that Matthews could tell them that he and his associates would seek to "put their party in peril"—that is, block the count in the House. The meeting ended and Burke left, determined to launch a strategy of delay, employing filibustering tactics to hold up the count in order to force a hands-off policy for Louisiana.[51]

In the ensuing controversy, Burke's delaying scheme worked at cross purposes with the efforts of Kellar and Boynton. They aimed to convince enough southerners in the House to vote with Republicans to prevent delays and keep the count on course. In Kellar and Boynton's version of the struggle, southern Democrats opposing the filibuster stood as the saviors of Hayes's victory from the revolutionary northern Democrats pushing for delay. Some southern Democrats did voice opposition to the filibuster. In the caucus of February 17, for instance, Kentuckian John Y. Brown, Texan John H. Reagan, Georgian Benjamin Hill, and Otho Singleton of Mississippi, among others, vigorously opposed dilatory tactics. But in fact, among House Democrats, antifilibuster southerners had only a slight impact. Indeed, southern Democrats formed the core of those *favoring* delay, and typically well over half of them voted against the Republicans on critical antifilibuster roll calls. In the end, neither Burke's nor Boynton's strategy proved particularly effective. Despite his boasts, Boynton was unable to deliver significant numbers of southern House Democrats *against* delay. On the other hand, because of defections of Democrats from outside the South, Burke could not consistently marshall enough forces *for* delay to shake the expectations of the Hayes people that their man would ultimately prevail. Moreover, although Republicans hoped to avoid a disturbing fight over delay in the House, in the last analysis, they knew, as one of Hayes's legal advisors wrote him on February 19, that in the event of obstruction, the president of the Senate could always "avail himself of his *reserved right* & open & count all the votes not counted when the filibustering commenced."[52]

The first test of Burke's strategy came in the House of Representatives on Monday, February 19. After the prolonged reading of their official protest against the Louisiana decision, the Democrats forced an immediate recess until the next day. Although the vote was close, 140–130, the recess won support from Democrats from every region, including 96 percent of the southerners. Brown, Reagan, Hill, and Singleton all voted for the delay, as did all three Democrats from Louisiana. A panicky Murat Halstead wrote Hayes that the Democrats were "behaving like idiots and lunatics." Boynton and Kellar considered the situation so "desperate" that it might be necessary for Hayes to give southerners assurances beyond his letter of acceptance, something Hayes consistently refused to do.[53]

But the delay proved short lived. Ominously for Boynton's purposes and for Burke's as well, nearly a quarter of the northeastern Democrats in the House vote sided with the Republicans against delay. Later that evening, when the Democrats met again in caucus, this group prevailed. The caucus witnessed some virulent profilibuster rhetoric, including an allegation by Speaker Randall that Hayes would reinstate bayonet rule in the South. Some southerners argued vigorously for obstruction while others were equally ardent against it—a division that could have pleased neither Boynton nor Burke. But as discussion proceeded, according to news reports, "it became apparent that the revolutionists were greatly in the minority" and that "the party which would stand by the Commission had so large a majority that opposition would be useless." Without even taking a formal vote, the Democrats refused to abandon their previous determination against obstruction. This determination held the next day when a motion for an early recess went down soundly, 57 to 192. The vote buoyed Republicans. Pennsylvania Congressman William D. Kelley wrote his wife that "it is now clear that Hayes is to be inaugurated." President Grant was so confident that the question of his successor "is now virtually determined" that he invited Hayes to stay at the White House before the inauguration.[54]

Still, the charge in the caucus that Hayes would pursue an antisouthern policy had rattled some antiobstruction southerners. Several of them approached the representative from Hayes's own district, Charles Foster, for a public reassurance about the governor's attitude. Foster reluctantly agreed to give a brief speech, but he did so only after substantial numbers of Democrats, northern and southern, went on record against an early recess on February 20. In a speech in the House, Foster vaguely assured southerners that Hayes would "administer the Government so patriotically and wisely as to wipe away any and all necessity or excuse for the formation of parties on a sectional basis and all traces of party color lines. . . . The flag shall float over states, not provinces; over freemen, and not subjects." But Foster offered no details and instead referred his listeners to Hayes's letter of acceptance. Moreover, he chided the Democrats that their original support for creating the Electoral Commission left them honor-bound "to carry out its findings in good faith." In addition, he told the southerners that a Hayes administration would expect "the patriotic co-operation of southern patriots in the great work of restoration through the Union, the Constitution, and the enforcement of the laws."[55]

Foster wrote Hayes that his speech had "been very kindly received by gentlemen from the South," but he may have overestimated its impact. The speech did help undermine the obstructionists' strength to the extent that they were unable to achieve a recess until the very late afternoon on February 20, and then only by a close vote of 97 to 88. But in that vote, 96 percent of the southern Democrats again voted for delay, with Brown, Hill, Reagan, and Singleton once more joining the Louisianians in taking the obstructionist position. This group also included Mississippi's L. Q. C. Lamar, who considered Foster's speech encouraging but insufficient. Later that evening Lamar urged Louisiana Representative E. John Ellis to go to Columbus to obtain more concrete assurances from Hayes himself. Ellis wired Nicholls in Louisiana about this suggestion, but he failed to receive instructions to visit Hayes. For their part, Hayes's associates in Washington wanted further assurances of southern good behavior. Stanley Matthews asked Burke to provide specific evidence that blacks in Louisiana would feel safe under a Nicholls regime. Burke promptly asked Nicholls to send him names of prominent Republicans and Republican newspapers endorsing his government. In addition, he urged Nicholls to get his "colored friends" to hold mass meetings and pass resolutions favoring his accession to power.[56]

In the next few days, a quasi-calm prevailed while the commission deliberated on Oregon, the last state from which Democrats had the remotest hope of securing the one vote necessary to put Tilden in office. The tranquility ended on Friday, February 23, when congressmen received copies of the previous day's *Ohio State Journal,* regarded by some as a Hayes mouthpiece, calling for the use of troops to uphold the Packard government in Louisiana. Matthews and Foster quickly obtained despatches from Ohio demonstrating that the paper in no sense spoke for Hayes, but the obstructionists exploited the alarm the story generated. That afternoon, when news spread that the commission had decided the Oregon vote for Hayes, they secured a recess of the House to block receipt of the report. Southerners voted for the recess overwhelmingly, while nearly a quarter of northeastern Democrats opposed it.[57]

Immediately after the recess, House Democrats were invited into a caucus, but fewer than two-thirds of them attended. Among those present, the obstructionists secured approval of a resolution stating that when the House convened on Saturday, the 24th, they would move for an immediate recess over the weekend. But many of those present indicated that they would not be bound by this resolution, and many of those absent were reported to have stayed away from the caucus to avoid approving such a move. According to newspaper reports, the sixty-six who voted in the caucus for delay represented the obstructionists' maximum strength, only two-fifths of the whole Democratic membership of the House. Moreover, while the caucus mulled the party's options, reports circulated through Washington that should this group succeed in tying up the count until March 3, the Republicans would have the Senate president open the remaining certificates and complete the count. Saturday morning Sherman assured Hayes, "There is no case now of doubt and every movement made by the Democrats to delay the count will be regarded as proof of a revolutionary intent, and need not be carried much farther to justify us in finishing the count without their assistance." Thus, despite much agitation, the obstructionists' power to frustrate the count remained limited.[58]

The crucial test of their strength came on Saturday, February 24. After the commission's Oregon decision was officially reported, they made an immediate move to recess until Monday, February 26, at 10 o'clock. Over objections, Speaker Randall ruled the motion in order, but the House rejected the delay by a vote of 112 to 158. Over 80 percent of the southern Democrats favored the motion, but nearly half the northeasterners and a third of border-state and western Democrats voted against them. When the motion lost, the obstructionists offered another to recess until 9:30 on Monday. Randall rejected this motion as "dilatory" and cautioned the House that "when the law under the Constitution of the United States enacted in obedience thereto directs any act by this House, it is not in order to make any motion to obstruct or impede the execution of that injunction of the Constitution and the laws." This ruling stood, and its implication was clear. "I accept to-day defeat, bitter as it is, rather than dishonor," said Kentuckian John Y. Brown, who had argued against obstruction in caucus but had voted for it several times in the House. Like other Democrats, Brown caustically denounced what he saw as the Republicans' fraudulent manipulation of the commission, but he advised that his colleagues "not take counsel of our passions." Abram Hewitt blasted the Republican commissioners' refusal to go behind the returns and receive evidence in their deliberations, but he too urged fellow Democrats to "stand up like men to principle, and not allow ourselves to be driven from the firm ground of truth and justice by any violation of it upon the other side of the House." Although many Democrats condemned Randall's ruling, others such as *Doylestown Democrat* editor W. W. H. Davis thought he was "right in not lending yourself to the filibustering programme of the extreme men. . . . We are in honor bound to submit to the verdict, as distasteful as it will be." On the Republican side, Garfield recorded in his diary, "we have made a good gain today, with a better hope of completing the count than we had when we assembled this morning." "The struggle among the Democrats has been fierce," Sherman wrote Hayes, "but the *acquiescents* have gained ground and I am now strongly of the opinion that your election will be quietly announced on Thursday next." (His prediction was off by just a few hours.)[59]

Thus, with substantial numbers of Democrats voting to proceed with the count and with Speaker Randall on record against dilatory motions, the obstructionists saw their options melting away. Outmaneuvered by the Republicans and abandoned by many northern Democrats, they felt a deepening desperation. Louisiana Congressman E. John Ellis wrote bitterly to his father:

> Timidity and cowardice has [*sic*] lost us the triumph we won. The great New York leader [Tilden] has proven himself without a plan or a policy. His chosen agents were men without capacity, or brain, or nerve. . . . Mr. Tilden uttered no word, and his sheep-headed backers, frightened for their stocks and bonds, sought refuge in this cowardly electoral bill which created a mere National Returning Board. . . . Now our struggle is for Nicholls and our Home Government. Hay[e]s' friends are profuse in promises. *He* has promised nothing. I believe his friends are lying in order to deceive and disarm the Democratic party—and particularly the men of the South.[60]

Feeling bereft of real power, the Louisianians were forced to rely more heavily on what Burke later termed "a bluff game." On Sunday, February 25, Foster showed Burke a letter he had received from Hayes approving Foster's House speech and stating that as soon as the count was settled, Hayes's southern policy should "be understood as Foster understands it." Burke reported this encouraging news to Nicholls, but he took a tough line with the Hayes people, requesting "direct assurances or action before House yields." Although Burke was in no position to determine when the House would "yield," his bravado had the desired effect. Garfield noted that "Foster is feeling very much depressed about the completion of the count. The Democrats are behaving very badly."[61]

With time running out and the leverage of disrupting the count diminishing, Burke accelerated his bluff game on Monday, February 26. That morning newspapers carried an Associated Press interview with Grant in which the president reiterated his intention to make no move in Louisiana or South Carolina that might "fix a Southern policy for my successor and thus embarrass him." "If I were to recognize the republican Governors they would have to be sustained by military force, and I think the entire people are tired of the military being employed to sustain a State government." Leaving nothing to chance, Burke went to the White House, where Grant reiterated the essence of the interview and added that he thought the Nicholls government should stand because it was "sustained by the most influential elements of the State." Grant assured Burke that public opinion would not sustain intervention to uphold a state government, but he also left open the possibility of interference if the Nicholls government were "carried away by the possession of power, [and] violent excesses were committed." Again he signaled his reluctance to adopt any course that might "embarrass" his successor.[62]

Encouraged by this exchange, Burke moved quickly to get the endorsement of the Hayes people for a troop withdrawal before the end of the count. From the White House he went to Capitol Hill, where he advised Ellis against going to Columbus to obtain concrete assurances from Hayes because Hayes could say nothing more definite than the intimations he had already made. Instead Burke saw the need to secure the cooperation of Republican leaders in Washington without whose support Hayes's conciliatory policy would have rough sledding. In a meeting with John Sherman, Matthews, and former Ohio Governor William Dennison, Burke asked the Ohioans to see Grant and tell him Hayes would not feel embarrassed if Grant withdrew the troops from Louisiana. When Sherman expressed skepticism that Grant would be willing to take such a step, Burke informed him of what Grant had said in their interview earlier that day. At this, the Ohioans agreed to speak with the president. But despite this concession, they did not see themselves as bargaining from a position of weakness. The House Democrats had, after all, voted to proceed with the count. Hence, in agreeing to see Grant, the Ohioans made additional demands on Burke. Sherman told Burke that Louisiana Republicans had complained to him that "it would be impossible for them to live in the State if the Nicholls government should prevail," and hence he wanted assurances that blacks and white Republicans would not be deprived of their rights. In response, Burke referred to the memorandum of guarantees he had given Matthews on February 18. Additionally, Louisiana was scheduled to elect two U.S. senators, one for a short term and one for a full six years, and Sherman noted that it would be problematic if just after the inauguration these seats should be contested in the Senate just as that body would be moving to confirm Hayes's cabinet members, some of whose support would be needed to implement the administration's southern policy. Burke responded that the election of the full-term senator could be delayed for several days. The meeting ended with no resolution beyond an agreement to meet again that evening at Wormley's Hotel with larger representation on each side.[63]

Meanwhile, Kentuckian John Y. Brown, who in Democratic caucuses had opposed dilatory tactics, also engaged in a bit of bluff. He and Georgia Senator John B. Gordon met with Foster, noted their past support for an expeditious count, but threatened to join the forces of delay unless some guarantees were given that Hayes would not perpetuate the Republican governments in Louisiana and South Carolina. Foster showed them Hayes's letter praising his House speech, but Brown requested a written assurance signed by Foster "that the policy of Mr. Hayes would be as indicated." Foster agreed to prepare a letter but wanted to consult Matthews about it first.[64]

For all Burke's later puffery about his role in the negotiations, his bluff game played directly into the hands of the Hayes people. They knew that as president,

Hayes intended to pull back from the intervention policy, and they also knew that the count would go forward. Indeed, that afternoon the House had voted overwhelmingly, 84 to 178, against taking an early recess. Over 60 percent of southern Democrats favored the delay, but they were abandoned by nearly 60 percent of northeasterners and more than two-fifths of the Midwestern and border-state Democrats. Later in the day, Senator Jones wrote his wife that the "electoral count seems to be progressing satisfactorily & I think now that the chances are largely in favor of the quiet inauguration of Mr. Hayes on Monday next." The business of the count proceeded until the House adjourned at 6:30, after which Boynton reported to Smith that he saw "no signs of southern men going back on us. . . . I consider the situation as bright & promising as need be."[65]

Later that night, at nine o'clock, when Hayes's representatives confronted Burke in the famous meeting at Wormley's Hotel, it was they, not Burke, who operated from a position of strength. As if to underscore the point, at 9:45, Boynton (who was not present at Wormley's) sent another gushing telegram to Smith, declaring that the "count went as far today as possible under the bill [and the] filibusters lost at every step. . . . You can readily see we have passed the dead point." Thus the key question regarding the negotiations that supposedly sealed what became known as the Compromise of 1877 is clear: If the virtual collapse of obstructionism and the consequent progress in the count had put the Republicans in such a strong position, why did they bother to proceed with the previously arranged meeting with Burke on the evening of February 26? Some of the Republican conferees, perhaps rattled by Burke's audacious bluffing, may have wished to leave nothing to chance; in Boynton's words that evening, "some of our men have a chronic panic."[66] But others read the situation as an opportunity. The inexorable progress in the count in effect defanged Burke's threat to delay it and consequently spurred his anxiety for an accommodation. With the possibility of a count by the Senate president always in the background, the Republicans knew that one way or another, Hayes would become president, and they did not need Burke's cooperation to put Hayes in the White House. Moreover, they knew that Hayes had already concluded to find some way to withdraw direct federal interference from Louisiana. On a flying trip to Columbus several days earlier, Sherman had discussed with the governor an "expedient" that would make "the Louisiana case easy of settlement."[67] Thus the real significance of the Wormley's gathering was that in Burke's desperate scramble to obtain assurance of "home rule" for Louisiana, Hayes's representatives seized the occasion to insist on still more conditions and promises to protect blacks' rights in return for a withdrawal policy Hayes intended to pursue anyway.

At the appointed hour, Sherman, Garfield, Matthews, Foster, and Dennison gathered at Wormley's, where they met with Burke and Ellis, with Kentucky journalist and Congressman Henry Watterson on hand to speak for South Carolina. Garfield, who apparently had not been privy to the previous discussions of the other men present, almost gave the Ohioans' game away. When Burke showed him the list of guarantees in his February 18 memorandum, Garfield said no one had authority to speak for Hayes. Moreover, he noted, "those Southern Democrats who are resisting filibustering are doing so on the ground of high public duty and honor; and any bargain would make their motives far lower." Matthews, who was more interested in gaining additional guarantees from Burke than calling his bluff, "did not like" Garfield's remarks, and the congressman left.[68]

As the conversation progressed, the Ohioans referred to Hayes's letter of acceptance and once again exhibited his letter to Foster praising his conciliatory speech. Ellis raised the question of how to deal with the anomaly of Hayes's receiving Louisiana's electoral vote while Nicholls was to be seated as governor. Matthews explained that Hayes could simply follow Grant's policy of neutrality, during which time Nicholls's support by the state's taxpayers would enable him to "sustain himself." Thus, should the point come for Hayes to "recognize either government, he will find one government perfect in all its organisms, and perhaps the shadow of another government, but something which amounts to nothing. In that way Mr. Nicholls will quietly succeed without any force or violence or act of interference by the Federal arm."

As Ellis later recalled the exchange, Hayes's representatives did not ask for an end of the filibuster, "nor did they require it as compensation for these guarantees." The Ohioans knew that the filibuster was toothless. Instead, Matthews insisted that "in order to bring about that state of affairs or that line of policy by Mr. Hayes, it would be necessary for us [the Louisianians] to assure them that the peace would be preserved, that there would be no violence, no bloodshed, and that nobody would be persecuted on account of any past political offenses." This was in addition to the guarantees in Burke's February 18 memorandum, which Ellis described as a commitment by the Louisianians that there would be "an equal and impartial administration of justice [and] that the rights of the people should be protected." The meeting ended with no further written agreement, but Burke and Ellis promised to get the necessary promises from the Nicholls camp in Louisiana, and the Ohioans said they would see Grant about a troop withdrawal.[69]

Burke immediately wired Nicholls requesting him to send an authoritative statement meeting the demands of the Hayes people. The next morning, February 27, betraying his growing sense of powerlessness, Burke urged the would-be governor to "act promptly" because the "organized movement to defeat count or save Louisiana and South Carolina" could "not be held together longer than to-day." In response, a caucus of the Nicholls legislators passed a resolution certifying "the guarantees asked for, of order, peace, and protection of law to white and black, no persecution for past political conduct, [and] no immunity for crime." Burke immediately wrote a letter for Matthews and his associates forwarding the guarantees telegraphed from New Orleans and also appending his own February 18 memorandum. Still, this was not enough for the Hayes people. Matthews insisted on the insertion of an explicit statement that the Nicholls government would guarantee, "1. The acceptance of the thirteenth, fourteenth, and fifteenth amendments to the Constitution of the United State, and will not attempt to deprive the colored people of any political or civil right."

Burke later testified that Matthews had demanded this addition to his original memorandum to meet the views of Senator Oliver Morton, thereby suggesting that the Hayes people were reluctant to move without an effort to satisfy the most radical opinion within the party regarding the future well-being of blacks. But this additional demand accurately represented Hayes's view as well. Two days earlier he had noted that if he broke his silence on the issue he would say, "What is required is: First, that for the protection and welfare of the colored people, the Thirteenth, Fourteenth, and Fifteenth Amendments shall be sacredly observed and faithfully enforced according to their true intent and meaning." Whether directly commanded by Hayes or not, Matthews's additional demand squared precisely with Hayes's desire to secure the southerners' specific pledge to uphold the constitutional amendments. From the Ohioans' standpoint, at stake in these negotiations was not the presidency; they knew the count would go forward and that Hayes would be inaugurated. Instead, they labored to secure promises as explicit as possible that the southerners would uphold blacks' constitutional rights.[70]

In return, Burke got nothing in writing from Matthews except a report of the latter's meeting with Grant the morning of the 27th, when the president adhered to his position that he would make no changes in the orders to the army at New Orleans until after the completion of the count. Foster did meet with John Y. Brown and present him with a brief letter expressing confidence that Hayes would adopt a policy giving "the people of the States of South Carolina and Louisiana the right to control their own affairs in their own way." When Brown objected to some passages, Foster consulted again with Matthews who insisted on inserting the statement that the southerners' behavior would be subject "to the Constitution of the United States, and the laws made in pursuance thereof." Thus Matthews once more required language that conveyed the substance of Hayes's views regarding the protection of the constitutional liberties of the blacks.[71]

The same day, Burke released to the Associated Press the substance of his communications with the Ohioans, including the guarantees passed by the Louisiana legislative caucus. But efforts to win endorsement by the U.S. House of Representatives of the Nicholls and Hampton governments failed to achieve the necessary two-thirds approval to suspend the rules. On Wednesday, February 28, the count inched forward, despite dilatory motions by a still-defiant band of Democratic obstructionists. Democrats voting against obstruction came from all regions, but in roll calls on four of the six motions, southern Democrats as a group were least likely to side with the Republicans to defeat delay. As Abram Hewitt later recalled, he and Randall had agreed that "in the last event filibustering should be suppressed and the count completed even though no understanding was reached in regard to the Louisiana case." Reports of political trouble no doubt confirmed Randall's determination, for a week earlier, in a municipal election in Chester, Pennsylvania, which many regarded as "a test" of the public's attitude regarding Democrats' flirtation with "anarchy," the outcome was that, "contrary to custom, not a democrat was elected to any office."[72]

The next day and night witnessed the obstructionists' final desperate efforts, including a challenge to the electoral vote of Vermont. Still, the Republicans remained confident. As Charles Devens, a Massachusetts lawyer who later became Hayes's attorney general, had reminded Congressman George Hoar, Republicans could always "let the Senate finish if the House does not and let us have Hayes in." Hayes himself set off for Washington, and en route his party received word that in the House the Republicans sat "quietly in their seats allowing [the] obstruction policy to die [a] natural death." On measures for delay in the House, the Louisiana Democrats voted with the Republicans, and at one point Congressman William M. Levy took the floor to reiterate once again the guarantees the Ohioans had demanded. Speaking for "the intelligent, the influential, the thoughtful, and the controlling element" in Louisiana, Levy pledged "the honest acceptance of the issues of the war which resulted in the enfranchisement of the colored race and the endowment of that race with all the rights of American citizenship under the Constitution and its more recent amendments." Hayes could scarcely have stated it better himself. The obstructionists' struggle came to its expected end at 4:10 in the morning of March 2, when in joint session the president of the Senate reported the final result of the Electoral Commission's work and declared Hayes and Wheeler the winners.[73]

While the drama in the House reached its denouement, Grant's promise to change the orders to soldiers at the Louisiana state capitol was not fulfilled. On March 1, Packard had desperately sought the president's military intercession and recognition of his government. Through a secretary, Grant refused, noting that troops would "not be used to establish or to pull down either claimant for control of the State" because public opinion would no "longer support the maintenance of State government in Louisiana by the use of the military."

When the commanding general on the scene in New Orleans, C. C. Auger, sought clarification, General in Chief William T. Sherman ordered him to keep the peace and use his "counsels" to "prevent any material change in the attitude of the contending parties till the new Administration can be fairly installed." Burke pleaded with Grant for more explicit instructions to Auger for a troop withdrawal, but because of confused communications and perhaps presidential foot-dragging, Auger never received such orders. To avoid an interregnum over Sunday, Hayes took the oath of office on the evening of March 3.[74]

Thus, after a months-long struggle, Hayes not only won election, but his representatives had secured public pledges by the Louisianians to accede to his core demand to guarantee the rights of blacks under the Thirteenth, Fourteenth, and Fifteenth Amendments. Moreover, he retained the freedom to direct his southern policy untrammeled by any last-minute changes by Grant. Grant's actions and sentiments over the last few years had, of course, pointed the way to a reduced federal role in the South. The hero of Appomattox, who had begun his administration with perhaps an inflated perception of what lay within a president's power, now fully recognized the political limits of the possible in the American Republic. Insofar as Louisiana and South Carolina were concerned, the retiring president left office having averted any irreversible step. What to do about those two states and about the South at large now rested in Hayes's hands. For a brief moment there was some hope that he might have to make no decision at all, for Stanley Matthews had written to Packard and South Carolina Republican D. H. Chamberlain, urging each to give up his claim to his state's governorship. Pending their replies (which would be negative), Hayes assured Burke on March 4 that his policy would be "conciliatory." But, he cautioned, he must have time to "remove difficulty and prepare the way." As it soon became clear, part of the purpose in Hayes's delay was to secure yet more assurances of southern good behavior and thus protect as best he could what he considered the key residual elements of the republican project in the South.[75]

Conciliation Is Not Mutual

Republicanism and the Southern Policy of Rutherford B. Hayes

The year 1877 stands in American historical memory as a moment of transcendent significance, the turning point when Rutherford B. Hayes's succeeding Ulysses S. Grant in the presidency marked the effective abandonment of Reconstruction. As is often the case with such shorthand understandings of the past, the reality was more complex. Grant had long before grown weary of using force to prop up Reconstruction regimes, and Hayes's "withdrawal" of the troops merely formalized a policy into which his predecessor had drifted. As for the broader republican project in the South, moreover, Hayes in some ways exhibited deeper commitment to its preservation than had Grant. Before his term ended, Grant had come to regard the Fifteenth Amendment as "a mistake" and had concluded that "it had done the negro no good, and had been a hindrance to the South." Hayes disagreed. Defense of the Reconstruction Amendments had formed a central component of his election campaign and of his demands during the electoral negotiations. He and other Republicans felt immense relief that the Democrats had not captured the national government, thereby removing any hope of restraining white southerners' actions. As he entered the White House, Hayes remained confident that a reordering of federal-state relations could proceed with the core of the Republican Party's policy—protection of the republican rights of the former slaves and their descendants—still intact. To render that purpose even more secure, the new president moved cautiously to procure yet more guarantees from southern leaders.[1]

As a first step, Hayes outlined his southern policy in his inaugural address. Naturally, he made no reference to the private negotiations in the final days of the count. Instead, he congratulated his countrymen on the peaceful outcome of the disputed election as a triumph of republican government. "It has been reserved for a government of the people," he said, "where the right of suffrage is universal, to give to the world the first example in history of a great nation, in the midst of the struggle of opposing parties for power, hushing its party tumults to yield the issue of the contest to adjustment according to the forms of law."

Hayes pronounced himself as "sincerely anxious to use every legitimate influence in favor of honest and efficient local *self*-government as the true resource of those States for the promotion of the contentment and prosperity of their citizens." He promised his "best efforts in behalf of a civil policy which will forever wipe out in our political affairs the color line and the distinction between North and South." Again, however, he insisted that home rule must rest on "a government which guards the interests of both races carefully and equally. It must be a government which submits loyally and heartily to the Constitution and the laws—the laws of the nation and the laws of the States themselves—accepting and obeying faithfully the whole Constitution as it is." Again alluding to the central tenet of republicanism, he said, "only a local government which recognizes and maintains inviolate the rights of all is a true self-government."[2]

Beyond these general sentiments, which echoed his letter of acceptance, Hayes indicated no specific action regarding Louisiana and South Carolina. Nonetheless, the speech's tenor reinforced the prevalent impression that the new president intended a turn in policy. So also did his cabinet selections, especially David M. Key as postmaster general, Carl Schurz as secretary of the interior, and William M. Evarts as secretary of state. William Henry Smith, Andrew Kellar, and others had pushed the selection of Key, a Tennessee Democrat and former Confederate general, as a way, in Smith's words, to "make the political break desired in the South." Key's appointment to head the department with the largest patronage signaled Hayes's intention to use the bestowal of office to woo conservative southern Democrats, especially those of Whig antecedents, to the Republican Party. Schurz had long opposed vigorous federal measures in the South. Evarts had a similar record, having served as Andrew Johnson's attorney general and having organized a protest meeting against Grant's Louisiana policy in 1875.

The choices shocked many Republicans. "A Southern Democrat, Carl Schurz, & the Counsel of Andy Johnson in the Cabinet," exclaimed outgoing

Secretary of State Hamilton Fish, "'tis done! The Bourbons are restored." Massachusetts Senator Henry Dawes wrote his wife that the cabinet and "the Southern policy of the new Administration" had created "a good deal of bad blood." "This new way is a new life or a *speedy* death to Republican control of public affairs."[3]

Although the general direction of Hayes's policy was set in his mind, the "bad blood" complicated the task of devising specific implementation. The immediate concern was Louisiana and South Carolina and their competing claimants for the two states' governorships. While the presidential count was still pending, Joseph Medill argued that the Republicans' attempt "for eight years to uphold negro rule in the South officered by Carpetbaggers" had "resulted in failure and almost ruin to our party. Statesmanship consists of *making* the *best use of* the *means* at command, and of *producing popular contentment*." In Medill's view, "To maintain Packard in place will make it impossible to secure southern conservative support for Haye's [*sic*] administration; it will spoil everything." On the other hand, William Henry Smith insisted that Hayes could not dismiss Packard and Chamberlain "with a waive [*sic*] of the hand. The questions involved . . . must be determined by considerations other than those of mere party expediency. Unless the decision shall be based upon Justice and truth it cannot stand. . . . At least we must have security for the future."[4]

The political complexity of the question was evident the day after Hayes's inauguration when James G. Blaine took the Senate floor to denounce the rumored arrangement whereby unauthorized agents had allegedly sacrificed Packard to ensure Hayes's election. Because the claims of each rested on the judgment of the same Returning Board in Louisiana, Blaine declared, if "Packard is not the legal governor," then "President Hayes has no title." The same day, Hayes convened a meeting of Grant's cabinet, during which outgoing interior secretary and Republican national chairman Zachariah Chandler similarly insisted that "the Packard Government was chosen on the same vote on which he [Hayes] was declared elected President." Hayes gave Chandler a severe dressing down for what Fish called "this great indecency," but the embarrassing dilemma remained: How could Hayes proceed with the new departure without besmirching the legitimacy of his own title?

The solution, Hayes believed, hinged on the perception of affairs within the two states. He asked the assembled secretaries whether there could be any "Constitutional right of military interference to sustain a State Government without violence having occurred," and the group considered it "doubtful." In the absence of such circumstances, the issue became a "question of the recognition of a 'de facto' State Government, as distinguished from one 'de jure,'" the existence of the de facto government having been determined not by external interference but by peaceful events within the state.[5]

Although Hayes privately described his policy as "trust, peace, and to put aside the bayonet," in the first few weeks of his administration, he still cast about for a workable plan. Further embarrassment threatened when newspapers printed Stanley Matthews's letters to Packard and Chamberlain urging them to resign their claims. Nonetheless, the Republican caucus in the Ohio legislature nominated Matthews for the U.S. Senate, an action that Hayes saw as "an endorsement of the policy of peace and home rule—of local self-government." Hayes faced limited options, for the political reality was that, as he put it, "the people will not now sustain the policy of upholding a State Government against a rival government, by the use of the forces of the United States. If this leads to the overthrow of the *de jure* government in a State, the *de facto* government must be recognized." The ideal was "to adjust the difficulties in Louisiana and South Carolina so as to make one government out of two in each State. But if this fails, if no adjustment can be made, we must then adopt the non–intervention policy, except so far as may be necessary to keep the peace." The president still avowed that the "real thing to be achieved is safety and prosperity for the colored people" and the "wish is to restore harmony and good feeling between sections and races." But, he concluded, "This can only be done by peaceful methods."[6]

In Louisiana and South Carolina, the claimants for the governorship were backed by rival legislatures. In each state the Democrats enjoyed fairly wide support, while the Republican regimes' authority extended hardly farther than the statehouses where they sat protected by federal troops. Hayes decided to deal directly with South Carolina, inviting both contenders for the governorship to meet with him in Washington. His aim, he said, was the organization of a single and undisputed state government and "an end as speedily as possible to all appearance of intervention of the military authority of the United States." Chamberlain urged Hayes to appoint a commission to determine the state's rightful government. The president declined. With his mind set on a troop withdrawal, he used his conferences with Democrat Wade Hampton to secure a pledge to uphold blacks' rights in South Carolina. Hampton complied. Recognizing that "the political rights of colored citizens" was "the subject of special anxiety" to Hayes, Hampton wrote the president that his government would "secure to every citizen, the lowest as well as the highest, black as well as white, full & equal protection in the enjoyment of all his rights under the Constitution." Accepting this promise, Hayes ordered an end to the military occupation of the statehouse at Columbia. The troops gone, Chamberlain promptly relinquished his claims, and Hampton and the Democrats assumed control.[7]

In Louisiana, Hayes pursued a strategy designed literally to "make one government out of two." This would take more time than the South Carolina case, and Congressman E. John Ellis and his two Democratic House colleagues grew impatient waiting, as Ellis's wife put it, for the president to do "something more than give his promise that the troops should be withdrawn from our State." After two and a half weeks, Hayes told the Louisianians that he contemplated appointing a commission to investigate affairs in the state. Fearful that this meant that he would "not keep his word to us," they responded with a written protest. Moreover, from New Orleans, Francis Nicholls, the Democratic claimant to the governorship, wired the congressmen that he was losing "confidence in the assurances given by you and others from the President himself & his confidential friends as to [the] purposes of [the] Administration." "I fear the President does not appreciate the situation here," Nicholls wrote. "If confidence is lost here either in me or the President, the consequences may be most serious." In Washington, Mississippi Senator L. Q. C. Lamar urged Hayes simply to withdraw the troops, writing the president, "Upon that subject we thought you had made up your mind and indeed *you so declared to me.*" Among Hayes's allies, Stanley Matthews was "very fearful of delays in the Louisiana business," but nonetheless cautioned the president, "If the troops are withdrawn can the peace and rights of the people be maintained and will they?"[8]

Hayes shared this anxiety and would not be deterred from his deliberate and judicious course. Despite objections, he decided to appoint a commission to visit Louisiana. Such a group, he told Hamilton Fish, could exercise "a strong moral influence, and might suggest a mode of arrangement whereby the contending parties may be brought together." Secretary of State Evarts instructed the commission, first, to work for "a removal of the obstacles to an acknowledgment of one government," and second, to gauge official and public opinion in Louisiana regarding "the protection of all legal and political privileges conferred by the Constitution of the United States upon all citizens. The maintenance and protection of these rights and privileges, by all Constitutional means and by every just, moral, and social influence, are the settled purpose of the President in his administration of the government."[9]

The commission succeeded on both counts, not only because Packard lacked support, but also because the forces backing Nicholls were eager to make a deal. Commissioner John Marshall Harlan found that the Democrats "talk more liberally" because they "feel that they must deal more liberally with the colored people before they can get the North to fairly consider the remedy" for the wrongs committed by the Reconstruction regime. After several days of negotiations, the Nicholls legislature passed a resolution echoing the pledges made during the electoral crisis. The Nicholls government would "accept in good faith the thirteenth, fourteenth, and fifteenth amendments to the Constitution of the United States, in letter and in spirit," and "the humblest laborer upon the soil of Louisiana, throughout every parish in the State, of every color, shall receive the full and equal protection of the laws in person, property, and political rights and privileges." A few days later a sufficient number of Republican legislators recognized the futility of expecting prolonged federal protection and agreed to sit with the Nicholls legislature, thereby making a quorum of members recognized by both sides. Nicholls forwarded the resolution to the commission and additionally promised that he would give a "vigorous and efficient enforcement of the laws, so that all persons and property will be fully and equally protected." The commission telegraphed these developments to Hayes, who promptly ordered the U.S. forces to leave the Packard statehouse and return to their barracks. Reconstruction was over.[10]

Hayes viewed this result as a consummation of the policy he had outlined nearly a year earlier in his letter of acceptance. As Andrew Kellar, who met with Hayes during this period, noted, "To secure peace and the protection of the weak, was dear to the President's heart."[11] "We have got through with the South Carolina and Louisiana [problems]," Hayes confided to his diary.

> At any rate, the troops are ordered away, and I now hope for peace, and what is equally important, security and prosperity for the colored people. The result of my plans is to get from those States by their governors, legislatures, press, and people pledges that the Thirteenth, Fourteenth, and Fifteenth Amendments shall be faithfully observed; that the colored people shall have equal rights to labor, education, and the privileges of citizenship. I am confident this is good work. Time will tell.[12]

Hayes continued to believe, as he had from the beginning of the campaign of 1876, that the success of such a policy hinged on continued Republican rule at the national level. On the same day he invited Hampton and Chamberlain to the White House, he met a group of black ministers and sought to allay their anxieties about his policy. They reminded him of his expressions of solicitude for blacks the previous November when it looked as if Tilden would become president. He responded that he had indeed "express[ed] anxiety with regard to the future condition of the colored people" and especially "that they could not be so well cared for, protected, and their best interests advanced under a Democratic Administration, however well-disposed toward them." Now he assured the ministers that "the race represented by you will never be neglected by my Administration."[13]

If Hayes hoped to remove the southern question as a bone of contention within the Republican Party, he was bitterly disappointed. In the midst of the negotiations, Blaine wrote a public letter expressing his "profoundest sympathy" for Chamberlain and Packard. "I can't go the new policy," Blaine wrote privately to Whitelaw Reid. "Every instinct of my nature rebels against it—and

I feel an intuition amounting to an inspiration that the North in adopting it, is but laying up wrath against the day of wrath." From Ohio former senator and deep-dyed Radical Benjamin Wade, who had seconded Hayes's nomination at Cincinnati, charged that the president had consulted with southern "malefactors how best he can put these colored people under the iron heel of their most bitter enemies, and reduce them to a condition infinitely worse than before they were made free." Zachariah Chandler feared that Hayes's policy meant "the destruction of the Republican Party" and republicanism as well. "I do not believe," he told William Chandler, "that the Republican party will endorse the doctrine that a successful mob constitutes a state government, or a government of any kind."[14]

Hayes's policy appealed most to Republicans who shared Chandler's concern for republicanism but who saw the old interventionist methods of Reconstruction as a threat to the nation's republican values. "Military government is not republican," Grant's former attorney general, Edwards Pierrepont, wrote the president. "If the whites do not treat the blacks with justice under the free working of our system of government then some other system will have to be adopted. I have faith that your plan will work well—certainly it ought to be fairly tried—the other way has not been successful." Philadelphia lawyer and future U.S. attorney general Benjamin Brewster applauded Hayes for "doing away with bastard governments in the South. . . . Such governments do not represent republican liberty. They are the worst form of oligarchy—despotic oligarchy verging on anarchy." Indeed, said Hayes's defenders, the interventionist policy of the previous administration had proven to be a signal failure. "Is there a 'new policy?'" Murat Halstead asked William Chandler. "Grant surrendered everything in the South but two untenable garrisons. Do you know that Hayes is liable to be the most *Radical* President we have ever had?"[15]

Some Republicans believed that Hayes might have saved himself a good deal of criticism if he had taken the position that in the absence of overt violence, the Constitution left him no choice but to withdraw the troops. Yet, as other Republicans realized, it was precisely the element of contingency that Hayes wished to preserve as leverage for good behavior from the southerners. "In any event," said Robert R. Hitt, "the Democracy would soon have gained control of S. Carolina and La. As it has turned out, the power there has passed to them under every sort of promise on their part, and their old practices there will hereafter be utterly without defense." Moreover, the president entertained high hopes that his policy would result in building the Republican Party in the South, especially among former Whigs. "Hayes . . . told me he expected to have 20 more Repubs. in the next house from the South than at present," Grant's postmaster general, Marshall Jewell, reported to Benjamin Bristow. "I told him I doubted it."[16]

Among the defenders of Hayes's policy was Senator Oliver P. Morton of Indiana. Over the years Morton had yielded to no one in his Radicalism, but now even he sensed the shift in party and public opinion. The former Republican Party chairman in his state told him that if Hayes was "successful in restoring peace and good feeling in the South, it will strengthen us in Indiana." In an open letter to a group of southern Republicans, Morton defended the legitimacy of the Packard and Chamberlain governments but declared that Grant's refusal to uphold them had left Hayes no choice but to "yield to the inevitable." Morton expressed the hope that "if the Democratic assurances to President Hayes, in Louisiana and elsewhere, of protection and equal rights, are executed in good faith, the system will not be a failure, but a grand success extorted from its enemies." But the senator harbored no illusions that southern Democrats "have been soundly converted and are honest advocates of the equal rights of men." Therefore, like Hayes, he emphasized the imperative necessity of preserving Republican control of the national government. "If Tilden had been elected President," he argued, "within his term of four years the fourteenth and fifteenth amendments would have been substantially overthrown." Now, "by the voluntary withdrawal of the army the South has been placed on her good behavior," and "should they fail to protect all classes and races in the enjoyment of their rights, the most conservative Republicans will see there is no security but to preserve the Government in the hands of the Republican Party."[17]

To underscore the point, Morton cited a recent violent outburst in Mississippi. The incident in Kemper County began with the arrest of Judge William Chisolm, a prominent merchant and Republican nominee for Congress in 1876, on trumped-up charges that he had murdered a political opponent. On April 29 a mob stormed the jail where Chisolm was held, and in the aftermath Chisolm, his thirteen-year-old son and nineteen-year-old daughter, as well as two other men lay dead. The incident raised an outcry, but this was just the sort of episode that the Hayes administration wanted southern state authorities to deal with. Treasury Secretary John Sherman warned Mississippi Senator L. Q. C. Lamar that "the Chisolm massacre has excited a more profound feeling in the North than any event since the close of the war. If the known murderers of this family, under the peculiar circumstances of atrocity stated, should go unchallenged and unpunished in Mississippi, it will deeply and injuriously affect the honor and credit of the people of your State." Although the administration concluded that the circumstances did not merit making it a federal cause célèbre, the Justice Department did mount an investigation, albeit a desultory one. That a local jury would convict the perpetrators was a slim prospect, reflecting, as the *New York Times* put it, "the helplessness of the Federal Government to protect its citizens within the sacred lines of State jurisdiction." Ultimately, the perpetrators were never punished by the state or federal government.[18]

The administration came in for further embarrassment when Louisiana authorities indicted members of the Returning Board for fraudulently altering returns from the 1876 election. As Sherman observed, "Nothing could be more injurious to the order and good will that is now springing up than this most unwise prosecution," and Governor Nicholls ought to "see the importance of arresting this proceeding." As in the Chisolm incident in Mississippi, the administration took a low-key approach, hoping that, as Sherman told one of the defendants, "if the liberality and generosity of the National government is to be abused and outraged in this way, . . . it will create a reaction in the mind of every just citizen of the United States that will secure your protection."[19]

But for Hayes's critics, such incidents merely confirmed the delusive error of his policy. Daniel Chamberlain used a speech at journalist Henry Bowen's Woodstock, Connecticut, July Fourth celebration, usually a Republican love feast, to condemn the administration. With a feint toward disinterestedness, the ousted South Carolina governor focused on Louisiana rather than his own state, but he pulled no punches in denouncing Hayes's policy as "a crime more wanton and unpardonable than the crime against Kansas." Hayes had conceded rule by "that class at the South which regarded slavery as a divine institution." Most important, he had failed in his duty as president to uphold "the constitutional guaranty to every state in this Union of a republican form of government." The Packard government had asked his intervention under the guarantee clause, but instead Hayes had appointed a commission to effect a change in the government's makeup. The president had asserted that in the absence of violence, the guarantee clause did not apply, but this was absurd, said Chamberlain, for the armed might of the Nicholls forces represented a violence only temporarily latent. "There was no more peace in Louisiana at this time than there was in Virginia in the winter of 1863 to '64, when the armies of General Meade and General Lee lay silently confronting each other on the banks of the Rapidan."

Chamberlain rejected the notion that "all this was inevitable, and, hence, right." "A victory won at the expense of principles is an irretrievable defeat." Ultimately, at risk was the ideal of republicanism itself. Hayes may have touted his course in the vocabulary of "local self-government," but the reality was that "the will of the majority of the voters of a state, lawfully and regularly expressed, is no longer the ruling power in our states." In a stinging peroration, Chamberlain invoked the shades of "Adams and Hancock and Jefferson of our earlier revolution" to "speak to us again your great lessons of patriotism, of courage, of self-sacrifice" against this "blow struck at the heart of the Republic." When he sat down, a local minister jumped to the platform, declared that such sentiments did not express the feeling of New England, and led three cheers for Hayes. In response, another listener led three cheers for Chamberlain. Such was the state of party opinion on Hayes's southern policy.[20]

Chamberlain's philippic did not go unanswered, and no one defended the president more stoutly than Treasury Secretary John Sherman. In a private letter to carpetbagger and former Alabama Senator Willard Warner, Sherman emphasized that Hayes had "fairly put upon the South the highest bonds for good behavior, and nothing can arrest the success of this policy except a gross and palpable breach of their promise of protection." Like many other Republicans, Sherman had come to believe that their party's attempt to reorder southern society and politics on the basis of black suffrage had proved problematic at best. Republicans' effort to reinvent the Republic with an equal franchise had born fruit that required careful tending if it were to nourish republican institutions. "We all know very well," he wrote Warner, "that the negroes, though in a majority, cannot of themselves secure personal or political rights. Unless they can find a party to befriend them among the whites they must relapse into a gross slavery, or will break out in open violence and civil war, which would be death to them and destruction to the South." Confronted with a situation of such grave complexity, Hayes was "doing all he can" to achieve a practical solution.[21]

Sherman also defended the president publicly in an Ohio campaign speech that portrayed Hayes alternately as having had no choice and as having chosen the right policy. On the one hand, the Treasury secretary declared that "the President is not made the judge of who is elected Governor of a State," nor did the Constitution empower him to use "the army of the United States in deciding a purely local election contest." Sherman argued that "the delay and hesitation of General Grant had been fatal to Packard," leaving Hayes little choice but to accept the Nicholls regime as "the *de facto* government of Louisiana, supported by the great body of the white men and nearly all the wealth and intelligence of the State, and by the tired acquiescence of a large portion of the colored people." But Sherman also claimed that Hayes had deliberately adopted a course that reflected his "broader motive" to "bring the North and South again into conditions of harmony and fraternity." No one, however, should be "foolish enough to talk of his abandoning the colored people and their constitutional rights." "Unarmed, unorganized, defenseless, and ignorant as they have been," blacks would find that Hayes's policy would enable them "to secure the aid and sympathy of an influential portion of the whites," and this would "do more to secure the full, practical enforcement of those rights than the employment of an army tenfold as great as the army of the United States." Because white southerners had given Hayes "their self-proclaimed promise that home rule means the equal protection in equal civil and political rights of all, they have to fulfill this promise or stand dishonored before the civilized world." Again underscoring the vital necessity of having a Republican in the White House, Sherman avowed that "if this fails," Hayes "will not be wanting in the exercise of the full powers of his great office to secure the civil rights of all, without distinction of race, color, or condition."[22]

Sherman's speech was widely circulated and won praise from Hayes's supporters. But many Republicans remained unmoved. "I almost ruined myself getting in Hayes," William Chandler wrote a friend, "& what have we to show for it. John Sherman abandoning Louisiana!!!" As Zachariah Chandler put it, "The Administration had the power to aid the Republican party in the south in its struggle for existence, but it chose the other course and the party vanished into thin air."[23]

Hayes was unshakable. "He believes in and is wedded to his policy," a New Hampshire Republican reported to William Chandler after an interview with the president. "He expects some reverses at first, but thinks the leaven will work and that the barriers of vice, ignorance and hatred will be overcome." During the summer, Hayes launched a public relations blitz, taking tours through New England, Ohio, and several southern states. In the South, citizens hailed him as an apostle of reconciliation. "Now," he told southern audiences, "you and I believe there is no real cause of quarrel between us." But again he stressed the requirement that white southerners keep their promises. In Louisville, he asked his audience point blank, "Do you intend to obey the whole Constitution and amendments?" When his listeners signaled their acquiescence with applause, he declared, "I believe you will, and that removes the last cause of dissension between us."[24]

In 1877, with the country still held in the grip of economic depression, Hayes defended his policy as essential to restore good times. "No part of our country can lack prosperity without affecting the prosperity of the whole country," he told a northern audience. "As long as discontent with the Government and with their fellow citizens of the North existed in the Southern States, we all know that politics would receive more attention than business. But now I think I am authorized to say to you that the whole Southern country begins to think more of industry, of improvements, of business, than of politics. . . . It is with ideas like these that we enter upon the work of pacification." Similarly, he told a southern audience, because "discord, discontent, and dissatisfaction are enemies of enterprise, . . . all our interests are for peace."[25]

Hayes was careful to include blacks within the peaceful circle of a reunited country. At Chattanooga he received a statement of support from a welcoming committee of blacks. He assured them that in formulating his policy, one of his "most anxious inquiries" had been how it would affect African Americans. He had concluded that "with the bayonets removed from the South the people of color would be safer in every right, in every interest, than they ever were when protected merely by the bayonet. (Applause) I rejoice that your address assures me that so far as you are concerned here the result is according to our anticipations." In September he congratulated a group of Atlanta blacks that "for no six months since the war has [*sic*] there been so few outrages and invasions of your rights, nor you so secure in your rights, persons, and homes than in the last six months." Hayes assured blacks that "your future will be brighter and brighter, your condition better and better," but he also frankly lectured them that along with the fruits of republican citizenship came responsibilities. "I trust, my colored friends, . . . that you will always remember that to command respect men must have the virtues to deserve respect; industry, good conduct, and intelligence are good alike for white men and for colored men."[26]

Perhaps the most remarkable feature of Hayes's campaign to conciliate white southerners was his glossing over the moral issues that had led to the Civil War. Time and again in addressing Confederate veterans, he likened the war to "a case of fighting between Greek and Greek" and the "party in that fight will always conquer that has the most Greeks. . . . So, with no discredit to you, and no special credit to us, the war turned out as it did." Although his metaphor ostensibly referred to military prowess, southerners could see in it an earnest that he was not going to berate them for past sins. Many Republicans bristled, however. As one put it, "The devil fly away with the patriotism which tells ex-rebels that the war for the Union was a question of Greek meeting Greek, and that neither side was entitled to praise or censure for the blood-bought result." By advocating such sentiments, Hayes would "blunder his party out of existence."[27]

Just the opposite was the president's aim, of course. Hayes had not given up the aim he had avowed during his campaign that the "rebellion" must at all costs be prevented from returning to power. But he had adopted a strategy whereby the rebellion's former adherents must now see that their best prospects lay with a new politics whereby men of similar ideas on nonsectional and especially economic issues could act together for the good of the whole nation. Hayes's southern policy was an extension of Grant's, but whereas Grant had witnessed the erosion of Republican power in the South under circumstances over which he had little control, Hayes sought to take hold of circumstances and direct them to his own ends, for the good of his party and of the country. The first step was to win southerners' goodwill for his administration, and, he hoped, for the Republican Party.

As other Republicans had done, Hayes depicted a regeneration of the Republic as his transcendent aim. The war, he told an audience of veterans at Dayton, had been fought to establish "a free nation where every man has an equal chance and a fair start in the race of life." Now, it was time to submerge sectional and racial animosities in order truly to renew the unified Republic of the Founding Fathers. "It occurred to me," he said, "that the American people would be glad to have such methods applied to the relation then existing between the States and between the whites and blacks as would, if possible, settle these differences peaceably and bring back the Republic to the condition in which it was 100 years ago, when the fathers were one on all questions." "In this pathway," he told a Virginia audience, "I am going [in] the pathway where your illustrious men led—your Jefferson, Madison, Monroe, and your Washington. Our hope is that the people of the whole country will unite to reconcile the feeling which prevailed when the Union was formed. We wish to see what the fathers gave us preserved and transmitted to those who come after."[28]

Hayes's supporters echoed these sentiments. Massachusetts editor Samuel Bowles believed "the practical wisdom and the great virtue of the presidential policies" to be "in utter sympathy with early republicanism."[29] Senator Henry Dawes told his constituents, "The very nature of our government, founded on the consent of the governed, leads us, it seems to me, this way, and this alone, in search of permanent reconciliation and peace. . . . Our government is so made that rebels unconvicted of their treason pass directly from the battlefield to the ballot box and the conquered share with their conquerors in determining the very policy which the victory necessitates. . . . This is all there is of the 'Southern policy.' "[30]

After his southern tour, Hayes felt confident that the "country does seem to be coming back to the ancient concord; and good people approve what I am doing." But Republican skeptics such as Wisconsin Senator Timothy Howe feared that the president was adrift in a "sea of gush." As the first electoral test of his policy loomed in state elections scheduled for the fall of 1877, Republican conventions in Massachusetts and Ohio, "cordially approve[d]" what he was doing in the South, but elsewhere, party members did not conceal their opposition. Iowa Republicans implicitly censured the president's apostasy by issuing a platform that repeated passages from the 1876 national platform calling for a chief executive who would show the "courage and fidelity to duty" to protect every citizen's rights. By a 3-to-1 vote, the New York convention rejected a resolution "heartily commend[ing]" Hayes's policy and instead expressed "no opinion." Pennsylvania Republicans, frankly admitting "differences of opinion existing among us as to the course pursued by President Hayes toward the South," could do no more than honor his "patriotic motives" and hope for good results. In contrast, Democrats, in the words of their convention in New York, believed that Hayes's having "reversed the vicious precedents of the Republican party" had "entitled [him] in that particular to the approval of all good citizens."[31]

Republican dissensions reverberated in Congress. James A. Garfield worried about the "great differences of opinion in regard to the President's policy" and feared that "the atmosphere of praise in which he lives" had "partially blinded the President to the dangers of his course." Taking occasion to "speak very plainly" to Hayes, Garfield complained that during his southern tour touting peace and goodwill, the president "no where spoke as though he did it as the representative of the people who elected him. He thus made his friends fear, and his political enemies hope, that he was acting as though he were not in alliance with his party, and when the South praised him, they dispraised his party. It would have been more just and more politic to have associated his party with his proffers of good will." In short, Hayes could not hope to govern effectively without a united party at his back, nor could he expect to win converts to an indigenous white Republican Party in the South with a policy perceived as merely personal.[32]

The outcome of the 1877 elections offered little solace. The voters' choices turned on a variety of issues, including Hayes's civil service reform policy, his aggressive actions against the Great Railroad Strike that summer, the currency question, and state issues such as prohibition, but the southern policy took a toll on party loyalty. Results were mixed. In some strongholds such as Maine, Iowa, and Kansas, the party easily retained power. In Massachusetts Republicans won but saw their vote decline substantially from 1876. The party lost New York, New Jersey, and Pennsylvania. Most disappointing, it also lost Hayes's home state of Ohio. "The President's Southern policy was distasteful to many," Cincinnati lawyer Warner Bateman confided to Sherman, "and some openly voted the Democratic ticket in expression of their disgust, while still more staid at home." Perhaps most damning were the results in Virginia where Republicans saw their 40 percent share of the vote in 1876 dwindle to 4.1 percent in 1877 and in Mississippi where the Republican vote declined from 30 to 1.2 percent.[33]

Such evidence convinced many Republicans that Hayes's policy would destroy the party's southern wing. Among the most alarmed was former national party secretary William E. Chandler, who went so far as publicly to accuse Hayes of having sold out Republican principles the previous winter to obtain the presidency. In a series of public letters, Chandler warned that the president's policy would lead inexorably to "Confederate generals who led the rebellion taking possession of both Houses of Congress and marching toward the White House . . . crushing out Republicanism and the right of suffrage at the South." Under Hayes, the Republican Party was "parting with its manhood, abasing itself before Southern rebels; wrapping itself about with the garments of self-righteousness, and saying to the negro and the carpet-bagger, 'We never knew

William E. Chandler
(Library of Congress)

you; make terms with the Democrats.'"[34] "The way this peace has been sought is not my way," black leader Frederick Douglass told a Washington gathering, "nor do I think it will or ought to succeed."[35]

Such criticism stung the administration. Republicans had "no occasion" to "drift into antagonism" against the president, John Sherman wrote a friend. Hayes still "desires to secure life and property and political rights to the colored people of the South," Sherman said, but he had concluded that the most effective way to do so was "through the active aid of white men living there, without whose aid the negro must for years be subject to cruel oppression and wrong." After an interview with the president, Senator Howe concluded that, despite the election outcome, Hayes was still "very confident he can revolutionize the South. . . . He is something of a fanatic." In his first annual message in December 1877, Hayes defended his policy as the one "most in harmony with the Constitution and with the genius of our people. . . . All apprehension of danger from remitting those states to local self-government is dispelled, and a most salutary change in the minds of the people has begun and is in progress in ever part of that section." Thus, he concluded, "in the brief period which has elapsed, the immediate effectiveness, no less than the justice of the course pursued is demonstrated, and I have an abiding faith that time will furnish its ample vindication in the minds of the great majority of my fellow citizens." "How the world loves to be humbugged!" exclaimed Hamilton Fish. "And no one ever put it on heavier than the present Administration. . . . Their 'Southern policy' has conciliated the Democratic party into a state of suspended (but still armed) hostility, & the Republican party (at least at the South) into a state of suspended vitality." James G. Blaine warned that the Administration's policy was not only naive but dangerous. "The Southern people are not, in fact, reconciled. . . . Their purpose is to get possession of the Government and rule it as they did before the war, and then all the established results of the war and reconstruction would be set aside."[36]

As Hayes moved into his second year in the White House the validity of these criticisms grew more apparent. In Louisiana, state officials proceeded with the prosecution of the federal collector of customs at New Orleans, Thomas Anderson, alleging that as a member of the 1876 Returning Board he had published a counterfeited public record as true. Republican leaders were outraged. Sherman, Garfield, and Stanley Matthews, all of whom had gone to Louisiana as "visiting statesmen" and had participated in the electoral crisis negotiations, joined in a telegram to Anderson expressing their support. Publicly, Sherman called Anderson's prosecution and conviction "an act of folly and madness" and a "terrible commentary upon the efforts of the President to quiet the turbulence and violence of Louisiana politics." Privately, Sherman warned Hayes that the prosecution tended "to show that this spirit of conciliation is not mutual, and cannot be successful."[37]

Hayes considered the Anderson case clearly within the set of promises of good behavior extended by Nicholls and his legislature, but he still hoped to trust to the "honor of Governor Nicholls" to secure Anderson's release. Rejecting a potentially disruptive showdown, he let it be known that he had instructed Attorney General Charles Devens to look into the federal government's options in the matter, while he also pursued a solution behind the scenes. He called on General Winfield Hancock, who was in New Orleans on an inspection tour, to meet with Nicholls and press him for a peaceful solution. The governor indicated that he would pardon Anderson but wanted to wait for an opportune moment. Meanwhile, some Democrats feared the episode would only result in reuniting the Republicans. After several weeks, the state supreme court defused the tension by overturning Anderson's conviction. Hayes took this outcome as a signal victory for his southern policy: "For the first time the better classes have overruled the violent. Pacification begins to tell."[38]

Others were less sanguine. Wisconsin Senator Timothy Howe took the occasion to deliver a long-anticipated speech against Hayes's southern policy. An early proponent of emancipation during the war and a strong advocate of blacks' rights since, Howe derided the Nicholls government in Louisiana as "born of presidential grace and not of popular choice." Hayes's refusal to defend the Republican Packard under the Constitution's guarantee clause had been a "matter of sincere regret to all who respect republican institutions." Hayes seemed to have forgotten that "self-government in a State is the government not of the strongest but of the greatest number." Howe conceded the value of sectional reconciliation, but said, "We cannot afford to purchase it by the sacrifice of the constitutional rights of majorities. Upon the protection of those rights hangs the perpetuity of our institutions. When they are sacrificed the American system is gone." Hayes dismissed Howe's speech as motivated by Hayes's refusal to appoint him to a Supreme Court vacancy.[39]

Nonetheless, Howe had tapped a well of anti–Hayes sentiment. Within days sympathetic party leaders requested 20,000 copies of his speech for distribution among their constituents. By the spring of 1878 the controversy over the "peace policy" had severely strained party unity. "Just so long as the old slaveholders and their ruffians can keep their heels on the necks of Republicans no doubt there will be a most delightful peace throughout the late Confederate Empire," a Vermont Republican wrote Senator Justin Morrill. "The party is dying, absolutely crumbling to dust," radical Maine editor Charles Boutelle complained to William Chandler. "The Republican masses cannot be rallied for a surrender, and that is all that is now offered them."[40]

The Democrats could reasonably expect to benefit politically from Republican divisions over Hayes's southern policy and his efforts at civil service reform, but they perversely took steps in the spring of 1878 that ultimately helped to reunite the GOP. In May House Democrats launched an investigation of alleged fraud during the election of 1876. Chaired by New Yorker Clarkson Potter and manned by Hayes foes, the House Committee focused on Republican activities in Louisiana and Florida immediately after the November balloting. Hayes saw the "shabby" move as "a partisan proceeding for merely partisan ends," which might backfire and "damage its authors." Still, the administration responded sharply. Postmaster General David Key denounced "this desperate attempt to Mexicanize our institutions" and cautioned his fellow southerners against following men who would "endanger the welfare of the country and the stability of republican institutions for the sake of revenge on political opponents." Key urged southerners to support in the upcoming congressional elections only men who pledged to sustain Hayes's title. Newspapers quoted Hayes himself as having said in private conversation that "such schemes cannot be carried out without war," that impeachment was the only mechanism for removing a president, and that he would "defend my office and the independence of the Executive against any intruder."[41]

The Potter Committee galvanized Republicans. "Like the first shot at Fort Sumter," said the *New York Tribune,* "the first overt act of assault upon the President's title will echo all round the world." Many Democrats considered the investigation unwise. Former Confederate Vice President Alexander Stephens predicted that it would "prove in the end either a contemptible farce, or a horrible tragedy." Within a month, large numbers of House Democrats joined the Republicans in passing two resolutions recognizing that the Forty-fourth Congress had definitively settled Hayes's election and asserting that neither Congress nor the courts had any power to reverse that outcome. Even so, the Potter Committee plowed ahead, although Hayes and other administration leaders remained confident that evidence before it was "too thin to do serious harm." By the end of June, Sherman concluded that "the general impression here is that it is fizzling out." A few months later the *New York Tribune* published the "cipher despatches" which implicated Tilden aides in bribery attempts during the election struggle, thereby largely neutralizing the Potter investigation's damage to the Republicans.[42]

As the congressional elections of 1878 approached, Republicans throughout the country rallied to a defense of Hayes's title. State party conventions denounced the Potter investigation, as Michigan Republicans put it, as "fraught with danger to Republican institutions." The attempt to oust the president, said the Indiana convention, amounted to a "revolutionary resistance to law" that would "destroy our institutions." And yet, party cadres betrayed little enthusiasm for Hayes's southern policy, and even his close associate Charles Foster admitted publicly that the "President's policy has lost him the sympathy of the great mass of the party." Most state platforms implicitly censured it in planks similar to Maine's declaration that "we hold it to be a primary and sacred duty of the National Government to protect and maintain the exercise of all these civil, political and public rights by every citizen of the United States." Iowa Republicans pulled no punches in condemning the "Democratic dogma of home rule" and the administration's "failure to enforce" Republican principles: "The armed conflict between traitors and rebels who sought to destroy the Republic, and the patriots who defended it and preserved it, was more than a mere trial of physical force between Greeks. It was a struggle of right against wrong—of a true civilization against a false one. Whoever regards the Republican and Democratic parties from other standpoints than this, fails to understand their character." This "stalwartness of the Republicans of Iowa" gratified Hayes antagonists such as William Chandler, who told Des Moines editor James Clarkson that the "Hayes surrender to rebel rule and the solid South is a fatal incubus and wherever it is not thrown off the party will go down."[43]

Nonetheless, during the congressional election campaign, Republicans remained divided over how much emphasis to give to the sectional issue. Many GOP leaders gave precedence to the currency debate, despite party divisions regarding that question as well. Hard times had stimulated movements for inflation, which both the Grant and Hayes administrations opposed. Earlier in 1878, administration forces in Congress had thwarted an effort to repeal the 1875 Specie Resumption Act, which mandated the payment of specie for greenbacks beginning in 1879. But in February, a veto by Hayes had failed to block passage of the Bland-Allison Act for the remonetization of silver. In the fall campaign, greenbackism posed a significant threat to the "sound money" forces of the Republican Party. Hayes concluded that the currency was "now the real issue before the country" rather than the southern question, and he took a speaking tour through several northern states to shore up Republican lines. At St. Paul, Minnesota, he told a large audience that financial matters were now the "most interesting questions in public affairs," and "a restored financial condition depends largely upon an honest currency." In usually Republican Maine, where the party confronted a serious threat from a Democratic-Greenback coalition, Blaine touted the issue as "the great question before the people," and warned that "the issuance of an unlimited amount of currency" would be "the most fearful thing that could happen to this country."[44]

But in the September elections, Blaine and the Maine Republicans received a shock, losing the governorship and two of five seats in the congressional delegation, which, with the exception of one single-term Democrat, had been solidly Republican since the 1850s. GOP critics of Hayes's policy, increasingly known as "Stalwarts," had no doubt about the blame. "I think the completeness of our defeat is owing to our recreancy on the Southern question," wrote William Chandler. "To insist upon the duty to maintain the nation's obligations to its creditors while justifying its abandonment of its duty to protect human life and a free ballot at the South seems absurd to me." Blaine defended the currency emphasis on the grounds that "nothing else was in the people's mind." But Stalwarts were not convinced. "Our party has played the comedy of the Almighty Dollar throughout the summer and fall," said George C. Gorham, and has "not even reminded the North of the suppression of the Republican vote of the South." As secretary of the GOP Congressional Campaign Committee, Gorham refused to authorize a printing of Hayes's St. Paul currency speech because it lacked any "word expressing a preference for the Republican Party over the Democratic Party." But more was at stake than the fortunes of party, for again the heart of the question was the fate of the nation's republican institutions. One New York Stalwart wrote Chandler, "We boast that this is a Republic. But it is a vain boast. To be ruled by a minority, no matter how large, attaining power by force, is no more republican than to be ruled by one man, king, emperor or sultan. I accuse the Republican party of having permitted this state of things by their cruel, I might almost say, treasonable apathy."[45]

As the fall campaign wore on, reports of renewed violence and intimidation by Democrats in the South underscored the Stalwarts' complaints. Black Congressman Joseph Rainey of South Carolina warned Hayes that whites were resorting to such methods in several of his state's counties to prevent blacks from organizing. Similar reports from several states prompted the Justice Department to instruct federal officials in the South to enforce the election laws vigorously, and in some locations, district attorneys initiated prosecutions even before election day. For his part, the president contemplated using his annual message to "make a clear, firm, and accurate statement of the facts as to Southern outrages" and to reiterate the demand for "exact justice, equality before the law, perfect freedom of political speech and action, and no denial of rights to any citizen on account of color and race." And yet events in the South did not move Hayes to abandon his basic assumption that lasting peace in the South depended on steering whites into divergent political attachments related to economic interests and other issues that transcended race. "The division there is still on the color line," he regretted after hearing from Rainey. "The whites have the intelligence, the property, and the courage which make power. The negroes are for the most part ignorant, poor, and timid. My view is that the whites must be divided there before a better state of things will prevail."[46]

The persistence of the color line was clear in the election results. In the new House of Representatives, the seventy-three members from the former Confederacy would include only three Republicans, none from any of the states with majority black populations. Republicans lost every southern Senate seat up for election and would have only two southern holdovers in the new Congress. Indeed, in the Senate as a whole, the Republicans lost their majority for the first time since before the war. In northern state contests, however, the party did well. Although Republicans lost state races in Indiana, they carried New York, Pennsylvania, Illinois, and Ohio, as well as several smaller states. In the aggregate of states outside of the former slave domain, the party gained three seats in the national House. Garfield calculated that had there been a presidential vote, the Republicans would have won by a margin of fifty-seven electoral votes (remarkably close to the fifty-nine-vote majority he himself amassed two years later). Clearly, the Republicans could win the presidency without the South. "This election changes the face of the political sky," said Garfield, "and gives an immense impulse to business by adding confidence to the sanctity of the public faith." Hayes likewise saw the primacy of the money question in the outcome and viewed the election as a "verdict in favor of a sound constitutional currency" and a "verdict against communism, socialism, and repudiation."[47]

How the outcome would affect the president's southern policy became a matter of intense interest. Hayes confessed that his "only regret" was "that the better elements of the South were not so organized as to have a share in the victory." He was disturbed by "grave charges" that by "state legislation, by frauds, by intimidation, and by violence of the most atrocious character, colored citizens have been deprived of the right of suffrage." Particularly galling was the violation of blacks' rights in Louisiana and South Carolina, whose Democratic leaders, he recalled, had "solemnly pledged" to uphold those rights. A week after the election, the Stalwart Washington *National Republican* printed a purported interview with Hayes in which he said that he was "*reluctantly forced to admit that the experiment was a failure.* The first election of importance held since it was attempted has proved that fair elections, with free suffrage for every voter in the South, are an impossibility under the existing condition of things." In a similar vein, Sherman told the national council of the Union League that "millions of people are now deprived of their political rights, in open violation of the Constitution," and unless they received protection "our political system will be overthrown."[48]

But even though these comments implied a change of direction, the election result sparked no fundamental alteration in the administration's policy. A Washington dispatch to the *New York Times* claimed that the "statement that the President has recently said that he had tried the plan of conciliation and found it a complete failure is untrue." Hayes himself offered no public clarification, but Secretary of State William Evarts told the *National Republican* that "President Hayes has never surrendered, abandoned, or changed any policy, because he has never had any to change." "The equality or parity of the States— all the States—was reinstated when he came into office," said Evarts, but his endeavors were not "in the nature of an experiment, unless it is an experiment to adhere closely to Constitutional requirements." The day after the election, Hayes listed "a sound national currency" as the Republicans' first priority, and he consoled himself that even though the party had suffered a crushing defeat in the South, among the Democratic victors in that region, "many good and conservative men have been elected. Probably a large majority are in their judgments and consciences opposed to the wild and dangerous [economic] doctrines which the better sentiment of Massachusetts and of the rest of the conservative States of the North have so decidedly condemned."[49]

Hayes did use his annual message to note that in Louisiana and South Carolina and parts of other states "the rights of the colored voters have been overridden." Pledging that the executive branch would vigorously pursue offenders of the election laws, he declared, "No means within my power will be spared to obtain a full and fair investigation of the alleged crimes and to secure the conviction and just punishment of the guilty." Nonetheless, he contemplated no return to military intervention and instead relied on prosecution in the federal courts. He called upon Congress for increased Justice Department appropriations, but he could have little hope that the Democrats in control would accede to that request. Moreover, when Attorney General Charles Devens thought of resigning in early December, Hayes considered appointing a conservative Virginian, A. H. H. Stuart, to the place, although he doubted "if our stalwarts would permit it. . . . The probability is that the attacks on such a course by the bitter brethren would damage the good cause of pacification, more than his appointment could benefit it." The Justice Department did pursue election cases in several states, but with scant prospect of securing convictions by southern juries.[50]

Conciliation and pacification, not confrontation, remained the core of Hayes's policy. "People are weary of sectional controversy," he wrote a friend. "It will gradually drop out of sight." In the House, Garfield declared that the "man who attempts to get up a political excitement in this country on the old sectional issues will find himself without a party and without support." Hayes called the remark "the true statement." By Christmas Day, seven weeks after the election, the president's faith in his original approach had so revived that he pronounced "the Southern policy safely vindicated." "My theory of the Southern situation is this," he wrote shortly thereafter. "Let the rights of the colored people be secured and the laws enforced only by the usual peaceful methods, by the action of the civil tribunals and wait for the healing influences of time and reflection to solve and remove the remaining difficulties. This will be a slow process, but the world moves faster than formerly, and it is plain that the politicians on both sides who seek to thrive by agitation and bitterness are losing rapidly their hold."[51]

Other Republicans were less optimistic. Even Vice President Wheeler frankly wrote his chief: "We *have* differed upon the southern question—mainly upon the measure of Confidence to be accorded to Southern men. *I* never had a particle of faith in their beguiling professions, and long before you leave the Ex[ecutive] Mansion any lingering confidence *you* may have in them will be fully dispelled." "I have not the slightest confidence that the present Administration will exhibit any real energy or determination to redress the outrages in the South," Charles Boutelle complained to Whitelaw Reid after Hayes's annual message. "The Lamars and Stephenses are the most dangerous of our enemies, as they pipe peace with the voice of Jacob, while they throttle human rights with the hand of Esau." For Boutelle, the issue at its core was a " 'conflict' between

Southern lawlessness and republican government," which was "as 'irrepressible' as was that between freedom and slavery."[52]

In Congress Blaine took the lead in voicing Republican ire at southern behavior in the recent election. When the new session convened in early December, even before Hayes's annual message reached the Senate, Blaine called for an investigation. Southern Democrats, he charged, had committed widespread fraud, intimidation, and even murder, thereby rendering blacks' suffrage rights "a hollow mockery." But the question had "taken a far wider range, one of portentous magnitude; and that is, whether the white voter of the North shall be equal to the white voter of the South in shaping the policy and fixing the destiny of this country." Thirty-five seats in the House (and hence thirty-five electoral votes) were based on the South's black population, but, said Blaine, the Democratic party had "seized and appropriated" the "entire political power" those seats represented. Blaine had emphasized the currency question during the 1878 campaign, but now he noted that as a result of "wanton usurpation" in the South, northern men "who have cared little, and affected to care less, for the rights or the wrongs of the negro suddenly find that vast monetary and commercial interests, great questions of revenue, adjustments of tariff, vast investments in manufactures, in railways, and in mines, are under the control of a Democratic Congress whose majority was obtained by depriving the negro of his rights under a common constitution and common laws." In sum, this "outrage upon the right of representation" equaled a "violent perversion of the whole theory of republican government." It had created "a Congress that lacks the warrant laid down by Jefferson to govern. It has not 'the consent of the governed.'" Blaine's motion carried, and a select committee undertook the investigation.[53]

Blaine's reference to "the whole theory of republican government" was more than just a rhetorical flourish. The outcome of the first congressional election after Hayes had "withdrawn" the troops from the South spurred misgivings in the minds of some Republicans about the wisdom of black suffrage in the first place. Secretary of State William M. Evarts, for instance, told an interviewer that the recent outrages in the South had made execution of the law "a stern necessity," but he also expressed sympathy for southern whites who had suffered from "the sudden interjection into their voting aggregate of an element of ignorance, and the consequent domination of uneducated and inexperienced power in their political affairs. It was," said Evarts, "perhaps a mistake that this was done by the Republican party of the North."[54]

Yet few Republicans would turn the clock back to disfranchise blacks. Evarts's misgivings shocked Republicans such as Charles Boutelle, who said the secretary had cast doubt on the value of the Civil War Amendments and had "assailed the very foundation on which the Republican party has builded." Daniel

Chamberlain, still smarting over his loss of the governorship of South Carolina, argued in the *North American Review* that the achievements of the Reconstruction regimes amply vindicated the blacks' innate capacity for self-government. Invoking "the cardinal doctrines of republican government," Chamberlain defended black suffrage as an "expression of the highest morality applied to the affairs of government, the recognition and protection of the natural and inalienable right of all men—the opportunity, without artificial shackles or hindrances, to run the race of life."[55]

The real threat to republican institutions, Republicans believed, was not the alleged political incompetence of blacks but the suppression of their right to cast an unfettered vote. Early in 1879 the whole question was aired in a symposium published by the *North American Review*, "Ought the Negro to Be Disfranchised? Ought He to Have Been Enfranchised?" Speaking for southern Democrats, Wade Hampton opposed any disfranchisement, arguing that the outcome of the recent elections had demonstrated that "as the negro is now acquiring education and property, he is becoming more conservative, and naturally desires to assist in the establishment and maintenance of good government and home rule." The irony, if not cynicism, of southern Democrats' new confidence in black suffrage was not lost on Blaine, who organized the symposium: "I do not recall any warm approval of negro suffrage by a Democratic leader so long as the negro was able to elect one of his own race or a white Republican. But when his numbers have been overborne by violence, when his white friends have been driven into exile, when murder has been just frequent enough to intimidate the voting majority, and when negro suffrage as a political power has been destroyed, we find leading minds in the Democratic party applauding and upholding it." Garfield, another symposium participant, placed the issue in the broader republican context:

> The ballot was given to the negro not so much to enable him to govern others as to prevent others from misgoverning him. Suffrage is the sword and shield of our law, the best armament that liberty offers to a citizen. . . . Our theory of government is based upon the belief that the suffrage carries with it individual responsibility, stimulates the activity and promotes the intelligence and self-respect of the voter. To accomplish these results the voter must be allowed to exercise his rights freely and without restraint.[56]

As if to underscore this position, the Republicans on the Senate committee investigating the 1878 elections in Louisiana and South Carolina reported in late February that murder, violence, and other intimidation had thwarted "the honest expression" of thousands of citizens. One committee member, Angus Cameron of Wisconsin, privately wrote Blaine that in Louisiana, "the Black man & independent white man is [*sic*] practically disfranchised; that no liberty of discussion is tolerated & that every pledge of Gov. Nicholls & his friends to President Hayes has been violated." Federal prosecution of the perpetrators of fraud and violence yielded meager results because Democratic state authorities arrested and jailed complainants on charges of perjury, libel, and disturbing the peace. With enforcement thus frustrated, the committee concluded that Congress should provide "by law for fair and free elections of members of Congress." With the Democrats in control of the House, however, the prospect of such legislation was nil. Senate Judiciary Committee Chairman George Edmunds secured Senate passage of a resolution reaffirming the validity of the Thirteenth, Fourteenth, and Fifteenth Amendments, but a bill his committee proposed to punish violators of citizens' constitutional rights got nowhere.[57]

Rather than strengthening enforcement, Democrats sought to weaken it. In the waning days of the Forty-fifth Congress, they moved to undermine enforcement laws by attaching repeal provisions to appropriations bills. The Republican Senate refused to go along, however, and Congress adjourned on March 3, 1879, without making appropriations for the army or for the legislative, executive, and judicial expenses of the government. As a result, Hayes called the new Congress into special session two weeks later. Now in control of both houses, the Democrats continued to attach riders to appropriations bills. The ensuing impasse vindicated Hayes's insistence in 1876 and 1877 on the absolute necessity of the Republicans' holding on to at least one branch of the federal government. With Democrats determined to roll back enforcement, Hayes noted, "Now the question will come to me."[58]

A year earlier Congress had passed an appropriations bill with a rider that barred use of the army to execute the law. Hayes had approved this rider, which came to be known as the Posse Comitatus Act, because it made exception for uses "expressly authorized by the Constitution or by act of Congress." In Hayes's view, this legislation meant that the military could not be used to "interfere" with an election, which he had no intention of doing, but civil authorities were still perfectly free to call in the troops whenever opposition to the law was "too powerful for the ordinary police or other civil officers to overcome." The key statutory authorization was Section 2002 of the *Revised Statutes*, originally passed in 1865:

> No military or naval officer, or other person engaged in the civil, military, or naval service of the United States, shall order, bring, keep, or have under his authority or control, any troops or armed men at the place where any general or special election is held in any State, unless it be necessary to repel the armed enemies of the United States, or to keep the peace at the polls.

Democrats now sought to excise the phrase "or to keep the peace at the polls."[59]

The Democrats' move sparked intense debate in Congress, with the unintended result of reuniting previously dissonant Republicans. As Providence Postmaster Charles Brayton told Congressman Nelson Aldrich, "There is a strong feeling growing with the debates in Congress among our people . . . for sustaining the Northern view at all hazards." In the Senate, Blaine dismissed Democrats' cries against "military despotism" as an "absolute farce," because the number of troops in the entire South amounted to just 1,155—less than one per county—"to intimidate, overrun, oppress, and destroy the liberties of fifteen million people!" The Democrats' real target, Blaine charged, was the "civil" officers mentioned in the law, as was doubly clear from another rider designed to repeal or revise several sections of the Ku Klux Klan Act and other laws in order to drastically reduce the powers of federal marshals and supervisors at elections. The Democrats' "avowed object," said Garfield, was "to destroy all the defenses which the nation has placed around its ballot-box to guard the fountain of its own life."[60]

Republicans rallied once more to defend the national government's power to regulate such elections. Connecticut's Joseph Hawley quoted arguments by Madison and Hamilton in the *Federalist* that the "definition of the right of suffrage is very justly regarded as a fundamental article of republican government." To leave the power of regulating national elections in the hands of the states "would leave the existence of the Union entirely at their mercy." According to Wisconsin Congressman Charles G. Williams, "two things are absolute and indispensable—*purity at the ballot-box; peace at the polls*. . . . If the laws be not enforced, there lies nothing beyond but the dark sea of anarchy, danger, and revolution. Is not this, rather than the sword, the first great cause which leads to the downfall of republics?"[61]

Nor was the issue limited to the South, for many of the election laws the Democrats hoped to repeal applied to big cities. Hayes believed that these statutes were "mainly employed in the densely-peopled regions of the North," and Roscoe Conkling accused the Democrats of a daring "partisan manoeuvre" to overcome their inability to carry New York "with a fair election and a fair count." "This is a struggle for power," said Conkling. "It is a fight for empire. It is a contrivance to clutch the National Government."[62]

At bottom, Republicans saw the Democrats' drive against the election laws as an assault on the Republic they had refashioned in the wake of the war. Pennsylvania Congressman John I. Mitchell spoke of "the new Republic" and warned that northern Democrats allied with the Lost Cause of the South were keeping "the ship of state—of the new state of freedom, equal rights, and equal opportunity for all men—floundering in a deep and troubled sea." White southerners, declared John A. Logan, "have never to this moment accepted the decisions of the war," and now the Democrats' election triumph in 1878 had robbed Republicans of "the power to continue peacefully their work of reconstruction upon the ideal hope of the Republic." "There is," said the *New York Tribune*, "a division of parties which goes to the very foundation of our system of government. . . . The Solid South wants, first, control of the Government for a minority of the people."[63]

Republicans also condemned their opponents' chief weapon in the crisis, the rider. The Democrats, said Hawley, "have put the thumbscrew on me here and tell me . . . that the whole Government shall go penniless for two years unless I shall vote against my conscience." Garfield labeled the misuse of the appropriations process as a "revolutionary method of legislation by coercion" whose objective differed little from the rebels' purpose in 1861. Then southerners tried to "shoot your Government to death"; now Democrats threatened to "starve the Government to death." Garfield reminded his House colleagues of the "vital importance" of "the voluntary element in our institutions." By attaching enforcement repeal to measures for indispensable appropriations, the Democrats tried to force the president to accept a policy against his will. Such legislative compulsion, said the Ohio congressman, "is revolutionary to the core, and is destructive of the fundamental element of American liberty, the free consent of all the powers that unite to make laws." Privately, Garfield wrote, "If this is not revolution, which if persisted in will destroy the government, I am wholly wrong in my conception of both the word and the thing."[64]

Hayes agreed, vowing to resist "to the last extremity" the Democrats' scheme to violate "the constitutional provision as to the President's participation in legislation." Momentarily he pondered whether he could accept a freestanding bill repealing laws permitting troops to keep the peace at the polls, but he quickly rejected the idea. "Experience has shown that the protection and conduct of national elections cannot safely be left to the States. I cannot consent to the repeal of the election laws enacted by Congress unless others equally effective are substituted." Hayes did "not care to use the military," he wrote William Henry Smith. "But the State Rights heresy that the Nation can not enact safeguards for national elections, and the still more dangerous doctrine that a bare majority in the two house[s] can absorb all the powers of all the Departments of the Government, cannot be under any conceivable circumstances approved when embodied in legislation."[65]

When Congress passed the army appropriations bill with its rider, Hayes issued a ringing veto. Such "coercive dictation," he insisted, would work "a radical, dangerous, and unconstitutional change in the character of our institutions."

Arguing that the "present laws have in practice unquestionably conduced to the prevention of fraud and violence at the elections," he said that the proposed bill "will weaken, if it does not altogether take away, the power of the National Government to protect the Federal elections by the civil authorities." This he could not permit. When Congress passed a freestanding bill barring troops from the polls, Hayes registered another strongly worded veto. Although he reiterated the position he had taken at the outset of his administration, that no troops "should be present at the polls to take the place or to perform the duties of the ordinary civil police force," he declared that "there should be no denial of the right of the National Government to employ its military force on any day and at any place in case such employment is necessary to enforce the Constitution and laws." Citing legislation dating back to the days of George Washington, Hayes insisted "that the Government of the United States possesses under the Constitution, in full measure, the power of self-protection by its own agencies, altogether independent of State authority, and, if need be, against the hostility of State governments."[66]

Before Congress adjourned, Hayes vetoed three more bills with riders designed to undermine federal protection of elections, either by repeal of statutory authority or by denial of necessary funds for enforcement. In his message of May 29 he declared, "On the day of an election peace and good order are more necessary than on any other day of the year." Citizens should feel "safe in the exercise of their most responsible duty and their most sacred right as members of society—their duty and their right to vote." In the end, Hayes accepted a rider that repealed the Reconstruction-era test oath for federal jurors and another that barred the use of troops as a "police force" at the polls. Hayes considered this latter provision meaningless because civil authorities could still employ troops to aid them "not at all as a police, but as part of the military power of the country." The special session adjourned without appropriating funds for U.S. marshals. Even so, Attorney General Charles Devens instructed them to perform their duties until they could be compensated for services rendered and expenses incurred.[67]

The Democrats' behavior in the special session confirmed the Republicans' worst fears about the Democrats' aim to reverse the reordering of the Republic the Republicans had wrought. Garfield cautioned his Ohio friend Burke Hinsdale not to "underestimate the prevalence of the wicked spirit of the Democratic party, especially the Southern wing of it. Their perfidious treatment of the President, their still worse treatment of the negroes, their persistent efforts to praise the 'lost cause'—and prophecy [*sic*] its ultimate success, their every day talk since they obtained control of both Houses, are forced upon our attention here constantly; and you mistake our resistance to them for an attempt on our part to re-awaken dead issues." Garfield thought Hayes's conciliatory policy had been "productive of good," but primarily for demonstrating "more clearly, the real character of the Southern people than the old policy could have done." Garfield even bridled at the conciliatory spirit promoted by so-called Blue and Gray veterans reunions, which he described as "meaningless gush" and "a stupid avoidance of all the meaning and spirit of the war." In an impassioned speech at the end of the special session, he declared that the Democrats' "destructive theory of government" was "filling the people with anxiety and indignation; and they are beginning to inquire whether the war has really settled these great questions."[68]

Similarly, Governor Shelby Cullom of Illinois saw the American system of republican government at the core of the rider controversy. "No principle in our form of government is clearer," Cullom wrote Hayes,

> than that the Constitution contemplates that the several departments shall exercise their respective functions free from either moral or physical duress or coercion by the others. If the right to do this is to be surrendered by one department in compliance with the usurpations of another, either in letter or in spirit, then will the equilibrium of the several parts of the government be overthrown, and we shall be on the high road to anarchy or the despotism of either a monarchy or an oligarchy. In either case the blood shed by the soldiers of the late war, and the thousands of millions of treasure expended in sustaining and strengthening the principles of republican freedom, established by the founders of the Republic, would have been spent in vain.[69]

The rider issue vindicated Hayes's belief in the crucial importance of the Republicans' maintaining control of at least one branch of the government. Only his vetoes had prevented a wholesale scrapping of national election laws. Personally, the controversy furnished the president "one of the '*ups*' of political life." "Party wise," said Garfield, "the extra session has united the Republicans more than anything since 1868." Galvanized for the 1879 elections, Republicans in state after state adopted resolutions saluting Hayes's steadfastness and condemning the Democrats' own brand of bloody-shirt politics. "The Republic of the United States is a nation and not a league," declared New York Republicans, who, despite Roscoe Conkling's patronage battles with Hayes, voiced their "hearty approval" of the president's vetoes. Massachusetts Republicans "deprecate[d] the course of the members of the Democratic party who have undertaken to revive sectional animosity for the purpose of securing political ascendancy in the Southern States, and who have revived the memories of sectional strife by the defiant declaration of the purpose to repeal laws made necessary by war and enacted to secure the results of the war." Ohio Republicans denounced southern

Democrats in Congress who were "now plotting to regain through the power of legislation the cause which they lost in the field, namely, the establishment of State sovereignty by the overthrow of national supremacy."[70]

Ohio was a key battleground, where Charles Foster, closely identified with the electoral negotiations two years earlier, headed the Republican ticket as the nominee for governor. Hayes himself participated in the campaign, most notably in a speech at Youngstown in which he traced the provenance of Republicans' nationalism back to the founding of the Union. Focusing on the meaning of republicanism, Hayes repeated Abraham Lincoln's paean to the American government as one "whose leading object is to elevate the condition of men; to lift artificial weights from all shoulders; to clear the paths of laudable pursuit for all; to afford all an unfettered start, and a fair chance in the race of life." That kind of government, Hayes warned, again confronted danger. Republicans had enhanced the republican polity by bringing within its bounds the former slaves, but the Democrats were still fighting against that reform. Their efforts to thwart the new-made elements in the Republic posed a grave threat not only to blacks but to the Republic itself. "The lawlessness which to-day assails the rights of the colored people will find other victims to-morrow," Hayes said. "The right of suffrage is the right of self-protection. Its free exercise is the vital air of republican institutions."[71]

In a speech at Cleveland, Garfield echoed those sentiments, noting that "the central thought in American political life" was "the principle that the freely expressed will of the majority shall be the law of all,—that all shall obey." Now, however, a reborn "spirit of Southern tyranny" had "arisen and killed freedom in the South." Moreover, "the Rebel brigadiers in Congress" wanted to eliminate federal election supervisors in the great cities and open the way for a southern alliance with northern cities that would give the South "the whole control of this republic." Garfield cast the great cities as pestiferous precincts lethal to republican virtue. Jefferson, he noted, had called them "the sores—the cancers—on the body politic." The urban Democratic party, said Garfield, was not unlike the party of Catiline described by Cicero: "all the thieves and robbers and murderers . . . 'the bilge-water of Rome.'" Should the Democrats succeed in overthrowing federal election laws, Garfield warned, they would make the cities "strongly enough Democratic to overwhelm all the votes that the green lanes of our country can grow," and "the vileness of New York city [would] pour its foul slime over the freedom of the American ballot-box."[72]

Clearly party managers saw the protection and purity of the ballot as an issue that tapped deep feeling in the North. Elihu Washburne told Blaine that campaigners should give the financial question only "a passing glance" and instead emphasize "the only real question—Shall the Government of the Country be turned over to the Rebels?" In 1879 Treasury Secretary John Sherman devoted his principal stump speech mostly to financial issues, but he also declared that "there is a question infinitely more important than money or bonds or property or silver or gold." Southerners were engaged in open "rebellion against constitutional rights," against which Republicans must "present a formidable and stern resistance." "Compared with this issue," said Sherman, "all other issues are secondary."[73]

Republicans carried the day throughout the North, winning a victory that Hayes considered a clear indication that the national executive would "be sustained in the faithful enforcement" of the election laws. And yet there was slim prospect that this popular endorsement would translate into any new policy. Hayes still had little inclination to use troops, and no southern governor or legislature would ask him to do so—the constitutional exigency he deemed necessary to take action. The Justice Department still faced discouraging prospects for securing election law convictions in the South. Hayes implicitly conceded these difficulties in his annual message in December. Beyond calling for the missing appropriation for marshals and deputies, he devoted only one paragraph to the ballot issue. The president called on the House and Senate to "supply any defects" in the election laws, with no chance that the Democrats of the Forty-sixth Congress would do so.[74]

Despite their victory, the intractability of the southern situation genuinely dismayed Republicans. Sherman believed that if white southerners could only rise above their prejudices, many would find that "their interests and feelings would incline them to act with the Republican party." But as long as they permitted violence and intimidation "to prevent the free and full discussion of public matters, . . . republican government is impossible." As for blacks, Sherman was tempted to conclude that the current exodus of many of them to Kansas and elsewhere offered perhaps "the best remedy for the fraud and violence practiced upon the Negroes." Nonetheless, "the people of the North who hate oppression" must stand by the Republicans' efforts to "support and maintain the equal rights of the humblest citizen." An equally pessimistic Garfield believed that "the betterment of the negro race must necessarily be the work of time." "The negroes have their fate in their own hands," he wrote a friend. "In spite of politics and its entanglements, if they shall prove themselves able to become self-supporting citizens, they will finally get their grip on the public mind and secure a permanent hold in the domain of citizenship."[75]

Although the Republican triumph in the North in 1879 did not spark a renewed vigor in the protection of blacks' rights, it did augur a Democratic defeat in 1880, with a potential long-term impact. "One more Republican triumph & the country will be safe," Hamilton Fish wrote. "After the next census, the strength of the 'Solid South' will be less, & the great West will be greater & mightier." Such a shift in electoral strength would not only permit a more effective southern policy. It would also provide greater security to the nationalistic economic policies that increasing numbers of Republicans saw as the more important focus for the party, especially with the return of better times after years of depression. "We have a great many things to do," Secretary of State William Evarts told a New York audience. "We have our manufactures, our agriculture, our commerce. We have the fostering and advancement of enterprise, of religion, of civilization, and we have our place among the nations of the world if we will step forward and take it. And we do not intend to be kept forever from these pursuits by having forced upon us, in a clear sky, these thunderbolts and threatenings of danger in the Southern heavens."[76]

Even so, party Stalwarts warned against any tendency to elevate the economic consequences of the southern question above its moral, political, and constitutional significance. On the eve of the 1879 election, Zachariah Chandler told a Chicago audience that "more important than all financial questions" was the question, "Are we, or are we not, a Nation?" "Through shot-guns and whips, tissue-ballots and violence," southern blacks were "absolutely disfranchised. . . . It ought not to be; it must not be; and it shall not be." Thanks to Republican policies, said Chandler, times were again good, but, he told Northerners, to defeat Rebel rule, they must "shut up your stores; shut up your manufactories, and go to work for your Country."[77]

Thus, as Hayes's third year in office neared its end, Republican priorities remained in flux. Many Republicans saw the coming national election in 1880 as a crossroads that would determine the party's direction in the ensuing decade. In accepting his nomination in 1876, Hayes had forsworn a second term, thereby clearing the way for a nomination struggle whose outcome could influence the party's ideological path. Many Republicans who deplored Hayes's southern policy saw the presidential race as an opportunity to return the party to a more intense and direct defense of the freedmen and the party's interests in the South. Many Stalwarts saw the party's salvation in a return to former President Grant. But many other Republicans recoiled from a Grant nomination, which would rekindle the corruption issue and violate the two-term tradition. "The Grant boom is a Stalwart boom and I hate to oppose it," William Chandler confessed, "but I should regard his nomination as a dangerous departure from republicanism."[78] Nonetheless, as 1879 drew to a close, the Grant boom continued to grow. Whatever its outcome, Grant's candidacy ensured that the southern question would be at the center of debate as the party chose its nominee and refined its vision for the new decade.

7

Confrontation with a Solid South
New Directions under Garfield and Arthur

As the nation entered the 1880s, fifteen years after the close of the Civil War, the Republicans' design for a new Republic with a broadened franchise and wider political liberty remained far from realization. Neither the aggressive intervention of the early 1870s nor Hayes's policy of conciliation had prevented the triumph of conservative white Democrats in the South. By 1880 Republicans confronted a South solidly in the grip of the Democratic Party. Even so, intractable as the problem seemed, Republicans did not lapse into defeatism. Instead, party leaders cast about for new strategies to revive the republican project. They continued to debate how best to deal with the southern question. That debate played a central role in the presidential campaign of 1880.

As the election year approached, former President Ulysses Grant appealed to Republicans disenchanted with the moderate policies pursued by the Hayes administration. Spearheading the general's candidacy were Stalwart Republican leaders, especially Senators Roscoe Conkling of New York, John A. Logan of Illinois, and J. Donald Cameron of Pennsylvania, who scorned Hayes's efforts at civil service reform as ruinous to the party. Republicans disgusted with the president's conciliatory policy toward the South also rallied around Grant. After four years of "Miss Nancy Jane Hayes," said one Indiana Stalwart, "I will sure willingly go in for Grant." And yet, such enthusiasm for Grant based on an anticipated revival of a more aggressive southern policy struck other

Republicans as unwarranted, if not altogether wrong-headed. Opponents such as Whitelaw Reid pointed to "the losses the Republican party experienced under Grant and the extent to which KuKlux outrages were tolerated under the 'strong man'—an extent much greater than has marked the subsequent career of the 'weak man' that followed him."[1]

But Grant's supporters showed a willingness to overlook a great deal. Soon after leaving the White House in 1877, he and his wife had embarked on a world tour that kept them out of the country for more than two years. They had received warm greetings from kings and potentates around the globe, and many at home saw Grant's experiences abroad as somehow giving him a preparation for the presidency he had lacked before his first term. Friendly newspaper coverage boosted his prestige and stimulated the boom for a third term. Grant returned to San Francisco in September 1879 and then traveled slowly eastward, accepting the plaudits of adoring crowds. As the year drew to a close, Henry Dawes noted that "the Grant boom soars," threatening to "sweep the Republican party and the country the *devil* knows where."[2]

But the general's boom was not invincible. Some observers believed that he had returned to the United States too early and that his supporters would be unable to sustain the popular zeal until the national convention in June. Moreover, other candidates showed no willingness to bow out or to concede any ground on issues. Although Hayes remained officially neutral, Secretary of the Treasury John Sherman based his candidacy in considerable measure on a defense of the administration, including its policy in the South. "The idea," Sherman wrote privately, "that Gen. Grant would be the strong man to aid us in our trouble will be met by the fact that during his Administration thousands of people were killed and bulldozed and deprived of their right to vote without any aid or assistance or redress from him." But more important, Sherman argued that it was time to shift the party's emphasis to economic issues. "While we should not in the slightest degree surrender any Republican principle or the full protection of every citizen in equal rights, we ought to direct the public mind from the questions growing out of the war to quieter questions of public policy." "If I am nominated," he wrote a constituent, "it will be from an earnest desire to maintain intact the financial policy of the Administration, the resumption of specie payments, the reduction of the interest of the public debt, and the development of our industrial resources."[3]

But Sherman's quest for national convention delegates rested largely on his control of patronage, especially in the South, and among Republicans in that region, financial issues took a back seat. Moreover, Sherman's Ohio supporters advised him that in the North, upholding national authority and protecting southern blacks' rights were "popular ideas now." Sherman conceded the difficulty in trying to shift popular attention to economic questions. The principal issues confronting the nation, he told a campaign group, included not only the "maintenance of a sound currency" but also the "full protection of every citizen of the United States by the National Government in every legal right . . . and against injustice and violence whether committed by authority of a State, or by a mob, or by a person."[4]

Grant's other major challenger was James G. Blaine. Vastly more popular than Sherman, the Maine senator posed a much greater threat to Grant's chances. Like Sherman, Blaine had recently given priority to economic issues. But as luck would have it, a bitter fight for power in his own state earned him broad respect in the party as a robust defender of the ballot. In the state elections of 1879 the Republicans won a clear majority in the legislature, but a fusionist band of Democrats and Greenbackers under Democratic governor Alonzo Garcelon sought to retain power by invalidating the returns of thirty-seven Republicans elected to the assembly. As Republican state chairman, Blaine marshaled his party's forces in a months-long struggle. Both sides even assembled units of armed men at the state capital, and though no violence occurred, few could miss the resemblance to the South earlier in the decade. When the state supreme court finally upheld the Republicans' claim, Blaine emerged with a refurbished image as a champion of free and fair elections. The Maine Republicans were "not merely fighting the battle of our own State alone," Blaine told an Augusta mass meeting. "The corruption or destruction of the ballot is a crime against free government. . . . I wish to speak for the millions of all political parties and in their name to declare that the Republic must be strong enough, and shall be strong enough, to protect the weakest of its citizens in all their rights."[5]

Back in Washington, Blaine found the issue very much alive. Despite the popularity of Hayes's vetoes and the Republican victories in the 1879 elections in the North, Democrats revived the tactic of using appropriations bills to try to vitiate the election laws. In the army spending bill, they included a section barring the use of troops as a police force to keep the peace at the polls. In response, Blaine offered a proviso making it a crime for any person to "carry a deadly weapon of any kind, openly or concealed, at the polls." The amendment had no chance, but Blaine scored the rhetorical point that "the whole question of elections in the South comes down to the one point of violence at the polls, of there not being a peaceable, lawful, protected ballot."[6] The bill passed and was signed by Hayes, who believed, as he had in approving a similar bill the previous year, that the section restricting the "police" use of troops was meaningless.[7]

Of greater significance was the festering issue of funding for special deputy marshals whose protective function at the polls Democrats sought to eliminate or curtail. In early March 1880 the Supreme Court bolstered the Republicans' position by upholding the constitutionality of the federal election laws, including the sections dealing with supervisors and marshals. Speaking for the majority in *Ex parte Siebold,* Justice Joseph Bradley declared that "if Congress has power to make regulations it must have the power to enforce them." "When duties are violated and outrageous frauds are committed, . . . the government of the United States may, by means of physical force, exercised through its official agents, execute on every foot of American soil the powers and functions that belong to it." The decision outraged Democrats, who charged that "the fires of partisanship burn beneath the ermine." Four days after the Court's opinion, Congressman John McMahon, an Ohio Democrat, reported a deficiency appropriations bill that specifically excluded payments to special election marshals. With an obvious swipe at Hayes's disputed election, McMahon dismissed the Court's opinion as "a sort of eight-by-seven decision" rendered "according to party lines."[8]

Such flippancy played directly into Republicans' hands. As Representative Joseph Hawley put it, Democrats' "hostility to the Supreme Court" was simply part of their larger "hostility to any attempt on the part of the General Government to protect the rights of the people in the sacred duty of voting." By ignoring the Court's decision as the "voice of the Constitution," said James A. Garfield, Democrats were committing a "cool, calm, deliberate, assassination of the law" that would "thwart the nation's 'collected will.'" The Democrats did change the bill, allowing for compensation of special deputies but changing their mode of selection in a way that drastically limited their authority. Hayes promptly vetoed the entire deficiency bill rather than accept these provisions.[9]

While the enforcement issue thus occupied all three branches of government, the southern question in general reverberated through the Republicans' preconvention campaign. Many of Grant's supporters continued to tout him as the indispensable "strong man." "If the lawful authority of the national Government is disputed," said his former treasury secretary, George Boutwell, "he will marshal and use all the resources of that Government for the maintenance of that authority. And if the constitutional rights of citizens are invaded, he will employ every constitutional power for their protection." But Grant's supporters could claim no monopoly over the issue. In New Hampshire, for instance, the state convention instructed its national delegates for Blaine but also adopted a forceful platform upholding "equal rights for every citizen, everywhere, and the securing of those rights, if absolutely necessary, by the strong arm of the General Government." Vermont Republicans supported their own senator and favorite of some reformist Republicans, George Edmunds, but they nonetheless devoted four of the six planks of their platform to the southern question, noting that the "overthrow of popular government in seven States of the Union by terrorism and ballot-box frauds" had raised "just alarm on the part of friends of a republican form of government."[10]

As the delegate contest continued with Grant unable to take a command-ing lead, the general's "strong-man" image did not thrill those who believed Hayes had followed a more appropriate policy. The *New York Tribune* point-edly asked, "Does the Republican party dare go back to the methods which, for eight years of wretchedness, lawlessness and massacre, were tried so vainly?" Grant's allies maintained that southerners had feelings of great respect for the general and that his nationwide popularity would help heal sectional wounds. Grant himself traveled through the South, and though usually preternaturally reticent, he gave several short speeches designed to calm fears of renewed na-tional government aggressiveness should he resume the presidency. "The past is gone," he told a New Orleans audience. What he now wished for the South was "increased and long-standing prosperity, believing and knowing that it is the best cure for disorders and sectional animosities." Back in Illinois, Grant told a crowd at Springfield that the southerners now exhibited "a returning love for the flag. . . . That is what we desire certainly; that there shall be no sectional feeling, that there should be a substantial, solid Union feeling in every section of the country." His supporters portrayed the former president as the very ava-tar of national harmony. Timothy Howe told Blaine that the applause showered upon Grant, North and South, represented "a proffer of reconciliation," and "the Chicago Convention ought to accept the proffer." Blaine disagreed, and the general's defeat remained a central objective of his own candidacy.[11]

When Republicans gathered for their convention in Chicago, the prospect for sectional reconciliation seemed remote to many delegates, some of whom had arrived fresh from the riders battle with the Democrats in Congress. On taking the gavel as chairman, Congressman George Hoar declared that the Democratic party, unchanged in purpose or character since the Rebellion, still waged "warfare upon the safeguards which the Nation has thrown around the purity of its elections." The platform included a strong antisouthern plank and made no mention of Hayes's southern policy. The document did "honor his ve-toes interposed between the people and attempted partisan laws," but otherwise accorded the president only a faint tribute for his "efficient, just and courteous discharge of the public business." As for the South, the platform declared un-equivocally, "The equal, steady and complete enforcement of the law, and the protection of all our citizens in the enjoyment of all privileges and immunities guaranteed by the Constitution, are the first duties of the Nation. . . . Whatever promises the Nation makes the Nation must perform."[12]

Roscoe Conkling's nominating speech for Grant depicted the general as a leader infinitely stronger than Hayes on the southern question. The coming election, Conkling declared, would be "the Austerlitz of American politics" and would "decide, for many years, whether the country shall be Republican or Cossack." If Grant were in power, "the poor dwellers in the cabins of the South should no longer be driven in terror from the homes of their childhood and the graves of their murdered dead." But the New Yorker also echoed the assertion of the preconvention campaign that the former president had a better chance than any other Republican to carry several doubtful states in the former Confederacy. His nomination would "dissolve and emancipate a distracted 'solid South'" and thus "break that power which dominates and mildews" the region. And that outcome could rescue the country at large from the benighted notions of the Democrats, especially in economic policy. The Democratic party was "a menace to order and prosperity," and Grant's nomination and certain victory would "overthrow an organization whose very existence is a standing protest against progress."

None of the other speakers who placed candidates in nomination attempted to portray their favorites as "stronger" than Grant on the southern issue. Robert Elliott, a black delegate from South Carolina, did, however, depict John Sherman as an "unyielding and consistent champion of human rights" who would protect "the rights of every citizen of the United States, without regard to their race or their nationality, without regard to their station or condition in life." More significantly, Elliott challenged Conkling's claim that Grant, or indeed any Republican, could carry some portion of the South. If the party made that "an element of calculation for success," said Elliott, "it cannot triumph." Such a judgment implicitly condemned past party policy that had brought the South to such a disordered condition. Only Garfield, in nominating Sherman, mentioned the issue in a way that partook of the spirit of Hayes's policy: "The Republican party offers to our brethren of the South the olive branch of Peace, and invites them to renewed brotherhood, on this supreme condition: That it shall be admitted, forever, that in the War for the Union we were right and they were wrong."[13]

In the end, the convention took none of the major candidates and instead nominated Garfield. In doing so, the party chose a man with a reputation for moderation on the southern question. Although Garfield had at times denounced suppression of the ballot as vehemently as any Republican, he had during the recent rider controversy advocated the appointment of an equal number of Democrats and Republicans as election deputy marshals. Privately he had worried that the "radical feeling on the part of Republicans" had "become in many respects unreasonable and dangerous." "I find myself suspected of being unsound," he confessed. Still, nothing in Garfield's record precluded a strong stand on the sectional question in the coming campaign.[14]

James A. Garfield
(Library of Congress)

In the wake of Garfield's nomination, the direction that he and the party would take was not immediately clear. John Sherman, smarting from his convention defeat, still wanted "to turn our political contests from war issues and recollections to business and financial interests and prosperity." But other Republicans believed that continued southern provocations offered ample reason to take a more aggressive stance on the sectional issue. Less than a week after Garfield's nomination congressional Democrats passed a marshals bill that largely replicated the provisions of the recently vetoed rider. Hayes promptly vetoed the new measure. Quoting at length from *Ex parte Siebold*, the president said the proposal would work a "radical change" in the national government's power over elections and hence was in "direct conflict with the judgment of the highest judicial tribunal of our country." The next day Hayes dashed off to Garfield a list of "The Issues" at stake in the election, assigning first place to "the attempt of the Democratic Party in Congress, in the Supreme Court and in the Country at large to reestablish the State Rights doctrine of Calhoun and the Rebellion, and the resistance to these reactionary movements by the Republican party."[15]

The following week the Democratic national convention underscored the dominance of that party's southern wing. Even northern Democrats such as New Yorker Smith Weed complained that "the old dictation of the South was prevalent." The delegates nominated General Winfield Scott Hancock, a northern general of Gettysburg fame, in an obvious attempt to defuse the Republicans' sectional arguments and cut into the northern vote. But Hancock had great appeal to white southerners because of his tilt in their direction during Reconstruction. Briefly in command in the military district of Louisiana and Texas, he had sympathized with Andrew Johnson's position and had overturned orders of his Radical-leaning predecessor, Philip Sheridan. He had enjoyed substantial southern support for the Democratic presidential nomination in 1868, and after twelve years, southerners still remembered his opposition to the Republicans' "military despotism." As the 1880 convention wound down, South Carolina's Wade Hampton rose to "pledge" to the cheering delegates that the "solid South" would deliver "its solid vote" for the Democratic ticket.[16]

For Republicans, this brazen boast that the election's outcome was preordained in sixteen states confirmed all they had alleged about the destruction of republicanism in the South. George Hoar told a meeting at Boston's Faneuil Hall that "Hampton will keep that pledge, you may be sure," and thus, "the question above all other questions in this country is the question of the free ballot . . . I have no patience with the men, whether they are Democratic politicians, whether they are independent essayists, or whether they are Republican doctors of divinity, who would seek to divert the attention of the people from this issue." Administration official John Defrees counseled Garfield that Hampton's insolent claim would "have a tendency to make an [*sic*] United North, if properly handled by our people." "I sometimes tremble for the result," Defrees confessed, "but, reflecting that there is a Divine Supervision over the affairs of Nations, I cannot believe that those who attempted to destroy the government will be permitted to control it."[17]

In his letter of acceptance, Garfield offered a balanced but firm statement of the Republican position on the South. He had, he declared, "no purpose or wish to revive the passions of the late war. . . . The best thoughts and energies of our people should be directed to those great questions of national well-being in which all have a common interest." "But," he added, "it is certain that the wounds of the war cannot be completely healed, and the spirit of brotherhood cannot fully pervade the whole country, until every citizen, rich or poor, white or black, is secure in the free and equal enjoyment of every civil and political right guaranteed by the Constitution and the laws." The guarantee of these rights would benefit white as well as black southerners, for wherever they were denied, "discontent will prevail, immigration will cease, and the social and industrial forces will continue to be disturbed by the migration of laborers and the consequent diminution of prosperity. . . . The prosperity which is made possible in the South by its great advantages of soil and climate will never be realized until every voter can freely and safely support any party he pleases."[18]

Garfield's call to the South to heed its own best interests mirrored the continuing discussions within Republican ranks about how to deal with the region in the campaign. The problem was that, as Hampton had proclaimed, the Democrats could rely almost certainly on 138 electoral votes from the South. If they could secure the two major northern swing states, New York with thirty-five electors and Indiana with fifteen, they would amass 188, or three more than enough to win. If, however, the Republicans could take at least one southern state's electoral votes, such as Florida's four, South Carolina's seven, or Louisiana's eight (all of which Hayes had received), Garfield could win without New York and Indiana. Republicans differed over which strategy to adopt, but it was clear that the emphasis chosen would influence how party figures would treat the southern question in speeches and campaign literature. An appeal to a "solid North," including New York and Indiana, would lay greater stress on white southerners' misdeeds, while a strategy to crack the Solid South would mute such discussions. The dilemma was compounded, moreover, by the Democrats' nomination of the Union hero Hancock.[19]

Ironically, chief among Republican leaders who favored a tough stance was Hayes. Although in a speech at Yale the president defended his early southern policy under which "the pacification of the country was the first duty," even he admitted that "all may not have followed and resulted as I or any one else hoped." Privately, he wrote that "the failure of the South to faithfully observe the Fifteenth Amendment is the cause of the failure of all efforts towards complete pacification. It is on this hook that the bloody shirt now hangs." Hayes believed that Republicans should show "by facts and figures how the Democratic party sanctions in both houses of Congress the practical nullification of the Fifteenth Amendment."[20]

Campaign strategy was much on the minds of members of the national committee and other leaders as they assembled for a conference in New York in early August. With Garfield, Blaine, Sherman, William Chandler, Benjamin Harrison, Thomas Platt, Thurlow Weed, George William Curtis, and more than 200 other Republicans crowding the corridors and rooms of the Fifth Avenue Hotel, this gathering was an extraordinary event. Scholars have usually focused on the meeting's principal purpose, which was to heal the party's factional wounds lingering after the convention and to secure the support of Conkling's powerful New York machine for the ticket.[21] But the conference's first day, August 5, witnessed a remarkable discussion about what general direction the campaign ought to take regarding the South. At issue was whether the national organization should send aid and speakers into southern states to try to win their electoral votes or simply write the South off and concentrate on winning the doubtful northern states. From the South itself, Republicans spoke with no united voice. When a congressional candidate from Tennessee called for "some earnest speakers from this [northern] section of the country to spread Republican truths in the South," a voice cried out only half in jest, "Well, then, you will have to get some men with ball-proof jackets to go down there." Another Tennessee delegate, Thomas J. Freeman, flatly predicted that "not a Republican electoral vote will be cast south of the Ohio River." "Nothing," said Freeman, "could suit the Democratic party better than to have you send speakers. After they have gone, the ballot-box stuffers and others with tissue ballots will be there to receive their orders. The only way you can beat them is to have a solid North."

Louisiana's black former governor, P. B. S. Pinchback, disagreed, admonishing the assembled Republicans that they could not claim to be a national party by campaigning only in the North. With notable candor, Pinchback cut to the heart of the problem. From the beginning of the ex-slaves' citizenship, northern attitudes, including Republican attitudes, toward blacks had rendered them helplessly vulnerable, dependent on outside aid for the assertion of their rights and for their very survival. "They have not been taught since the hour of their enfranchisement the way to exercise their manhood," Pinchback declared. Instead, "black men have been continually advised against a war of races, and it has been said to them, in effect, 'You must submit to every kind of outrage, rather than give offense to the dominant classes.'" Against this history, it would not do now for northern Republicans to abandon their southern black brethren and say "they must now assert their manhood." Rather, the party should send leaders such as Blaine, Conkling, and Sherman into the South to "let these poor ignorant black people see that Republicanism is not a farce, and that liberty for them is not only a name but a fact."

Blaine responded that no northern Republicans advocated abandoning their southern counterparts, but, he argued, it was more important to focus on winning the early state elections in Maine, Indiana, and Ohio to build the momentum for national victory in November. In Blaine's view, "the practical thing in hand is to get the Northern States and you will get Southern support then." John Sherman accepted Pinchback's premise that "you cannot expect men, but so recently emancipated from slavery, without arms and discipline, to stand up against the rebel army," but he reached a contrary conclusion: "All the resources, all the power, all the money, all the energy of the Republican party should be aimed at the weakest point in the enemy's line"—that is, the three or four doubtful states of the North. Winning Indiana, he argued, would "help every Republican State" and "do far more than wasting money and energy in doubtful experiments against the power of the Ku-Klux to cheat and defraud." Sherman agreed that money and speakers might help in some parts of the South, but he "would not waste money . . . where it would not do good." Later in the day the Republican Congressional Campaign Committee adopted essentially this view, deciding to dispatch speakers and documents only to those southern districts where there was a possibility of success.[22]

Thus the thrust of the Republican campaign would emphasize arousing a solid North, as was clear from speeches at a mass meeting in New York the next day. "It is to the North we look," declared Edwards Pierrepont, "to the intelligent, the loyal, the patriotic North." "Break up those treasonable associations in your Southern States," said Benjamin Harrison, "give free voice to the Republican electors in all those States, and let them have their due political influence; and then we will consider the question of dividing in the North."[23]

If this was "waving the bloody shirt," Republicans believed that Southern Democrats' behavior had left them no choice: Despite their talk of sectional reconciliation, the Democrats were more than willing, as Wade Hampton's promise of a Solid South suggested, to keep the country bifurcated politically. "Their machinery is now so perfect," said John Hay, "that even murder, the cheapest of all political methods in the South, will hardly be necessary this year." The Democrats had attempted to repeal election laws and had vilified the Supreme Court for upholding them. On the floor of the House, Missouri Democrat Aylett Buckner had flatly denied "that because the Supreme Court has decided the election law constitutional we are under any obligation to change our opinions or our action to carry it out in any form whatever." Pending in Congress was legislation to enlarge the Court, which would, should a Democrat be elected president, permit him to pack it with Democrats who would make short work of the elections laws. But even if the Court were not reorganized, no one could expect a Democratic attorney general to enforce those laws. Thus, in the Republicans' view, the Democrats were still determined to do whatever was necessary to thwart the achievement of the republican project that Republicans had championed since Appomattox. "What we fought for was to make us one people," Hayes wrote in his diary, "a free people with an equal start and a fair chance in the race." Unfortunately, he told a veterans' reunion at Columbus, the South still persisted in its "refusal to accept the results of the war for the Union." "Until the Democracy renounces the idea of denying the right of the people to rule," declared Senator George Edmunds, "it is unworthy of confidence."[24]

This general theme echoed throughout the Republican campaign. When the Republican Congressional Committee issued its *Campaign Textbook* in September, twelve of its nineteen issue chapters dealt with the sectional question. The same topic predominated in the 12 million documents the Committee distributed and in party leaders' speeches. "I believe we shall succeed," William Chandler told a Boston audience, "because I believe we are on the right platform with reference to the Southern question, because we plant ourselves upon the broad position that justice shall be done to the Southern Republicans, [and] to every living being in the country, black or white."

Nor did Republicans merely package sectionalist rhetoric for public consumption; most were truly fearful of a return to power by the Democratic South. Former Vice President Schuyler Colfax confessed his deep anxiety over "our imminent danger now of being ruled by the Rebels, & becoming, after all our sacrifices, the Confederate States of America." When Grant was criticized for making campaign speeches, he wrote a friend, "If we had two National parties, neither dangerous to the prosperity and wellfare [*sic*] of the country, I would agree with them in saying that it would be much more dignified for me to keep out of the arena of politics. But our sacrifice of blood and treasure has been too great to loose [*sic*] all the results now to save a little dignity. I sincerely believe that a democratic success now would be almost as disastrous as a war, and that the disaster would be no less to our section, or to our party, than to the other."[25]

Republicans' focus on the southern question in 1880 ranged beyond reciting past atrocities against blacks and white Republicans in the South. They also warned of the dire economic consequences of rule by the Democrats dominated by their southern wing. Democratic capture of the presidency as well as the Congress would usher in economic policies deeply detrimental to the nation. The Republicans' greatest asset in the campaign was the general prosperity that had returned in 1879. After six long years of depression, Americans generally were back on their feet and making money. Democratic economic heresies, Republicans warned, could destroy the fragile recovery. In August Treasury Secretary John Sherman told a campaign audience, "An honest and faithful administration of the Government; a firm adherence to the resumption and refunding act; the maintenance of the public faith as against fiat money, and the protection policy embodied in our tariff laws, are the human agencies, the work of the Republican party, that have contributed to our prosperity. . . . Certain it is that we owe no part of our prosperity to the Democratic party."[26]

The significance of the economic issue seemed clear from the mid-September state elections in Maine, where a Democratic-Greenback fusion candidate for governor narrowly defeated the Republican incumbent. In 1880 prosperity had not yet reached Maine, whose shipbuilding and lumber industries remained depressed. But what struck Garfield immediately about the Maine returns was that the Republicans "lost in the shipping towns and gained in the manufacturing towns." That outcome, he believed, reflected the influence of the party's arguments on the tariff issue. As Maine party leader A. L. Morrison told the candidate, "Were it not for the protection afforded by the tariff the whole state would be beggared." Morrison urged that henceforth tariff documents "be spread broadcast at every meeting." National Republican chairman Marshall Jewell saw a silver lining in the Maine cloud: "I think this will open the purses, the pockets, and the eyes of our business men to the danger which immediately threatens," he told Garfield. "We shall pull you through, I believe, for the reason, and the reason only, that the business of the country can not afford to have you defeated." Garfield had reached a similar conclusion, telling Sherman, "I think our friends should push the business aspect of the campaign with greater vigor than they are doing, especially the Tariff question which so deeply affects the interests of manufacturers and laborers. The argument of the 'Solid South' is well enough in its way and ought not to be overlooked, but we should also press those questions which lie close to the homes and interests of our people."[27]

Historians of the 1880 campaign have often noted that after the Maine election the Republican focus switched from the southern question to a concentration on the tariff and kindred economic issues. Blaine allegedly stormed into Republican headquarters, commanding party workers to "fold up the bloody shirt and lay it away" and "shift the main issue to protection."[28] But at most the shift was one of emphasis. Republican campaigners had discussed the tariff, the currency, and other economic issues before the Maine state balloting. In August Jewell had told the *New York Tribune*'s Whitelaw Reid that the "strong point in this campaign is the 'business man's fight' of it," and he had urged the editor to stress that "merchants, manufacturers, investors, wealthy men, [and] laboring men are equally interested in continuing these good times." Three weeks before the Maine election, F. X. Schoonmaker had told a New York audience that to "a great number of American voters, the Tariff Question is the most important one to be decided in the coming Presidential election."[29]

By the same token, the southern question persisted as a key element of the Republicans' campaign after the Maine election. Two weeks before the general vote in November, addressing a Brooklyn audience on the "Dangers of a Solid South," Secretary of State William Evarts asked, "How long can it be maintained in this country, that 138 electoral votes are taken out of politics and are wielded, not by liberty and justice, but by power and oppression?" On the same night, Emery Storrs told a Cooper Union audience that the free ballot was "the supreme question in our politics." "If the ballot of the black men down South cannot be collected in any other way, except on the point of a bayonet, and cannot be put into the ballot-box by any other piece of machinery, I am in favor of employing the bayonet for that purpose."

During September and October Sherman carried on a heated exchange of letters with Wade Hampton on the issue, in one instance telling the South Carolinian that the Democrats' "power in the southern states rests upon the actual crimes of every grade in the code of crimes—from murder to the meanest form of ballot-box stuffing committed by the Ku-Klux Klan and its kindred associates, and, as you know, some of the worst of them were committed since 1877, when you and your associates gave the most solemn assurance of protection to the freedmen of the south." When Sherman published the letters two weeks before the election, the result was electric. A Treasury Department official wrote the secretary from St. Louis, "A distinguished 'Stalwart' here today remarked that we would now have to add to your soubriquets [*sic*] of 'Old Resumption' and 'Old Prosperity' the new one 'Old Stalwart,' as Zach Chandler's successor."[30]

That combination of Sherman's sobriquets in fact mirrored the dual emphasis of the Republicans' campaign. More important than any supposed shift from the southern question to economic issues was the way in which Republicans interwove the two. Both before and after the Maine election, Republicans excoriated Democrats, especially southerners, for their low tariff views, opposition to resumption of specie payments, repudiation of debts, hostility to the national banking system, designs on the national treasury to pay bogus war claims and build unnecessary public works, and other attitudes that threatened the prosperity wrought by Republican policies. In one of the most powerful speeches of the campaign, Roscoe Conkling warned that "whenever the hour strikes that the veto power is in Democratic hands—put there by Southern votes—whatever the 'solid' caucus decrees will be written." Because southerners dominated the Democratic congressional caucus, Conkling declared, "the broad issue at this election is whether our colossal fabric of commercial, industrial and financial interests shall be under the management and protection of those who chiefly created and own it, or shall be handed over to the sway of those whose share in it is small, and whose experience, antecedents, theories and practices do not fit them or entitle them to assume its control."[31]

Emerging as the most salient economic issue in the campaign was the tariff, and Republicans quickly seized upon the Democratic platform's declaration in favor of "a tariff for revenue only," which had long been the South's position on customs duties. "The South is tired of what it calls 'paying tribute to Yankee factories,'" said the *New York Tribune*. "For all purposes of shaping Government policy the South is the Democratic party, now as it was before the war. . . . A Democratic victory this year means the destruction of the protective tariff system."[32]

This focus on the economic consequences of southern rule permitted the Republicans to portray the indisputably loyal but inexperienced Hancock as a dupe for southern interests. If Hancock were elected, said Indiana's Benjamin Harrison, he would be indebted to the Solid South, and because the general was "utterly without experience in public life, he will be delivered to the control of the caucus, which is itself controlled by the South." When Republicans pilloried the Democrats' for their unfortunate tariff plank, Hancock made matters worse by asserting in an interview that "the tariff is a local question" and "a matter that the general government seldom cares to interfere with." Republicans pounced on this evidence of Hancock's obvious ignorance of civil affairs, which, said Emery Storrs, was like the effect "in a mathematical debate if somebody had jumped up and disputed the multiplication table." Hancock soon backtracked in a public letter asserting that he was "too sound an American to advocate any departure from the general features" of the protective policy. But this move simply underscored the issue's importance and convinced few that Hancock could reverse his party's stand. "The people, at all events," said the *New York Tribune,* "know that the record proves that the Democratic party cannot be trusted on this matter. And General Hancock has now shown that he is either too insincere or too ignorant to be trusted to restrain his party."[33]

Ultimately, Republicans were able to connect the Democrats' tariff stance with the South's old defense of slavery, which taken together bespoke a fundamental hostility to the republican ideal of free labor. Protective tariff laws, said Evarts, "are intended to preserve the dignity of labor. The South never desired the dignity of labor to be preserved under the old system—I do not see that they have much care to preserve its dignity under the new. But in this country of ours, where intelligence and thrift and domestic virtue and personal pride are just as generally and just as clearly the possession of the laboring men as they are of the learned and the powerful and the rich, no peace, no prosperity can exist if we undertake to put our labor . . . upon the level of the labor of countries where its dignity and its political power are not accorded."[34]

Thus, at issue once again, Evarts and other Republicans argued, was the republicanism they had reinvented in the wake of Appomattox. "We have changed the old aristocratic system," Nathaniel Banks told an Indianapolis audience. "We have put the power into the hands of the people—of all the people. Shall those plantation masters take back again that power which we have wrung from them?" Southern Democrats, said George Edmunds, "would deny, if they could, the right of the people at large to govern. They want to rule by an aristocracy." To achieve that purpose, Republicans claimed, the Bourbons of the South had found the ideal candidate in the elitist, antirepublican Hancock. Not only had the general supported the former master class during Reconstruction, but he also shared their fundamental values. According to George Hoar, Hancock exhibited an unfeeling elitism acquired in part at West Point, where the typical cadet entered "the world as one of a favored caste." Garfield, by contrast, epitomized "the brave soldier who learned his knowledge of the rights of men, of the genius of the American people, of the feelings of the poor and lowly in the carpenter's shop and on the towpath." "Such men as Hancock," said Hoar, "are the natural product of the military schools of Europe, of monarchical countries," trained "in keeping the people in subjection. Such men as Garfield are the product only of a republic. It is that such men may exist, and grow, and may go from the bottom to the top, that republican institutions exist." Edwards Pierrepont portrayed Garfield and Hancock as the personification of republicanism and its antithesis: "the one is a noble representative of the principle of equal rights and the Christian civilization of the North;—the other fairly represents the privileged class of the old slave-holding South."[35]

As ever, the sine qua non of republicanism was the right to vote, which Evarts described as "an act of sovereign intelligence and moral uprightness." "How long," he asked, "can the rest of the country tolerate this unequal partition of power" represented by the Solid South? As party orator Robert Ingersoll put it, "Unless we see to it that every man who has a right to vote votes, and unless we see to it that every honest vote is counted, the days of the Republic are numbered." At a mass rally at Warren, Ohio, Grant declared, "There is not a precinct in this vast nation where a Democrat can not cast his ballot and have it counted as cast," but in fourteen states, "Republicans have not this privilege." To correct this egregious wrong, he said, was one of the main reasons he was a Republican.

But Grant and other Republicans defended the right to vote not only as an end, but also as a means. A broad-based suffrage, they believed, must inevitably lead to a more equitable, more truly republican society. Hence, Grant was a Republican also because the party "encourages the poor to strive to better their condition; the ignorant to educate their children, to enable them to compete successfully with their more fortunate associates, and, in fine, it secures an entire equality before the law of every citizen, no matter what his race, nationality, or previous condition. It tolerates no privileged class. Every one has the opportunity to make himself all he is capable of." On the eve of the election, Ingersoll told a New York audience that when he looked at the South, "I want to see their towns prosperous; I want to see school-houses in every town; and I want to see books in the hands of every child, and papers and magazines in every house; I want to see all the rays of light of the civilization of the nineteenth century enter every home of the South; and in a little while you will see that country full of good Republicans."[36]

But, alas, in 1880, the South was by no means full of Republicans, or at least Republican votes. Hancock won every one of the former slave states. He also took New Jersey, Nevada, and five of six electoral votes from California, but this was insufficient to deny the prize to Garfield, who won all the rest of a nearly solid North. Moreover, the Republicans won a clear majority in the House of Representatives and replaced a nine-seat deficit in the Senate with a tie with the Democrats. Party leaders believed that the triumph more than justified the strategy they had followed. "The distrust of the Solid South and of adverse financial legislation have been the chief factors in the contest," Garfield wrote Sherman.[37]

Conversely, in the initial euphoria of victory, Republicans also thought that the result should demonstrate beyond dispute the futility of southern political sectionalism of the type Wade Hampton had proclaimed. The South, without substantial help from the North, could not elect a president. "The most promising & hopeful result of the last contest," said Hamilton Fish, "is the prospect that hereafter, political parties throughout the whole country will divide upon the material issues of the time."[38]

In his last annual message, Hayes agreed that "sectionalism as a factor in our politics" should give way to "internal improvements, the tariff, domestic taxation, education, finance, and other important subjects." Only one dark cloud obscured this bright prospect: southerners' "disposition to refuse a prompt and hearty obedience to the equal-rights amendments." As long as southerners "flagrantly violated or disregarded" those amendments, Hayes said, "the people who placed them in the Constitution, as embodying the legitimate results of the war for the Union" would "continue to act together and insist that they shall be obeyed." Once again, violations of the election laws had marred the southern elections, and the Justice Department, with its meager resources, pursued prosecutions in several southern states. With an eye to the incoming administration, Hayes noted that it "will be the duty of the Executive, with sufficient appropriations for the purpose, to prosecute unsparingly all who have been engaged in depriving citizens of the rights guaranteed to them by the Constitution." At stake was "the fundamental principle of our Government."[39]

Indeed, the election of 1880 had not settled the southern question, and for many Republicans, it remained the great task before the party. Insisting that Republicans were "sacredly bound to do all we can" to protect the right of suffrage, William Chandler urged the president-elect not to "let the deep and undying sentiments of the northern people receive under your administration any such shock as President Hayes inflicted." "I trust you may be spared in full health of body and mind to lead the Nation in the great work of securing Free Suffrage in all its domain, without which we are no Republic."[40] Garfield spent much of the transition period contemplating the problem and consulting with others. In the election, the Republicans had prevented the southern Democrats from taking the government and undoing Republican civil rights and economic policies, but what could the new president and Congress do to move toward resolving the lingering sectional and racial conundrum? Garfield's assassination prevented his developing a fully fledged response, but as he launched his administration, the question loomed large in his calculations.

In the short term, personnel matters, especially the assembling of a cabinet, took precedence. With some difficulty, Garfield secured what he considered a suitable southerner for the group: William Hunt as secretary of the navy. A native white southern Republican, Hunt had stood with Stephen Packard during his losing struggle for the Louisiana governorship four years earlier. Southern party voices hailed Hunt's appointment, but in fact, as head of the navy, he would have little to do with southern policy.

For attorney general, the cabinet officer most concerned with southern affairs, Garfield chose Wayne MacVeagh, a Pennsylvania lawyer with reform credentials. MacVeagh had served on Hayes's Louisiana Commission that brokered Packard's defeat, and he was an outspoken critic of Grant. Thus, his appointment hardly seemed calculated to mollify southern stalwart Republicans who had bridled at Hayes's policy. Therefore, "to supplement MacVeagh on the southern side," Garfield chose William Chandler to be solicitor general, the Justice Department's chief litigator. Chandler was one of most vigorous defenders of the freedmen, and the president thought his appointment would "confirm the support of the election laws." But MacVeagh, threatening to resign, vehemently opposed Chandler, as did some reform senators, and the Senate rejected his nomination. This imbroglio and its outcome did not augur well for an aggressive administration offensive against election law violators in the South. As matters later turned out, although MacVeagh carried forward some prosecutions, he focused his attention on the case against Garfield's assassin and on prosecution of the so-called Star Route frauds in the Post Office Department.[41]

As Garfield turned from offices in Washington to federal patronage in the South, he was hardly confident that he, or anyone, could devise an appointments policy that would successfully nourish a Republican Party in the region as well as render the results of the war more secure. He had seen Grant's support for carpetbaggers result in a steady loss of states to the Democrats, and he thought Hayes's strategy of giving offices to southern Democrats had "proved a dreary failure." Former Congressman Robert Elliott, who headed a delegation of blacks visiting Garfield in Ohio, insisted on "the appointment to public trusts of men who will enforce the United States laws." Former South Carolina Governor Daniel Chamberlain emphasized respectability in appointees, but Garfield replied that the intense factionalism that plagued southern Republicans often made the selection of worthy officials "very difficult." Most important, he doubted that any appointments could do much to alleviate "the apparent inexpungable hostility of the Southern Democrats to the Republican Party."[42]

The difficulty was compounded by the even partisan balance in the Senate, which jeopardized the approval of any nominees whom southern Democrats opposed. The upper house in the Forty-seventh Congress comprised thirty-seven Republicans, thirty-seven Democrats, Independent David Davis, who said he would vote with the Democrats to organize the body, and Virginian William Mahone. Mahone had won his seat as head of the Readjuster movement, whose advocacy of a scaling down of Virginia's prewar debt smacked of repudiation, in the view of "sound money" champions. If Mahone could be persuaded to act with the Republicans in the Senate, Vice President Chester Arthur could break any resulting ties in the party's favor. The most potent form of persuasion, of course, was control of the state's federal patronage, and this Garfield was reluctant to give to Mahone. Long a foe of debt repudiation in any form, Garfield was loath to countenance the Readjuster movement. But Chandler and others argued that enlisting Mahone's help was "essential, even vital to the success of the work now again commenced of securing a free and honestly counted ballot at the South. Senators elected only through the agencies of murder and fraud will not consent to the confirmation of officers who will faithfully and courageously labor to abolish those crimes as political agencies."[43]

Mahone's power was clear when he voted with the Republicans on Senate committee assignments, including the appointment of Republicans to the powerful chairmanships.[44] By that time Garfield had concluded that if the Readjusters would continue to support public schools and other essential public functions while applying the remnant of Virginia's revenues to pay its debt, he could regard the movement as "defensible." He envisioned awarding patronage to both the Readjusters and the regular state Republican organization as a way to forge an alliance against the state's Bourbon Democrats and in favor of "protection and justice for the blacks." As matters turned out, the distraction of a heated battle with the New York Stalwarts over customhouse appointments, followed by Garfield's assassination, prevented any real test of his Virginia policy.[45]

In any event, Virginia was a special case, and Garfield was skeptical that patronage was anything more than a short-term measure, with a slim prospect of effecting a fundamental alteration in the condition of the South. The problem, he believed, was at bottom a matter of culture. In a letter to his friend Burke Hinsdale, he offered one of the era's most trenchant analyses of the intractable predicament Republicans faced in their attempt to reinvent republicanism in the South:

In my opinion the real trouble can be summed up in this: Our Government is a modern republic; the South was rooted and grounded in feudalism based on slavery; and the destruction of slavery has not yet destroyed the feudalism which it caused. Nothing but time can complete its dissolution. I do not know a better way to treat people than to let them know that this is a modern free government, and only men who believe in it, and not in feudalism, can be invited to aid in administering it; then give the South, as rapidly as possible, the blessings of general education and business enterprise; and trust to time and these forces to work out the problem.

"I have no doubt," he concluded, "that the final cure for the 'Solid South' will be found in the education of its youth, and in the development of its business interest, but both of these require time."[46]

During his campaign, Garfield had cited the importance of educating southern youth and had called for national aid to education. The Republican national platform made a similar call. Indeed, the plank citing "the duty of the National Government to aid" popular education "to the extent of its constitutional power" represented the first time a major party had taken such a stance in its national convention.[47] In part, the Republicans' endorsement of federal aid to education, with its prospect of success only over the long haul, reflected the frustration they felt over the failure of other southern policies. In 1880, however, they were not inventing a new idea but instead reviving one they had embraced in the past but which circumstances had now come to make more apposite.

Ten years earlier, upon the ratification of the Fifteenth Amendment in 1870, President Grant urged members of Congress "to take all the means within their constitutional powers to promote and encourage popular education." Grant cited President George Washington's support of such aid and noted that the "framers of our Constitution firmly believed that a republican government could not endure without intelligence and education generally diffused among the people." In Congress that spring, Representative George Hoar of Massachusetts proposed legislation that would induce states to establish public school systems by threatening to impose a federally run system in states that refused to do so. Basing his proposal squarely on the Constitution's guarantee of a republican form of government in the states, Hoar argued that if national authority ensured each citizen "his equal share in the Government[,] surely there is implied the corresponding power and duty of securing the capacity for the exercise of that share of Government." Hoar's draconian measure never reached a vote in the House.[48]

Republicans gave more support to a bill introduced in 1872 by Mississippi carpetbag Congressman Legrand Perce to use the proceeds from federal land sales to help finance common-school education in the states. Reiterating Hoar's arguments, Perce declared that a "republican Government, based upon the will of the people, . . . presupposes an amount of intelligence in the citizen necessary to grasp the various questions presented to him for action." Democrats, however, opposed Perce's bill as an unconstitutional violation of states' rights. Although the measure passed the House on a largely party-line vote, it received no consideration in the Senate.[49]

During the depression of the 1870s the issue lay dormant in Congress, although Presidents Grant and Hayes regularly urged action in their annual messages. But the failure of military intervention, patronage policy, or the attempted enforcement of the election laws to effect much change, and the consequent increasing solidity of Democratic control in the South, underscored arguments for longer-term measures such as education, not only for blacks but for whites as well. The future direction of the South lay in the training of the young of both races, and data emerging from the 1880 census underscored the need. As Hayes told a Columbus audience in August, the census showed the South to be lagging in population growth from immigration or otherwise, largely because those states had failed to provide adequate schools or good order. The Peabody Educational Fund reported that 2 million children in the South had no means of instruction. In these dire circumstances, said Hayes, the national government must give its help, either through funds from the public land sales or, if necessary, direct appropriations from the Treasury. "The work of the schoolmaster is now in order," he declared. "Wherever his work shall be well done, in all our borders, it will be found that there, also, the principles of the Declaration of Independence will be cherished, the sentiment of nationality will prevail, [and] the equal rights amendments will be cheerfully obeyed."[50]

Hayes repeated this call in his last annual message, and Republicans in the Senate responded. After just three days of debate, that body passed a bill to earmark the public lands proceeds for a fund whose interest income would be distributed to the states for schools. Although the initial pecuniary contribution to each state would be modest, the bill included the important stipulation that the state must maintain schools for all children six to sixteen years old for three months (four months after 1885) each year, and the state must provide annual reports of its public school operations to the U.S. commissioner of education.

In support of the bill, Vermont Senator Justin Morrill appealed to the republican ideal that in "the great, peerless experiment of man's self-government . . . the voting population shall have the means of improvement and intellectual advancement." But, anticipating Booker T. Washington's Atlanta Compromise approach a decade and a half later, Morrill also argued that blacks needed "extensive primary and technical education" in order to find employment "beyond 'the shovel and the hoe.'" Moreover, he argued, "They should be made to comprehend that duties go hand in hand with privileges, and that self-restraint makes liberty possible." Black leader Frederick Douglass thanked Morrill and agreed that there could be "no great or happy future for my race or for the Republic outside general education." The Senate passed the bill by a bipartisan vote of 41 to 6. But while two-thirds of the Republicans voted for it and none against, only 43 percent of Democrats voted aye, all but one of them representing the South. The bill's champions could not muster this level of support in the House, which took no action before the expiration of the Forty-sixth Congress on the eve of Garfield's inauguration.[51]

As president-elect, Garfield emphasized the educational theme in a meeting with blacks at his Ohio farm in January 1881, telling them that "the education of your race, in my judgment, lies at the base of the final solution of your great question."[52] In his inaugural address, he argued that although both the states and the nation must keep "the ballot free and pure by the strong sanctions of the law[,] . . . the danger which arises from ignorance in the voter cannot be denied." Citing census reports of a "dangerously high . . . tide of illiteracy" among voters and their children, he warned that if the rising "generation comes to its inheritance blinded by ignorance and corrupted by vice, the fall of the republic will be certain and remediless." The problem was particularly acute in the South, but it was not the South's alone to resolve. The national government had extended the suffrage and therefore was "under special obligations to aid in removing the illiteracy which it has added to the voting population." "In this work," he said with more hope than expectation, "sections and races should be forgotten, and partisanship should be unknown."[53] As was true with his southern patronage policy, the brevity of his administration denied Garfield the opportunity to follow through on his notions about federal aid to education, but both would form part of his legacy to his successor.

Before becoming vice president, Chester A. Arthur had never held office at Washington and had played virtually no role in the formulation of national Republican Party policy, regarding the South or any other issue. But in 1880 he had devoted nearly half his letter of acceptance to the southern question, declaring that "the Republican party holds, as a cardinal point in its creed, that the Government should, by every means known to the Constitution, protect all American citizens everywhere in the full enjoyment of their civil and political rights." Upon assuming the presidency, however, Arthur quickly found, as had his predecessors, that the realities of politics placed limits on his power to translate that creed into practice. A few months after he took office, his first annual message included a passage on the southern question that made no reference at all to the issue's relation to fraudulent or violent elections or to the denial of rights. Instead it focused exclusively on federal aid to education, calling upon Congress to supplement state and local spending "by such aid as can be constitutionally afforded by the National Government," to be distributed to the states "according to the ratio of illiteracy."[54]

Although Arthur forbore treating the elections issue in his first or subsequent messages, his administration did make efforts to enforce the election laws on the books. Arthur appointed as his attorney general Benjamin Brewster, an experienced prosecutor, who determined upon a vigorous prosecution of election cases still pending from 1880. Brewster instructed one special U.S. attorney to go after prominent men who not only violated the law but encouraged others to do so as well. "The abuse of the right of suffrage," he declared, "is a practical treason against the dignity of the people." But, as had been true during past administrations, these efforts resulted in few convictions. Before the 1882 congressional elections, Brewster sent circular letters to U.S. attorneys and marshals with detailed instructions for enforcing the election laws. Their main efforts should be directed toward protecting the right to vote, preventing unlawful voting, and ensuring lawful procedures in the handling and counting of the vote. Despite these precautions, nearly every southern state in 1882 witnessed some form of election fraud or intimidation, aimed not only against blacks but against anti-Democratic Independent party movements as well. And once again federal officials had meager success in securing convictions. In 1882 they won 32 convictions out of 256 cases, in 1883, 12 out of 287. The problem, as one U.S. attorney in Alabama put it, was that "public sentiment justifies these acquittals on the ground that they are necessary for the supremacy of the white race, and the juries who thus acquit, instead of being condemned, are sustained by public opinion."[55]

Clearly, the prosecutorial effort would bring no fundamental reordering of the political condition of the South. Hence, the Arthur administration worked toward that goal by also supporting so-called Independent movements that challenged the hegemony of the Bourbon Democrats. Whereas Garfield had flirted with the Mahonites in Virginia, his successor embraced them and similar Democratic bolters in other states. The chief mastermind of Arthur's southern strategy was William Chandler, who entered the cabinet as secretary of the navy. Chandler had been one of the most vocal critics of Hayes's policy of giving patronage to southern Democrats in hopes of luring them away from their former political allegiance, a policy whose failure Chandler had correctly predicted. Instead, Arthur and Chandler decided to reward the Independents, those Democrats already disenchanted with the Bourbon leaders, in hopes of securing their cooperation with Republicans to break the Bourbons' lock on the Solid South.[56]

In the case of Mahone and some of the other Independents, however, this strategy entailed a seeming endorsement of their ideas about debt refunding, currency expansion, and similar issues that violated standard Republican precepts of financial orthodoxy. Most vocal in condemning this approach was James G. Blaine, who had served briefly as Garfield's secretary of state. Blaine warned that it would be "a great political blunder to unite the Republican Party with the Readjusters. The Republican Party," he said, "has been always devoted to upholding the public faith, and this fact contributed powerfully to the victory of 1880."[57]

To Chandler, at least, the risk was worth taking. In the midst of the 1882 congressional campaign, Chandler urged Blaine not to be "narrow minded," for "the safety of the colored race while exercising the suffrage depends upon this new departure." "Every independent democrat or coalition candidate at the South fully and sincerely pledges himself in favor of a free vote, an honest count, the obliteration of race distinctions, and popular education by a common school system; while in every case the Bourbon democratic candidate is in fact against all the[se] principles and depends for his success upon their suppression. Shall we fail to follow our principles when they are so vital[?]" Although some African Americans in the South viewed Arthur and Chandler's patronage policy as a denial of their own claims to preference, most black editors and national leaders endorsed the coalition strategy. Frederick Douglass pronounced himself "heartily in favor of the Mahone movement" or "any decent movement looking to the abolition of the color line in American politics."[58]

The administration did not discount the impact of federal internal improvements on its overall southern strategy. Arthur called for appropriations to improve navigation on the Mississippi River and to close gaps in the river's levees to protect surrounding farmland. He noted the value of such projects to the people of both the Old Northwest and the Mississippi Valley, and thus underscored the Republicans' new effort to emphasize consanguinity between northern and southern interests and to play down the sectionalist rhetoric of the past. Former Treasury official George Tichenor wrote John Sherman that it was "high time to bury forever some of the old disturbing war issues and prejudices, and to invite the cooperation of patriotic southern Democrats and northern Democrats in such movements as appear best calculated to advance the material interests of the Nation as a whole." Republican state platforms during 1881 and 1882 typically made only the briefest reference to "a free ballot and a fair count," if they mentioned the southern question at all. From the northern reformist wing of the party, Carl Schurz observed, "The 'solid South,' as a dangerous political power, is rapidly losing, or has already lost, its terrors in consequence of the evident tendency of political forces in that section to divide, and thus to be solid no more. . . . The Southern question is, therefore, practically eliminated from our party contests."[59]

The first real test of the administration's strategy came in the midterm congressional elections, and the result seemed to validate Arthur's approach. Although nationwide the party lost nearly three dozen seats, in the South, it picked up one seat for a total of fourteen, and the number of Readjusters or Independents rose from three to seven. These cracks in the Solid South encouraged those Republicans who believed that the GOP should abandon sectionalist appeals and move on to other issues to build the party in the South and elsewhere. After the election, a Pennsylvania Republican wrote to the clerk of the national House, "The waving of the bloody shirt can never again rally the Republican masses to victory. All along the line thinking, intelligent and active Republicans are demanding that the *column shall move forward.*"[60]

For many Republicans, funding for education represented the ideal issue to move the column forward, as a complement to the administration's patronage policy. The president himself used his 1882 annual message to issue an emphatic call for "immediate and substantial aid" for the South's school systems. The political value of such a program was clear to men such as John Mott, a member of the party's state executive committee in North Carolina, who told a northern senator that "neither party can afford to vote against it; and the effect of it coming from our party would be tremendous through the south, and would break it up politically and ensure the country against the Bourbons in '84." Several aid bills were pending in Congress, but none survived the short second session of Forty-seventh Congress in the winter of 1883.[61]

That session devoted much more time to tariff legislation, which many Republicans believed offered the party an even brighter prospect for cracking the Solid South. Indiana Senator Benjamin Harrison argued that with the growth of cotton mills, minerals extraction, and iron production, the "industrial question threatens to dominate the race question, and that bodes no good to the Democratic party in the South." But whether they focused on education or tariff protection, many Republicans in 1883 clearly saw value in turning away from the traditional approach to the southern question. As Republicans still struggled with truly reworking republicanism in the South, the wisdom of President-elect Garfield's prescription seemed even more apparent three years later: "give the South . . . the blessings of general education and business enterprise; and trust to time and these forces to work out the problem."[62]

But a series of events in late 1883 shattered the relative calm prevailing on racial and sectional issues and cast doubt on the efficacy of the party's new approaches. In September the growing restiveness of blacks with Arthur's policies burst forth at a national meeting of race leaders in Louisville. Some delegates at

Frederick Douglass
(Library of Congress)

the stormy convention favored independent political action for blacks, although the leading black Republican, Frederick Douglass, opposed such a move. But even Douglass took the opportunity to put party leaders on notice that blacks felt abandoned on the voting-rights front and snubbed by Arthur's patronage policies. "Follow no party blindly," he told the gathering at Louisville. "If the Republican party cannot stand a demand for justice and fair play it ought to go down. We were men before that party was born, and our manhood is more sacred than any party can be." The convention rejected resolutions affirming blacks' devotion to the Republican Party or endorsing the Arthur administration.

It was clear that growing numbers of blacks thought the Republicans were taking them for granted, but it was equally clear that they had no viable alternative in politics. On the eve of state elections in October, Douglass issued a public statement clarifying his earlier remarks. "For the life of me I cannot see how any honest colored man, who has brains enough to put two ideas together, can allow himself, under the notion of independence, to give aid and comfort to the Democratic Party. . . . My advice to colored men everywhere is to stick to the Republican party. Tell your wants, hold the party up to its professions, but do your utmost to keep it in power in state and nation."[63]

Blacks' disillusionment grew, however, when a week later the Republican-dominated Supreme Court dealt them a devastating blow in the Civil Rights Cases, which overturned Sections 1 and 2 of the Civil Rights Act of 1875. Those sections had outlawed discrimination in transportation, lodging, theaters, and other places of public amusement. The only dissent came from Justice John Marshall Harlan, appointed by Hayes in 1877. The court majority ruled that the law could not be justified by the Fourteenth Amendment, which pertained only to state action, not to discriminatory behavior by private citizens. Nor did the Thirteenth Amendment abolishing slavery apply, for such discrimination, contrary to the assertions of the statute's defenders, did not represent a continuing "badge of slavery." That all but one of the Court's Republican members sustained the majority opinion was not lost on black leaders such as Douglass, who said the decision had "swept over the land like a moral cyclone, leaving moral desolation in its track." Accusing the Court of a logic chopping that ignored the original purpose of the Fourteenth Amendment, Douglass pointedly asked, "What does it matter to a colored citizen that a State may not insult and outrage him, if a citizen of a State may? The effect upon him is the same, and it was just this effect that the framers of the Fourteenth Amendment plainly intended by that article to prevent."[64]

Reaction by Republican Party leaders was mixed. An outraged Robert G. Ingersoll told a mass meeting of blacks in Washington that the Court's two main assertions were dead wrong. The prohibitions of the Fourteenth Amendment did apply to individuals as well as state governments, because, he declared, "the word 'State' embraces and includes all the people of a State." As for the Thirteenth Amendment, he flatly stated, "A man is in a state of involuntary servitude when he is forced to do, or prevented from doing, a thing, not by the law of the State, but by the simple will of another." But Ingersoll went further, locating the citizen's rights and liberties in the original Constitution's guarantee to the states of a republican form of government. "If distinctions are made between free men on account of race or color, the government is not republican."[65] John Sherman agreed that the Court's decision "undermine[d] the foundation stone of Republican principles." "Inequality made by law is tyranny and should be resisted by constant opposition and agitation."[66]

Other Republicans, however, although not particularly pleased by the decision, were unwilling to contradict the Court's pronouncement on the law. Senator Benjamin Harrison told a meeting of blacks at Indianapolis that, "judging as a lawyer," he could see "very strong reason" for the Court's interpretation of "the scope and effect of the Fourteenth Amendment." But Harrison sought to assuage his listeners' anxiety by minimizing the decision's impact. It had no effect on blacks' right to vote, serve on juries, or attend public schools, and if they did suffer discrimination by railroads or hotels, they could seek redress under state laws or in suits at common law. Still, Harrison conceded that a new constitutional amendment might be necessary. Although he doubted "whether in the present condition of parties in this country, we could ever pass such an amendment again," if it were possible, blacks would "find the Republican party ready to do it." Harrison's remarks did not altogether placate his listeners, who went on to pass a resolution condemning the Court ruling as "narrow and partisan" and at variance with the positions taken by Charles Sumner, Abraham Lincoln, Oliver P. Morton, and other Republicans.[67]

For many white Republicans as well, the Court's ruling rekindled old feelings of moral indignation. A constituent wrote John Sherman, "From my understanding of republican government, the history of our nation, and *Justice*, as we aimed to establish it, I consider the Supreme Court has acted disgracefully." Indiana party leader Louis Michener reported to a member of Arthur's cabinet that "the decision of the Supreme Court has created considerable stir here. It has proven that Republicans still have the old feeling, though it has not been stirred for some time. We hope here that the President will take a stand in his message in favor of adopting a Constitutional amendment which will embody the fundamental idea of the civil rights bill. The discussion of the question in 1884 will appeal strongly to the moral and liberty-loving element of our party, which is so strong when aroused, and so indifferent when not aroused."[68]

That element of the party was further aroused by reports of renewed political violence in the South. In Virginia, Bourbon Democrats determined to defeat the Mahonites in the 1883 legislative elections resorted to the crudest sort of racist demagoguery, which, three days before the election, helped spark a riot at Danville. The fighting left at least four blacks dead, and the Democrats went on to win a two-thirds majority in the legislature. Copiah County, Mississippi, also witnessed an upsurge of violence, culminating in the election-day murder of Republican leader J. P. Matthews by a Democratic poll watcher, apparently with the encouragement of local Democratic leaders. These outbreaks stunned northern Republicans. Even the *New York Tribune*, which had earlier said that in the Civil Rights Cases the Supreme Court had "simply done its duty," now reacted sharply. "The Tribune cannot shut its eyes to facts. If men are murdered in the South because of their political opinions, if negroes are still intimidated and deterred from voting by threats and violence, The Tribune cannot ignore such things, because it wishes well to the Southern people. If to denounce political outrages is to 'wave the bloody shirt,' we shall wave it as long as the outrages are committed." Some Republicans saw a direct link between the election violence and the Supreme Court's decision, which, said one former U.S. attorney, "let loose the Devil" and "handed over the colored men" to the whites' "tender mercies."[69]

When Congress convened in early December 1883, President Arthur raised the issue at the close of his annual message, asserting that "the special purpose" of the Fourteenth Amendment was "to insure to members of the colored race the full enjoyment of civil and political rights." He noted the Supreme Court's decision and then promised to give his "unhesitating approval" to "any legislation" that would secure to all citizens equal enjoyment of "every right, privilege, and immunity of citizenship." Arthur made no mention of the recent political violence, however, and Navy Secretary Chandler again assumed the lead in voicing the administration's concern. A week after Arthur's message, Chandler attended a meeting of the Republican National Committee in Washington, where he secured passage of a resolution that condemned "the recent attempts to suppress human rights and to destroy free suffrage" as a "war with humanity and civilization." The secretary encouraged Republican journalists such as the *New York Tribune*'s Whitelaw Reid to maintain a steady drumbeat in the "struggle against Bourbon Democracy in favor of free speech, free education, free suffrage, and an honest counting of ballots."[70]

No sooner had the clerks finished reading Arthur's message than Republicans in Congress began to propose constitutional amendments to repair the supposed defect in the Fourteenth Amendment. One of the most strongly worded of such proposals, offered by Indiana Congressman William Calkins, declared, "No State, public or private corporation, or person, shall deprive any citizen of the United States of the equal protection of the law, nor abridge his rights, privileges, or immunities, on account of race, color, or previous condition of servitude." Republicans also introduced several bills to replace the legislation invalidated by the Supreme Court. The aim, said Senate Judiciary Committee chairman George Edmunds, one of the sponsors, was to secure "protection of the colored citizens of the United States against the inhuman, and, as I believe, wicked and cruel and prejudicial, distinctions that in some of the States are still made against them in respect of their civil rights." None of these measures had any chance for passage by the Forty-eighth Congress, however, for the House, where the Democrats held a nearly two-to-one majority, would give no countenance to civil rights legislation.[71]

In the Senate, Republicans held a slight majority, which afforded them the power at least to try to raise voters' consciousness by publicizing events in the South, particularly the recent violence in Virginia and Mississippi. A subcommittee of the Committee on Privileges and Elections conducted an investigation, and the Republican majority found the violence and murders to be part of a larger pattern of politically motivated intimidation in the interest of the Democratic Party. The committee recommended passage of Edmunds's civil rights bill and also cited the Fourteenth Amendment's provision calling for the reduction of congressional representation of any state that denied the right to vote to a portion of its eligible citizens. Again, however, as long as at least one house remained in Democratic hands, the prospect for such measures was nil.[72]

Nevertheless, congressional Republicans did harbor some hope for southern Democratic support for federal aid to education, a program that promised not punishment but cash outlays. At the opening of the session New Hampshire Senator Henry W. Blair, chairman of the Committee on Education and Labor, reintroduced the measure and quickly emerged as its most ardent and steadfast champion. As amended in committee, the Blair bill called for the distribution over a period of years of $105 million (later scaled back to $77 million) to the states on the basis of the illiteracy in their population. In advocating his bill, Blair went to the heart of Republicans' notions about republicanism. Common schools, he argued, were the principal institutions for educating citizens in "the practical duties of public and private life."

> By the public life of an American citizen I refer to his life as a sovereign; to his constant participation in the active government of his country; to the continual study and decision of political issues which devolve upon him whatever may be his occupation; and to his responsibility for the conduct of national and State affairs as the primary law-making, law-construing, and law-executing power. . . . The degree of education which the citizen must acquire is commensurate with the character and dignity of the station which he occupies by the theory of the government of which he is part. By so much and so far as he is deficient he will fail, and either become a nonentity or a source of danger and misrule.[73]

The bill enjoyed bipartisan support, including backing from many Southern Democrats who momentarily laid aside their states rights scruples. Most Senate Republicans favored the bill, but some were skeptical, most notably John Sherman, who always kept a watchful eye on expenditures. Sherman seconded Blair's notions about the need for an educated electorate in a republic, but as a member of the Copiah and Danville investigating committee, he believed that if southern state leaders received federal money, it might not "be properly used for the education of all classes." Sherman conceded that the federal government "should cooperate with the several States in educating the illiterate children of the United States," but he insisted on "conditions that will insure the application of that fund to the impartial education of all classes of illiterate children."[74]

Henry W. Blair
(Library of Congress)

Senator Benjamin Harrison led the way in drafting amendments to tighten Blair's bill. Most important, he secured a provision to bar funding to any state that could not certify in advance that it provided "free common schools for all of its children of school age, without distinction of race or color." Although his amendment did not mandate integrated schools, Harrison insisted that "unless the black boy and girl in the South can share equally in the privileges of education, then I am opposed to the bill, because it will not reach the evil that we are endeavoring to eradicate." Not unexpectedly, some southerners bridled at this proposal. But Blair told southern whites that federal aid to education would help them control an anomalous and potentially dangerous element among them. "The colored youths now," he said, were "rapidly becoming demoralized, an idle, thriftless population, with a tendency to violence. . . . In twenty-five years from now this Southern colored population, unless something is done to restrain, improve, and elevate them, are quite likely to be a source of violence and of turmoil in this country." Hence, Blair argued, "the more they know the greater will be their personal power and the better will they govern themselves." In the end, whether out of altruism or notions of racial self-defense, thirteen Democrats, all southerners, joined twenty Republicans to pass the bill. In its final version the bill required each state to spend as much of its own money on education as it received from the national government and required detailed reporting on the state's educational operations to substantiate compliance with the bill's conditions.[75]

After Senate passage on April 7, 1884, Blair's bill went to the House of Representatives, where the idea of federal aid to education enjoyed considerable support. Indeed, earlier in the session, both the majority and minority of the Committee on Education had prepared bills essentially similar in purpose to Blair's. But in the Forty-eighth Congress, none of these bills had any realistic chance of House passage because of the adamant opposition of Speaker John G. Carlisle. Although Carlisle's fellow Kentucky Democrat, Albert S. Willis, spearheaded the House campaign for the legislation, the Speaker consistently refused floor recognition to anyone proposing to bring the measure up for consideration.[76]

Still, despite Carlisle's obstructionism, Blair, Harrison, and their like-minded colleagues could take some pride in their achievement. They had garnered serious consideration, and Senate passage, for a measure to appropriate from the national treasury substantial sums of money for purposes historically viewed as the particular province of state and local government. Recognizing widespread illiteracy as a social and political problem of enormous proportions, they argued for a wider federal role to achieve its amelioration. Their arguments carried with them the implicit admission that they could do little else to rectify the condition of blacks in the South. Because military intervention in elections no longer availed as a way to protect the region's newly created republican institutions, the most realistic alternative seemed to be a better preparation of new citizens to participate in those institutions.

Reaction to the Supreme Court's Civil Rights decision and to the recent election violence in Virginia and Mississippi suggested the continuing relevance of the southern question in the nation's political life. Despite efforts of the Arthur administration to break the Solid South, it remained a potent threat to Republican prospects. As the presidential election year 1884 approached, Republicans cast about for a strategy and a candidate equal to the challenge. "The man who is most likely to succeed," a Cleveland constituent wrote John Sherman, "is the one who can make the strongest fight on the civil rights question—for that battle has to be fought again."[77]

8

The Fundamental Question in a Republic

Republicanism, Economics, and Electoral Stalemate in the 1880s

In the mid–1880s, Republicans continued to debate the party's approach to the southern question. Should they assault the Solid South directly by focusing on the suffrage issue, or should they endeavor to divide the South by appeals to economic interests? The latter approach, stressing sectional reconciliation and the benefits to the region wrought by Republican economic policies, gained favor among party leaders. The strategy came close to working—but only close—and its ultimate failure underscored Republican demands for a renewed defense of the republican project in the South.

As Republicans began to map strategy for the 1884 presidential election, many agreed with North Carolina party leader John Mott, who wrote John Sherman that in light of recent election violence, "This question of providing the states of the South with a republican form of government should be prominent in the coming campaign." Among the conspicuous aspirants for the Republican nomination, Sherman assumed the strongest position on the issue, both in launching the Copiah and Danville investigations and in demanding conditions for the Blair bill. In doing so he won the gratitude of southern and northern Republicans who considered the question paramount. "Please permit me to express my gratification that you have offered your resolutions of inquiry into the horrible butcheries said to have occurred in Va & Miss," wrote former Tennessee Congressman William Moore. "I tell you that tariffs, banks, and other questions of economics are matters of trifling concern compared with the question of owning and controlling one's own manhood." Xenia, Ohio, lawyer B. Nesbitt agreed: "If the eventful campaign of this year shall be fought by the Republicans upon the sentimental nonsensical 'Goody-Goody' theory, *'Do come and shake hands with us across the bloody chasam* [*sic*]*,' 'Let us bury the bloody shirt'* ad noiseum [*sic*], then in my opinion we shall be defeated."[1]

Yet the front-runner for the presidential nomination was not Sherman, but James G. Blaine, who still believed, as he had argued in 1880, that the party's best hope lay in emphasizing economic issues that would not only appeal to northerners but also potentially divide the white vote in the South. Since leaving the cabinet in late 1881, Blaine had devoted himself to writing. The result was *Twenty Years of Congress,* a massive history of the period from 1860 to 1880, which had much to say about the pre-1860 period as well. The first volume appeared in April 1884, just as the preconvention delegate hunt intensified. That Blaine aimed at winning southern support as a potential presidential nominee seemed evident in his book's generous treatment of the South. Antebellum southern leaders, Blaine wrote, "were, almost without exception, men of high integrity" who "guarded the Treasury with rigid and unceasing vigilance against every attempt at extravagance, and against every form of corruption." As the Civil War approached, southern leaders were "not mere malcontents. They were not pretenders. . . . They had ability and they had courage." During the war, Blaine wrote, the Confederate soldiers "fought with an absolute conviction, however erroneous, that their cause was just; and their arms were nerved by the feeling which their leaders had instilled deeply into their minds, that they were contending against an intolerable tyranny and protecting the sacredness of home." So attuned was Blaine to southern sensibilities that one Republican wrote William Chandler, "I really think if the book should be put in the hands of any one who had never heard of our war, & knew nothing of the antecedent history of the country, he would come to the conclusion that Lincoln and the North were the moving influences, and that the south had been greatly outraged in some occult way not fully explained by the author."[2]

Blaine's book was hardly calculated to garner much convention support from the embattled Republicans of the South, most of whom rallied behind President Chester Arthur. In many parts of the region the party had shrunk to little more than the corps of federal officeholders. Many owed their very livelihood to the administration and were thus among the president's most ardent supporters. Arthur entered the national convention at Chicago second to Blaine in delegate strength, with 70 percent of his supporters coming from the South.[3]

At the convention, the delegates gave relatively little attention to the southern question. The resolutions committee, under the leadership of Blaine men

James G. Blaine
(Library of Congress)

William McKinley as chairman and William Walter Phelps as secretary, produced a platform that devoted six paragraphs to the tariff issue and only two to southern affairs. The party "denounce[d] the fraud and violence practiced by the Democracy in the Southern States, by which the will of the voter is defeated, as dangerous to the preservation of free institutions," and it favored legislation to "secure to every citizen, of whatever race and color, the full and complete recognition, possession and exercise of all civil and political rights."[4]

Compared with the oratory of conventions past, the nominating speeches said little about the southern question. Speaking for Blaine, William West declared that no "electoral gun can be expected" from the South. Economic issues held the key to victory, for which "the Republican States of the North must furnish the conquering battalions from the farm, the anvil, the loom; from the mine, the workshop, and the desk." Still, said West, Blaine represented "that Republicanism that can not regard with indifference a despotism which, under the flaunting lie of *Sic semper tyrannis,* annihilates, by slaughter, popular majorities in the name of democracy." One of Arthur's seconders, Henry Bingham of Pennsylvania, warned that ignoring the party's "legends of liberty" would leave it "a flag without faith, proclaiming only material prosperity and material success." Speakers for John Sherman accentuated his record on financial issues, but Joseph Foraker also praised him as "a man who can find . . . some method whereby the brutal butcheries of Copiah and Danville may for the future be prevented." Advocates of the reformers' favorite, George Edmunds, generally ignored the South, believing, as George William Curtis put it, that "the old issues are largely settled."[5]

In the convention voting, Blaine led on all the ballots. The great bulk of his strength came from northern states, and few southern delegates switched to his column as he marched to victory. From the first to the fourth and last ballot, 82 percent of Arthur's supporters from the states of the old Confederacy stuck by the president. Two weeks later, at Augusta, the official notification committee frankly told the nominee, "At an early stage of the proceedings of the Convention, it became manifest that the Republican States [that is, the northern states], whose aid must be invoked at last to insure success to the ticket, earnestly desired your nomination."[6]

The committee also declared that during the previous twenty-three years, "the Republican party has builded a new Republic," and it now welcomed Blaine as the party's new "architect-in-chief." Blaine accepted that assignment with relish. In his letter of acceptance, he made clear his belief that henceforth the party's foundation must rest firmly on economic issues. He devoted nearly all of the letter to such matters, over half to the protective tariff alone. He played down sectional antagonism and instead stressed the common economic destiny of North and South. "Any effort to unite the Southern States upon issues that grow out of the memories of the war," he said, would inevitably meet an assertion of nationality by a solid North. Fortunately, however, the "Southern Commonwealths are learning to vindicate civil rights, and adapting themselves to the conditions of political tranquility and industrial progress." With no mention of Copiah or Danville, Blaine noted that "if there be occasional outbreaks in the South against this peaceful progress, the public opinion of the country regards them as exceptional and hopefully trusts that each will prove the last."[7]

These passages met a mixed reaction within the party. Speaking for Republicans who welcomed a shift in emphasis, the Newark *Daily Advertiser* was gratified that "those who hope for a new unfurling of 'the bloody shirt' will find no encouragement in Mr. Blaine's generous and manly utterance concerning the South and its relation to the whole Union." Others disagreed. From Blaine's own state, Congressman Charles Boutelle told the nominee that he "would have preferred not to have had the settled policy of Southern proscription referred to as 'exceptional' and 'occasional.' I should also place the establishment of political and civil rights and the vindication of the ballot as the foremost issue—taking precedence of merely material and economic questions." "But," Boutelle concluded, "I suppose I am behind the times."[8]

With the last point, Blaine no doubt concurred. As his campaign unfolded, he stressed intersectional unity, urging southerners to recognize the great material benefits they derived from Republican economic policies. In part this southern strategy reflected Blaine's realization that winning New York would be difficult, given the lingering opposition of his factional enemies there led by Roscoe Conkling, as well as the likely bolt by the so-called mugwumps turned off by Blaine's scandal-tainted record. Compounding the problem was the Democrats' nomination of New York Governor Grover Cleveland to run against Blaine. Without New York, Blaine would need help from the South, and hence he sought to win favor in the region's more progressive states.

But Blaine's southern strategy derived not only from his drive for election but also from his sincere belief that Republican economic policies were best for southern development. A division of the southern vote along economic rather than racial lines was the key to political and social, as well as economic, progress for the region. And that could benefit the North as well, for as soon as southerners began thinking like enlightened northerners on economic questions, so soon would they cease to block the kinds of programs Blaine and other Republicans advocated for national development. Thus, in his campaign Blaine spoke particularly of "the new South" with its "awakened liberal sentiment which is striving for the industrial development of that naturally rich section of the Union, which recognizes the necessity of a tariff for protection, which casts the bitter memories of the civil conflict behind," and which "naturally affiliates with the Republican party." He invited southerners to "join in a union not merely in form, but a union in fact, and take your part in the solution of the industrial and financial problems of the time."[9]

Following Blaine's lead, other Republican campaigners generally emphasized economic issues, especially the tariff. Speakers and pamphleteers pointed to high protective duties as the key to American prosperity. Not all party members agreed with Blaine's priorities, however. As one Massachusetts Republican complained to John Sherman, "In the days of slavery the tariff question was agitated to call attention from the 'nigger question.' So today, the tariff question is raised to divert attention from the 'nigger question.' The right to vote is 'the right preservative of all rights,' and unless we can have 'a free ballot and a fair count' the Republic has failed." In August, Green B. Raum, former Illinois congressman and U.S. Commissioner of Internal Revenue, published a book entitled *The Existing Conflict between Republican Government and Southern Oligarchy,* which presented a graphic account of southern political violence from the end of the war through Copiah and Danville. Clearly disagreeing with Blaine's treatment of the South in *Twenty Years of Congress,* Raum hoped that his own book would "exercise a strong influence favorable to the Republican party in the next election."[10]

Like Raum, Arthur's postmaster general, Walter Q. Gresham, thought that "the force of race prejudice" would prevent Blaine's economic appeals from winning many converts in the South. Instead, the key to victory was "to arouse the people of the North to the importance of the southern question and the enormity of the outrages perpetrated in that region." Nonetheless, as the campaign wore on, Blaine stuck by his southern strategy. He particularly targeted West Virginia, whose October state elections would serve as a test of his approach. He spoke at several points in the state. "Under the protective tariff," he declared, "your coal industries, and your iron industries, and the wealth of your forests have been brought out, and it is for you voters of West Virginia to say whether you want this to continue or whether you want to try free trade." He appealed "to West Virginia not to vote upon a tradition or a prejudice" but to lead the whole South "in a great National movement which shall in fact and in feeling, as well as in form, make us a people with one union, one Constitution, one destiny."[11]

The West Virginia strategy failed. In the October election, the Democratic nominee for governor defeated a candidate running on a Republican–Greenback fusion ticket, and the Democrats took a majority in the legislature. On the same day, Republicans carried the state elections in Ohio. Blaine's initial reaction was to stand by his tariff emphasis; two days later, he told a Michigan audience that that question remained "the one absorbing and controlling issue" of the campaign. Yet as he crossed into the important doubtful state of Indiana, he conceded that the West Virginia and Ohio elections had "put a new phase on the national contest, or rather they have reproduced the old phase. The Democratic party, as of old, consider now they have the South solid again." Now the danger was that the Democrats would capture 153 electoral votes from the sixteen southern states and work mightily to add the key doubtful states of Indiana and New York to "seize the Government of the Union." Decrying the persistence of the Solid South, Blaine warned Hoosier voters that rule by the Democrats, dominated by their southern wing, would mean "the breaking down of the great industrial system which has enriched the United States so marvelously in the last twenty-three years." He carried the same message to New York, where he turned up the heat in his denunciation of the Solid South: "The proposition of the Democratic party of the Nation is to have New York join this alliance, and, taking advantage of this wholesale crime against free suffrage in the South, to seize the Government of the United States by a gross violation of the plainest

"Blaine's Funeral" democratic campaign flyer, 1884 (Library of Congress)

rights of citizenship. . . . It is startling to reflect that by an election thus carried the great domestic policies of the country may be overturned." Most fundamentally, he declared, "A crime against the suffrage is a crime against the Republic."[12]

Blaine's loss to Cleveland in November was so narrow that any number of influences could have caused it. Blaine lost the entire South, but results in several individual states demonstrate that his southern strategy was not necessarily mistaken. He lost all four northern doubtful states—New York, Indiana, Connecticut, and New Jersey—where he gained an average of 47.94 percent of each state's popular vote. But in Virginia, Tennessee, and West Virginia he garnered an average popular vote of 48.16 percent. Had Blaine won Virginia and Tennessee, he could have taken the presidency without any of the four northern swing states. The closeness of the vote in these southern states (and a few others, including Florida and North Carolina) highlighted the apparent appeal of Blaine's southern campaign. Still, it also raised the imponderable question as to whether local and state election officials, who were Democrats, would have permitted the counting and reporting of a Blaine victory. In any event, many Republicans remained convinced that the culture of political intimidation in the South had thwarted their legitimate claim to the presidency.[13]

Blaine himself subscribed to that belief, as he told his neighbors at Augusta, Maine, in an impassioned speech after the election. Harkening to the economic emphasis he had followed during the campaign, he said that "the transfer of the political power of the Government to the South is a great National misfortune . . . because it introduces an element which cannot insure harmony and prosperity to the people." But he also decried the spurious result, "because it introduces into a Republic the rule of a minority." As Republicans had done in the past, Blaine condemned the political condition of the South as being at war with the fundamental principles of the American Republic, especially as Republicans had sought to recreate that Republic in the postwar decades:

> The first instinct of an American is equality—equality of right, equality of privilege, equality of political power—that equality which says to every citizen, "Your vote is as good, and as potential as the vote of any other citizen." That cannot be said to-day in the United States. The course of affairs in the South has crushed out the political power of more than six million American citizens and has transferred it by violence to others.

Moreover, political proscription of blacks allowed white southerners to "exert an electoral influence far beyond that exerted by the same number of white people in the North." "Such a condition of affairs," said Blaine, "is extraordinary, unjust, and derogatory to the manhood of the North. . . . Gentleman, there cannot be political inequality among the citizens of a Free Republic." "Your speech strikes the keynote of the party struggle of the next four years," wrote former North Carolina carpetbagger Albion Tourgée, who thanked Blaine for advancing "a policy which is not only in harmony with the instincts and traditions of the party, but is founded on an immutable principle."[14]

But mugwump Republicans, who abjured the southern question as much as they condemned Blaine's alleged corruption, dismissed the candidate's postelection analysis as the bitter outburst of a disappointed "demagogue" from whose grasp the country had narrowly escaped. Carl Schurz exulted that Blaine "has dug his grave by his serenade speech." For Republicans who believed in the primacy of the suffrage question, however, Blaine's speech represented a return to the true faith. "What a pity Mr. Blaine did not deliver his Augusta speech of yesterday in July last!" M. Woodhull wrote to William Chandler. "He would now be President Elect, if he had done so."[15]

More than ever before, Blaine's loss and Cleveland's victory brought home to northern Republicans the meaning and impact of southern political villainy. For the first time, an election in which they directly participated was carried by what they saw as the southern Democrats' fraudulent methods. Previously, northern Republicans had been sympathetic observers of the losses their southern allies had suffered in state, local, and congressional elections. Now, many northerners believed, the suppression of Republican votes in the South had frustrated the expression of their own will and had violated republican principles in the nation at large. "It is time," wrote small-town banker Edward Squire, "for all fair minded men to reflect and ask, is not the very foundation stone of our Republic, the power of the majority, in danger?" Ohio editor John Hopley wrote John Sherman that "the statesman who takes the lead in contending against the southern methods whereby the presidency is *usurped,* will be the leader of this outraged and cheated Republican party."[16]

Again, Sherman stepped out front on the issue, as he had done with the Copiah and Danville investigations a year previously. During the Ohio state election campaign in 1885, Sherman decried the Solid South as a "specter that now haunts American politics." He disclaimed any intention to revive the old passions of the war, which were subsiding. Instead he focused on the continuing postwar political transgressions by which the "rebels are in as absolute mastery in the South as they would have been if the Confederacy had succeeded." The Democratic party had been "the chief agent in organizing the frauds in elections" and thus had "done more to sap the foundation of republican government than all the parties that have existed." "If such wrongs can thus be condoned," Sherman warned, "and there is no protection to the citizen against similar occurrences, the time will soon come when elections will cease, by the general confession of the people that free government by elections has failed, and the 'man on horseback' will be called upon to repeat again his role in history." In effect, he charged, the nation confronted a "second rebellion of the South."[17]

Sherman's reelection to the Senate turned on the makeup of the legislature elected in 1885, and Democrats accused him of "waving the bloody shirt" in order to divert Ohio voters from the prohibition question and other issues that threatened Republican success. But when Sherman took a campaign swing through Virginia in late October, he pulled no punches. "The great and pressing issue," he told a Petersburg audience, "involves the fundamental principles of our government; that elections must be free and open and fair; and every honest voter should be permitted to cast his vote, and every honest vote should be counted, and no others. If this principle is once overthrown republican government is at an end, and the war of the Guelphs and the Ghibellines, the war of civil strife between factions and of riots will commence, and there will soon be an end of all elections." "Any violation of the purity of elections," he declared, is "the greatest crime against a republic."[18]

Sherman's electioneering rhetoric may have been overheated, but it nonetheless reflected the deep frustrations he and other Republicans felt. "I have read your speeches," wrote Charles Holstein, former U.S. attorney at Indianapolis, "& believe with you that the right to vote must be recognized & respected in & by every voting precinct in the land, South as well as North, & that as long

John Sherman
(Library of Congress)

as that right is denied even the humblest citizen, there is wrong to be righted. If the principle involved is not worth fighting for, there is none that is." As J. C. F. Beyland of *Der New York Republikaner* put it, the issue of suffrage was "the *question* underlying all other questions at issue. Its correct interpretation means a *republican government,* its violation nothing short of revolution & disorder."[19]

Nonetheless, with Cleveland in the White House and the Democrats in control of the House of Representatives, Republicans had few options beyond calling attention to the debased state of southern politics. "What can we do?" asked Senator Benjamin Harrison. Even if a Republican should win the presidency and station marshals at the polls, he observed, it had "been demonstrated that local sentiment is such that convictions for any violations of election laws is impossible." Nor was there much chance that Congress would ever follow through on the threat to reduce southern representation in the House and the Electoral College. Hence, Harrison believed, "A division of the white vote in the South furnishes the only solution possible. That may come about from the tariff or some other financial question." In March 1886 Senate Republicans again passed the Blair education bill, with Democratic support, but again the measure failed in the Democratic House.[20]

Still, Republican leaders were unwilling to admit defeat on the southern question. In the congressional elections of 1886 George Hoar urged Blaine "not [to] let this campaign pass without one emphatic statement of protest and indignation at the suppression of the Republican vote in the South. . . . If it be supposed that we mean to abandon political resistance, the heart will be taken out of the Republican party." The Maine leader had been emphasizing the tariff and that issue remained the focus of his speeches in 1886, but in an address at Bangor a few days after hearing from Hoar, he "surprised his hearers with a burst of eloquence on Southern outrages." Noting the continuing violation of the nation's fundamental republican tenets, Blaine declared that the Democrats' suppression of the black vote of the South enabled them to "cast from 35 to 40 votes in Congress to which they have no moral title, nor legal title, nor no constitutional title, and no title at all, except that which is founded upon force and fraud." In the November elections, the Democrats retained their majority in the House, but the Republicans gained eleven seats; in the new Senate, however, Republicans saw their majority cut from eight to two seats.[21]

The outcome offered little guidance for GOP strategists. If the party wanted to do better in the future, Ohio Republican Warner Bateman wrote William Chandler, Republicans should not "waste their time and dry up on past issues merely. . . . The old questions as to the South, in my judgment, are substantially solved." But Chandler insisted that while the party "must be right on new issues, . . . we must not cease to talk about the southern question. Whether we can do anything for the suppressed voters until we have elected a President and obtained possession of both Houses of Congress is doubtful, but we should continue to agitate."[22]

John Sherman, who aspired to head the Republican ticket in the next campaign, agreed with Chandler about the need to "agitate," but he also harbored some hope that an "appeal to the people of the South to correct this enormous wrong . . . will not be in vain." In late March, 1887, he tested that approach in an invited address to the Republican members of the Tennessee legislature in Nashville. "I was glad to hear," he told the group, "in passing through several of the southern States, conservative citizens say that public sentiment now revolts at the unlawful methods to defeat the free exercise of equal rights of citizens." He warned that sectional feeling would persist "as long as such methods are resorted to" and as long as large numbers of people "are denied their rights to share in self-government." But, he said, "I gladly turn to those questions of

National politics which alike affect all parts of our country," issues such as taxation, currency, commerce, and internal improvements. He cautioned the Tennesseans and southerners in general that Democratic party ascendancy based on a combination of the Solid South with free-trade New York would inevitably yield economic policies that would "confine your industries to the growth of cotton and keep you out of the profitable development of your resources." Better that southerners should join in "a union of the manhood and patriotism of the country, North and South, in the support of what Henry Clay called the American policy of developed industries and internal improvement."[23]

Reaction to Sherman's Nashville speech varied. The *New York Tribune* observed that he said "in Tennessee precisely what Mr. Blaine said years ago in West Virginia, and appeals in precisely the same spirit to the more progressive and enlightened sentiment of the 'New South.'" John Hay wrote the senator, "If the men of the South could be brought to look at their opportunity in this way, I would feel that the great age of American politics—from 1850 to 1890—had had its legitimate course, and that our system was secure for many generations to come." From Marshall, Texas, R. W. Thompson Jr., son of a former colleague of Sherman in the Hayes cabinet, reported that the Republicans' protective tariff principles were "attracting the attention of the young men of the south to a remarkable degree" and that "the time is now near when the 'Solid South' can be broken."[24]

Others were less confident, however. From Belton, Texas, J. P. Osterhout wrote the senator that the "Democrats in the South are so *set* in their hostility to the Republican party, that it is doubtful if any argument, or any feeling of self interest will ever move them to change their views." Louisville publisher John Finnell sent Sherman a copy of the platform of the recent Kentucky Democratic state convention, which he described as "a rehash of the resolutions of '98, on the powers of the Federal government and an attempt to revive the issues upon which the South made war upon the Government." Finnell urged Sherman to cite the Kentucky platform in a speech he was scheduled to give to the Illinois legislature in early June. Green B. Raum similarly urged Sherman to hit the southern issue hard in his Springfield speech. Raum sent citations from his book, *The Existing Conflict*, including a quotation from the Supreme Court's 1884 decision, *Ex parte Yarbrough*, which upheld the federal government's "power to protect the elections on which its existence depends from violence and corruption."[25]

Sherman took Finnell's and Raum's advice in preparing his Springfield speech. Noting the "revolting details" of political violence that Raum had cataloged, Sherman conceded that the white southern conservatives had apparently won the guerrilla war they had waged since Appomattox. No intelligent man could deny that "Mr. Cleveland is now President of the United States by virtue of crimes against the elective franchise, including murder, arson, ballot-box stuffing, forgery and perjury." But beyond determining who would be president and fill the subordinate offices, such crimes had enormous policy consequences. The "vital controlling difference between the two great parties now, as during the war," Sherman said, was that "one theory tended to belittle, degrade and lessen the authority of the National Union," while the "opposite theory was that the Government formed by our fathers was a National Government, that the constitution was an indissoluble bond of union, defining the powers of the Government, to be construed liberally, so as to carry into effect the purposes of its framers." The illegitimate triumph of the Democratic theory jeopardized numerous economic policies, including the protective tariff, internal improvements, aid to education, and trade expansion. But the gravest threat was to republicanism itself. "In the later days of the Roman Republic the controlling elements in elections were bribery, force and corruption, and this was the cause of its fall. So in ours, if elections are controlled by the meanest frauds and crimes instead of the popular will, it will be the end of free government."[26]

As had his previous utterances on the issue, Sherman's Springfield speech met a varied response. The *New York Tribune* declared that if the American people "were careful to preserve republican institutions for their children, they would consider this array of facts with the deepest solicitude." J. W. Dimmick, clerk of the U.S. Circuit Court at Montgomery Alabama, thought "Sherman's boldly proclaiming a political truth affecting as it does the very existence of the Republic [ought to] endear him to Republicans and make him their leader." Chandler paid Sherman the compliment of imitation, warning a New Hampshire audience a week later to be wary of the "commercial spirit" that "creates a seeming indifference to the vital question of a free ballot," for "a nation which puts money and its uses before man and his liberty cannot long endure as a republic."[27]

But Sherman's speech also came in for severe denunciation, especially in New York. According to Associated Press manager William Henry Smith, "many Republicans here do not want to dwell on the southern question" because the "influence of trade is the same as before the war." The mugwump press generally condemned the address. "Certainly," said *The Nation*, "the transformation of Dr. Jekyll into Mr. Hyde was not more remarkable than the change which makes the Nashville apostle of conciliation in March preach the gospel of hate at Springfield in June." Of the Springfield speech, Sherman himself confided to a friend, "I feared at the time it would be a little too strong for public sentiment, although it expresses every word of my own earnest feeling. I do not want to be cheated any longer by criminals, North or South." Publicly, the senator steadfastly maintained that his two speeches exhibited no material difference. "I do not see," he told an interviewer, "how the arraignment of election methods that confessedly destroy the purity of the ballot box, and deprive a million of people of their political rights, can be ignored or silenced in a republic by the shoo-fly cry of 'bloody shirt.'" A few weeks after the Springfield speech Sherman called for new legislation "fixing the time, manner and circumstances of electing members of Congress, defining and providing for the rights of every citizen at such an election."[28]

As matters turned out, the seeming extremism of Sherman's position was mitigated by newspaper accounts of President Grover Cleveland's approval of an order that Confederate battle flags, heretofore stored in the War Department, should be returned to the individual southern states. This gesture toward sectional rapprochement aroused the ire of many northern veterans, who were already angered by Cleveland's vetoes of pension bills and now saw his flag order as hallowing the symbols of rebellion against which they had fought. In his speeches Sherman had carefully differentiated between inciting old war animosities and condemning current political depredations committed by "cowards and criminals, not in war, but in peace." But in the minds of many northerners, particularly members of veterans groups such as the Grand Army of the Republic, Cleveland's order blurred this distinction. From as far away as Washington Territory, party member John Gowey advised Sherman that the flag order had aroused "the old-time spirit and enthusiasm in the hearts of Republicans, and has brought home to them in a most convincing way the fact that the 'South is in the saddle.'" Even in New York, former Senator Warner Miller reported to Sherman, Cleveland's order had "done much to . . . show some people that the Springfield speech was justifiable."[29]

Sherman himself said little about the flag order and instead deferred to his fellow Ohioan, Governor Joseph Foraker, a passionate orator who hammered against Cleveland in several speeches. In an article for *The Forum* on "The Return of the Republican Party," Foraker excoriated Cleveland for treating the flags "as though they were not still the emblems of treason, of which the people of the South should be forever ashamed." Although Foraker discussed a broad range of issues in his article, he argued that "the question of 'a free ballot and a fair count' . . . outranks all others, because it affects directly the very existence of our government. The theory of our institutions is, that the people are the source of all rightful authority. The only sovereignty we have is their lawfully expressed will. Whatever defeats or interferes with that expression is, at least, moral treason."[30]

Despite the momentary furor over the battle-flag incident, however, as the next presidential election year approached, Republicans confronted a political landscape that was essentially unchanged since 1884. Democrats' hold on the South seemed just as solid, and the pivotal northern state of New York remained as "doubtful" as ever. To many Republicans, the "southern question" remained chained to the ineluctable state of race relations. "Race prejudice," Sherman wrote privately, "is the root of most of the evils we are suffering. It is this that induces the criminal overthrow of the rights of the colored people in the South and the same prejudice tends to produce indifference in the North."[31]

How to overcome that persistent prejudice was the party's central conundrum, and many Republicans saw little utility in continued rhetoric about violations of the suffrage. H. H. Leavitt, a leader of the New York City Republican Club, laid out an alternative for Sherman. Leavitt argued that making speeches on "the subject of the negro vote is wasting time and powder in firing salutes. The noise is heard, but the only effect is from the recoil, and the Republican party receives it." Instead, echoing Blaine's 1884 strategy, Leavitt advocated an appeal to white southern economic interests, especially those in the growing manufacturing sector eager for tariff protection. Once these interests recognized that their prosperity depended on Republican party policies, "they will be desirous of seeing that party victorious," and the best way for them to achieve a majority was "by seeing that every negro vote is freely cast and honestly counted." Hence, "protectionists of the South will then take up the fight which thus far has been so unsuccessfully waged by the Republican party." Although Sherman himself had sought to steer Republican emphasis from sectional to economic issues, he found Leavitt's reasoning less than persuasive. If, he insisted, Republicans ignored "the question of a fair vote and an honest count, . . . we will lose the support of great masses of earnest and honest men as well as the colored vote, and we will lose our own self-respect when we allow a Constitutional provision to be utterly ignored and trodden under foot."[32]

If Republicans were uncertain about what to emphasize in the coming presidential election, President Cleveland helped to focus the contest by devoting his entire annual message in December 1887 to the tariff. Advocating substantial reductions in customs duties, the message mirrored the long-standing views of southern Democrats and the New York mercantile community, precisely the economic axis that Sherman and other Republicans had warned threatened to undermine the protective system. Republicans such as Blaine found Cleveland's appeal to the South particularly ironic, for "the South above all sections of the Union needs a protective tariff." No doubt recalling his own futile southern strategy in 1884, Blaine feared that "the truth has been so long obscured by certain local questions of unreasoning prejudice that nobody can hope for industrial enlightenment among their leaders just yet." Still, most Republicans welcomed the sense of clarity Cleveland's message brought to partisan competition. "The

President has thrown down the gauntlet," said Wisconsin Senator John Spooner, "and there seems to be a general feeling among Republicans, and among a great many Democrats, here that our chances are infinitely better for carrying the country than they were a month ago."[33]

But the southern question was by no means dead. Indeed, Cleveland himself helped keep it alive with the nomination of Mississippian Lucius Q. C. Lamar to a vacancy on the Supreme Court. A former senator now serving in Cleveland's cabinet as secretary of the interior, Lamar would be the first Confederate veteran to sit on the high court. Lamar's fitness for the appointment aroused doubts, for he was of advanced age (at sixty-two, the second oldest person ever nominated), suffered precarious health, had never held a judicial position, and had not even practiced law since the early days of his career, although he had been a law professor briefly two decades earlier. Most Republicans could see only one motive behind Cleveland's move: a desire to give recognition and representation to the South. Hence, if in the president's view Lamar's chief qualification was that he was a southerner, Republicans felt fully justified in judging him on that ground. Some observers and later historians dismissed the Republicans' opposition to the appointment as raw partisanship, but Cleveland's selection of the marginally qualified Lamar for sectional, partisan reasons invited the response it received.[34]

William Chandler readily conceded the political nature of the dispute, noting that because the Senate was "the only branch of the national government controlled by the Republicans, the members of the party throughout the country are looking to the Republicans of the Senate to sound the keynote of the coming conflict." "That Lamar was a rebel is not the argument," Chandler wrote Whitelaw Reid; "that he still advocates the doctrine of secession as right and is a bulldozer is a potent argument."[35]

In Washington and the nation, Lamar had acquired a reputation as a southern moderate, most notably for his affecting House eulogy for Charles Sumner. Nonetheless, over the years, he had clung to the essential southern Democratic position on suffrage and related issues. In 1879, for instance, he had voted against a Senate resolution upholding the Thirteenth, Fourteenth, and Fifteenth Amendments and the power of the federal government to enforce them. As Senator Spooner explained to a constituent, "No man ought to be confirmed to the Supreme Court whose *status* as to the validity of the Constitutional amendments growing out of the war is open to question." Moreover, said Spooner, "The 'Mississippi plan,' which drove the Negroes to the swamps and, by assassination and threats, suppressed the Republican vote, I do not find that he ever condemned." "There is something so incongruous," said Reid's *New York Tribune*, "in the idea of a man being nominated to one of the highest judicial places in the land who owes all his prominence to crimes, oppressions and fraud."[36]

Many rank-and-file Republicans seconded these objections. Cleveland GAR member L. S. Fish wrote to Sherman, "These men are placed on the most lofty and advanced 'picket posts' at the outer confines of the republic, and none but the most patriotic and known law abiding citizen should ever be placed on duty there." In the end, two Senate Republicans, William Stewart of Nevada and Leland Stanford of California, plus Independent Harrison Riddleberger of Virginia voted with the Democrats to confirm Lamar by a vote of 32 to 28.[37]

Lamar won confirmation in mid-January 1888, and the brief but sharp controversy over his appointment did not alter the drift of opinion that the tariff issue would dominate the coming presidential election campaign. Among many Republicans a sense of resignation was setting in regarding the southern question. Conditions had not materially improved in the South, but the prospect of arousing northern public opinion against them progressively dimmed. Iowa Republican editor and national committeeman James Clarkson frankly declared that "there is no longer a majority in the North to respond to the nobler issues on which the Republican party has so long stood." He noted that every four years the nation gained a million new voters "to whom the war is history and not a personal experience." "Not swayed by sentimental issues or the historic grandeur of the Republican party," these young men wanted "to fight present politics on present issues." By stressing the southern issue, said Clarkson, the party managed only to keep "itself out of power, and therefore unable to protect in the least degree any interest of the loyal people." Clarkson advocated an appeal to business interests north and south on issues such as the tariff.[38]

But other party leaders believed Clarkson's ideas misrepresented the true feelings of average Republicans, who still bridled at the continuing violation of republican precepts in the political life of the South, and hence of the nation at large. "We must remember," Foraker wrote privately, "that it is not what a few men, who imagine they control parties, think, but what do the rank and file of the party think. Every man who is acquainted with the sentiment of the Republican masses, by going among them and making speeches to them, knows that it is their determination that the Constitution shall be obeyed and that we shall have a free ballot and a fair count, that has stirred the spirit of Republicanism as nothing else has done since the war. Tariff is good; but what's the use of talking about it or anything else until we have first settled it that after the argument, the people are to be allowed to express their conclusions[?]" In Foraker's view, not more than 10 percent of northern Republicans favored emphasizing the tariff issue, whereas "the other ninety per cent are demanding a settlement of the other question."[39]

Chandler, of course, agreed with Foraker's assessment. No sooner had Congress come into session in December 1887 than Chandler, now representing New Hampshire in the Senate, introduced legislation for the federal regulation of elections in several southern states. With Democrats controlling the House and the presidency, the proposal had no chance of becoming law, but a month later, Chandler secured passage of a resolution calling for a Senate investigation of the recent municipal election in Jackson, Mississippi, during which Democratic federal officials allegedly participated in a movement to bar blacks from voting. By devices such as these, Chandler aimed to keep the southern question alive and before the public view.[40]

Needless to say, for southern blacks the issue was very much alive. P. B. Thompkins, a student at Lincoln University in Pennsylvania described for John Sherman conditions in his home town of Meriwether, South Carolina:

> The Negroes of the South are natur[al]ly Republicans, but we have no fair election. They (the Democrats) say that the law says that the Ballot boxes must be in a small room & only 2 doors and one voter in at the time. They generally have all Democratic judges, 7 or 8 boxes in which to vote. Our people as a general thing cannot read or write their own names and consequently when they go in to vote are confused and vote in the wrong box. Besides that the judges move the boxes every 2 or 3 minutes. Ignorant Republicans outside ask what box did you vote in? Reply such and such box. The inquirer will go in and vote as instructed. By the time he gets to the boxes they are removed. In South Carolina (my home) they prevent them from going to the polls. "A New South!" Does this favor it? If the Republican party could arrange some plane [*sic*] so as to have a fair election, we the Negroes of S. C. could carry it Republican by an enormous majority. Our people have loyal hearts. They do not sell their votes for rum. The fact is they are not free. How long shall we be oppressed? How long shall we be denied the rights of having a free vote and fair count?[41]

State elections in Louisiana held in April 1888 offered further evidence of the Democrats' continued suppression of the black vote. From New Iberia Parish, former New Orleans postmaster William Merchant reported to Sherman, "At this poll they assaulted, beat, wounded and ill-treated several colored men, and ran every white Republican away." Chandler again called for an investigation, and the day after the election, Sherman denounced such methods on the floor of the Senate. He was particularly appalled by the attitude of Louisiana Senator James B. Eustis. In a preelection campaign speech Eustis had said that "we have to determine whether the negro shall govern and rule the white man, or whether the white man shall govern and rule the negro," and "the sooner we let the northern people understand that their opinions on this race question will not influence or control our action in any degree, the better it will be for our safety." "The Constitution says that this is a republican form of government, not a government of caste or race," Sherman declared. "It is not a republican government when a majority of the people are deprived of plain constitutional rights. When you say in Louisiana that the black men shall not rule, you say the majority shall not rule. . . . Therefore, when you say that it shall be a white man's government in Louisiana you make it an anti-republican government, and overthrow republican government."[42]

With the Republican national convention little more than two months away, Sherman was clearly angling for delegate support from the rotten boroughs of the South. Even so, black Republicans were nonetheless grateful for the prominent role he played in championing their cause. A week after his Senate speech, Frederick Douglass wrote Sherman that "there is no man living with any chance of being president of the U. States whom I would rather see in that quality than yourself. You know the sad condition of my people, and I believe you have the head, hand, and heart to help them."[43]

Sherman entered the convention with considerable southern support, but from the beginning, it was clear that the southern question would play a relatively minor role in the gathering's deliberations. The tone was set by the temporary chairman, John M. Thurston of Nebraska, who declared, "The Republican party turns to the new South with wide-open arms. It offers loyal assistance in the development of its agriculture, the opening of its mines and the upbuilding of its manufactories. It proposes to break down the barrier of unpleasant memories with the hope of a new prosperity. The distinctive issue of the present campaign is that of the tariff." Most speakers echoed Thurston, but Douglass was on hand, and in an impromptu address cautioned the delegates not to be "deterred from duty by the cry of 'bloody shirt.'" He reminded them of the past services of blacks in war and peace and called for a platform plank to "remember these black men now stripped of their constitutional right to vote. . . . A government that can give liberty in its constitution ought to have power to protect liberty in its administration." The platform reported by William McKinley's resolutions committee and unanimously adopted gave twice as much space to the tariff issue, although it did mention the suffrage question first and in fairly strong language. It charged that the Democrats owed their current hold on power to "a criminal nullification of the Constitution and laws." The platform upheld free elections and equal representation as "the foundation of our Republican government" and demanded "effective legislation to secure the integrity and purity of elections, which are the fountains of all public authority."[44]

The nominating speeches for presidential candidates said little about the southern question. The principal exceptions were two seconders for Sherman. Foraker told the delegates, "We are just aching up in Ohio to get a man into the Presidential chair, who will have courage enough to vindicate the rights of the Republicans of South Carolina. . . . What is the use of talking about how you are going to reduce the surplus or anything else, until you have first settled it that, when the argument is concluded, the people shall be allowed to express the conclusions they have reached?" John Mercer Langston, the distinguished black leader representing Virginia in the convention, flatly declared, "Seven millions of negroes to-day in this country ask you to nominate John Sherman to the Presidency of the United States. . . . . The name of John Sherman is a wonderful thing in the South to-day. It is a tower of strength to the negro, the poor white man and the Republicans in the South, too."[45]

Southerners at the Chicago convention repaid Sherman's loyalty in the balloting. Half the delegates from Dixie cast their votes for the Ohio senator on the first ballot, and most stuck by him to the end. But, unfortunately for his chances, that bloc constituted nearly two-thirds of his total vote, with virtually all the remainder coming from only two northern states, Ohio and Pennsylvania. Although Sherman's southern strength helped him to lead the first six ballots, he was never able to attract much more support from the North, and on the eighth ballot, the delegates turned to Benjamin Harrison from the doubtful state of Indiana.

In the selection of the vice presidential nominee, some support emerged for choosing a southerner. In offering the name of William O. Bradley of Kentucky, George Denny said his nomination "would fruitfully and correctly answer the heretofore Sphinx riddle of what can be done to break the solid South." But most delegates heeded the strategic advice offered by Mississippi's James R. Chalmers that "the best interests of a suffering people in the South demand that you shall nominate a man from New York to stand by the man from Indiana." New Yorker Levi P. Morton, a former congressman and minister to France, handily took the nomination on the first ballot.[46]

Although their favorite lost the nomination, southern Republicans could take heart from Harrison's record. A deeply religious man who had fought for the Union, he once declared that the nation's commitment to protect the freedmen was "an obligation [as] solemn as a covenant with our God." During the preconvention campaign he had said, "This is a republican government," and "the one overwhelming, towering first question of the day is the restoration of equal suffrage throughout this land." Although in years past he had spoken of the need to divide the white South through appeals on issues such as the tariff,

Benjamin Harrison
(Library of Congress)

he had never been comfortable with subordinating the suffrage issue to economic questions: "Do we hear from New York and her markets of trade that it is a disturbing question and we must not broach it? I beg our friends, and those who thus speak, to recollect that there is no peace, that there can be no security for commerce, no security for the perpetuation of our Government, except by the establishment of justice the country over." Even though Republicans might be powerless to effect an immediate solution, Harrison nonetheless believed that "we should at least lift up our protest; that we should at least denounce the wrong. . . . I believe we greatly underestimate the importance of bringing the issue to the front."[47]

But no sooner had Harrison won the nomination than he began to receive advice, as Cleveland lawyer T. B. McKearney wrote, to "come out square upon the tariff issue" and "let the 'Bloody Shirt' drop." Leaders in control of the party's campaign apparatus concurred. Heading the national committee was Pennsylvania Senator Matthew S. Quay, who had been pushed for the chairmanship by the highly protectionist steel interests of his state and elsewhere. Vice chairman of the committee was James Clarkson, who wrote Harrison that "the tariff issue is the one issue to depend on," especially in the East, where "wage-earners are intensely interested in the tariff & in nothing else." Under these leaders, the national committee and other campaign groups focused almost exclusively on the tariff issue. In large measure, this emphasis grew out of the marathon debates in Congress over the Democrats' tariff-reduction Mills bill passed by the House and alternative protectionist legislation sponsored by Senate Republicans. Press and public alike followed the debates closely, with the result that Clarkson could confidently tell Iowa Senator William B. Allison that thanks to the Mills bill discussion "everybody who is now for Protection and willing to make it a paramount issue, is ready to vote the Republican ticket."[48]

But not all Republican leaders agreed with this emphasis. Chicago Mayor John A. Roche wrote Harrison that the suffrage issue "strikes deeper than the surface and strata of material things, and reaches to the very marrow and life of Republican institutions." Foraker wrote privately, "I believe in a free ballot and a fair count, and my conscience will not allow me to be still about so grave a matter as Southern Democrats have made this question to be." Wisconsin Senator John Spooner complained that the "National Committee has refused to allow one dollar of its funds to be used by the Congressional Committee in distributing literature upon the subject. They think it will deter Democrats, who are likely to come to us on the tariff question, from coming. I think they are mistaken." While the Senate tariff debate dragged on, Spooner drew attention to the southern question by calling for an investigation of the politically motivated murder of Joseph Hoffman in Texas. Hoffman, a Republican county officeholder, had testified in a previous Senate investigation of election fraud and was scheduled to testify again when he was murdered. Just such events as this convinced Spooner that "the real issue in this campaign is the suppression of the ballot, by force and fraud, in the South." The suffrage question, he wrote a friend, "lies at the very foundation of what is put more prominently to the front—the tariff issue. . . . The South, by means of the suppression of the ballot, is ruling this country today, and attempting to force free trade upon it. Their labor there is degraded, and it is to their interest, as they understand it, and it is their desire, to keep it so."[49]

Chandler similarly called attention to the issue by his move for a Senate investigation of the spring election in Louisiana. In a long, detailed speech, he accused the Democrats of a sustained program of fraud and intimidation to carry the state. But, Chandler argued, the misdeeds in Louisiana were simply part of a larger pattern: "No colored citizen votes and has his vote counted in any Southern State where that vote will affect the result of the election."

With this avowed and universal defiance of the fifteenth amendment is the American Republic confronted on the threshold of the momentous Presidential election of 1888. The question thus presented is of more importance than any other now pending or which can be imagined as likely at any time to arise. It is the fundamental question in a republic. Shall all legally qualified voters be allowed to vote as they choose and to have their votes honestly counted? If the answer is to be in the negative, there is no republic. The Government is either that of a despot or of an oligarchy. . . . If the nation will not meet and rightly settle this issue, which is above and beyond all other issues, it cares not for republicanism; it is unworthy of either liberty or prosperity.[50]

Although nearly all Republicans subscribed to Chandler's beliefs, a great many doubted the political utility of such rhetoric during the campaign. Ohio Congressman Benjamin Butterworth urged Harrison not to "say anything about the 'Solid South,' nor use any expression which would tend to cement those together in the battle against us, whom we are desirous of tearing apart." Shortly after his nomination Harrison received similar counsel from New York boss Thomas Platt, who urged him to give "careful consideration" to advice offered by businessman William Henry Wood, a Democrat and Confederate veteran living in New York. Described by Platt as a "valuable acquisition" for the party, Wood believed fervently in protection and claimed that "at least five southern states are ready and willing to join the protection ranks." He advised Harrison to take a campaign tour through the South, adopting the line that "the time has come to let bygones be bygones absolutely and forever, and it is the time to join hands on the only real issue before the country, the protection of American Industries and American labor." In addition, Wood suggested "that you simply ignore entirely the plank in the platform about a free ballot at the South, for by all of the best people of the South this has always been regarded as an unfair charge of the Republican party."[51]

Wood assured Harrison that the South was full of Confederate veterans and their sons ready to vote for him "if the canvass is so conducted that they can do so without doing violence to their own self respect." But Harrison had also to consider his own self-respect and that of his party. He took the proposal seriously enough to invite Wood to visit him in Indianapolis. But in the end, no such meeting occurred, and although Harrison devoted most of his front-porch campaign speeches to the tariff issue, he continued to make reference to the suffrage question. A few weeks after hearing from Wood, he told an audience, "The theory upon which our Government is builded is that every qualified elector shall have an equal influence at the ballot-box with every other." Although

Harrison devoted most of his letter of acceptance to the tariff and other economic issues, he also forthrightly declared, "The right of every qualified elector to cast one free ballot and to have it honestly counted must not be questioned." He promised to use "every constitutional power . . . to make this right secure." "Our colored people," he said, "do not ask special legislation in their interest, but only to be made secure in the common rights of American citizenship."[52]

Although Wood made little headway with Harrison, Wood clung to the notion that the less said about the issue the better. In New York, he appealed to *Tribune* editor Whitelaw Reid to "let the whole Southern question alone." Reid had kept the paper's editorials focused on the tariff issue, but news of renewed bad behavior in the South troubled him. In early September evidence of fraud and intimidation in the Arkansas election surfaced, and Reid forwarded to Harrison a letter from former Congressman Logan Roots, which detailed instances of ballot-box tampering sanctioned by local Democratic officials. In light of this and "several other things," Reid asked Harrison to let him "know, privately, how far you think it is likely to be useful to deal with this Southern question."[53] Harrison replied unequivocally. Discussion of the issue "ought to be *temperate*" and "separated from any war associations." But, he affirmed,

> I feel very strongly upon the question of a free ballot. It is one of the few essential things. I have never failed in any campaign to speak upon it and to insist that the settlement of that question preceded all others in natural order. There would be no tariff question now, if the labor vote of the south had not been suppressed. My opinion has been that this question should be discussed with firmness; that the facts relating to southern election methods should be carefully laid before northern readers; and that the south itself should be asked to consider the question, what the end of all this is to be for it.

As for his own course, Harrison told Reid, "I would not be willing myself to purchase the Presidency by a compact of silence upon this question."[54]

Reid replied that he took "great satisfaction" from Harrison's position, even though it was "in direct opposition to the view which an officer of the [National] Committee expressed to me." The editor promised "to indulge in a little temperate discussion of Arkansas." For the remainder of the campaign, Harrison continued to accentuate the tariff, but, as other Republicans had tried to do, he also sought to connect the two issues. "I believe," he told a campaign audience, "that this great question of a free ballot, so much disturbed by race questions in the South, would be settled this year if the men of the South who believe with us upon the great question of the protection of American industries would throw off old prejudices and vote their convictions upon that question." Should they do so, "the question of a free ballot, so far as it is a Southern question, will be settled forever, for they will have the power to insist that those who believe with them shall vote, and that their votes shall be counted."[55]

In the November balloting, Harrison took New York and Indiana and defeated Cleveland, but he carried none of the former slave states. In the upper South, where the Republicans' tariff arguments held the greatest appeal, Harrison, like Blaine four years earlier, did well. He won more than 49 percent of the vote in both Virginia and West Virginia, losing the former by just a half percent and the latter by just three-tenths of a percent of the total vote cast. In both North Carolina and Maryland, Harrison garnered more than 47 percent of the ballots. But in the states of the lower South, where large black populations would have yielded Republican majorities had the elections been free, Harrison lost heavily. In Alabama, Georgia, Louisiana, and Mississippi, he received less than a third of the votes. In South Carolina, his total was a bare 17 percent of the votes reported. This suppression of the black vote in the South enabled Cleveland to amass a national popular-vote plurality of more than 90,000.

That fraud and intimidation had made Harrison a "minority" president naturally heightened his and his party's outrage at the South's contempt for republican values. But the party did win majorities in both houses of Congress, and in the House of Representatives, Republican inroads in the upper South made the difference in the party's attaining control. Republicans won twenty-five seats in the old slave states, nine more than in the previous Congress, and nearly all came from the upper South. For the first time since 1875, the Republicans would control the presidency, the House, and the Senate. Their congressional majorities were slim, but—potentially, at least—they would have the power at last to do something about the southern question.[56]

Republicanism Defeated
The Lodge Federal Elections Bill

The disparate election results in the South in 1888 presented Benjamin Harrison and his party with no clear signal about how to treat the region once they resumed control of the national government in March 1889. Again, the question was whether to stress the New South notions of the common economic objectives the region shared with the North or to give first priority to a restoration of a free ballot. Harrison's campaign utterances had suggested that he found these strategies not incompatible, but other Republicans were less confident that they could reconcile the two. With majority control for the first time in fifteen years, congressional Republicans joined with Harrison in a valiant attempt to enact legislation that they believed would at last secure the republican project in the South. In the end, the defeat of the Lodge Federal Elections bill, perhaps even more than the Compromise of 1877, spelled the doom of the new Republic.

In the four months before Harrison's inauguration, advice on the issue flooded in. The president-elect refused to declare in advance for any specific action, but he did try to allay white southerners' fears with a public letter denying any "unfriendliness toward the South." Moreover, he said, if southerners "who in their hearts believe with us" on economic questions "would act with us, some other questions that give you local concern would settle themselves."[1]

But many Republicans saw their return to power as a grand opportunity to resume the work of perfecting the republican results of the Civil War, work that had met with increasing resistance while the Democrats had held control in the House of Representatives. Most basically, these Republicans pushed for greater federal government protection for black suffrage. William Chandler wrote the president-elect that the white Democrats' dire warning of "negro supremacy" was a "great bugbear." Indeed, wrote Chandler, "there is no Southern question except the question whether the 15th amendment of the Constitution shall be obeyed." At the least, Chandler advised the appointment of a strong attorney general to ensure the vigorous enforcement of the law.[2] In his heart, Harrison seems to have agreed. A week later, in an emotion-filled appearance before the local GAR post in Indianapolis, the former general told his comrades that a "free ballot, honestly expressed and fairly counted is the main safeguard of our institutions, and its suppression under any circumstances cannot be tolerated."[3]

Yet among white Republicans in the South, doubts had been growing about blacks' ability to meet their obligations as citizens and voters. Many questioned whether they had yet attained the requisite capacity and virtue. From Mississippi, Federal District Judge Robert Hill wrote Harrison that "the colored race in this state, in their present condition are not as a race, capable of governing our public affairs." Tightening the election laws would not improve matters, Hill argued, for long years on the bench had taught him that "it is impossible, through the Courts, to enforce for any considerable time, any law against public opinion." Hill and others urged Harrison to give little patronage recognition to blacks and instead to confer appointments on whites drawn to the Republican Party by its stand on economic issues.[4]

Black Republicans such as Frederick Douglass dismissed white southerners' admonitions against political domination by "ignorant negroes" as the "veriest affectation." The issue of black suffrage, Douglass declared, "affects the fundamental principles that underlie the whole system of our republican government." Harrison should take whatever action necessary to secure "a genuine republican government in the south." Former minister to Haiti John Mercer Langston led a delegation of blacks to Indianapolis to implore the president-elect to appoint an attorney general who would make the Justice Department "what it was meant to be, the bulwark of the equal rights of free citizens." The question, the group said, was "not only of vital concernment to us as colored voters of the South, now practically disfranchised, but of profoundest and most substantial concernment as regards free institutions themselves in our Republic."[5]

Among the party's leaders in Congress, blacks still looked to John Sherman as one of their principal champions. In the District of Columbia they formed the John Sherman Republican League, which in late December presented him with an address of thanks for his past labors in their behalf. In response, Sherman counseled blacks to be patient and to cultivate the true virtues of republican citizenship:

> It is for you to show that you have caught the spirit and will observe the obligations of liberty. It is the first duty of your people to avail themselves of all opportunities for education and improvement, to seek to acquire property by industry and economy, and to enjoin respect for the property of others. You must yourselves win your own way by a strict observance of moral and legal obligations. You must value your rights as citizens above all money or price, and treat as the highest insult all attempts to influence your vote. Like all other citizens your standing and influence will depend upon your virtue, morality, integrity, and industry.

But Sherman also told the black Republican League, "We must have fair elections in this country or our institutions will become a mockery and a sham." In early January 1889 he introduced legislation for federal control of congressional elections, "containing all such safeguards as will secure to every legal voter one honest vote and no more, and to have that vote counted." Although his bill had no chance of passage in the waning days of the Fiftieth Congress, Sherman hoped to set the stage for such legislation once the GOP took power. As Republicans prepared for the transition, many agreed that the time was soon at hand when they could do something about the South.[6]

Between Harrison's election and inauguration, many in the country saw his appointments to the cabinet and subordinate positions as a marker of his southern policy. Former Alabama Senator Willard Warner thought Harrison should appoint two southerners to his cabinet, one from the border states and the other from the Gulf region, but both "fully convinced that Republican supremacy in the south can be secured only by a division of the white vote and not by building on the Negro alone." Taking a harder line, Augustus Willson advocated a cabinet slot for his fellow Kentuckian, Stalwart William Bradley. "There is war now and greater war ever smouldering," Willson told Harrison, and the new administration must take action to end "oppression, denial of rights, crime and murder [in the] South." Blacks and their white Republican champions emphasized the need for a strong attorney general. As Supreme Court Justice John Marshall Harlan told Harrison, "Much that you will aim to do in order to protect the elective franchise against fraud and violence will depend upon the wisdom & efficiency which characterizes the Department of Justice."[7]

In the end, the closest Harrison came to tapping a southerner was his selection of his old college friend, Missourian John W. Noble, to be secretary of the interior. Noble, a native of Ohio, had commanded an Iowa regiment in the war and had practiced law in Missouri since 1867. He hardly met the expectations of southerners who wanted one of their own in the cabinet. For attorney general, Harrison appointed his law partner and longtime friend, William H. H. Miller. Like Miller, all other members of the cabinet were northerners.[8]

In his inaugural address, Harrison disavowed any intention to pursue "a special Executive policy for any section of our country," but he nonetheless registered his continued support both for the New South notions of economic development and for further protection of the right to vote. He urged southerners interested in economic advance not to let "the prejudices and paralysis of slavery continue to hang upon the skirts of progress." Entrepreneurs in mining and manufacturing should see "that the free ballot of the workingman, without distinction of race, is needed for their defense as well as for his own." White southerners who espoused Henry Clay's tariff ideas should "make the black man their efficient and safe ally, not only in establishing correct principles in our national administration, but in preserving for their local communities the benefits of social order and economical and honest government." But if the promptings of interest failed to move white southerners to act justly, Harrison declared that the "freedom of the ballot is a condition of our national life, and no power vested in Congress or in the Executive to secure or perpetuate it should remain unused upon occasion." He condemned those who "regard the ballot box as a juggler's hat," and argued that if the states refused to defend the right to vote, Congress should act. "The people of all the Congressional districts have an equal interest that the election in each shall truly express the views and wishes of a majority of the qualified electors residing within it. The results of such elections are not local, and the insistence of electors residing in other districts that they shall be pure and free does not savor at all of impertinence." In short, republicanism was indivisible.[9]

Although Harrison's failure to appoint a southerner as attorney general disappointed some Republicans from the region, he nonetheless expected the Justice Department to act to protect the ballot. In a draft of his inaugural address he had stated his intention "to use every power vested in me by the Constitution to enforce the laws, to bring every violator of them to trial and punishment, and to secure every citizen in the free exercise & enjoyment of all his civil and political rights." The new attorney general agreed. Miller lost little time in ordering federal district attorneys in several southern states to initiate prosecutions of alleged violations of the election laws during the election of 1888. As in the past, however, such efforts yielded few convictions. Moreover, whereas in previous administrations trial juries had frustrated prosecutors' work, now in many instances grand juries refused to hand down indictments.

Miller's most vigorous effort came in response to events in the northern district of Florida, where the U.S. attorney reported "flagrant" violations of the election laws during the 1888 election. Local armed groups resisted the serving of arrest warrants and the calling of witnesses, and at least one potential witness and a deputy marshal were murdered. As the situation in the state worsened, Harrison ordered Miller to "employ such civil posse as may seem adequate to discourage resistance or to overcome it." Declaring that "this condition of things cannot be longer tolerated," Harrison threatened to invoke "every resource lodged with the Executive by the Constitution and the laws," and he took the unusual step of giving his order to the press. At the same time Justice Department officials drafted a presidential proclamation preparatory to dispatching federal troops to the region. Harrison did not issue the proclamation, in part because a newly appointed marshal proved more successful in making arrests. Ultimately, however, the Florida prosecutions resulted in only three convictions.[10]

The frustrations that Harrison and Miller felt in these and other election cases underscored their belief that further federal legislation was needed to render the ballot truly secure. Harrison called for congressional action in his first annual message, but he also advocated federal aid for education to render the African Americans of the South more capable of a judicious exercise of the franchise. In making this latter recommendation, he conceded that southern states had made some progress in educating the former slaves and their descendants, but, he said, "a great work remains to be done, and I think the General Government should lend its aid." At stake was the responsible participation of these new citizens in the affairs of the Republic: "No one will deny that it is of the gravest national concern that those who hold the ultimate control of all public affairs should have the necessary intelligence wisely to direct and determine them."[11]

The day after the president's message, Senator Henry W. Blair of New Hampshire was ready to reintroduce his bill for federal government support of the nation's common schools. During the winter of 1888 the Senate had passed the bill for a third time, but again it had died in House committee. Now Blair once more asked for an appropriation of $77 million spread over eight years, distributed among the states in proportion to the illiteracy in their population. This time, however, signs pointed to trouble. The managing editor of the Cleveland *Leader* reported to Sherman "a disposition on the part of a number of Republican newspapers to change front in regard to the Blair Education Bill." Before long, Blair complained to Harrison of "a strong & very dangerous effort among Republican Senators including some who have hitherto given their support to the measure to secure its defeat."[12] In response, Blair engaged in what amounted to a filibuster in its favor, speaking almost every day for nearly three weeks. He marshaled masses of statistical information and endorsements in the measure's behalf, and he also defended it on the score of republicanism. A republic, where the people are sovereign, he maintained, "requires on the part of each individual man the possession of the same virtues and intelligence which are the primary qualities in the good king."

> To ordain and establish a republican form of government, then, is to ordain and establish that those things shall be provided without which republican government can not be. It follows that in the very act of ordaining and establishing the Constitution to be forever[,] the fathers ordained and established that the means of perpetuating virtue and intelligence should be provided. . . . Without education, the means through which intelligence is obtained, there can be no republican form of government.[13]

Few if any Republican senators would disagree with Blair about the value of an enlightened electorate, but many questioned whether the South now needed aid from the federal government. John C. Spooner of Wisconsin argued that the South was "abundantly able to educate her own children." Citing the republican virtues of "thrift, integrity, and work," he argued that no people "should be helped out of the public Treasury who can help themselves." Similarly, Kansas Senator Preston Plumb asserted that it was wrong "to tax the willing and patriotic for the benefit of the slothful."[14]

Defenders of the bill denied that the South was now prosperous enough to give adequate support to education. "Would it do," asked William M. Evarts, "for a benevolent bystander to refuse to cast a rope to a struggling and drowning man on the ground that it would enfeeble his self-help?" Nor, said William Chandler, should constitutional arguments about violating states rights or restrictions on expenditures have any bearing. After 100 years of "the practical adaptation of the Constitution," the federal government could spend money "for any purpose deemed by Congress useful for the public welfare." Most important, Chandler argued, education offered "the only remedy for the difficulties of what is called the Southern question. . . . With education and with increased religious sentiment at the South, developed by education, will come greater forbearance towards each other on the part of the two races. The great lesson, as it seems to me, for the Southern whites to learn in dealing with the black man is forbearance and justice."[15]

The measure won support from many groups around the country, including the Women's Christian Temperance Union, whose Ohio superintendent wrote Sherman that "*Illiteracy* is a dangerous foe under our form of government." Both the Union League and the Republican Club of New York petitioned Congress in favor of the measure. Although some blacks bridled at its acquiescence in segregated schools, in general they applauded the bill, and the national convention of the Afro-American League formally endorsed federal aid to education. Indeed, as the president of the black Boston Republican League wrote to Sherman, he and other African Americans were "very much aroused as to the cold manner in which the Republican representatives and senators are acting towards this very important matter."[16]

That "cold manner" on the part of some Republicans reflected resistance among segments of public opinion. Opposition was spearheaded by *New York Evening Post* writer Edward Clark, who gathered his scathing editorials in a pamphlet entitled *A Bill to Promote Mendicancy*. The *Chicago Tribune* charged that the "pestiferous measure" would thwart "all effort to develop the school system" of the South by destroying the "quality of self-reliance." Catholic leaders denounced it as a threat to parochial schools. Moreover, ardent black rights advocate Albion W. Tourgée argued that Blair's bill would permit southern state governments to syphon federal aid intended for black illiterates to white schools. In the end, most Republican senators stuck by the bill, but enough Republicans and former southern Democratic supporters defected to defeat it. The bill failed in the Senate by a vote of 31 to 37. Counting pairs as well as actual votes cast, Republicans favored the measure by a margin of 27 to 18, and Democrats opposed it, 12 in favor to 25 against.[17]

The defeat greatly discouraged Blair and his allies. Evarts privately called the loss "a great disaster in our politics and in the condition of the country." Blacks leveled much of their criticism against John Sherman, who had long stood as a champion of their cause but now voted against the Blair bill. When the editor of the Cleveland *Gazette* asked for an explanation, Sherman replied that conditions had changed since he had voted for the bill in 1888 and that the "South is now prosperous and is making fair and reasonable efforts to educate its illiterates."[18]

Many blacks found this answer evasive at best, but some others found it reasonable and saw the issue of southern elections as a more important concern. In the course of the debate, Sherman had in fact said little about the Blair bill itself but instead asserted that it was more important "to secure to every man in the United States entitled to vote one free, honest vote, and to have that vote counted." As John Spooner put it, with the "vicious" Blair bill out of the way, "the southern debate will open in earnest."[19]

The Republican victory in both the presidential and congressional elections of 1888 gave Spooner and other party leaders their first real opportunity in more than a decade to carry on that fight by toughening national election legislation. Although Republicans were unable to unite behind an education bill in the Fifty-first Congress, most were convinced of the need to take action against the continued violation of the free ballot in the South. Before Harrison took office, the movement received a shocking impetus in January with the cold-blooded murder in Arkansas of John M. Clayton, a Republican candidate for Congress defeated in November. Clayton was shot while investigating the disappearance of a ballot box whose theft had cost him the election.[20] According to the *New York Tribune,* the question concerned "not merely this latest murder, not merely other murders or political crimes, but the entire system of fraud and crime by which free elections at the South have been prevented." As William Chandler put it, "if a country nominally a republic is not really so, wrongs once established must be perpetually endured or thrown off by a revolution." In his inaugural address, Harrison welcomed the heightened "general interest now being manifested in the reform of our election laws."[21]

No action could occur, however, until the first session of the Fifty-first Congress convened in December 1889. In the interim, party spokesmen continued to denounce the deplorable state of affairs in the South. In May Chandler published a letter to the editor of the *New York Tribune* that cataloged a number of murders and other "disgraceful incidents." Many Republicans believed that, as one of Chandler's informants wrote John Sherman, "there is a rapidly growing revolutionary tendency in the South, tending towards a guerrilla system of warfare." In late summer the *Tribune* cited "an epidemic of outrages against negroes . . . sweeping across the South," and no less a figure than General William T. Sherman told a Cincinnati audience that "these negroes must have the rights which the Constitution gives them, . . . and the war won't be over until that is done." The general's brother John warned that the crisis "threatens to subvert republican government and justifies the most extreme measures of resistance."[22]

Sherman's alarm seemed justified by events in Virginia, where former Readjuster governor William Mahone ran for his old office on the Republican ticket in 1889. Although Virginia Republicans suffered from internal dissension, they also confronted a desperate foe in the Democrats. Indiana Congressman Joseph B. Cheadle, touring the state for Mahone, found that at several places Democratic officials banned Republican meetings and speeches. "It takes courage to be a Rep[ublican] here," Cheadle reported to the White House. After Mahone's loss, Cheadle charged that Democrats had deleted 20,000 Republican names from the registration lists and had barred from voting or had refused to count the votes of another 25,000. "The National Government undertakes to guarantee a republican form of Government to every state," Cheadle wrote Harrison. "There is not even a semblance of such a Government in Virginia." Cheadle urged the president to use "brave and bold words" in his upcoming annual message to alert Congress and the country "to the imperative duty of securing to the humblest citizen his right of suffrage."[23]

"The Serious Problem of To-Day." Uncle Sam: "Wake up gentlemen! Here is a vital issue which must be settled, or the Republican party will be held responsible!" *Judge,* October 5, 1889.

Harrison's political adviser Louis T. Michener sent similar pleas after a meeting with black leaders in Indianapolis. The men complained that African Americans had received inadequate patronage recognition from Harrison. "But what they want especially," Michener wrote the White House "is some action upon the part of this administration which will give to the colored people of the South, some protection in the exercise of their rights as citizens. . . . They told me what had been recited to them by the preachers who recently came here from the South, and my blood boiled while I listened." Michener conceded that new voting rights legislation might cause bloodshed, "but better bloodshed than slavery and outrages and murder for political reasons in this civilized nation." Like Cheadle, he urged Harrison to make an "earnest recommendation" in his message and thereby "touch the conscience of every good man regardless of party."[24]

Harrison needed little prodding. When Congress convened in December 1889, he urged it to use "its well-defined constitutional powers" to "secure to all our people a free exercise of the right of suffrage." Blacks, he observed, "have their representatives in the national cemeteries, where a grateful Government has gathered the ashes of those who died in its defense." In civil life, African Americans were "now the toilers of their communities, making their full contribution to the widening streams of prosperity." And yet those same communities

Henry Cabot Lodge
(Library of Congress)

barred blacks from exercising their political rights. "When and under what conditions is the black man to have a free ballot?" the president demanded. "When is that equality of influence which our form of government was intended to secure to the electors to be restored? This generation should courageously face these grave questions, and not leave them as a heritage of woe to the next."[25]

As Harrison's plea suggested, Republicans believed their party and the country stood at a critical moment. Most understood that they must either seize the opportunity to complete their reinvention of the Republic or reconcile themselves to a polity not truly republican. Among the leaders of reform in the House was Henry Cabot Lodge of Massachusetts, scion of an old abolitionist family, who as a boy had imbibed a sense of justice from Charles Sumner, a frequent visitor at his house. Lodge eagerly sought the chairmanship of a special committee on federal elections because, he wrote to his mother, it "gives me control of our greatest measure, the Election law." Kansas Congressman Harrison Kelley, an equally ardent champion of blacks' rights, told Albion Tourgée, "If the Republican party allows this opportunity to pass without effecting a remedy, I fear its opportunity will not return." Connecticut Senator Joseph R.

Hawley wrote privately that the elections issue was "a matter that civilization, Christianity, and our pledges for the last twenty-five years will not allow us to abandon."[26] Assistant Postmaster General James S. Clarkson, who during the 1888 campaign had favored emphasis on the tariff over the southern question, now returned to the view that Congress must act to purify elections. The son of abolitionists who had kept a station on the Underground Railroad, Clarkson confessed to Michener,

> If we do not protect the Republicans of the South at the polls and in their homes we shall show ourselves too cowardly as a party to be worthy to live. . . . I believe so firmly in the ruling of God in the affairs of men that I think this opportunity has been given us to prove whether the party has the right and the courage to live, the courage to defend its own, and to stand by the weak and lowly, and by Republican principles. If we do not fulfill the expectation of the Divine Power I think we shall be cast down and thrown out, as we ought to be, and pass away as a party to have the contempt of the future. There is no other real question in present politics but this.[27]

From the South, party leaders heard a mixed message. Former Senator Powell Clayton, brother of the murdered John Clayton, wrote George Hoar that the "feeling here in Arkansas among Republicans is that if Congress fails to make good the pledges of the party in this respect, that we might as well disband our organization in the South at once and that the party will not deserve National success in that case." "The question is simple," former Tennessee Congressman William Moore told Sherman. "Negroes are citizens or they are not. If they can be called into the country's service, they *must* be protected by the government claiming such service." But Cyrus Drew of New Orleans warned that new elections legislation would serve only "as an excuse for lawless villains to assassinate citizens." Atlanta lawyer L. J. Gartrell, who had served in Congress with Sherman in the 1850s, predicted that "the result will be very disastrous to the best interests of the whole country, I mean in retarding the good will, harmony, and reciprocity of commerce now existing between the sections." Sherman appreciated "the importance of maintaining and encouraging the good will, harmony and reciprocity now existing between the North and the South," but, he told Gartrell, one could not ignore that "more than a million of legal voters are substantially disfranchised by the Democratic party where their votes would change the result. . . . Before the South can complain of an injustice and wrong they ought to do what is just and right."[28]

A flood of election disputes at the beginning of the Fifty-first Congress underscored the urgency of the problem. Since 1863 the House of Representatives had been forced to decide more than 200 contested elections. The new House confronted eighteen such disputes, all but one from the South or Border states. In the words of one Republican elections committee member, "No fair man can sit in Committee as I have done and hear the testimony and arguments in seventeen contested cases without becoming thoroughly *convinced* of the absolute lawlessness in elections in a large portion of the South." The Republican majority ultimately ejected eleven southern Democrats. These investigations fed the Republicans' drive for election reform and spurred the Democrats to resist it at all costs.[29]

Elections to the House were the focus of a host of reform bills Republicans sponsored at the outset of the session. These elections most clearly fell within Congress's purview to regulate. Sherman favored having the federal government take over completely the management of congressional elections in every district in the country and conduct them "with every safeguard and at the expense of the United States."[30] But many Republicans considered this approach too expensive, especially since the reform was needed in only a portion of the 325 districts nationwide.[31]

In the House, Lodge proposed a bill that would have federal officials conduct registration and elections only in districts where 500 residents petitioned for such intervention. This approach would be less costly than universal control, but some from the more radical wing of the party considered it inadequate. Albion W. Tourgée told Lodge's committee that in the South "it would unquestionably be a perilous thing for voters to petition" for federal control. As a result, the law would be invoked far more often in the North than in the South where federal intervention was needed. Tourgée drafted an alternative bill, introduced by Harrison Kelley, which mandated federal control of registration and voting in congressional elections throughout the country and prescribed stiff penalties for interference with individuals' right to vote or with candidates' or parties' right to electioneer. "I think," Tourgée wrote Lodge, "the government should give the citizen the best known weapons for achieving the most difficult task civilization has imposed—government by the people."[32]

President Harrison agreed with that goal, but like others, he was skeptical about a complete absorption of congressional elections by the federal government. Although he had no doubt that Congress had every constitutional right and power to take such a drastic step, the president thought that a strengthening of existing laws regarding federal supervision of elections would produce "better results" than absolute control. In the Senate, several Republicans agreed and called for augmentation of the enforcement legislation of the early 1870s. The party eventually adopted this approach.[33]

What came to be known as the Lodge Federal Elections bill was the work of many hands. Republicans labored to find a formula that would effect real reform in the South in a bill that had a chance to pass. Their painstaking effort testified to their sincerity and seriousness of purpose. Lodge's special House committee deliberated for several weeks and in mid–March 1890 reported his bill for out-right federal control. The day after Harrison's message in early December, John Spooner introduced two bills in the Senate. The first embodied the supervisory principle, outlining procedures for the selection of federal supervisors for con-gressional elections in districts where they were requested. Spooner's second bill outlawed fraudulent voting and other crimes against the franchise, whether committed by local election officials or other individuals.

These and other proposals went to the Senate's Committee on Privileges and Elections chaired by George F. Hoar. Hoar, who had originally favored Sherman's approach to federal control of elections, now worked closely with Spooner and Chandler to formulate a new measure, taking Spooner's first bill as a starting point. Their labors drew heavily on the advice of John I. Davenport, who had served for two decades as chief federal supervisor of elections in New York City. In late April, Hoar reported a bill that built on Spooner's, elaborat-ing the procedures for selecting election supervisors, raising their number from two to three per precinct, and greatly expanding their powers and duties. Most important, Hoar's bill called for a federal board of canvassers, appointed by the federal circuit judge in each state and empowered to declare congressional elec-tion winners according to the supervisors' returns. The provision for a canvass-ing board mirrored a similar stipulation in Sherman's bill.[34]

Hoar's bill did not win universal approval among Republicans. Tourgée la-beled it "unjust, evasive, insufficient, irritating and unmanly." A supervisory law, he told Harrison, "is only repeating the worst folly of Reconstruction legis-lation, making a show of force with no force behind it." House Speaker Thomas Reed told a Pittsburgh audience that "the only wise course is to take into Federal hands the Federal elections," to "cut loose from the State elections, do our own registration, our own counting and our own certification." But the likelihood of passing such a measure was slim. Chandler, whose bona fides as a supporter of blacks' rights were unquestioned, reminded Reed that the existing supervisors law had worked well in New York. Hoar's bill, "whatever may be its faults, has this merit:—that it provides for the extension of an existing system which has been tried and tested, and therefore is less likely to have defects developed when put in operation than any newly-devised law." Moreover, Chandler added, a su-pervisors bill "has the practical merit of being the method upon which we are most likely to secure an agreement of Republicans so as to secure its passage." Reed was nothing if not pragmatic, and soon wrote Tourgée, "I am not at all sure that we can get through such an election law as you and I desire."[35]

Lodge and other representatives believed that any bill dealing with House

George F. Hoar
(Library of Congress)

elections should originate in their chamber. Hoar conceded the point, and two weeks later, Jonathan Rowell, a member of Lodge's committee from Illinois, offered a bill that largely duplicated that of the Massachusetts senator. In early June the Republican caucus, under the commanding hand of Reed, accepted the basic thrust of this measure and instructed Lodge's committee to prepare a composite bill that would embody the supervisory principle and also throw additional safeguards around the ballot. After "toiling all day & every day with might and main to get my committee in line," Lodge reported the new bill on June 14. Borrowing heavily from the Hoar/Rowell verbiage, this bill was more than seventy pages long. It went into minute detail regarding the supervisors' duties and also incorporated most of the criminal offenses set forth in Spooner's second bill in December. Although it later underwent further refinement, this bill, ultimately bearing the number HR 11045, was what contemporaries and later historians labeled the Lodge bill.[36]

Previous statutes had called for federal judges, upon petition by a small number of citizens, to appoint supervisors in towns or cities of more than 20,000 population. The new bill would extend the procedure to smaller jurisdictions as well. The supervisors would observe all phases of registration, voting, and counting in congressional elections. They would report any irregularities and make their own return of vote totals in addition to the tally made by state officials. As Hoar's bill had done, HR 11045 called for a federal board of canvassers. Moreover, in its final House version, the bill stipulated that if the canvassers' decision were challenged, a federal judge would determine and certify the winner.[37]

The bill would reaffirm the president's existing power to use the military to uphold the law, but it was unlikely that any president would take the politically suicidal step of sending troops at election time. Indeed, despite their rhetoric about a return to bayonet rule, southern Democrats were most disturbed by the prospect of losing the power of certification in congressional elections to federal canvassers or a judge appointed by a Republican president. This was the real heart of the bill, which threatened to work a fundamental reordering of power. As Spooner observed, this provision would deprive "the partisan State Governors in the South of the power, which they have heretofore abused, of issuing certificates of election. This feature of the bill is dreaded and hated, and will be bitterly fought, by the southern Democracy."[38]

Spooner was right; debate was passionate. Republicans' sense of urgency intensified with unsettling reports from Mississippi, where intimidation in the recent state election had forced the withdrawal of the Republican ticket. Early in the session, Kansas Senator John J. Ingalls quoted at length from the gubernatorial nominee's statement, which declared that because of "nameless killing on creek and bayou, on highway and byway. . . . we dare no longer carry our battered and blood-stained Republican flag." "This," said Ingalls, "I consider as one of the most tragic utterances that ever occurred in political history."[39]

Equally provoking was the undisguised and defiant racism exhibited by southern congressional Democrats. According to South Carolina's George Tillman, "Nearly every decent white man in South Carolina is a Democrat and will remain so till you cease trying to put white men under negroes." As Tillman's colleague John Hemphill put it, whites would not again submit to being "over-ridden and down-trodden by a race whom God never intended should rule over us." Speaking of his own state, Hemphill declared that "the honest and intelligent people must either rule it or we must leave it; and . . . I swear we will not leave it." "That gentlemen's speech," retorted Republican David Henderson of Iowa, "was a declaration to the people of the country that the black citizens of South Carolina should not exercise the rights guarantied them by the Constitution of the United States. Who wants more proof?"[40]

Lodge led off the speaking on the Republican side. He had already begun the battle for public opinion in an article in *Frank Leslie's* which declared that "if anything is wrong with our elections the very life of the Republic is in peril."

In the House, Lodge argued at length the bill's constitutionality based on Article One's directive that Congress may "make or alter" regulations made by states regarding the "times, places, and manner of holding elections for Senators and Representatives." True to his reputation as a scholar in politics, Lodge quoted from James Madison's notes of the Constitutional Convention, George Ticknor Curtis's *Constitutional History of the United States,* and the Supreme Court decisions in *Ex parte Siebold* and *Ex parte Yarbrough.* "If," said Lodge, "citizens of the United States entitled to vote for Representatives in Congress are deprived of their rights, it is the duty of Congress to see that they are protected." Other Republicans also cited the court cases, and some referred as well to the *Federalist* Number Fifty-nine, in which Alexander Hamilton had argued that the power to regulate congressional elections was "reserved to the National Government, so that it may not be abused [by the states], and thus hazard the safety and permanence of the Union." It was clear, said Marriott Brosius, that Congress could make or change regulations "to any extent necessary to the full protection of the voter and the complete defense of the existence of the Government."[41]

Lodge used his opening remarks to reiterate what had become a staple in Republican thinking on the elections issue: suppression of the votes of blacks and other Republicans in the South gave the southern Democrats disproportionate influence in Congress and the electoral college. He and others presented tables of statistics to demonstrate that southern members represented far fewer voters than did northern members from districts of comparable population. Moreover, said Lodge, the imbalance gave southerners lopsided representation and leverage on committees. "The State of Alabama," said Joseph H. Sweney of Iowa, "has no right to send a Representative to this Chamber with twelve or fifteen thousand votes back of him while the State of Iowa requires thirty-six thousand for every one upon this floor. It is a fraud upon their rights. . . . The issue here involved is the perpetuation of self-government among men, government under Magna Charta, Declaration of Independence, and Constitution."[42]

The question of race permeated the debate. "The negro," said Lodge, "is not thrust out from his rights merely because he is ignorant and unfit to use them, as is constantly charged, but because his skin is black. It is this distinction which gives the lie to every principle of American liberty that is at the bottom of the difficulty and of the problem which we all deplore." In Lodge's view, "The Government which made the black man a citizen of the United States is bound to protect him in his rights as a citizen of the United States, and it is a cowardly Government if it does not do it!" If ignorance were the real issue, said Robert Kennedy of Ohio, then southern conservatives "should at the same time disfranchise black ignorance and white ignorance alike." They did not do so, because, Edmund Waddill of Virginia argued, the whole notion of inferiority was nothing more than a political ruse used "by the Democratic party to set itself up as the white man's party, and with that as its shibboleth, and with practically no other issue, to whip everything and everybody into line."

Wisconsin's Nils P. Haugen argued that the white southern oligarchy raised the "cry of 'negro supremacy'" simply as a means to further the oppression of the lower classes generally: "It is a hollow pretense, used by the self-styled and self-appointed leaders to detract attention from their insidious attacks upon the rights of the common people to control and manage their own affairs." Daniel Kerr of Iowa concurred in this class analysis, noting that "ignorance in the voter is much less dangerous to society than organized and educated selfishness. Selfishness combined for oppression, as to retain class supremacy, has been the great foe of human freedom and human progress in all ages."[43]

For many Republicans, the time was long past when whites should have begun thinking of the former slaves in a new light. As Jonathan Rowell put it, "These men, lately bondmen, ignorant, semi-civilized, unaccustomed to self-reliance and independent judgment, ought not to be judged by their mistakes, but rather by their successes under adverse circumstances." "Fair play is the foundation stone of our citizenship," said David Henderson. "Why are we to ignore the rights of a man because God made him black? . . . The members of the colored race have the same instincts, the same great impulses as ourselves. . . . Let us try a little justice by our fellow-man and see how it will work." And, as Henry L. Morey of Ohio argued, far more was at stake. "The preservation of the rights of the strong and powerful can be permanently maintained only by a jealous protection of the rights of the ignorant and weak. There can be no safety for the Republic and republican institutions when the rights of the people can be disregarded and trampled upon under a plea of race inferiority."[44]

Nearly every Republican defender of the measure emphasized this theme of republicanism. Daniel Kerr cited the definition of republicanism offered by the Founders, noting that James Madison had argued in the Thirty-ninth *Federalist* that republican government must "be derived from the great mass of society, not from a portion or a favored class." Central to republicanism, Robert Kennedy argued, was the notion of government by consent, for as "one of the parties to the compact," each citizen in a republic "is entitled to be heard in establishing its terms and formulating its requirements." Equally important, Kennedy maintained, was the principle of majority rule. "Any attempt to subvert the will of the majority, in whatever manner made, is an attempt to overthrow and defeat the will of the people, and in a measure to destroy the very foundations of our republican institutions." With the Lodge bill, said Haugen, Republicans were "legislating in the line of popular government" and were, therefore, the real " 'Democrats' in the true sense of that much-abused word."[45]

For the Republic to endure, Republicans argued, the right to vote must be secure. "Fraud upon the ballot-box is a species of treason," said Charles A. Hill of Illinois. "Wink at it, apologize for it, tolerate it, let it spread, and sooner or later this great Republic will totter to its fall." Republicans frequently invoked organic metaphors in upholding the republican principle. "A free ballot and a fair count are the very breath of the nation's life," said Marriott Brosius. "The ballot is the heart of the Republic," insisted Joseph D. Taylor of Ohio; "stab it and the Republic will die. The election machinery is the life blood of the nation, and if it is poisoned our national existence must come to an end." Switching the metaphor, Taylor warned that unless the president, "who holds in his grasp the pilot-wheel of this great Government," and Congress, "which forges the statutory chains which bind 65,000,000 of freemen," were "chosen fairly and justly, . . . the Republic will go down amid the fires of anarchy and the bloodshed of communism." Taylor's colleague Elihu Williams similarly cautioned that if the people lost confidence "in the ballot-box as an expression of the will of the majority, . . . you sow the seeds of discord that will ripen and grow into the harvest of revolution and anarchy."

Four years after the Haymarket Affair, the specter of "revolution" retained great rhetorical potence, and some Democrats charged that Republicans aimed to revolutionize the government with the Lodge bill. Frederic Greenhalge of Massachusetts turned the argument around, however, noting that the American people had long been "accustomed to associate with the term 'revolution' the idea of independence, of political equality, of civil liberty. If this measure is revolutionary it is in the high sense in which the Declaration of Independence is revolutionary, in the same sense in which the Virginia Bill of Rights is revolutionary, in the same sense in which the Constitution itself is revolutionary." To label the bill revolutionary, Greenhalge argued, was "a contradiction in terms," for "its whole aim and purpose is to conserve, to defend, to save the Constitution, and to give equal political rights to every one of the people of the United States." William E. Mason of Illinois asserted that the "use of the power of citizenship makes a better citizen" and warned that when he loses his "citizen's right . . . he becomes an enemy to the law, disheartened, discouraged, and in his heart an alien to our institutions."[46]

House Democrats solidly opposed the Lodge bill and were joined by a handful of Republicans. Hamilton Ewart of North Carolina claimed that elections in his state were fair and that southern Republicans generally were "not demanding the passage of this measure." Instead of new laws, Ewart advocated a stricter enforcement of existing legislation by federal district attorneys with "nerve and backbone enough to do their whole duty." Ewart noted that southern blacks were profoundly disappointed by the Republican Senate's "cowardly" abandonment of the Blair bill, which belied Republicans' arguments that white Democrats kept blacks in ignorance for political reasons. Any new elections legislation, he argued, would only result in solidifying the white vote, whereas economic issues had added to the southern Republican delegation in Congress. "We will continue to increase our numbers if you will let us alone." In a similar vein, Hamilton Coleman of Louisiana said that far more than any new elections bill, "every furnace and every rolling-mill and every factory established in the South makes friends and recruits for the Republican party of protection."[47]

But the vast majority of House Republicans rejected such arguments. As the debate neared its end, William McKinley, the avatar of the Republican protection policy, implored his colleagues to do "our supreme duty to enforce the Constitution and laws of the United States and 'dare to be strong for the weak.'" "God puts no nation in supreme place which will not do supreme duty," he insisted. "He will not long prosper that nation which will not protect and defend its weakest citizens." A few moments after McKinley spoke, on July 2, 1890, the House voted to pass the bill, 155 to 149. Not a single Democrat voted in its favor, and counting pairs, only three Republicans opposed it. It was a triumphant moment. "It is a *satisfaction*," wrote Harrison Kelley, "to be an actor, though ever so humble, in the drama of liberty." A grateful Chandler praised Lodge for his "labor, energy, courage, and success."[48]

Attention now turned to the Senate. Hoping for a speedy consideration by the upper chamber, Lodge told Chandler that the Republican Senators would "make a terrible mistake if they fail to act now." But even though the idea of new elections legislation enjoyed wide support in the Senate, not all Republicans were happy with the version that passed the House. Even so staunch a supporter of free elections as Spooner considered it "too cumbersome and rasping." Hence, he and Hoar set about revising "the Lodge bill to remove from it the objectionable features, and generally to improve it." Maine's Eugene Hale confidently reported to Chandler, who was ill and absent from Washington, that Hoar's committee was "going to report a good election bill that we can all vote for when the time comes."[49]

While this labor proceeded, public interest and debate mounted. From Arkansas, the editor of the Pine Bluff *Echo* reported to Sherman, "All classes of Republicans in the South, especially colored, are waiting with bated breath. . . . If some such law is not passed it would be better for the colored people and the Republican party that they be legally disfranchised." Ohio's secretary of state, Daniel Ryan, told the senator that "the one subject over which the most Re-

John C. Spooner
(Library of Congress)

publican enthusiasm can be aroused right now, is the Federal Election Law. Its importance appeals to every Republican."[50]

But in both sections Republican support for the measure was far from universal. From Birmingham, Alabama, a petition by a mass meeting of protectionist Republicans warned senators that the bill would "destroy the better element" in the state's Republican Party. Passage of the measure would "lead to a race conflict, and thus imperil our present grand industrial system which is just starting on its career of unequaled progress." Cincinnati lawyer Warner Bateman reminded Sherman that the party had "carried a number of the districts in the South in 1888 on economic issues, and [by] putting out of sight to a considerable degree the question of negro suffrage." Pushing the election bill now would only bring "exasperation and trouble without profit." Another constituent warned the senator that the bill would "hurt trade for us and all other people in the North and injure our credits [in the] South."[51] Business and financial journals echoed these dire predictions. "It is time," said the *American Grocer*, "for the business men of the United States to protest in the name of the country's welfare against such legislation as the Force bill, and that they will protest earnestly and vigorously, the leaders of the Republican party will find out in 1892, if they do not before."[52]

But leading party journals defended the bill. Voicing the fundamental republican tenet at stake, the *Chicago Tribune* declared, "Where fraud prevails at the polls the country is not to be ruled by the people. . . . The governing power would not be vested in the majority of the lawful voters, but in a criminal class of ballot corrupters." The *New York Tribune* urged Republican legislators not to fall for the specious notion that passage of the bill would somehow damage commercial relations between the sections: "As rebellion blundered in 1861, imagining that Northern men loved the Almighty Dollar too much to possess a grain of patriotism, so the vote-stealing party mistakes now if it expects Northern men of enterprise to uphold crime, lest their profits should be endangered." The paper reprinted election-reform planks from past national and state platforms and avowed that Republicans in Congress should feel "bound by such pledges and obligations, especially when they have been so many times repeated as to have become party doctrine." As an Ohio editor told Sherman, "The Republican party is pledged to this legislation and our people pray for it with a deep and forever-increasing fervency. Now is no time for the Republican party to be withheld from its duty by any consideration, prudential or otherwise."[53]

But even while the bill's Senate managers worked to revise Lodge's bill to make it acceptable, they recognized that, as Spooner put it, "there are two or three Republican Senators who do not like to vote for any federal election bill. The almighty dollar obscures their vision. I mean by that, that the commercial spirit which held back the anti-slavery men is holding them back against anything that might sacrifice commerce to the rights of citizenship." Such men "care more for their ease, or for the trade of their localities with the south, than they do for justice, honest elections, and a manly redemption of the pledges of the Republican party." Although such apostates in the Senate were relatively few, just enough might combine with the Democrats to scuttle the measure. Spooner and his allies were determined, therefore, to make any defectors "vote in the open Senate in the presence of all the people, not to take up the bill. We are determined that it shall not be left a question of doubt who in the Senate among Republicans are in favor of redeeming the party pledges, and protecting the integrity of our Government, and who are not."[54]

By the first week in August, Hoar was ready to report Lodge's bill as amended. The committee's substitute simplified the vote-counting procedure, reduced the sections related to criminal interference with registration or voting, and eliminated wording that had empowered supervisors to pass on the qualifications of would-be voters. The new version acknowledged the ultimate power of the House itself to overturn a judge's decision in an election dispute, and it eliminated a provision to punish the House clerk for refusing to place a declared winner on the roll. The Senate committee also deleted reference to the reaffirmation of the president's power to employ the military, because, as Spooner explained, it "would be the introduction of a power to use force which no man on the committee and, I think, no man in the Senate, was prepared to sanction." Lodge could live with this change, as he wrote, "I do not believe that bayonets are in the least needed to make a proper election law march." With these and other changes to the bill, Hoar and his colleagues hoped to improve its chances in the upper chamber.[55]

The timing, however, could hardly have been less propitious. For weeks, the Senate had been debating the McKinley Tariff bill, which had passed the House on May 21. Consideration of the highly protectionist measure had moved at a snail's pace, in large part because of delaying tactics pursued by low-tariff Democrats, who capitalized on the Senate's rules inhibiting restrictions on debate.[56] While opponents droned on, exasperated businessmen pressured Republican Senate leaders for action. Pennsylvania businessman Samuel Lee complained to Sherman: "Mills continue to fail and the Senate does about as much in a week as a set of men in business would do in half an hour. You are killing the Republican party as fast as you can."[57]

As pressure mounted, Republicans hunted for a way to escape the stalemate. The Republican caucus discussed the problem at length, and Nelson Aldrich, floor manager for the McKinley bill, asked the Library of Congress to investigate the experience of European legislatures in invoking cloture. Limiting debate in the Senate would require a rule change, which would require the concurrence of a majority of the whole Senate, or forty-three members. Republicans held forty-seven seats, but, as Connecticut senator Orville Platt reported to Chandler, the "question whether we can pass an election law I think depends on whether we can change the rules, and the persons who don't want to pass an election law don't want to change the rules, and are re-inforced by two or three Senators, like Mr. Edmunds, who do want to pass an election law." Two days after reporting the bill, Hoar submitted a resolution to amend the rules so that after a measure had been debated for "a reasonable time," a majority of senators present could vote to cut off debate except for a final speech of thirty minutes by each member desiring to speak. George Edmunds, leery of so broad a change in the rules, proposed an order limiting debate on the tariff bill to five minutes per senator per item in the bill. Henry Blair proposed a rule change to permit the motion of the previous question on any measure that had been under debate for two days. Because three Republicans were absent from Washington and a handful of others opposed a rule change, passage of such a move was problematic without Democratic support, and Democrats could see no reason to help Republicans expedite legislation they opposed.[58]

At this juncture, Matthew Quay offered a resolution to break the impasse. Quay maintained close relations with Pennsylvania industrialists, and as chairman of the national committee he had emphasized the tariff issue over the southern question during the 1888 campaign. He concluded that the best way to persuade Democrats to scale back the tariff debate was to alleviate their fears of election legislation after the McKinley bill had passed. On the morning of August 12 he conferred with Democratic floor leader Arthur P. Gorman, and near the end of that day's session Quay proposed a resolution setting August 30 for the end of debate on the tariff. In addition, the resolution would limit the Senate's other action that session to general appropriations, bills relating to public buildings and public lands, and Senate or concurrent resolutions, and it would postpone consideration of all other bills until the second session of the Fifty-first Congress. The Lodge bill would be among the bills thus delayed. Quay's aim was to wind up the tariff debate through a combination of Democrats who adamantly opposed the Lodge bill with those Republicans who gave the tariff priority over elections legislation.[59]

Proponents of the elections bill were stunned. Many believed that delay of the bill until the next session would kill it. Calling the Quay resolution "a cowardly surrender," Spooner wrote, "It looks as if Aldrich and Quay had sold us out." Aldrich defended the move, telling reporters that "it is perfectly well known" that "there is a sufficient number of Republican Senators opposed to the Elections bill to prevent its passage. They will be glad of an opportunity to pass the Tariff bill and go home." But the Lodge bill forces would not surrender without a fight. The next day, Hoar moved to amend Quay's pending resolution by adding the election bill to the list of measures the Senate would consider in the present session. The night of August 14, Senate Republicans held a stormy caucus that was largely a shouting match between Quay and his backers on one side and Hoar and Spooner on the other. Hoar tried to convince his colleagues to endorse his amendment to Quay's resolution, but his motion failed by a single vote. Bitter feeling prevailed at the caucus and no solution emerged. Over the next several days Quay angled for support among particular senators by tacking on to his resolution additional subjects to be considered in the first session, including bills on pensions, agriculture and forestry, the U.S. courts, and the postal service. Meanwhile, Ohioan Charles Foster reported to Sherman that "Republicans generally are well nigh disgusted with what appears to be the effeminacy of the Senate" reflected in its "reverence for 'time honored' rules that only hamper and retard action by the majority."[60]

The principal leverage the Lodge bill supporters possessed was the unwillingness of most Republicans to go on record as seemingly against the bill by voting for Quay's resolution. Hoar and Spooner had help from Speaker Reed, who buttonholed senators on the floor in favor of the House's bill. Representative Robert Kennedy of Ohio mounted a petition campaign among his colleagues to refuse to adjourn until both the elections bill and the tariff bill had passed.[61]

President Harrison, who considered the situation in the Senate "very annoying and discouraging," also weighed in. He summoned several senators to the White House, and newspapers described him as "leaving no stone unturned to let the Republican Senators know that he wants the Force bill passed." He told each senator he met that voting for the bill was "his highest duty." Moreover, the White House worked on public opinion by distributing to newspapers extracts from Harrison's inaugural address and annual message endorsing elections legislation. Papers such as the *Chicago Tribune* complied. The paper printed the elections plank from the 1888 platform and declared, "The President believes still that that pledge, which heads the list of those made by the Republican party, and which it deemed the most important, shall be kept."[62]

The administration's united front appeared compromised by rumors that Secretary of State James G. Blaine had ghostwritten the Quay resolution. Privately, Blaine told Harrison and Lodge that the charge was untrue, although he confessed that he did "not have great faith" that the elections bill could remove a disease that, "deepseated and poisonous as it is," would "have to be left to self-cure." But Harrison was unwilling to lose without a fight the Republicans' first opportunity in fifteen years to enact new civil rights legislation. "It can be authoritatively stated that President Harrison's views have undergone no change whatever," reported the Washington correspondent for the *Indianapolis Journal*, the president's hometown newspaper. "He believes in a federal election bill, and is very deeply concerned in the prospect of a failure to pass the bill."[63]

Quay maintained that his sole object was to secure early passage of the tariff bill and that he still favored enactment of elections legislation. But other Republicans rejected his notion of priority. Gideon Moody of South Dakota told reporters that he and other senators from the Northwest had received a flood of telegrams from constituents more anxious for the elections bill than the tariff bill. The president of the Afro-American News Company, a black correspondents association, warned Sherman that the "probability that the Lodge Federal election bill will not pass the Senate this session is causing an uneasy excitement amongst Afro-Americans all over the country," who would "hold the party guilty of being false to the pledges which they claim to make to them." William Moore told Sherman that the Senate's "failure to pass the tariff bill *and* the election bill means *inevitable* future Republican defeat. It places us in one of two categories, namely, either a party of imbecile incompetents, or else of *unprincipled cowards* who are afraid to do what each of us has a thousand times vociferously promised." Even some fervent protectionists regretted Quay's priority. Albert Clarke, secretary of the Boston Home Market Club, wrote to Hoar, "It is difficult to see why the Tariff bill and the Elections bill need antagonize each other. . . . The Republican party is as much committed to the one policy as to the other. Indeed, a protective tariff, or any other wholesome measure, can have but an uncertain tenure unless the freedom and purity of elections can be guaranteed." As Clarke put it, "The rule of an honest majority is fundamental. Even revenue measures and appropriations are secondary."[64]

With no settlement in sight, Hoar took to the Senate floor on August 20 and beseeched his colleagues to redeem their solemn pledges. He cited Madison, Hamilton, and other early statesmen on the power of Congress to regulate national elections and insisted that in "proposing this measure we are doing exactly what the framers of the Constitution expected of us." He quoted at length from Supreme Court decisions upholding that power. He cited addresses and messages from several presidents as well as planks from national and state party platforms as undeniable proof "that the Republican party, by everything which can bind a party, is pledged to this policy." Hoar particularly resented the mischaracterization of the measure as a "force bill." "There was never a more senseless utterance than to call that a force bill which transfers the settlement of a great public question from the shotgun to the court." Nor would he accept the charge that its proponents merely waved the bloody shirt: "Was cheating at elections an issue of the war? Did Jackson die; did Lee go through that struggle more bitter than death, between his allegiance to his country and his love for his State, that ballot-boxes might be stuffed, that naturalization papers might be forged, that returns might be altered, and that votes might be falsely counted?"

Hoar reiterated his devotion to the protective tariff, but he could "take little satisfaction in it if it is to be [at] the price of the dishonor of my country or the broken pledges of my party." In his peroration he appealed to the republican values that both the tariff and the elections bill aimed to guard. The protective tariff was designed not "that capital may be gathered to capital," but to "increase the wages of American labor, that thereby American citizenship and American manhood may be exalted. . . . We can bring it to pass that the American workman shall live in a comfortable dwelling; that his wife shall be at church and his child shall be at school; above all, that he shall have his equal share in the government of his country, and everywhere through the whole land cast his vote in freedom and in honor."[65]

The next day Spooner was prepared to denounce Quay's methods in a speech so impassioned, he admitted, "that after its delivery we probably could not have gotten together in the Senate." To forestall any further damage to the party's image and its legislative program, Maine Senator Eugene Hale and others persuaded Spooner to desist until after one more private attempt at reconciliation. On the evening of August 21, Republican senators gathered informally at the house of their colleague James McMillan of Michigan and at last reached an understanding. Quay would not press his resolution, and Republicans would pledge themselves to begin consideration of the elections bill on the first day of the next session of Congress (less than four months away), to the exclusion of other matters until it was settled by a vote. The assumption, soon confirmed by informal contacts with Democrats, was that the Democrats, no longer fearful of elections legislation hard on the tariff's heels, would accede to a relatively early end to the tariff debate so that the present session could adjourn. After the McMillan house meeting, Hoar and Spooner secured the signatures of nearly all the Republican senators to an explicit pledge to begin consideration of the elections bill on the first day of the second session and to support a rule change to secure a vote.[66]

This maneuver broke the logjam. On September 10 the Senate passed the McKinley bill. Two weeks later, when Quay's resolution, which had gone to the bottom of the calendar, was reached, the Pennsylvania senator let it be indefinitely postponed, because it had "fulfilled its purpose." On the other side, Spooner took immense satisfaction that "we have succeeded in defeating . . . the Quay resolution to barter the cause of honest elections for the speedy passage of a tariff bill for *Pennsylvania reasons*." "It would have been a humiliating spectacle indeed," he believed, "for a few Republicans to have voted with the solid southern Democracy in the Senate of the United States to abandon for all time, for that is what the proposition meant, a Federal elections bill. In lieu of it we have no trade with the Democrats, but an agreement among ourselves which has brought the Republicans of the Senate into harmony, which will secure the passage of the Federal election bill at the next session." Similarly, William Evarts assured a constituent that the election bill would "occupy immediate and constant attention at the next session till it is passed."[67]

But not all Republicans were so optimistic. In a scathing speech, Ohio Congressman Robert Kennedy told the House that the "great party of the Republic," which had "never yet assisted in riveting the shackles on a human being, . . . is about to prove false and its repeated promises are not to be redeemed." A local party leader from York, Pennsylvania, wrote Chandler that "all true Republicans" were "humiliated by the cowardly surrender of the Republican majority to a Rebel minority. . . . It is time for Republicans to ask themselves the question why vote the Republican ticket, when we are betrayed by our public servants." Frederick Douglass thanked Hoar for having "kept the faith of the Republican party," but he warned that if the bill were finally defeated, it would "disappoint the hopes of an oft deceived, betrayed and deeply wronged people. . . . What if we gain the tariff and many other good things if in doing it the soul of the party and nation is lost?"[68]

In the aftermath of the agreement for delay, Republican senators recognized its potential for damage in the upcoming congressional elections, and several favored the convening of a special session to deal with the ballot issue before the regular session in December. Expressing "a profound interest in the enactment of an Election law," Maine's William P. Frye told President Harrison that "an extra session, called before the November election, to meet about the fifteenth of that month, would be a most excellent political move" that "would wonderfully strengthen and solidify our party for the November election." But the current session dragged on until October 1, and the enthusiasm for a return to Washington before December waned.[69]

In the interim, Republicans suffered enormous losses in the 1890 congressional election. In the new House they saw their membership cut almost in half, down to a scant 88 compared with 235 Democrats. Reasons for the defeat varied. Democrats had effectively exploited fears of high prices due to the McKinley Tariff, and in some midwestern states certain ethnic groups recoiled against Republican temperance legislation or laws mandating the use of the English language in schools.[70] But the Lodge bill also affected the outcome. It proved a godsend for southern Democrats, who raised the specter of a revived Reconstruction. As a result, Republicans saw their congressional representation from the old slave states fall from twenty-five to four seats. Some southern Republicans blamed the pro–Lodge forces for handing their Democratic opponents an insurmountable advantage. One Alabama Republican told Quay, "The Republican party must get out of the 'Negro Rut' if they desire any success in this country. . . . It is high time the Republican party of the North were looking after the *White people* of the South."[71]

But other southern party members saw the outcome as an object lesson in favor of the Lodge bill. Writing from the second district of Georgia, Edward Wade told Sherman that the Republican candidate for Congress had been defeated "by the old methods of fraud, violence, etc. with which you are as familiar as I am. The Lodge bill, in my judgment, ought at once to become a law without amendment, otherwise it will be nonsense to run a Republican electoral ticket in the rebel states in 1892." Some northerners echoed this sentiment. C. L. Poorman, one of fourteen Republicans defeated in Ohio's congressional elections, told Sherman, "In this part of Ohio nothing did more to create indifference among Republicans and reduce their votes at the late election than the attitude of the Senate upon the election bill. . . . Many of them will cease to be Republicans unless the party makes an effort, at least, to prevent the great wrongs now perpetrated with impunity." "If the Senate will stand fast," former governor Harrison Reed of Florida told President Harrison's secretary, "the revolution can be arrested & the Republic preserved."[72]

Although Harrison considered the election a "disaster," he was in no mood to retreat on the Lodge bill. When Congress convened for its second session on December 1, the president offered an impassioned endorsement of the pending bill. The constitutionality of such legislation, he noted, had already been affirmed by the Supreme Court. Indeed, over the years Congress had already passed numerous regulations of national elections. But, he said, the current laws on the books stopped "just short of effectiveness," because they left to state authorities "all control over the certification which establishes the *prima facie* right to a seat in the House of Representatives." It was this defect that the Lodge bill aimed to cure. The president brushed aside the "force bill" label, declaring that "every law," whatever its subject, "has force behind it." He decried "the fact that some electors have been accustomed to exercise the franchise for others as well as themselves." "The qualifications of an elector must be sought in the law, not in the opinions, prejudices, or fears of any class, however powerful." Ultimately, at the heart of the issue was the viability of republican institutions. "Equality of representation and the parity of electors must be maintained or everything that is valuable in our system of government is lost."[73]

Harrison's stand sparked wide approval from Republicans. Albion Tourgée, who had come around to support the Lodge bill as the best that could be obtained, thanked Harrison for his "courage and statesmanship," especially after the election loss, "which would certainly have demoralized a man of less firm convictions." James Clarkson, vacationing in Asheville, North Carolina, wired Harrison his congratulations for the message's "firmness, self-respect and courage," and noted that "of the hundreds of Southern republicans I have met here in [the] last month every one strongly endorses [the] elections bill."[74]

Be that as it may, the fate of the bill lay with the Senate, where Hoar brought it up for discussion the day after Harrison's message. Although Lodge wrote privately that he "believe[d] more deeply in the cause than in anything I ever thought of," he nonetheless feared that the Senate debate would be "only dress parade."[75] Indeed, bolstered by the November elections, the Democrats were determined that the bill should fail. The American people had registered "their expressed, emphatic, resounding condemnation," declared Virginia's John W. Daniel. "Neither the Senator from Massachusetts nor any other man can, in this high noon of our country's history, warm the cold fingers of this cadaver at the dying embers of sectional hatred." Daniel set the tone for a Democratic filibuster that occupied most of the ensuing month. Democrats condemned the bill as unconstitutional, outrageously partisan in intent, and designed, as Georgia's Alfred Colquitt put it, "to take possession of the Southern States and subject them . . . to negro ascendancy and party despotism."[76]

Although the Democrats aimed to eat up time, Republicans felt the need to respond to their opponents' attacks. Spooner gave a long point-by-point defense of the bill, answering each of the objections to its provisions. He particularly denied that partisanship motivated its Republican supporters. He noted that the original election supervisor law of 1871, of which the Lodge bill was an expansion, had over the years been invoked by both Republicans and Democrats and had been defended by such Democratic party luminaries as Congressman Samuel S. Cox and Navy Secretary William C. Whitney. Hoar echoed these points. Indeed, far from being partisan itself, the bill sought to counteract the brazen partisanship of election officials appointed by Democratic governors in the South by lodging the selection of supervisors in the federal circuit judges, who, said Hoar, "are admitted to be the class of officers furthest removed from partisan influence."[77]

Race figured largely in the discussion. When Democrats raised the specter of a return to Reconstruction with "negro domination," Republicans reminded them that the bill dealt not with local or state elections but solely with congressional elections. In Hoar's words, "There never were in the times of which you so much complain, when, as you say, the negro ruled the whole South, more than seven or eight members of that race in the Congress at one time." New Yorker Frank Hiscock conceded "the superiority of the Anglo-Saxon race over the negro," but he maintained that Anglo-Saxons were "a just people, generous to the weak and ever ready to extend to them a helping hand. . . . Our people recognize the strong foundation upon which manhood suffrage rests; it is an armor and a defense to the poor, ignorant, and weak against the arrogance, selfishness, and oppressions of the rich, learned, and strong." Similarly, Spooner asserted that suffrage had originally been granted as "the colored man's shield against wrong and injustice at the hands of his old masters who no longer owned him, but who could not forget that they had owned him." "It may be hard," said Hoar, "for two populations differing in race and color, in political opinion, yet locally intermingled, to dwell together in amity under republican government, but in the present case the crime, the blame, the barbarism, have been on the side of the superior race. . . . The fundamental error of the Democratic party of the South in dealing with this problem, is in their assumption that race hatred is the dominant passion of the human soul; that it is stronger than love of country, stronger than the principle of equality, stronger than Christianity, stronger than justice." Rhode Island's Nathan Dixon cited the tenets of equality embodied in the Declaration of Independence and claimed that the Republican Party was "animated with the belief that man is endowed with certain unalienable rights," one of the most essential of them being the right to government by consent.[78]

Although nearly all the Republican senators touched on the republican theme, its fullest exposition came from Oregon's Joseph Dolph. During the debate, Louisiana Democrat Randall Gibson, a Yale graduate and president of Tulane University's board of administration, had lectured Dolph that "intelligence and education are considered necessary to the safe maintenance of republican institutions" and that "the whole theory of republican government rests upon the idea that intelligence and virtue and character and property rule in every well-organized State." Dolph was a self-made man and successful railroad lawyer who favored women's suffrage as well as voting rights for blacks.[79] He took vigorous exception to Gibson's elitist notions:

> The theory of republican government is that those admitted by the constitution and laws to have a voice in the control of the government are equal, and that the vote of the college president and the unlettered man, of the millionaire and the day laborer, of the moral and immoral (if not disfranchised for crime), are equal in their effect, and that the will of the majority legally expressed controls. In a republic, so far as political rights are concerned, there is no aristocracy of learning, of wealth, or even of virtue. . . . Whenever one class of citizens can say to another class of citizens entitled in a republican government to the elective franchise; "I am intelligent and you are ignorant; I am wealthy and you are poor;" or "I am holier than thou and I will do your voting for you, and you shall not vote;" that government is no longer, in fact, a republican government.

Whenever any voters were deprived of a free ballot, Dolph argued, "that government is no longer a government of the people, but a government of a class."[80]

Republican support for the bill in the Senate was not unanimous. The principal dissenters were senators from western silver-mining states who looked to Democrats for support for free coinage of the white metal. Colorado's Edward Wolcott, among the most forceful of the Republican silverites, conceded that the right to vote was "the very foundation and corner stone of our Republic," but he argued that "there are many things more important and vital to the welfare of this nation than that the colored citizens of the South shall vote." Blacks were now protected in life and property, and although they were "slowly but surely coming up out of the ignorance imposed by bondage," they "can afford to wait. And so can the Republican party afford to wait." For Wolcott, an even "weightier" argument against the bill was the emergence of the South "from poverty and despair" on to "the solid rock of material prosperity." In view of the region's "marvelous growth and transformation now taking place," he asserted,

"The Political Crisis.
To back-down would be
death to the elephant."
Judge, January 31, 1891.

"it would be unwise and unpatriotic for us to interfere in the conduct of its internal affairs." As for the safety of republican ideals, Wolcott took the position that the Lodge bill "should not become a law because it involves Federal interference and espionage at other than national elections, and such interference is contrary to the spirit of our institutions and an obstacle to the right enjoyment of our liberties."[81]

As the debate dragged on with no settlement in sight, Harrison worked behind the scenes to bring the bill to a vote. "The President is anxious to take the responsibility if he is given the power," Harrison Kelley wrote Tourgée. "He feels deeply the humiliation, and I believe he would rather die trying to protect the rights of American citizens, than to live and not make the effort." In the Senate, Nelson Aldrich, who had backed Quay's resolution in the first session, now pushed a move toward cloture similar to the one Hoar had proposed in August.[82]

But before Aldrich could secure a vote on his motion, Nevada Senator William Stewart surprised the bill's advocates on January 5, 1891, with a motion to take up a pending free coinage bill. Hoar protested the interruption of the elections debate, but by a vote of 34 to 29, the Senate agreed to Stewart's move. According to Chandler, "The Democrats are so hostile to the Elections bill that they are about all willing to vote for free coinage in order to get the desired Republican votes against the Elections bill." Indeed, at least three Democrats who actually opposed free coinage nonetheless voted to take up Stewart's bill. One, Arthur Gorman of Maryland, said that he "would have voted for the free coinage of lead" to block Lodge's bill. Included in the majority were the two Republican senators from the new silver-producing state of Idaho, one of whom had taken his seat only moments earlier. William McConnell's first word on the Senate floor was his "aye" in favor of Stewart's motion. All told, seven silver-state Republicans plus Minnesota's William Washburn joined the Democrats in derailing the Lodge bill. As Stewart's Nevada colleague, John P. Jones, observed, this vote "caused a decided sensation & engendered considerable bitterness of feeling especially among Eastern Senators against the Republican silver Senators of the West." Nine days later the coinage bill passed, but immediately afterward it required the tie-breaking vote of Vice President Levi Morton for the Senate to decide to return to the Lodge bill. This time, five silver senators and Washburn voted with the Democrats.[83]

The bill's supporters saw little hope of success against what Spooner saw as a combination of "the confederates" and a "few Republicans representing the mining camps." Most disappointing was the behavior of Stewart. Two decades earlier, the Nevada senator had played a leading role in the passage of both the Fifteenth Amendment and the voting rights legislation of 1870 and 1871. Now he was a leader of the small group working with Gorman and other Democrats against augmenting his earlier handiwork. Before the silver bill was taken up, Stewart argued against the Lodge bill on the grounds that it was unworkable. Given the refractoriness of white southerners, he said, the program could not work without military force, and no one was willing to sanction that. White southerners would go to any length to resist, and individuals who petitioned to invoke the bill's provisions would find themselves "marked men." For blacks it would bring "persecution, misery, and, if need be, death." Thus, Stewart argued, the measure "ought not to pass, because it never will be enforced; because it will consolidate the Southern whites; because it will bring further misery upon the southern blacks, and because it will increase sectional animosities and kindle anew the discords of the past."[84]

But after the free coinage vote, during which all but one of the Democrats voting sided with the silver Republicans, Stewart shifted his opposition to the Lodge bill from an argument based on its inexpediency to one that roundly echoed Democrats' notions of states rights. Place this scheme in operation, he declared, and "a spectacle will be presented of the imperial power of the General Government dominating local elections throughout the United States." Turning aside the bill's proponents' arguments that protecting the right to vote was essential to republicanism, he argued rather that the Lodge bill would itself mark "the beginning of the end of free government."

> If the Federal authorities can have at all the polls in the United States paid retainers to govern and control the local elections, you have gone very far towards changing the form of this Government from a republic to a monarchy. There is no excuse for saying that you can manage these elections better than the people. That is always the plea of tyrants. That is the reason given by despots for the exercise of imperial power. Their excuse for governing is that they are wiser than the masses. Local self-government is the foundation of free institutions. It is the only guaranty against despotism. This bill if enacted into a law would not only violate the Constitution, but also the fundamental principles of free institutions.[85]

In private correspondence, Stewart reiterated his belief that enactment of the bill would change "our form of Government" and prepare "the way for a monarchy in this country." "Local self-government has its defects," he wrote, but "the people must be permitted to do wrong or they will never be able to do right. If you take from them the power to abuse the elective franchise, you have nothing left but imperialism."[86]

With the bill's opponents again bent on obstruction, Aldrich and his allies labored mightily to limit debate and keep the legislative wheels in motion. Once more, however, their opponents prevailed. The matter came to a dramatic end on January 26, when Wolcott interrupted debate with a motion to take up a pending apportionment bill. Wolcott's motion carried by one vote, 35 to 34, with four silver-state senators plus Washburn and J. Donald Cameron of Pennsylvania voting with the Democrats. The Lodge bill was dead.[87]

Supporters of the bill were livid, none more than John Spooner. "I am too angry to write," he told J. M. Bundy, editor of the New York *Mail and Express*. "We are fallen upon bad times for the party. The Confederacy and the Western mining camps are in legislative supremacy. Think of it—Nevada, in 1870 about 45,000 people, in 1880 about 65,000, and in 1890 about 47,000—barely a respectable county, furnishes two senators to betray the Republican party and the rights of citizenship for silver." William Evarts, who made his last great effort in the Senate on the bill's behalf before his term expired, saw the outcome as evidence of the resurgence of "the ante-bellum Democracy which is planning to reverse the triumphs of the Republican party." George Edmunds saw it as a victory for the "unrepublican system" by which the southern "oligarchy" kept its lock on power. In a rare newspaper interview, President Harrison expressed similar apprehensions. "That the majority shall rule is an underlying principle of our institutions," he asserted. "It will not do for the people of any section to say that they must be let alone; that it is a local question to be settled by the States of whether we shall have honest elections or not." On the other side, Stewart insisted that the "defeat of the elections Bill has saved the country from a great danger. The supervision of local elections by Federal officers, whatever the excuse, will ultimately lead to a monarchy."[88]

No one was more disappointed at the bill's defeat than Hoar, who rushed an article on "The Fate of the Election Bill" for the next issue of *The Forum*. Hoar cited past party platforms as well as the statement signed in August by Republican senators pledging to support the Lodge bill. "To keep that promise," he avowed, "is the one essential thing that constitutes Republicanism." Privately, Hoar blamed the loss on the "treachery of a very few men," but in his article he forbore denouncing the silver-state apostates and instead condemned "larger forces which have made possible the overthrow of popular elections in this country." Over the long haul, the real culprits had been businessmen who had put their selfish interests ahead of principle and mugwumps who had abandoned the party's core faith. "If the body of northern business men, the body of self-styled 'reformers,' the body of educated and wealthy men, who are indifferent to their political obligations, had acted for the past fifteen years with the Republican Party, election practices which have made so many States of the South solid against the wishes of a majority of their own people, would have been unavailing." The great irony was that "those classes will be the first to experience the penalty," for the artificially large Democratic representation in Congress would continue to make possible the passage of destructive economic legislation such as the free coinage bill.[89]

The prospect for erecting any further shield for the new Republic during Harrison's term died with the adjournment of the Fifty-first Congress on March 3, 1891. Hoar insisted that the "question will not down. Nothing is settled that is not right." Nonetheless, the opposing forces he had identified remained insuperable. "The Lord only knows," Spooner wrote, "when, if ever, we shall have another chance to pass an election bill." For his part, Stewart expressed satisfaction that the defeat of the bill "has terminated the unnatural strife between the North and the South. I trust [that] the bonds of union and friendship, which existed in the better days of the Republic, will now be restored." Although Stewart would temporarily abandon the Republican Party over the silver question, his observation, more than those of Hoar or Spooner, captured the party's notion of the Republic as it evolved in the 1890s.[90]

Surrender of the New Republic

Reconstruction Undone and the Nationalism of Reconciliation

Defeat of the Lodge bill dealt a devastating blow to Republican efforts to fulfill their republican aims in the South. In national political discourse, the Democrats tarred the measure with the odious label "Force bill," and the chastened Republicans drew back. In the southern states, Democrats proceeded to adopt measures for "legal" disfranchisement of blacks, and when they captured control of the national government under Grover Cleveland, they promptly repealed most of the federal election protections passed during Reconstruction. Even when the Republicans returned to power, however, they saw no real hope of reviving the republican experiment in the face of implacable racism, endemic in the South and at least acquiesced in elsewhere. Republicans began to preach the republican virtues of hard work and self-help to blacks, and party leaders quickly embraced Booker T. Washington's affirmation of those ideals. At the same time, as segregation took root in the South, the Supreme Court set its imprimatur on the doctrine of "separate but equal." Finally, under William McKinley, sectional reconciliation became the party's new hallmark. In the end, the republican project in the South became one more victim of the nationalistic outburst as the century drew to a close.

Among the most discouraging results of the Lodge bill struggle was the impetus it gave to conservative white southerners determined to devise methods to disfranchise blacks beyond the reach of federal legislation. In the fall of 1890, a convention in Mississippi wrote and promulgated a new state constitution that required a voter to be able to read a passage of the state constitution or understand and interpret such a passage read to him. The acceptance of the interpretation, and hence the determination of the right to vote, rested solely with the state election official. George Hoar asserted that any state restrictions on voting ought to be applied equally, but even he was forced to admit that "all that the Constitution of the United States declares is that you shall not deny [suffrage] to any man whom in all other respects you find fit for it simply because he is a negro." Hence, opponents of the Lodge bill such as Colorado's Henry Teller maintained that enacting it would succeed only in inspiring the adoption of "Mississippi constitutions in other States than Mississippi, which will be clearly beyond our control." As it happened, even without the passage of the Lodge bill, over the next decade, states throughout the South followed Mississippi in the enactment of legal disfranchisement.[1]

In the wake of the Lodge bill's defeat, President Harrison was not hopeful that election reform could again become a dominant issue. "It depends on how much the public conscience is quickened regarding the principle of right" concerning the "inequality of representation in the administration of National affairs." A month after the Fifty-first Congress adjourned, the president headed south on the first leg of a month-long national speaking tour that took him all the way to the West Coast. In speeches in several southern states, he focused on economic advances the region had made, clearly implying that such development owed much to Republican policies such as the tariff. On such a tour glorifying the shared economic progress of North and South, Harrison saw little utility in reopening the debate over the Lodge bill. Nonetheless, he took occasion to underscore the basic principles that the bill had represented. "As God shall give us power to see truth and right," he told 10,000 citizens of Atlanta, "let us do our duty, and, while exacting all our own rights, let us bravely and generously give every other man his equal rights before the law." At Chattanooga he declared that Americans should "resolutely maintain the great idea upon which everything else is builded—the rule of the majority, constitutionally expressed, and the absolute equality of all men before the law." Back in the East for a Decoration Day speech at Philadelphia, Harrison more pointedly asserted that northerners demanded nothing of white southerners beyond that "they shall obey the law, and that they shall yield to every other man his full rights under the law."[2]

As the months wore on, however, it became apparent that the southern question was rapidly fading from American political discourse. To Republicans, the consummation of the new Republic for which they had long labored never seemed more remote. In the face of new exclusionary methods like those embodied in the Mississippi constitution, Republican calls to arms against injustice gave way increasingly to confessions of frustration and resignation. Speaking at a Fourth of July gathering in 1891, journalist Murat Halstead said it now seemed "that the war settled nothing more than that slavery should be political rather than personal." William McKinley told the same audience that there were "wrongs in the United States to-day, crimes against the Constitution and the organic law," but it was "not manifest to the statesman of the present what the true remedy is or shall be." Perhaps, he declared, someone in his audience would some day "point the way which is not now clear to the vision of the best and wisest." With more hope than conviction, McKinley insisted that "what at this moment seems insurmountable can only for a little while lie in cold obstruction across the pathway of a Republic."[3]

In the state election campaigns in 1891, Republicans said little about the issue. Party platforms in Ohio, New York, and even once-radical Iowa contained only brief mention of the ballot issue and devoted much more space to the tariff and currency. William Chandler commiserated with black editor T. Thomas Fortune about conditions in the South, but he underscored the need for blacks themselves to "stand up & say that they will not allow the suffrage to be taken from them. . . . The Lord helps those who help themselves." In August Harrison told citizens in Vermont that the "compact of our Government is a rule by the majority" and throughout the whole country "we must insist that the behests of the Federal Constitution and of the laws written in the Federal statute-book shall be loyally obeyed." But in a speech the next day he acknowledged that "the prejudices of generations are not like marks upon the blackboard, that can be rubbed out with a sponge. These are more like the deep glacial lines that the years have left in the rock; but the water, when that surface is exposed to its quiet, gentle, and perpetual influence, wears even these out, until the surface is smooth and uniform. And so these influences are at work in our whole country, and we should be hopeful for it, hopeful for its future."[4]

When the first session of the Fifty-second Congress convened in December, Harrison gamely sought to reverse the drift of public opinion that the Republicans' 1890 loss seemed to represent. He coupled the elections issue with the problem of gerrymandering and declared, "We must not entertain the delusion that our people have ceased to regard a free ballot and equal representation as the price of their allegiance to laws and to civil magistrates." Indeed, he insisted, "Our chief national danger lies . . . in the overthrow of majority control by the suppression or perversion of the popular suffrage." It remained unclear, he said, whether the failure of the Lodge bill in the previous Congress resulted from opposition to particular features or objections to such corrective legislation in general. But in the face of the overwhelming Democratic majority in the new House, he forbore recommending a reconsideration of the bill. Instead he proposed creation of a bipartisan commission, to be appointed by the Supreme Court, to investigate the whole question of elections "with a view to securing to every elector a free and unmolested exercise of the suffrage."[5] Even this modest proposal had no chance of enactment.

While prospects for federal action in defense of suffrage faded, the physical safety of blacks grew more precarious. The 1890s witnessed an upsurge of lynching, principally in the South but elsewhere as well. Harrison deplored this "appalling" development and was the first American president to attack it publicly. He urged black leaders to compile and publicize a record of the killings, in the hope that the "frightful aggregate could not fail . . . to arouse public attention and indignation." In May 1892, in a public response to a memorial from a group of black religious leaders, the president decried lynchings as "a reproach to any community; they impeach the adequacy of our institutions for the punishment of crime; they brutalize the participants and shame our Christian civilization." He noted, however, that as president he had no jurisdiction over murders committed in violation of state laws. (Harrison was bound to this position by a festering international dispute with Italy that had begun the previous year over the lynching of eleven Italians and Italian Americans at New Orleans. He and Secretary of State James G. Blaine had maintained that the nation's federal structure would not permit the national government to take direct action.) Nonetheless, Harrison assured the black ministers that in any cases within federal jurisdiction the Justice Department would make "the most strenuous endeavors to bring guilty persons to punishment." He promised to give "my voice and help . . . to every effort to arouse the conscience of our people and to stimulate efficient efforts to reestablish the supremacy of the courts and public officers as the only proper agency for the detection and punishment of crime and the only security of those who are falsely accused." These attempts at moral suasion had virtually no effect in slowing the course of vigilante violence in the South.[6]

As the 1892 presidential election season heated up, Republicans differed over how much attention their campaign should devote to the southern question. "There seems to be just now," George Hoar lamented, "an indifference on the part of many good men, including many Republicans . . . to the question of honest elections." But when the national convention met in Minneapolis, the resolutions committee came under the influence of its chairman, Joseph Foraker of Ohio, long known for his ardent support of federal elections legislation. To prepare a plank on the subject, Foraker appointed a subcommittee dominated by southerners, including Edmund Waddill of Virginia, who during the Lodge bill debate had predicted that unless the free ballot were protected, "our

Government, in its present form, must in the near future tumble and fall to the dust." Foraker and the committee reported a platform that called for elections legislation to be "enacted and enforced." "The free and honest popular ballot, the just and equal representation of all the people, as well as their just and equal protection under the laws, are the foundation of our Republican institutions," the plank declared, "and the party will never relax its efforts until the integrity of the ballot and the purity of elections shall be fully guaranteed and protected in every State." T. Thomas Fortune hailed the platform as "republican through and through."[7]

The convention approved Foraker's platform without debate, but the unanimity masked the uneasiness some Republicans felt over the elections plank. E. P. Branch, an Ohioan who had lived in Florida for the past six years, told John Sherman that renewing elections-bill "agitation in the coming campaign will gain the party no votes but will lose hundreds of them. A conciliatory course toward the Southern people will be much more effective toward breaking up the Solid South than a dozen Force bills." "As for the race problem," Branch continued, "it can only be solved by the people who have their homes alongside those of the colored race. . . . It will work itself out in due time. Its solution cannot be precipitated by New England politicians, no matter how wise and just, who are without actual experience as residents in the Southern States." But other Republicans resisted what seemed a growing attitude of surrender. In a private letter to President Harrison, Connecticut Senator Joseph Hawley lamented the "systematic, avowed, determined & bulldozing violence and fraud that accompany southern elections" and urged Harrison, who was seeking re-election, to use his letter of acceptance to condemn the "great wrong." "That much can be said and should be repeated continually."[8]

Some party leaders, however, urged Harrison to back away from the strongly worded plank, believing that the convention had handed the Democrats an easily exploitable issue. Indeed, Democrats did seize upon the elections plank. Their national convention warned that Republican victory would "mean the enactment of the Force Bill and . . . despotic control over elections in all the States," thereby creating dangers "scarcely less momentous than would result from a revolution practically establishing monarchy on the ruins of the Republic." Leading the Democratic assault was the New York *Sun,* which charged that Republican victory followed by passage of the "Force bill" would lead to "negro domination." During the Democrats' preconvention campaign, *Sun* editor Charles A. Dana had vehemently opposed the nomination of Grover Cleveland, but after the convention chose the former president, Dana grasped the elections issue as a way to unify the Democratic party. "Better vote for the liberty and the white government of the Southern States, even if the candidate were the Devil himself, rather than consent to the election of respectable Benjamin Harrison with a Force bill in his pocket!" Cleveland himself joined in the invective, condemning the "Force bill" as "a most atrocious measure" and "a direct attack upon the spirit and theory of our Government."[9]

Many Republicans who regretted their platform's southern plank believed the party should resist being drawn into a defense of the bill. Democrats were divided on the tariff and currency questions, Virginian V. D. Groner wrote Harrison, and could "be united on *only one* issue under which the negro 'bug-a-boo' can be perpetuated." Moreover, Groner warned, holding elections under federal supervision would reawaken "all the slumbering ashes of the race hatred, . . . and the negro would suffer incalculably through agencies which could not be reached by any Federal law." Harrison considered Groner's advice in preparing his letter of acceptance. Meanwhile, a few days later, Secretary of the Treasury Charles Foster told reporters that although the Democrats were "trying to make a 'Force bill' issue," they were "not succeeding. The life is all out of that."[10]

Compounding the problem was the Republicans' effort in several southern states to form coalitions with Farmers' Alliances or Populists to lure dissatisfied white farmers away from the Democratic party. Again, this strategy suggested that Republicans should soft-pedal issues such as the "Force bill" that might serve to unite white southerners behind the Democrats. An early test of the fusion strategy occurred in Alabama, during the August contest for state offices. Republicans ran no candidate for governor and instead threw their support to the anti-Democratic candidate Reuben Kolb, with the expectation that Kolb's supporters would vote for Harrison electors in November. But even though Kolb won a majority of the white counties, Democratic frauds cost him all but one of the black counties, and he lost the election by a narrow margin. Ironically, this Democratic trickery against Kolb in black areas could potentially inure to the Republicans' benefit, for it permitted them to broaden the elections issue beyond the question of race. As Groner told Harrison, Republicans should cultivate "active allies" among the white farmers who would of necessity collaborate with the black voter "to guarantee his rights *at the ballot box*." After the election, the Alabama Alliance told Harrison through an intermediary that "the elective franchise under the election laws of Alabama is a failure and that some federal protection is necessary to secure to the people here protection against the frauds of the democratic party." Echoing the language that Republicans had long invoked, the Alliance called on the president to "secure to them a Republican form of Government in Ala[bama]."[11]

Watching these developments closely, Harrison believed that if the Alliance protest "takes shape," it would "go far to take the Force Bill out of the campaign." Hence, he carefully fashioned the elections section of his letter of acceptance. He quoted his annual message's call for a bipartisan commission to study the elections question "upon absolutely fair non-partisan lines." He referred specifically to the Democrats' cheating of the Alliance candidates in Alabama, which simply underscored "the demand that every man found to be qualified under the law should be made secure in the right to cast a free ballot and have that vote honestly counted." Emphasizing the common plight of southern Republicans and Populists, he declared, "Our old Republican battle cry, 'a free ballot and a fair count,' comes back to us not only from Alabama, but from other States and from men who, while differing from us widely in opinion, have come to see that parties and political debate are but a mockery if, when the debate is ended, judgment of honest majorities are to be reversed by ballot box frauds and tally sheet manipulations in the interests of the party, or party faction, in power." Harrison did not explicitly call for federal legislation but instead argued that "these new political movements . . . encourage the hope that the arbitrary and partisan election laws and practices which have prevailed may be corrected by the States, the law made equal and non-partisan, and the elections free and honest."[12]

Thus, standing Dana's strategy on its head, Harrison sought to use the elections question to divide Democrats, or at least the whites in the South, rather than unite them. But still, he signaled no heightened emphasis of the issue and regarded the tariff as "the most important" issue in the campaign. Vice presidential nominee Whitelaw Reid, releasing his letter of acceptance a month after Harrison's, concurred and said that the Democrats' attempt to divert attention from the tariff and currency issues "to an alleged force bill scarcely calls for notice." "It failed lately anyway," Reid added, "and the Southern white men who were its chief, as they were its most interested opponents, now begin to wish it revived to protect them from being themselves counted out of elections they have fairly won—as the other day in Alabama—by their own white fellow Democrats."[13]

The official campaign textbook issued by the National Committee declared that the "Republican party holds nothing so dear as free and fair elections," but it took the defensive against the Democrats' charges of favoring a "Force bill." The textbook contained a brief summary of the Lodge bill and asserted that it "was no more a 'Force Bill' than are the Ten Commandments." Moreover, the book's compilers added, the Republican Party "is in no sense committed to this bill, or to any other particular method of curing the evil of dishonest elections." The simple truth was that Republicans had concluded that public opinion would no longer sustain a call for federal intervention in elections. The white South had in effect won on this issue. As Republican journalist James P. Boyd conceded, it was "doubtful whether the time has arrived for legislative insistence on a method of voting in advance of that which prevails. . . . Prejudice is yet profound among the lower strata of voters. The race instinct is hard to eliminate. The tradition of state-rights has survived the war to an alarming extent. Upon these can be built an opposition which is susceptible of withstanding any onslaught, as things exist." Real change in the South would be the work of generations.[14]

The result of the election seemed to confirm that pessimistic conclusion. In his victory over Harrison, Cleveland once again enjoyed the support of a Solid South. Although the Democrat carried the four northern doubtful states of New York, Indiana, New Jersey, and Connecticut, plus the traditional Republican states of Wisconsin, Illinois, and California, he racked up his substantial national popular-vote margin over Harrison primarily in the South. In the former slave states, Cleveland garnered 805,974 more votes than Harrison, whereas outside the region Harrison ran ahead of Cleveland by 442,895. The result also illustrated the efficacy of the disfranchisement schemes launched in Mississippi and elsewhere. In Mississippi, 1,398 votes, 2.66 percent of the total, were counted for Harrison. The only ray of sunshine for the Republicans was Harrison's showing in the upper South. In Delaware, Missouri, North Carolina, and West Virginia, Cleveland won only a plurality of the popular vote. Harrison did not run as well in the upper South as he had in 1888, but his 1892 performance again lent credence to the argument that Republicans should emphasize economic appeals to the New South rather than demand election reform.[15]

In election postmortems, a few Republicans, such as former Michigan Senator Thomas Palmer, argued that the "republican party would have done much better if it had made the election bill, commonly called the force bill, more prominent." "The "demoralization upon this question," Palmer lamented "is already apparent in the indifference with which northern people seem to regard the neutralization of the rights of millions in the south. . . . When our people become satisfied that there is no free ballot and fair count, the empire is not far off." Others, however, reached the conclusion that any effort to impose reform on the South from the outside was futile. "That time will not come," former New Hampshire Senator P. C. Cheney wrote Harrison, "until they teach *each* other that an *honest ballot* and an *honest* count is essential to the perpetuity of our republican form of government." For Civil Service Commissioner Theodore Roosevelt, the election simply confirmed "the inadvisability of legislation providing for Federal control of elections," because "the people at large, whether rightly or wrongly, would not sustain such an attempt." In a sense, the Republicans' struggle to secure a free ballot and a fair count had become their Lost Cause.[16]

In his last annual message Harrison again denounced lynching and called for "the strongest repressive legislation" wherever the practice came under Federal jurisdiction. On the elections issue, he renewed his call for a bipartisan commission. He urged Republicans and Democrats to "come together upon the high plane of patriotism" to "devise methods that shall secure the right of every man qualified by law to cast a free ballot."[17] But with Democrats in control of the House and about to take over the Senate and presidency as well, Harrison's suggestion had no prospect of enactment.

The death of Supreme Court Associate Justice L. Q. C. Lamar on January 23, 1893, raised the southern question again in the closing weeks of Harrison's administration as the president searched for a suitable replacement who could win confirmation. That Lamar was from Mississippi led many, including the president, to conclude that his successor should also come from the South. Many Republicans favored the selection of Circuit Judge Don Pardee, a twelve-year veteran of the federal bench at New Orleans. But the Republicans' slim majority in the Senate made problematic the confirmation of Pardee or any other Republican if Democrats followed through with threats of delaying tactics. Hence, Judiciary Committee Chairman George Hoar urged Harrison to appoint another circuit judge, Democrat Howell Jackson of Tennessee. At first reluctant to appoint a Democrat, the president eventually conceded the unlikelihood of the Senate's confirming a Republican and named the Tennessean.[18]

In many ways Jackson was an ideal choice. He and Harrison had served in the Senate together and had become good friends; members of the upper chamber would, moreover, incline to accept a former colleague. Most important, however, Jackson subscribed to legal and constitutional beliefs basically consonant with Harrison's. A Whig before the Civil War and an opponent of secession, Jackson had held a nonmilitary office under the Confederacy, but after the war he emerged as a moderate Democrat who did not embrace the extreme states rights notions of most of his party colleagues. Indeed, shortly before his nomination, Jackson had upheld the indictment of three Tennessee men under the Enforcement Act of 1870 for conspiring to violate the civil rights of federal officials (three of whom had been killed) searching for an illegal still. Many southerners criticized Jackson for expanding the application of the Reconstruction-era law, but the decision represented precisely the attitude Harrison was looking for in a new justice. As he explained to a fellow Republican, "I know Judge Jackson to hold constitutional views more nearly like ours than any southern Democrat. . . . In the trial of Democrats for election frauds in Tennessee he has shown the most vigorous and honest indignation at such crimes."[19]

But not all Republicans were convinced. Former national chairman James Clarkson saw Harrison's choice as "party perfidy" and "little short of moral crime." Clarkson denied that Jackson had "in any way" suppressed election frauds and declared that he should "not go upon the Supreme Bench to help declare unconstitutional legislation to protect the rights of the Republicans and black men in the South." Representative John Houk, one of two House Republicans from Jackson's home state, agreed that the nomination was "an outrage and a betrayal of Republican principles." More significant, however, was the fact that Tennessee Democrats, including the state's two senators, also opposed Jackson. Newspapers reported that his party colleagues regarded him as "a strong Federalist and never a good party man as a Democrat." Similarly, Senator George Vest, a leading Democrat on the Judiciary Committee, was reported to oppose Jackson as "too much of a Federalist to make an acceptable member of the Supreme Court."[20] Such criticism from Democrats merely confirmed Hoar and Harrison's original judgment about the role Jackson would play on the bench, and nearly all Republican senators accepted their reasoning. Still, in a private letter to Jackson before his confirmation, the president made clear the sort of justice he expected Jackson to be:

> I would not, of course, appoint to the Supreme Bench a man who held views of the Constitution and of the powers of the general government that I thought subverted or diminished those necessary powers. I have believed from my knowledge of you and representations of others that you were a believer in the nation and did not sympathize with the opinion that a United States Marshal was an alien officer or that election frauds or any other infraction of the Federal Statutes were deserving of aught but indignant condemnation and punishment.[21]

Two weeks later, the Senate confirmed the appointment. As matters turned out, Jackson never had much chance to live up to Harrison's expectations. Ill health curtailed his activities on the bench until he died of tuberculosis in August 1895. Moreover, the Democratic administration of Grover Cleveland exhibited no great enthusiasm in pushing voting or other civil rights litigation that might find its way to the Court. In his inaugural address, Cleveland did aver that equality before the law, "unimpaired by race or color," should be "justly and in good faith conceded in all parts of the land," but few Republicans expected action to follow these words. Indeed, of one thing Republicans were fairly certain: the Democrats would use their power to dismantle the new Republic they had built during Reconstruction.[22]

Republicans could do little more than attempt a rearguard action. Addressing the national meeting of the League of Republican Clubs early in the Cleveland administration, Clarkson devoted a third of his speech to the southern question and the issue of blacks' rights. He noted that in some places in both the North and the South, the Democrats allowed black voting and even officeholding in places where white Democrats clearly maintained control. But in those areas of the South—eight states, according to Clarkson—where white and black Republicans constituted a majority, Democrats held a grip on power "through State election laws, or Force Bills of the most ultra form of despotism, and the most complete disregard of local or majority rights." Moreover, Clarkson linked the protection of blacks' rights with the defense of northern white laborers. "Democratic policies and Democratic conditions in the South" had created a pool of cheap labor, and some northern manufacturers were substituting blacks for whites in their factories, while other employers cited the "nearness of such cheap labor in our own land as a reason for the reduction of high wages in the North." "Thus," said Clarkson, "the negro question is passing from a purely party question, or from any form of Sectionalism or the Bloody Shirt, and becoming one of the most serious labor questions of the present time and condition." Ultimately, this exploitation of the working class, North and South, threatened the fundamental tenets of republicanism:

> No Republic is stronger in actual liberty than its weakest home. If hosts of free men may be disfranchised in the south at this time because they are weak, or black, or poor, or Republican, and degraded beyond that into a form of servile and cheap labor, the time may come when free men in the North may also be disfranchised and degraded. . . . Gentlemen may cry for peace on this question; still there will be no peace until it is settled according to the decrees of God, & not the prejudices of men.[23]

Despite Clarkson's speech, the League convention's resolutions said virtually nothing about the question beyond the call for a committee to investigate and report annually on the condition of the party in the South. Among those present in Louisville was William Ball, a transplanted northerner from Greensboro, North Carolina, who attended the meeting at Clarkson's behest. Ball hoped to obtain financial help to publish a book he had written on southern "outrages" and the new state disfranchisement measures, but he found few sympathizers. He soon abandoned his project because of "an utter indifference on the part of the people regarding the southern question."[24]

For their part, the Democrats moved quickly to expunge voting rights legislation from the federal code. In the wake of a financial panic in the spring of 1893, Cleveland called Congress into special session in August to repeal the Sherman Silver Purchase Act. Although the purpose of the session was to deal with the currency, House Democrats seized the opportunity to launch an effort to repeal the election laws. On September 11, Virginia's Henry St. George Tucker introduced a bill to eliminate nearly forty sections from the Revised Statutes. Originating in the enforcement legislation of 1870, 1871, and 1872, these sections dealt with federal election supervisors and deputy marshals and set penalties for violating the right to vote. Democrats claimed that these statutes were unconstitutional, trenched on rightful power of the states, and unfairly benefitted the Republican Party. They made no secret of their desire that "every trace of the reconstruction measures be wiped from the statute books." The House approved Tucker's bill before the special session ended. Although the Senate did not take it up until the regular session in December, it passed the bill two months later, and Cleveland promptly signed it.[25]

The fate of the repeal was never in doubt. It seemed, as William Chandler wrote a Senate colleague, that the Democrats were "ramming down our throats a bill to promote fraud and violence in congressional elections."[26] With no prospect of derailing the effort, Republicans used the debate to put themselves on record against what most saw as an enormous step backward. The argument was the last significant effort Republicans in Congress made on the elections issue as the nineteenth century drew to a close.

Republicans took great pains to refute the Democrats' argument that the election laws of the 1870s were unconstitutional. Any notion that the power to conduct elections for national offices was somehow among the reserved powers of the states was absurd, because no such offices had existed before the adoption of the Constitution. Moreover, although Article One, Section 4, directed that states could regulate the "times, places, and manner" of holding congressional elections, it also stipulated that "the Congress may at any time by law make or alter such regulations." Republicans rejected the Democrats' claim that this provision meant that Congress could exercise the power only when a state had failed to do so.[27]

To buttress their constitutional position, Republicans quoted at length from the Founders, including Alexander Hamilton, who asserted in the *Federalist* that "nothing can be more evident than that an exclusive power of regulating elections for the National Government in the hands of the State Legislatures would leave the existence entirely at their mercy." In addition, Republicans never tired of invoking the authority of the Supreme Court, which especially in *Ex parte Siebold* and *Ex parte Yarbrough* had upheld Congress's power to legislate to protect federal elections. Ohio Congressman Charles Grosvenor cited no less an authority than Democrat Howell Jackson, who as circuit judge had declared that the "constitutionality of this legislation has been fully established by the highest tribunal in the land." It was "a glorious thing," Grosvenor said, for Harrison to appoint to the Court "a Democrat who had passed away from the fog and the mist and the doubt and the confusion of the teachings of Jefferson and Jackson and others, out into the open sunlight, out into the clear sailing, out upon the pathway of national unity and national power."[28]

The defense of national authority against "the pernicious doctrine of State rights" formed an important motif in the debates. Henry Blair argued that if the Democrats were right that only a state could define a voter and that "the nation has no voter, then it follows logically and inevitably that neither has the voter any nation. Therefore there is no nation at all and the war was waged in vain." Henry Cabot Lodge, now in the Senate, found the existing laws "incomplete and insufficient," but he nonetheless opposed their repeal because it represented "a direct blow to national sentiment and to the right and authority of the nation. If they serve no other purpose, except as an expression of national right and authority, these laws ought not to be touched."[29]

Lodge's Massachusetts colleague George Hoar dismissed the Democrats' constitutional appeals as mere claptrap. "This is not a question of States rights," he argued. "It is a question of fraud or no fraud. There is nothing else to it." Hoar and other Republicans argued that the Democrats disregarded their own vaunted principle of local self-government by the enactment of state "force laws" that arrogated the selection of local election officials to the state government, where the dominant Democrats made sure that only Democrats would receive such positions. William Chandler, the ranking Republican on the Senate Committee on Elections, conducted a survey among trusted observers in the South that showed that in state after state, the governor or other state officials exercised control over the appointment of local election officials. By "these extraordinary and undemocratic laws, which are totally destructive of 'home rule' and 'local self-government,'" Chandler concluded, "year after year, unscrupulous oligarchies perpetuate their absolute political control of the States." Similarly, the House Minority Report argued that though "occasional instances of violence" still occurred, it was no longer necessary because the southern force laws were "so framed that the Democrats can keep themselves in possession of the governments in every Southern State." With the election machinery thus rigged, said Delaware's Anthony Higgins, "it can not be claimed that it is a popular institution."[30]

Republicans emphasized the centrality of race in the subversion of southern elections. In the words of Charles Grosvenor, Democrats had carried election after election by waving "in the face of the Southern people this black specter of negro domination." Moreover, disfranchisement based on this bogus justification was only the beginning of the menace to blacks. Once the Democrats had repealed the election laws, Chandler argued, they would not only "take the suffrage away from the black man" but "also little by little in this process of reaction and retrogression, come to reduce him virtually to a state of slavery." Chandler cited the hundreds of lynchings that demonstrated that the "colored people have not only been deprived of the suffrage under the fifteenth amendment, but they are deprived of the privilege of being protected by the laws which protect the white people of the North and the South." As George Murray, a black representative from South Carolina, put it, "Everything—economics, finances, laws, customs, morality, and religion—is subordinated to the false teachings of white supremacy."[31]

The most eloquent defense of African Americans came from Lodge. His position was not without irony, for the Massachusetts senator had already become known for his theorizing about the diverse character traits exhibited by different European "races" (that is, nationalities), and he had emerged as a champion of literacy tests to bar immigration by "undesirable" types from abroad.[32] Yet Lodge pulled no punches in his defense of blacks. Tracing the problem to "the evil legacies of slavery," he held northerners as well as southerners culpable for the "great wrong" inflicted on the enslaved Africans and their descendants. "The fact that their condition as a race has improved by their enforced contact with our civilization does not diminish in the least the debt we owe them for the countless wrongs we inflicted upon them." Blacks were not demanding to be wards of the nation, but they did legitimately demand their rights as citizens. Lodge dismissed the bogey of "negro domination" as "absurd." Federal law could apply only to national elections, and blacks could send to Congress no more than twelve to fifteen of their race, out of 354 representatives and 88 senators. To the argument that blacks should not vote because they were illiterate, Lodge conceded that his own state had set a literacy requirement for voting. But he argued that such measures in the South had been so framed "that all negroes may be excluded and all white men admitted." Indeed, the black man "is not disfranchised because he is ignorant, but because he is black." "Every right-minded man draws the distinction between the misfortunes which lie within our own power of remedy and those which are beyond our reach," Lodge concluded. "It is this discrimination against a man on account of his color which is repugnant to justice and honesty."[33]

But blacks were not the only victims. Again Republicans decried the disproportionate representation in Congress that southern whites enjoyed as compared with their northern counterparts. In 1892, for instance, as a result of black disfranchisement, the seven congressional districts of Mississippi posted an aggregate vote that was less than the total in a single district in New York. But within the South itself, other whites besides blacks' Republican allies suffered from the Democrats' lock on the election machinery. As Chandler noted, in states where the Populist uprising and similar revolts challenged the Democrats' dominance, "the freedom of white voters . . . is shamefully impaired by the unrepublican laws." Indeed, said Anthony Higgins, "the Populists find themselves in the iron grasp of the fetters which, as Democrats, they themselves helped to forge."

Moreover, "this anaconda–like conspiracy against human rights," which permitted "the remorseless grip of the Calhounist, the Mugwump, and the free-trade doctrinaire," ruined the prospects for an economic New South.[34]

These policy implications affected the whole nation. In Congress ex–Confederates held virtually all the major committee chairmanships. Chandler noted that the black population in the South gave the region 39 of its 127 House seats, but Republicans held only 7 of them. If the other 32 had gone Republican in the last election, as a free vote likely would have permitted, the Wilson tariff bill, which the House recently passed and which reduced customs duties, would in all likelihood have failed. For Republicans, such a turn of events epitomized "retrogression," against which President Harrison had solemnly warned in his last annual message.[35] The Democrats, possessed of power illicitly gained, seemed determined to halt the forward march of national potential. Ohio Republican Stephen Northway lectured colleagues across the aisle:

> What do you think you are doing for the rising generation in condemning, to them, and before their eyes, all that the General Government shall do? Don't you know that you can accomplish more to perpetuate the glories of our institutions by teaching your sons, your daughters, and your families to love and revere the Federal Government and the Federal Constitution than you can by teaching them to despise it, by teaching them that it is a monster of tyranny to them?[36]

Republicans had no chance of defeating the repeal bill. As Northway's comments suggested, they witnessed the undoing of the election laws with a sense of foreboding mingled with melancholy. Higgins ruefully noted that the great turning point in the southern question had actually come three years earlier when Republican votes had helped defeat the Lodge bill in the Senate. Now, Chandler warned, "If the Republican party abandons the fifteenth amendment and forsakes the colored man . . , it will die the death of all parties which are faithless to their professions and to their trusts, and it will die a deserved death." In the final tally virtually no Republicans voted for repeal, but it made no difference.[37]

For the present and an indeterminate future, white southerners had won their long twilight struggle to undo the results of the Civil War. From outside the Senate, George Edmunds wrote his former colleague Justin Morrill that repeal of the election laws would "leave the southern aristocracy again the masters of the country, as they were before their rebellion, until the people of the rest of the U.S. again wake up to the principles & practices of fair play." "How persistently and consecutively," cried Maine Representative Charles Boutelle, "the armies paroled by Grant and Sherman have succeeded in evading, avoiding, or overthrowing nearly every one of the guaranties which the country thought it had established for the safety of the Republic." Once the southerners had been "admitted in full power within the temple of our liberties," they had proceeded "to tear the great structure down upon our heads."[38]

Thus, Republicans had come to realize that insofar as the South and African Americans were concerned, their attempt to reinvent the Republic had failed. As Marriott Brosius put it, government by consent was "the only reason for the existence of our form of government," but in the "nonsuffrage States" of the South, the "Constitution and the law are paralyzed. Consent has no expression, and . . . authority is not conferred by lot or consent, but by force." In Chandler's estimate, "the legal effect and real result of the [repeal] legislation will be wholly pernicious and injurious to popular government throughout the United States." It is, he declared, a "fearful danger to a republic when the suffrage is so destroyed that there can not be a change of political control from one party to another as the result of successive elections. It is to that condition of things that we are coming in this country."[39]

The result augured ill for blacks in the South. Lodge noted that the "future of the negro race in the United States" was "one of the gravest problems to be met by the American people," a problem that could not "be settled this year or next" but would "remain with us and with our children's children for many years to come." John Sherman even expressed "grave doubt" whether the Fifteenth Amendment had been "wise or expedient." Without it, Congress's power under the Fourteenth Amendment to reduce the representation of states limiting the suffrage would have convinced white southerners that an untrammelled black vote was in their own interest. Now, however, southern states employed "ingenious provisions" to exclude blacks from voting without technically violating the Fifteenth Amendment, and "no way is pointed out by which Congress can enforce this amendment." Hence, Sherman concluded, "I can see no remedy for this wrong except the growing intelligence of the negro race, which, in time, I trust, will enable them to demand and to receive the right of suffrage."[40]

Similarly, George Hoar later recalled that "it became clear to my mind, and to the minds of many other Republicans, that it was better to leave this matter to the returning and growing sense of justice of the people of the south than to have laws on this subject passed in one Administration, only to be repealed in another." He began advising black correspondents that for now it was best for them to "cultivate the virtues of integrity, industry, frugality, [and] chastity. . . . The negro question is to be settled in this country by the personal worth of the negro. When he attains that, all other things will be added unto him." Thus,

Sherman, Hoar, and other Republicans had come around to the view that it was best for blacks first to acquire and cultivate republican virtues before they exercised their republican rights.[41]

This gradualism soon received the stamp of approval in the Atlanta Compromise speech of Booker T. Washington in September 1895. A leading black educator and, after Frederick Douglass's death the previous February, the preeminent spokesman for his race, Washington used the occasion of the Atlanta Cotton States Exposition to call for a new turn in southern race relations. Asserting that blacks had mistakenly sought political preferment with the first rush of freedom, Washington now urged them to focus their attention and energy on work in "agriculture, mechanics, in commerce, in domestic service, and in the professions." The address won widespread acclaim. Even W. E. B. DuBois, who later came to disagree with Washington, initially declared that it "might be the basis of a real settlement between whites and blacks in the South" if the two races could cooperate in economics and politics. For Republicans convinced of the futility of further agitation in behalf of voting rights, Washington's speech served to sanction the party's redefinition of the southern question in a way that deemphasized federal government intervention. James Clarkson wrote the black leader that his speech "made clear to your people that the negro problem is a different one since the close of the war and that it is constantly changing and must be met constantly from different standpoints of view."[42]

Clarkson's comment came during the preliminary skirmishing for the 1896 presidential nomination. His letter solicited Washington's support for Iowa Senator William B. Allison. Clarkson pledged patronage recognition for southern blacks, but it was clear that Allison, though long a champion of blacks, would not mount any crusade to reverse the ebbing of their rights. Neither, apparently, would front-runner William McKinley, who aimed his southern delegate hunt primarily at whites whom he hoped to attract to his economic ideas. State conventions in New York, Indiana, Massachusetts, and elsewhere issued platforms that said nothing about the southern question and concentrated instead on the tariff and currency issues.[43]

Moreover, while the preconvention maneuvering accelerated, yet another event operated to relieve Republicans from saying much about section and race in the coming campaign. In May the Supreme Court issued its opinion in *Plessy v. Ferguson*, which upheld a Louisiana state law segregating the races in railroad cars and sanctioned the "separate but equal" practice in other contexts as well. The case attracted little immediate attention, less because it lacked long-term legal significance than because it merely codified a prevailing sentiment. Among the few protesting voices, the Republican Chicago *Inter Ocean* condemned the

Booker T. Washington
(Library of Congress)

opinion as the last in a series of Court decisions that completed "the denial [of] the fourteenth amendment."[44]

No one mentioned the *Plessy* case a month later when the Republican national convention met in St. Louis. This was the first time Republicans held their national convention in a former slave state, thereby accenting sectional reconciliation over concern for blacks. Not surprisingly, the choice raised some embarrassment, for despite city leaders' pledges of fair treatment, some hotels refused accommodations for black delegates, who were forced to make alternative arrangements. But this disturbance had no impact inside the convention, where the tariff and currency issues received nearly exclusive attention. In his opening address, chairman John Thurston said nothing about the southern question except to call for the "abolition of sectionalism." Joseph Foraker chaired the platform committee as he had in 1892, but this time he did not renew his fiery plank on the elections issue. In 1896 the great fight in the committee concerned

William McKinley
(Library of Congress)

the money question, and the platform contained merely a perfunctory demand in the passive voice that every citizen "shall be allowed to cast one free and unrestricted ballot, and that such ballot shall be counted and returned as cast." In stronger language, the convention did register its "unqualified condemnation of the uncivilized" practice of lynching.[45]

The convention's reconciliationist spirit perhaps showed most clearly in speeches nominating southern men for vice president. Advocating James Walker of Virginia, D. F. Bailey said that his hope was for "the people of the South to feel within the folds, under and beneath the protection of the old Republican party" so that they "can move out on the same lines as the people of the North." "Now is the time," said Tennessean W. M. Randolph, nominating his colleague, H. Clay Evans, "for the great Republican party to make its first serious effort to build itself up and put itself in a position of impregnable strength among the people of the South." In a seconding speech for Evans, Wisconsin's Robert La-Follette agreed that the party should move to rework the "line of cleavage that separates the two great sections of this country." The second spot on the ticket went to a northerner, New Jersey's Garrett Hobart, but these speeches nonetheless reflected the party's determination to highlight sectional rapprochement.[46]

Presidential nominee William McKinley embraced this view, especially in his use of economic arguments to attract southern support. His letter of acceptance said nothing about the ballot issue or African Americans generally and instead congratulated the country on "the almost total obliteration" of sectional lines. McKinley rejoiced that the "era of reconciliation, so long and earnestly desired by General Grant and many other great leaders, north and south, has happily come, and the feeling of distrust and hostility between the sections is everywhere vanishing." Whereas Republicans had for decades demanded a protected ballot and government by consent as indispensable ingredients of American republicanism, McKinley now declared that "nothing is better calculated to . . . add to the permanency and security of our free institutions than the restoration of cordial relations between the people of all sections and parts of our beloved country." His front-porch campaign continued this spirit. Sectional lines "have been happily obliterated," he told one visiting delegation, "and no part of this great Republic can now be justly called 'the enemy's country.'" Such sentiments won warm commendation from at least some southern Republicans, including Virginia editor A. P. Funkhouser, who assured McKinley that the conditions that had once made Republicans advocate federal intervention "are happily now passing rapidly away. We do not now look to what our home enemies call a 'force bill' to secure our rights, and we feel it is unjust to our party, our platform and our splendid candidate to urge that it is the policy of our party to renew the efforts to pass such an election law." Funkhouser noted that white southerners took "special pleasure" from a recent interview with Benjamin Harrison in which the ex-president reportedly said that "the force bill is a dead issue. The Republicans will leave all that business to the local authorities." A few days later Funkhouser led a pilgrimage of a thousand Confederate veterans to McKinley's home, where the nominee preached "the gospel of peace and of National unity."[47]

McKinley's conciliatory approach to the South held out little to African Americans. When delegations of blacks from his own county called on him to pledge their support, McKinley referred to Abraham Lincoln's famous letter in 1864 to Michael Hahn, the first free-state governor of Louisiana, suggesting the right to vote for blacks who were "very intelligent" or had fought in the Union ranks. But McKinley gave his black neighbors no hint that he would use federal intervention to uphold suffrage. He told another group of blacks that "equality of privilege and equality in political power" had "long ago found expression in the Constitution," but he suggested no means for securing that equality. Instead, he hailed African Americans as "among the most conservative of the citizens of this great Republic." Again he quoted Lincoln, this time on the republican virtues of hard work, thrift, and self-improvement: "That some should be rich shows that others may become rich, and hence is just encouragement to industry and enterprise. Let no man who is homeless pull down the house of another, but let him work diligently and build one for himself, thus by example assuring that his own shall be safe from violence when built." Similarly, he told a group of black ministers that their race had made "wonderful progress" and that the Constitution "protects and defends all alike and accords to each civil and religious liberty." But he offered them nothing beyond "my prayer for still greater progress in the future."[48]

McKinley's southern strategy paid off, at least in the upper portion of the region. Winning the border states of Delaware, Kentucky, Maryland, and West Virginia, he was the first Republican since Hayes to carry a southern state. In the lower South, however, the effects of disfranchisement were glaring. Despite heavy black populations, the Republicans polled just 21.8 percent of the vote in Louisiana, 24.3 percent in Florida, 13.5 percent in South Carolina, and 6.9 percent in Mississippi. But this anomalous circumstance received scant attention in the general exultation over Republican victory. A few weeks after the election, the *New York Tribune* gladly noted that blacks had "passed through that unfortunate era" in their history when their "conception of progress was to hold political office." In an editorial entitled "The Negro in Industry," which was redolent of the spirit of the Atlanta Compromise, the paper reminded its readers of Washington's "wholesome truth" that "industrial capacity is the first requisite for any race or nation that would advance along the path of civilization."[49]

McKinley's administration sealed the Republicans' effective abandonment of blacks' rights. His inaugural address indicated that the new president would give a much higher priority to sectional reconciliation. Indeed, though reminding citizens that the "great essential to our happiness and prosperity is that we adhere to the principles upon which the Government was established," he said nothing about disfranchisement and instead claimed that "free and fair elections are dearer and more universally enjoyed to-day than ever before." He declared that "lynchings must not be tolerated in a great and civilized country like the United States," but he reserved for his peroration a stirring encomium to sectional rapprochement. He congratulated the country that the recent election had not only "demonstrated the obliteration of sectional or geographical lines, but to some extent also the prejudices which for years have distracted our councils and marred our true greatness as a nation." Most pointedly, he assured southerners that he would favor no policy that partook of either the letter or the spirit of a force bill. "It will be my constant aim to do nothing, and permit nothing to be done, that will arrest or disturb this growing sentiment of unity and co-operation, . . . but I shall cheerfully do everything possible to promote and increase it."[50]

This approach was clear in McKinley's distribution of patronage, in which he walked a thin line between extending due recognition to blacks for their party services but not going so far as to alienate too many whites. He did appoint a few blacks to fairly visible jobs and more to lesser positions in the South, but never in numbers commensurate with their proportion of the population. Moreover, in some instances when such appointments sparked white complaints, McKinley bowed to the objections and made other selections. Successful black applicants such as Treasury official Blanche K. Bruce thanked the president for doing "more for this class of our fellow-citizens than any of your distinguished predecessors," but such appointments never reached numbers sufficient to render the Republican Party in the South an effective advocate for blacks' rights.[51]

McKinley returned to the issue of lynching in his annual message to Congress in December 1899. Those who "constitute themselves judges and executioners," he said, "should not escape the severest penalties for their crimes." Mostly, however, when he referred to such vigilantism, he decried the international complications raised by attacks against foreign nationals, usually Italians. As for the lynching of blacks, he never permitted the issue to hinder his drive to nourish fraternal feeling between North and South.[52]

To foster that sentiment, McKinley set off early in his term on the first of several goodwill tours. He set the tone for these trips in a speech in June 1897 at the Tennessee Centennial Exposition in Nashville, where he avowed that northerners and southerners were "once more and forever united in heart and purpose under one flag in a never-to-be broken Union." Nor did he limit such expressions to the old Confederacy. A few months later he told a Buffalo audience that the two sections were "one now in faith, in hope, in fraternity, in purpose, and in an invincible patriotism." Indeed, he declared, "The army of Grant and the army of Lee are together." The literal merging of northern and southern fighting units the next year in the Spanish-American War served to ratify McKinley's vision of national solidarity, forging what he called a "holy alliance" between the sections. "No development of the war has been more gratifying and exalting than the complete unification of the nation." At the war's end, he told a St. Louis audience that "not since the beginning of the agitation of slavery has there been such a common bond in name and purpose, such genuine affection, such a unity of the sections, such obliteration of party and geographical divisions."[53]

Many blacks did not share this sense of triumphant nationalism, especially when the Spanish war gave way to the suppression of the inhabitants of the Philippines. As John P. Green, an African American official in the Post Office Department, reported to the president, the Philippine war was *"exceedingly unpopular amongst all colored people, without regard to condition."* McKinley did his best to bring blacks into the national effort. They served in segregated units during the Spanish-American War, and he praised their bravery. He also advocated the appointment of black officers for black units in the Philippines. Nonetheless, most blacks remained unaffected by such advances. Indeed, most remained mired without hope of advancement in second-class citizenship in the increasingly one-party South. It was for this majority that Reverdy C. Ransom, a leading black clergyman and critic of Booker T. Washington, spoke when he wrote Green that even if McKinley could not constitutionally intervene in the South, he could "at least use the influence of his great office by saying some word of condemnation against wholesale lawlessness and crime. . . . Let the President remember that the poor, the lowly, the disfranchised need his practical sympathy far more than the trusts, the moneyed interests and the unreconstructed southerners whom he is trying to win from the error of their way."[54]

In part Ransom was reacting to McKinley's seeming indifference to renewed violence against blacks in the South. A crisis of sorts came in November 1898 with an outburst of racial savagery in Wilmington, North Carolina. There in 1897 a coalition of Republicans and Populists had won control of the city government, including the election of some blacks to local offices. The next year, Democrats mounted a white supremacy campaign that reached fever pitch after a local black newspaper editorial had dared to equate the sexual mores, or lack thereof, of poor black women and poor white women. The Democrats won the 1898 election, and two days later, on November 10, enraged whites destroyed the black newspaper building, ousted the holdover Republicans from city offices, and replaced them with Democrats. The result was a spasm of murderous violence that left at least fourteen and probably many more blacks dead.[55] The White House received telegraphic reports of these events, and blacks in Wilmington pleaded with McKinley to intervene. The president referred these pleas to the attorney general, who also received information from Justice Department lawyers in North Carolina, calling for an investigation. In the end, however, no one was ever indicted in connection with the riot. Nor did McKinley send troops to the scene, because the state's Republican governor had made no request for such intervention and the overt violence quickly subsided.[56]

After the riot, George Hoar expressed his "deep sense of mortification and wrong that such things should be possible in our Republic," but he counseled blacks to adhere to the teachings of "your great and wise leader, Booker Washington." "I believe," Hoar wrote a black minister, "that integrity, industry, chastity, [and] education will in the end secure for the colored man his rightful place in the Republic and his equal share in the functions and privileges of citizenship. Every man of your race who is an example of these things helps the coming of the good time." A month later, in a speech in Charleston, Hoar noted, "We have not yet solved the problem how men of different races can dwell together in the same land in accordance with our principles of republican rule and republican liberty," but "on the whole, we are advancing quite as rapidly as could be expected to the time when these races will live together on American soil in freedom, in honor and in peace, every man enjoying his just right."[57]

Nonetheless, the Wilmington riot alarmed blacks and their sympathizers around the country, who demanded some response from McKinley. John Milholland of the *New York Tribune* wrote the president, "The Black man must be protected in his rights and the Administration failing in this will make a terrible blunder. Stand by him and the Nation will stand by you." Yet those who expected McKinley to use his upcoming annual message to Congress to condemn the Wilmington riot and similar violence in South Carolina were disappointed. He said nothing about the outrages or about blacks at all. Indeed, preparations were under way for another goodwill trip during which McKinley expected to reemphasize the unity of North and South. Five weeks after the riot, at Atlanta, he again hailed the "magic healing" wrought by the common war effort, thanks to which "sectional lines no longer mar the map of the United States." In a dramatic gesture, the president told the Georgia state legislature that the sections had settled their differences "long ago," and "the time has now come, in the evolution of sentiment and feeling under the providence of God, when in the spirit of fraternity we should share with you in the care of the graves of Confederate soldiers." Perhaps more than anything else McKinley said regarding the ideal of national unity, this equation of the Union and Confederate dead touched the heartstrings of white southerners.[58]

From Atlanta, McKinley went to Washington's Tuskegee Institute in Alabama. There he said nothing about blacks' exclusion from the governance of the Republic; rather, he saluted the Institute's leaders for offering "instruction in self-reliance and practical industry" and for not "attempting the unattainable." In the spirit of the Atlanta Compromise, the president touted not republican participation but republican virtues to America's blacks. "Patience, moderation, self-control, knowledge, character will surely win you victories and realize the best aspirations of your people," he told the Tuskegee students. "Integrity and industry are the best possessions which any man can have, and every man can have them. . . . They give one moral and material power." Two days later he told a similar black audience in Savannah, "Nothing in the world commands more respect than skill and industry. . . . Keep on. You will solve your own problem."[59]

Washington naturally welcomed the president's endorsement. "Your visit to Tuskegee," he wrote soon afterward, "has resulted in bringing about a sympathy and union between the races of this section that is almost marvelous. . . . You have helped every black man and white man in the South." Other black leaders disagreed. T. Thomas Fortune confided to Washington his feeling that McKinley was "a thoroughly despicable character." Addressing a meeting of blacks in Washington, D.C., Fortune charged that the president had turned his back on the African Americans who had stood by him. During his recent trip through the South, McKinley had done nothing for blacks but instead had spent his time "glorifying rebellion, mobocracy, and the murder of women and children."[60]

The second half of the 1890s witnessed an acceleration of black disfranchisement in the South by methods such as literacy tests, poll taxes, and the grandfather clause. Just a few months before the Wilmington riot, this process won the approval of the Supreme Court in *Williams v. Mississippi*. In an opinion written by Joseph McKenna, a Republican appointed by McKinley, the unanimous court held that the provisions of the 1890 Mississippi constitution, under which Democrats had drastically curtailed black voting, did not violate the Fourteenth Amendment because they did "not on their face discriminate between the races." This decision, added to McKinley's reconciliation policy, could only exacerbate blacks' sense of political abandonment and isolation.[61]

In early 1899 these feelings found expression in a speech by North Carolina Representative George White, the last African American elected to Congress for thirty years. Citing the liberation of Cuba from Spain, White noted the willingness of the American people "to extend a helping hand to the oppressed, to the outraged" in other lands. Now, he importuned his House colleagues, "remember those who are at our own door." Decrying the treatment of American blacks, White showed little affinity for the Atlanta Compromise. "We are told to be still; to keep quiet," he said. "How long must we keep quiet, constantly sitting down and seeing our rights one by one taken away from us?" He particularly denounced southern disfranchisement schemes, which reflected "the wrong conception of American citizenship" and the "wrong conception of a civilized government." He implored Republicans not to forsake the republican principles they had refashioned after the war so that government by consent would embrace black as well as white. "Shall the nation stand by listlessly, or shall it uphold the principles that it has established?" White asked. The problem not only touched blacks but "affects every citizen of the American Republic. . . . How long will you sit in your seats here and see the principles that underlie the foundation of this Government sapped little by little, but nevertheless surely sapped away?" Less than a month after White spoke, the legislature in his home state of North Carolina passed a constitutional amendment instituting a literacy test, a poll tax, and the grandfather clause, thereby joining other southern states in the disfranchisement of black citizens.[62]

In the U.S. Senate, North Carolina Republican Jeter Pritchard, elected four years earlier by a Republican-Populist legislature, sought to persuade his colleagues to condemn this proposed state amendment as a violation of "a fundamental principle of our republican form of government." Pritchard especially denounced the grandfather clause, which he said attempted to "confer the right of suffrage by inheritance" and thus "ignore[d] all that is sacred and dear to a free and independent people." Adoption of the scheme would "result in the complete overthrow of that republican form of government to which we are entitled under the Constitution." Speaking for most southern senators, however, Alabama Democrat John T. Morgan charged that Pritchard's resolution once more raised the specter of "negro domination." "In physical, mental, social, inventive, religious, and ruling power the African race holds the lowest place, as it has since the world has had a history, and it is no idle boast that the white race holds the highest place. . . . Whoever has supposed or has endeavored to realize that free republican government has for its task the undoing of what the Creator has done in classifying and grading the races according to His will overestimates both the powers and the duties of its grand mission."

Pritchard scoffed at Morgan's mock dread of black rule, noting that in North Carolina whites outnumbered blacks two to one. Rather, Pritchard asserted, the real aim of Morgan and his allies was not merely to disfranchise blacks but also to repress poor whites who challenged Bourbon control with movements such as Populism. The "real intent and effect of the Democratic methods in those states" was "to restore the rule of the classes and to ignore the masses." "Before the war it was the slaveowners and the aristocratic classes who dominated the politics of the Southern States, and we are rapidly drifting to a point where only the favored few will be given political preferment." Urging his party colleagues to meet this new assault against republicanism, Pritchard declared, "The Republican party can not afford to fold its hands and permit the Democratic party to again secure political ascendancy in the nation by resorting to such unrepublican and unconstitutional methods." His pleas stirred little response, however. William Chandler joined briefly in the debate, but in part he did so to chide Morgan and his allies for "reopening the . . . whole Southern question," which he had "supposed was forever dead," and for pursuing the issue "without the slightest occasion for it." Near the end of the congressional session, Chandler reworked Pritchard's resolution into one calling for an investigation of disfranchisement, but he failed to bring the new version to the floor for debate.[63]

Pritchard and other North Carolina Republicans found no greater success in trying to convince McKinley to wield the moral force of his office against the proposed state constitutional amendment. Indeed, after the racial violence in the fall of 1898, the president stuck by his theme of national unity. Choosing to ignore the virulently racist rhetoric that marked the white supremacy campaign in North Carolina and elsewhere, the president told an Iowa audience, "Old prejudices are but a faded memory. The orator of hate, like the orator of despair, has no hearing in any section of our country." "All sections are united," he told another group in Illinois, "and passion, hate, and prejudice have totally disappeared." Such observations seem bizarrely astigmatic in light of Morgan's depiction of blacks as a race as "lowest in the scale of intelligence and capacity," or Benjamin Tillman's sneering remark in the Senate, "If you read the thirteenth, fourteenth, and fifteenth amendments at me I certainly should yell 'nigger' back at you, because they are chock-full of 'nigger,' and nothing else."[64]

When McKinley proclaimed that prejudice had totally disappeared, he referred to sectionalist rhetoric and chose to overlook the race baiting that shamed the Senate and had become rampant on the southern political stump. His decision thus to avert his and the nation's attention could only have contributed to the growing "invisibility" of African Americans' plight during much of the first half of the twentieth century. Thus, with entire equanimity he could boast that the avenues of upward mobility were open to all American citizens, so that "no matter about their race or their nationality, they all have an equal opportunity to secure private and public positions of honor and profit." By the same token, the president saw republicanism intact as well. "Has the republic lost any of its virility? Has the self-governing principle been weakened?" he asked a Chicago audience. Such questions brought "but one answer. The republic is sturdier and stronger than ever before. Government by the people has not been retarded, but advanced." McKinley made such assertions in answer to critics of imperialism, but again, he simply drew no connection between the degradation of blacks' citizenship and the success or failure of the republican experiment. Clearly McKinley followed a different set of priorities. "If I have been permitted in the slightest degree," he told a northern audience, "to help in the work of reconciliation and unification, I shall hold it the greatest honor of my life."[65]

In this, as in many other things, McKinley proved a fitting representative of his party. In 1900 the Republican national convention labeled devices to circumvent the Fifteenth Amendment "revolutionary" and said they "should be condemned," but the gathering resisted calls by black leaders for stronger language against disfranchisement and lynching. McKinley said nothing on either subject in his letter accepting renomination or in his second inaugural address. In the latter speech, he again affirmed that "sectionalism has disappeared. Division on public questions can no longer be traced by the war maps of 1861." McKinley, the last veteran of the northern army to serve in the White House, had come to place the highest premium on national unity, while he strove to implement economic policies and foreign adventures in the interest of the nation at large.[66]

Even before McKinley's administration had begun, a confluence of forces had conspired to defeat the Republicans' attempt to create a new Republic. In the late 1860s they had devised a new republican blueprint for the South, but they soon found that erecting a sturdy edifice was enormously difficult, and securing its future was all but impossible. On the scene in the South, for a variety of reasons, the Republican coalition of freedmen, scalawags, and carpetbaggers proved to be poor material for the delicate task of building a viable new polity. But more important, conservative white southerners were willing to go to any length to make certain that it failed. Over the years, Republicans deployed a number of different methods to secure their handiwork, including military intervention, judicial prosecution, amnesty and conciliation, patronage enticements, and the promise of economic development—all to no avail against an implacable and vengeful foe determined to wreck the republican project.

From the beginning the project also suffered from quarrels among the party's leadership in Washington about aims and methods. After the election of 1874 gave the Democrats a share of the national government, Republicans found it increasingly more difficult to present a united front and rally northern public opinion. Over time, ineffectuality on the southern question bred indifference. Competing issues, especially economic questions, moved to the head of the party's agenda, and business leaders who looked to the party to advance their interests pushed for an end to sectional strife. When the Republicans at last held the Congress and the presidency again, they made a valiant effort with the Lodge bill to revive the republican project, but it was too late; the effort failed. Partly in reaction to that attempt, Democrats moved swiftly to complete the destruction of the postwar republican edifice by the repeal of national election laws and the widespread disfranchisement of blacks in the South. Racist notions of black capacity made it easier for northerners to yield to the South's degradation of republican principles, especially after the Atlanta Compromise and *Williams v. Mississippi*. In the McKinley years Republicans at last acquiesced in a defeat that neither they nor the nation had the will to reverse.

In the end, most party leaders found ways to accommodate themselves intellectually and morally to the frustration of their earlier ideals. In his 1903 *Autobiography*, George Hoar, principal architect of the Lodge bill, still maintained that it "is a bad thing that any man who has the Constitutional right to vote should fail to have his vote received and counted." But, he added,

My opinion is that as the colored man gets land, becomes chaste, frugal, temperate, industrious, veracious, that he will gradually acquire respect, and will attain political equality. Let us not be in a hurry. Evils, if they be evils, which have existed from the foundation of the world, are not to be cured in the lifetime of a single man. The men of the day of reconstruction were controlled by the irresistible logic of events; by a power higher than their own. I could see no alternative then, and I see no alternative now, better than that which was adopted.[67]

Other Republicans were more despairing. Albion Tourgée, one of the "men of the day of reconstruction," wrote President McKinley after the Wilmington riot that the southern race question was

> one of those questions which are beyond remedy by any human means, that it has so cankered the political and moral sentiment of the American people, that no organized resistance to it is possible. It seems to be one of those questions which only God can handle. I have no doubt that He will sometime take it in hand, and it is quite possible that the American Republic may pay the price of its own injustice, by finding in the Race Problem the end of its liberties and the destruction of its organic character.

"There was a time," Tourgée concluded, "when we had a conscience upon this subject, when the American people believed that Liberty and Justice were essential elements of republican freedom and prosperity. That time has passed away."[68]

NOTES

ABBREVIATIONS

AHR	*American Historical Review*
ANB	*American National Biography* (ed. John A. Garraty and Mark C. Carnes; New York, Oxford University Press, 1999, 24 vols.)
ATA-UVA	Amos T. Akerman Letterbooks, University of Virginia Library
AWT-CCHS	Albion W. Tourgée Papers, Chautauqua County Historical Society, Westfield, New York
BFB-LC	Benjamin F. Butler Papers, Library of Congress
BHB-LC	Benjamin H. Bristow Papers, Library of Congress
BH-LC	Benjamin Harrison Papers, Library of Congress,
BH-Walker	Benjamin Harrison Papers, Collection of Benjamin Harrison Walker, privately held
CG	*Congressional Globe*
CR	*Congressional Record*
CS-HU	Charles Sumner Papers, Harvard University Library
CS-LC	Carl Schurz Papers, Library of Congress
EBW-LC	Elihu B. Washburne Papers, Library of Congress
EF-LSU	Ellis Family Papers, Louisiana State University Library
EGH-LC	Eugene Gano Hay Papers, Library of Congress
EM-LC	Edward McPherson Papers, Library of Congress
EP-Yale	Edwards Pierrepont Papers, Yale University Library
FTN-LSU	Francis T. Nicholls Papers, Louisiana State University Library
GFH-MHS	George F. Hoar Papers, Massachusetts Historical Society
GSB-LC	George S. Boutwell Papers, Library of Congress
HCL-MHS	Henry Cabot Lodge Papers, Massachusetts Historical Society
HF-LC	Hamilton Fish Papers, Library of Congress
HLD-LC	Henry L. Dawes Papers, Library of Congress
HM-LC	Hugh McCulloch Papers, Library of Congress
HPC	Hayes Presidential Center
HW-LC	Henry Wilson Papers, Library of Congress
JAG-LC	James A. Garfield Papers, Library of Congress
JAG-WRHS	James A. Garfield Papers, Western Reserve Historical Society
JAH	*Journal of American History*
JAL-LC	John A. Logan Papers, Library of Congress
JBF-CHS	Joseph B. Foraker Papers, Cincinnati Historical Society

JBF–LC	Joseph B. Foraker Papers, Library of Congress
JCS–LC	John Coit Spooner Papers, Library of Congress
JGB–LC	James G. Blaine Papers, Library of Congress
JPJ–HL	John P. Jones Papers, Huntington Library
JRH–LC	Joseph R. Hawley Papers, Library of Congress
JSH	*Journal of Southern History*
JS–LC	John Sherman Papers, Library of Congress
JSC–LC	James S. Clarkson Papers, Library of Congress
JSM–LC	Justin S. Morrill Papers, Library of Congress
LTM–LC	Louis T. Michener Papers, Library of Congress
MVHR	*Mississippi Valley Historical Review*
NCB–IHS	Noble C. Butler Papers, Indiana Historical Society
NPB–LC	Nathaniel P. Banks Papers, Library of Congress
NWA–LC	Nelson W. Aldrich Papers, Library of Congress
NYH	*New York Herald*
NYT	*New York Times*
NYTr	*New York Tribune*
OPM–ISL	Oliver P. Morton Papers, Indiana State Library
RBH–HPC	Rutherford B. Hayes Papers, Hayes Presidential Center
RBH–LC	Rutherford B. Hayes Papers, Library of Congress
SB–Yale	Samuel Bowles Papers, Yale University Library
SJR–HSP	Samuel J. Randall Papers, Historical Society of Pennsylvania
SJT–NYPL	Samuel J. Tilden Papers, New York Public Library
TOH–WHS	Timothy O. Howe Papers, Wisconsin Historical Society
USG–LC	Ulysses S. Grant Papers, Library of Congress
WBA–SHSI	William B. Allison Papers, State Historical Society of Iowa
WDK–HSP	William D. Kelley Papers, Historical Society of Pennsylvania
WEC–LC	William E. Chandler Papers, Library of Congress
WEC–NHHS	William E. Chandler Papers, New Hampshire Historical Society
WHS–IHS	William Henry Smith Papers, Indiana Historical Society
WHT–LC	William Howard Taft Papers, Library of Congress
WM–LC	William McKinley Papers, Library of Congress
WME–LC	William M. Evarts Papers, Library of Congress
WME–Yale	Evarts Family Papers, Yale University Library
WMS–NHS	William M. Stewart Papers, Nevada Historical Society
WQG–LC	Walter Q. Gresham Papers, Library of Congress
WR–LC	Reid Family Papers, Library of Congress
ZC–LC	Zachariah Chandler Papers, Library of Congress

INTRODUCTION

1. *NYT,* July 15, 18, 2005.

2. For other works, see the notes to chapters. Vincent De Santis, *Republicans Face the Southern Question—The New Departure Years, 1877–1897* (Baltimore, Md.: Johns Hopkins University Press, 1959); Stanley Hirshson, *Farewell to the Bloody Shirt: Northern Republicans and the Southern Negro, 1877–1893* (Bloomington: Indiana University Press, 1962); William Gillette, *Retreat from Reconstruction, 1869–1879* (Baton Rouge: Louisiana State University Press, 1979); Richard Abbott, *The Republican Party and the South, 1855–1877* (Chapel Hill: University of North Carolina Press, 1986); Heather Cox Richardson, *The Death of Reconstruction: Race, Labor, and Politics in the Post–Civil War North, 1865–1901* (Cambridge, Mass.: Harvard University Press, 2001); Brooks D. Simpson, *The Reconstruction Presidents* (Lawrence: University Press of Kansas, 1998); Xi Wang, *The Trial of Democracy: Black Suffrage and Northern Republicans, 1860–1910* (Athens: University of Georgia Press, 1997).

3. *CR,* 42-1, 651.

4. *Speeches of Benjamin Harrison,* comp. Charles Hedges (New York: United States Book Company, 1892), 543.

5. *Speeches and Addresses of William McKinley from March 1, 1897, to May 30, 1900* (New York: Doubleday & McClure, 1900), 168.

CHAPTER 1: Regeneration of a Nation

1. Wm. R. Moore to Elihu B. Washburne, November 17, 1868, E. H. Derby to Washburne, November 10, 1868, EBW-LC.

2. Donald Bruce Johnson and Kirk H. Porter, comps., *National Party Platforms, 1840–1972* (Urbana: University of Illinois Press, 1975), 38, 39; Edward McPherson, *The Political History of the United States of America during the Period of Reconstruction* (Washington, D.C.: Philp & Solomons, 1871), 381; Eric Foner, *Reconstruction: America's Unfinished Revolution, 1863–1877* (New York: Harper and Row, 1988), 340; Lawrence Grossman, *The Democratic Party and the Negro: Northern and National Politics, 1868–92* (Urbana: University of Illinois Press, 1976), 7–13.

3. Alfred Barstow to William E. Chandler, July 16, 1868, John Sherman to Chandler, October 4, 1868, WEC-LC; *Text Book for the Republican Campaign* (New York: American Literary Publishing Association, 1868), 98–100.

4. *The Works of James Abram Garfield,* ed. Burke A. Hinsdale (Boston: James R. Osgood, 1882), 1:397.

5. William T. Sherman to Ulysses S. Grant, October 22, 1868, USG-LC; Wm. R. Moore to Elihu B. Washburne, November 17, 1868, EBW-LC; Edward Atkinson to Hugh McCulloch, November 6, 1868, HM-LC.

6. James D. Richardson, *A Compilation of the Messages and Papers of the Presidents, 1789–1902* (Washington, D.C.: Bureau of National Literature and Art, 1903), 7:6–8.

7. Historians have long debated Republicans' motives and purposes in the origin and drafting of the Fifteenth Amendment. The first century of the historiographic controversy is summarized in LaWanda Cox and John H. Cox, "Negro Suffrage and Republican Politics: The Problem of Motivation in Reconstruction Historiography," *Journal of Southern History* 33 (1967): 303–330. See also William Gillette, *The Right to Vote: Politics and the Passage of the Fifteenth Amendment* (Baltimore, Md.: Johns Hopkins University Press, 1965); Glenn M. Linden, "A Note on Negro Suffrage and Republican Politics," *Journal of Southern History* 36 (1970): 411–420; Michael Les Benedict, *A Compromise of Principle: Congressional Republicans and Reconstruction, 1863–1869* (New York: W. W. Norton, 1974), 325–336; Earl M. Maltz, *Civil Rights, the Constitution, and Congress, 1863–1869* (Lawrence: University Press of Kansas, 1990), 142–156; Xi Wang, *The Trial of Democracy: Black Suffrage and Northern Republicans, 1860–1910* (Athens: University of Georgia Press, 1997), 39–48.

8. *CG*, 40-3, appx., 104; Allen W. Trelease, *White Terror: The Ku Klux Klan Conspiracy and Southern Reconstruction* (New York: Harper and Row, 1971), 113–185; George C. Rable, *But There Was No Peace: The Role of Violence in the Politics of Reconstruction* (Athens: University of Georgia Press, 1984), 69–80.

9. *CG*, 40-3, 538, 553.

10. Wang, *Trial of Democracy*, 41–42.

11. *CG*, 40-3, 904; Gillette, *Right to Vote*, 48; Wang, *Trial of Democracy*, 42.

12. *CG*, 40-3, 672, 904, 983, appx., 99; James G. Blaine, *Twenty Years of Congress* (Norwich, Conn.: Henry Bill Publishing, 1884, 1886), 2:412.

13. *CG*, 40-3, 863, 902, and passim, January–February 1869; McPherson, *Political History*, 402–403; Grossman, *Democratic Party and the Negro*, 16–17.

14. *CG*, 40-3, 553, 861, 903, 1004, appx., 200, 294–295.

15. *CG*, 40-3, 858, appx., 95, 105.

16. *CG*, 40-3, appx., 93, 96, 146, 241, 295.

17. *CG*, 40-3, 709, appx., 94; Barbour Lewis to William E. Chandler, November 5, 1868, WEC-LC.

18. *CG*, 40-3, 997, 998.

19. *CG*, 40-3, 982.

20. *CG*, 40-3, 903, 911, appx., 200.

21. *CG*, 40-3, 557, 558, 862, 978, 982, appx., 97; Charles Sumner to Edward Pierce, June 25, 1868, CS-HU.

22. *CG*, 40-3, 693, 862.

23. *CG*, 40-3, 1039, 1628, appx., 98, 99; John Sherman, *Recollections of Forty Years in the House, Senate and Cabinet* (Chicago: Werner, 1895) 1:101–105, 369–372.

24. *CG*, 40-3, 709, 710, 862, appx., 94.

25. McPherson, *Political History*, 402–403, 406; *CG*, 40-3, 1629.

26. *CG*, 40-3, 857, 984, appx., 294.

27. *CG*, 40-3, 561, 672–673, appx., 93, 94–95.

28. *The Papers of Ulysses S. Grant*, ed. John Y. Simon (Carbondale: Southern Il-

linois University Press, 1967–), 20:91, 137; Richardson, *Messages,* 7:56; Wang, *Trial of Democracy,* 51; J. Langdon Ward to Benjamin F. Butler, February 26, 1870, BFB–LC

29. Foner, *Reconstruction,* 412–415, 425–430; Wang, *Trial of Democracy,* 53–55; Trelease, *White Terror,* 189–284; Jas. W. Stephenson to Benjamin F. Butler, February 26, 1870, BFB–LC; *CG,* 41-2, 3492, 3668–3669.

30. *CG,* 41-2, 3883, appx., 420.

31. *CG,* 41-2, 3607–3610.

32. *CG,* 41-2, 3568, 3570, 3611.

33. McPherson, *Political History,* 546–550.

34. *CG,* 41-2, 3490, 3492, 3516.

35. *CG,* 41-2, 3489, 3519, 3613–3614.

36. Hamilton Fish, diary, July 10, 11, 1870, HF–LC; *CG,* 41-2, 5121, 5123; Wang, *Trial of Democracy,* 68–73.

37. *CG,* 41-2, 5155–5157, 5161, 5169, 5177.

38. *CG,* 41-2, 5125, 5151, 5152, 5159, 5168–5169.

39. *CG,* 41-2, 5152, 5155, 5156, 5161, 5169, 5176.

40. Garfield, *Works,* 1:610–614; Hamilton Fish, diary, October 18, 21, 24, 28, November 1, 1870, HF–LC; Trelease, *White Terror,* 223, 240–242, 270–273, 385–386; Samuel Shellabarger to Washburne, September 10, 1870, EBW–LC; Richard H. Abbott, *The Republican Party and the South, 1855–1877: The First Southern Strategy* (Chapel Hill: University of North Carolina Press, 1986), 211; *Statistical History of the United States, from Colonial Times to 1970* (New York: Basic Books, 1976), 1083; Kenneth C. Martis, *The Historical Atlas of Political Parties in the United States Congress, 1789–1989* (New York: Macmillan, 1989), 122–125; Richardson, *Messages,* 7:96, 112.

41. *CG,* 41-3, 1280, appx., 307.

42. Everette Swinney, *Suppressing the Ku Klux Klan: The Enforcement of the Reconstruction Amendments, 1870–1877* (New York: Garland, 1987), 126–137, 144–147; Grant to James G. Blaine, March 9, 1871, USG–LC; Hamilton Fish, diary, February 24, 1871, HF–LC; *NYT,* March 24, 1871; George F. Hoar, *Autobiography of Seventy Years* (New York: Charles Scribner's Sons, 1903), 1:204–206; Richardson, *Messages,* 7:127–128; *CG,* 42-1, 340.

43. *CG,* 42-1, 374, 517, appx., 264, 266.

44. *CG,* 42-1, appx., 110, 111, 254, 256; John Sherman, *Ku Klux Outrages. Speech of Hon. John Sherman of Ohio, Delivered in the Senate of the United States, March 18, 1871* (Washington, D.C.: F. & J. Rives & Geo. A. Bailey, 1871), 5, 11.

45. *CG,* 42-1, 576, 578, 579, appx., 112, 117, 256.

46. *CG,* 42-1, appx., 83, 84.

47. *CG,* 42-1, 332, 370.

48. *CG,* 42-1, 367, 368, 413, 487–488, 691–692, 695.

49. *CG,* 42-1, 375, 692.

50. *CG,* 42-1, 383, appx., 154.

51. *CG,* 42-1, 414, 691, 697, appx., 183.

52. *CG,* 42-1, 690, appx., 256.

53. Garfield to Burke Hinsdale, March 30, 1871, JAG-WRHS; *CG,* 42-1, 651, appx., 73, 74; Sherman, *Ku Klux Outrages,* 11.

54. *U.S. Statutes at Large* 17 (1871): 13–15; *CG,* 42-1, 702.

55. John Sherman, *Speech of Hon. John Sherman at the Ratification Meeting, Wednesday Night, June 21, 1871* (n.p., n.d.), 8; *Speech of Carl Schurz, Delivered at Farwell Hall, Chicago, August 12th, 1871* (n.p., n.d.), 6; Richardson, *Messages,* 7:134–135.

56. Robert J. Kaczorowski, *The Politics of Judicial Interpretation: The Federal Courts, Department of Justice and Civil Rights, 1866–1876* (New York: Oceana Publications, 1985), 83–96; Foner, *Reconstruction,* 457–459; Amos Akerman to Alfred Terry, November 18, 1871, ATA-UVA.

57. Grant, *Papers,* 20:312–313.

CHAPTER 2: Republicanism Contested: The Election of 1872

1. Xi Wang, *The Trial of Democracy: Black Suffrage and Northern Republicans, 1869–1910* (Athens: University of Georgia Press, 1997), 87–89; Edward McPherson, *A Hand-Book of Politics for 1872* (Washington, D.C.: Philp & Solomons, 1872), 90–91.

2. *CG,* 42-2, appx., 542.

3. *CG,* 42-2, appx., 494, 544, 581; Amos Akerman to Benjamin Conley, December 28, 1871, ATA-UVA.

4. James Ford Rhodes, *History of the United States from the Compromise of 1850* (New York: Macmillan, 1892–1906), 6:324; James G. Blaine, *Twenty Years of Congress* (Norwich, Conn.: Henry Bill, 1884, 1886), 2:512; *CG,* 42-1, 102, 104, 562; McPherson, *Hand-Book of Politics for 1872,* 78.

5. James D. Richardson, *A Compilation of the Messages and Papers of the Presidents, 1789–1902* (Washington, D.C.: Bureau of National Literature and Art, 1903), 7:153; *CG,* 42-1, 561–562, 42-2, 237.

6. *CG,* 42-2, 246, 698, 699, 700, 701, 703.

7. *CG,* 42-2, 522, 523, 525.

8. *CG,* 42-2, 247–248, 490, 920, 3193.

9. *CG,* 42-2, 488–489, 920, 928, 3260, 3263; Charles Sumner to George William Curtis, December 30, 1871, CS-HU.

10. *CG,* 42-2, 272, 382, 386, 846.

11. *CG,* 42-2, 3192, 3264.

12. *CG,* 42-2, 892–894, appx., 1, 3, 5.

13. *CG,* 42-2, 436, 761.

14. *CG,* 42-2, 3189, 3195, 3257, 3262.

15. *CG,* 42-2, 384, 921, 3193, 3259.

16. *CG,* 42-2, 919, 928–929; McPherson, *Hand-Book of Politics for 1872,* 81.

17. Donald Bruce Johnson and Kirk H. Porter, comps., *National Party Platforms, 1840–1972* (Urbana: University of Illinois Press, 1975), 44; *CG,* 42-2, 3268, 3270.

18. *CG*, 42-2, 3381–3382, 3727–3743, 3932, 4321–4323. As noted below, a civil rights bill eventually passed in 1875. For a treatment that stresses northern skepticism regarding such legislation, as indicated by press opinion, see Heather Cox Richardson, *The Death of Reconstruction: Race, Labor, and Politics in the Post-Civil War North, 1865–1901* (Cambridge, Mass.: Harvard University Press, 2001), 122–144.

19. McPherson, *Hand-Book of Politics for 1872*, 154, 165–166; Erik S. Lunde, "The Ambiguity of the National Idea: The Presidential Campaign of 1872," *Canadian Review of Studies of Nationalism* 5 (Spring 1978): 1–23.

20. Earle Dudley Ross, *The Liberal Republican Movement* (1919; reprint, Seattle: University of Washington Press, 1970), 1–68; Johnson and Porter, *National Party Platforms*, 44.

21. McPherson, *Hand-Book of Politics for 1872*, 209; Blaine, *Twenty Years*, 2:525–526; Johnson and Porter, *National Party Platforms*, 41; *NYT*, July 24, 1872.

22. *NYT*, September 20, 22, 24, 25, 1872.

23. Richardson, *Messages*, 7:176–177; Johnson and Porter, *National Party Platforms*, 47; McPherson, *Hand-Book of Politics for 1872*, 205; Hamilton Fish to Thurlow Weed, August 3, 1872, HF-LC; Washburne, to Geo. F. Baker, August 9, 1872, William E. Chandler to Washburne, August 29, 1872, EBW-LC.

24. Roscoe Conkling, *Grant and His Defamers: Deeds against Words. Speech of Hon. Roscoe Conkling, at Cooper Institute, New York, July 23, 1872* (Buffalo: Commercial Advertiser, 1872), 21; Edwards Pierrepont, *Speech of Hon. Edwards Pierrepont, Delivered before the Republican Mass Meeting, at Wilgus Hall, Ithica, N.Y., October 11th, 1872* (New York: Evening Post Steam Presses, 1872), 14.

25. George S. Boutwell, "Speech at Greensboro, N.C., July 1872," GSB-LC; *Extract from a Speech of Hon. Gerrit Smith, to His Neighbors, in Peterboro, New York, June 22, 1872* (New York: n.p., 1872), 2.

26. Eric Foner, *Reconstruction: America's Unfinished Revolution, 1863–1877* (New York: Harper and Row, 1988), 506; *NYT*, September 24, 25, 1872; Horace Greeley to Mrs. J. S. Griffing, September 7, 1870, in *NYT*, October 25, 1872; B. Gratz Brown, *Speech of Gov. B. Gratz Brown, of Missouri, Delivered in the Academy of Music, Indianapolis, Ind., Wednesday Evening, September 11, 1872* (Indianapolis: Indianapolis Sentinel Print, 1872), 6; *Letters and Literary Memorials of Samuel J. Tilden*, ed. John Bigelow (New York: Harper and Brothers, 1908), 1:311.

27. William S. McFeely, *Grant: A Biography* (New York: W. W. Norton, 1981), 352–353; McFeely, *Frederick Douglass* (New York: W. W. Norton, 1991), 277; Frederick Douglass, *U. S. Grant and the Colored People* (Washington, D.C.: n.p., 1872), 7; Brooks D. Simpson, *The Reconstruction Presidents* (Lawrence: University Press of Kansas, 1998), 145–146; Grant to "Gentlemen," May 9, 1872, in *NYT*, May 13, 1872; Charles Sumner, *Republicanism vs. Grantism . . . Speech of Hon. Charles Sumner, of Massachusetts, Delivered in the Senate of the United States, May 31, 1872* (Washington, D.C.: F. & J. Rives & Geo. A. Bailey, 1872).

28. Charles Sumner, *Letter to Colored Citizens by Hon. Charles Sumner, July 29, 1872* (Washington, D.C.: F. & J. Rives and Geo. A. Bailey, 1872).

29. James G. Blaine to Charles Sumner, July 31, 1872, printed with *Extract from a Speech of Hon. Gerrit Smith*, 8; H. O. Wagoner to Elihu Washburne, August 2, 1872, John Jay to Washburne, August 12, 1872, EBW-LC; *NYT,* August 12, 1872.

30. William G. Shade and Ballard C. Campbell, eds., *American Presidential Campaigns and Elections* (Armonk, N.Y.: M. E. Sharpe, 2003), 2:458; Blaine, *Twenty Years,* 2:535–536; Patrick W. Riddleberger, "The Break in the Radical Ranks: Liberals vs. Stalwarts in the Election of 1872," *Journal of Negro History* 44 (1959): 156; John G. Sproat, *"The Best Men": Liberal Reformers in the Gilded Age* (New York: Oxford University Press, 1968), 87–88.

31. Washington *National Republican,* November 28, 1872; John Jay to William E. Chandler, November 12, 1872, WEC-LC.

CHAPTER 3: The Republican Project under Siege: The Grant Administration and the Trial of Enforcement

1. James D. Richardson, *A Compilation of the Messages and Papers of the Presidents, 1789–1902* (Washington, D.C.: Bureau of National Literature and Art, 1903), 7:199; Eric Foner, *Reconstruction: America's Unfinished Revolution, 1863–1877* (New York: Harper and Row, 1988), 528, 547–548; Robert J. Kaczorowski, *The Politics of Judicial Interpretation: The Federal Courts, Department of Justice and Civil Rights, 1866–1876* (New York: Oceana Publications, 1985), 109–113; *CG,* 42-3, 1893.

2. Hamilton Fish, diary, December 12, 1872, HF-LC; Edward McPherson, *A Hand-Book of Politics for 1874* (Washington, D.C.: Solomons & Chapman, 1874), 100–107; Richardson, *Messages,* 7:212–213; Ted Tunnell, *Crucible of Reconstruction: War, Radicalism, and Race in Louisiana, 1862–1877* (Baton Rouge: Louisiana State University Press, 1984), 170–171; George Rable, "Republican Albatross: The Louisiana Question, National Politics, and the Failure of Reconstruction," *Louisiana History* 23 (1982): 109–112; William Gillette, *Retreat from Reconstruction, 1869–1879* (Baton Rouge: Louisiana State University Press, 1979), 110–112.

3. *CG,* 42-3, 541–551.

4. *CG,* 42-3, 633–641, 1520–1521, 1746, 1850–1851, 1853–1854; Senate Report No. 457, 42nd Cong., 3rd sess.

5. Richardson, *Messages,* 7:212–213.

6. *CG,* 42-3, 1744–1745, 1747, 1874, 1876, 1889, 1891, 1896, appx., 199, 208, 211; Oliver P. Morton to William R. Holloway [circa March 1873, misdated by archivist "c. 1872"], OPM-ISL.

7. *CG,* 42-3, 1852, 1872, 2041; George C. Rable, *But There Was No Peace: The Role of Violence in the Politics of Reconstruction* (Athens: University of Georgia Press, 1984), 124–125; Richardson, *Messages,* 7:221–222.

8. Tunnell, *Crucible of Reconstruction,* 189–193; Rable, *But There Was No Peace,* 125–129; Joel M. Sipress, "From the Barrel of a Gun: The Politics of Murder in Grant Parish," *Louisiana History* 42 (2001): 303–321.

9. Richardson, *Messages*, 7:223–224; Rable, *But There Was No Peace*, 129–131; Gillette, *Retreat from Reconstruction*, 116; *The Diary of James A. Garfield*, ed. Harry James Brown and Frederick D. Williams (East Lansing: Michigan State University Press, 1967–1981), 2:184–185; Henry L. Dawes, manuscript speech, Greenfield, Massachusetts, May 30, 1873, HLD–LC.

10. *Slaughter-House Cases*, 83 U.S. (16 Wall.) 36 (1873) at 77, 78; *CG*, 42-1, appx., 84. See also Ronald M. Labbé and Jonathan Lurie, *The Slaughterhouse Cases: Regulation, Reconstruction, and the Fourteenth Amendment* (Lawrence: University Press of Kansas, 2003).

11. *Slaughter-House Cases*, 83 U.S. at 71, 82; *CR*, 43-1, 4116; Geo. S. Boutwell to Hamilton Fish, September 19, 1873, HF–LC; Benjamin Bristow to Morton, May 6, 1873, BHB–LC.

12. Richardson, *Messages*, 7:255; McPherson, *Hand-Book of Politics for 1874*, 206, 208; *CR*, 43-1, 379–380, 408, 409–410.

13. *CR*, 43-1, 412, 455–456.

14. *CR*, 43-1, 3453, 3454, 4149.

15. *CR*, 43-1, 3452, 4116, 4168, 4172, 4173.

16. *CR*, 43-1, 4081, 4151, 4152, 4176.

17. *CR*, 43-1, appx., 478, 5328–5329; McPherson, *Hand-Book of Politics for 1874*, 207–209; Alfred H. Kelly, "The Congressional Controversy over School Segregation, 1867–1875," *AHR* 64 (April 1959): 552–553.

18. Matthew Carpenter to H. C. Warmoth, March 16, 1874, Henry C. Warmoth Papers, Southern Historical Collections, University of North Carolina, Chapel Hill; *CR*, 43-1, appx., 43, 93, 95, 347.

19. *NYH*, January 18, 1874; William P. Kellogg to Morton, January 17, February 10, 23, 1874, Morton to William R. Holloway [circa February 1874, misdated by archivist "c. 1872"], OPM–ISL; William E. Chandler to the President, January 22, 1874 (draft), Chandler to Kellogg [January 22, 1874] (draft telegram), Kellogg to Chandler, January 22, 1874 (telegram), WEC–LC; L. J. Higby to Grant, January 13, 1874 (telegram), S. B. Packard to Grant, January 23, 1874 (telegram), C. C. Antoine to Grant, January 24, 1874 (telegram), USG–LC; Hamilton Fish, diary, January 27, 1874, HF–LC.

20. Hamilton Fish, diary, December 10, 1872, HF–LC; McPherson, *Hand-Book of Politics for 1874*, 85–87, 108–112; Michael Les Benedict, *The Fruits of Victory: Alternatives in Restoring the Union, 1865–1877* (Philadelphia: J. B. Lippincott, 1975), 60–61; Gillette, *Retreat from Reconstruction*, 96–99; *NYH*, January 18, 1874; Grant to Gov. Davis, January 12, 1874, USG–LC; *NYT*, January 13, 1874.

21. Earl F. Woodward, "The Brooks and Baxter War in Arkansas, 1872–1874," *Arkansas Historical Quarterly* 30 (Winter 1971): 315–323.

22. McPherson, *Hand-Book of Politics for 1874*, 87–100; Hamilton Fish, diary, April 17, 21, May 5, 8, 12, 14, 1874, HF–LC; Richardson, *Messages*, 7:272–273; Woodward, "Brooks and Baxter War," 326–336.

23. Kaczorowski, *Politics of Judicial Interpretation*, 179–184, 187–189; Rable, *But There Was No Peace*, 132–133, 137; Gillette, *Retreat from Reconstruction*, 117–118; Foner, *Reconstruction*, 550–551.

24. *NYTr,* August 21, 1874; Morton to Henry Wilson, August 23, 1874, OPM-ISL; John Marshall Harlan to Bristow, August 28, 1874, BHB-LC; Edward McPherson, *A Hand-Book of Politics for 1876* (Washington, D.C.: Solomons & Chapman, 1876), 21; Gillette, *Retreat from Reconstruction,* 225; Rable, *But There Was No Peace,* 133–136; Tunnell, *Crucible of Reconstruction,* 198–202.

25. McPherson, *Hand-Book of Politics for 1876,* 21–22; Richardson, *Messages,* 7:276–277; Rable, *But There Was No Peace,* 138–140.

26. Marshall Jewell to Elihu Washburne, September 19, 1874, EBW-LC; Hamilton Fish, diary, September 15, 16, 1874, HF-LC; McPherson, *Hand-Book of Politics for 1876,* 25.

27. Gillette, *Retreat from Reconstruction,* 224–225; *Speeches, Correspondence and Political Papers of Carl Schurz,* ed. Frederic Bancroft (New York: G. P. Putnam's Sons, 1913), 3:93; John Sherman, *Selected Speeches and Reports on Finance and Taxation, from 1859 to 1878* (New York: D. Appleton, 1879), 455; Henry Dawes, manuscript speech, October 8, 1874, HLD-LC; *Address of the Union Republican Congressional Committee* (n.p., [1874]), 12.

28. Gillette, *Retreat from Reconstruction,* 252; John W. Forney to Washburne, November 6, 1874, Medill to Washburne, November 1, 1874, Jewell to Washburne, December 5, 1874, EBW-LC; Bristow to William Bell, November 12, 1874, BHB-LC; Gerrit Smith to Henry Wilson, December 20, 1874, HW-LC.

29. Hamilton Fish, diary, December 1, 4, 1874, HF-LC.

30. Richardson, *Messages,* 7:296–299; *NYT,* December 8, 1874.

31. Rable, *But There Was No Peace,* 148–149; Richardson, *Messages,* 7:322–323; McPherson, *Hand-Book of Politics for 1876,* 28.

32. Tunnell, *Crucible of Reconstruction,* 204; Hamilton Fish, diary, December 29, 1874, HF-LC; John Sherman to Isaac H. Sturgess, December 28, 1874, JS-LC.

33. McPherson, *Hand-Book of Politics for 1876,* 30–31; *NYT,* January 16, 1875; *CR,* 43-2, 366.

34. McPherson, *Hand-Book of Politics for 1876,* 29.

35. Newspaper clipping enclosed in Edwards Pierrepont to Grant, January 10, 1875, USG-LC; *Garfield-Hinsdale Letters: Correspondence between James Abram Garfield and Burke Aaron Hinsdale,* ed. Mary L. Hinsdale (Ann Arbor: University of Michigan Press, 1949), 309; Dawes tb Samuel Bowles, January 7, 1875, SB-Yale; Hamilton Fish, diary, January 8, 1875, HF-LC.

36. *CR,* 43-2, 366–367, 368, 370.

37. *CR,* 43-2, 248, 340, 371, 696.

38. *CR,* 43-2, 339, 371, 430.

39. Hamilton Fish, diary, January 8, 1875, HF-LC; Bristow to John Marshall Harlan, January 11, 1875, BHB-LC.

40. Hamilton Fish, diary, January 10, 11, 12, 1875, HF-LC; *CR,* 43-2, 371, 374; Bristow to Harlan, January 11, 1875, BHB-LC.

41. Richardson, *Messages,* 7:305–314.

42. James G. Blaine to Grant, January 14, 1875, W. W. Holden to Grant, January 14, 1875, USG-LC.

43. *NYT,* January 14, 1875; John Sherman, *Self-Government in Louisiana. Speech of Hon. John Sherman of Ohio, in the United States Senate, January 16 and 22, 1875* (Washington, D.C.: Government Printing Office, 1875), 22–23; Bristow to Edwin W. Stoughton, January 15, 1875, Stoughton to Bristow, January 14, 1875, BHB-LC.

44. *NYT,* January 16, 1875; Richardson, *Messages,* 7:314; E. A. Merritt to Whitelaw Reid, January 17, 24, 1875, WR-LC; Joseph Medill to Washburne, January 17, 1875, EBW-LC.

45. *CR,* 43-2, 490, 695, 836, 879; Sherman, *Self-Government in Louisiana,* 41, 42–43.

46. *CR,* 43-2, 488; *NYT,* January 19, 1875; D. A. Goddard to Dawes, January 27, 1875, HLD-LC.

47. Fish to Bristow, February 3, 1875, HF-LC; James T. Otten, "The Wheeler Adjustment in Louisiana: National Republicans Begin to Reappraise Their Reconstruction Policy," *Louisiana History* 13 (Fall 1972): 359–360.

48. Gillette, *Retreat from Reconstruction,* 265–267; William Vincent Byars, *"An American Commoner": The Life and Times of Richard Parks Bland* (St. Louis: H. L. Conard, 1900), 94–96; Garfield, *Diary,* 3:16–17; *CR,* 43-2, 785–829, 880–902; *Garfield-Hinsdale Letters,* 316; Dawes to Bowles, February 2, 1875, SB-Yale.

49. Byars, *"American Commoner,"* 93; *CR,* 43-2, 944, 945, 959, 1001.

50. *CR,* 43-2, 940, 980, 982, appx., 157.

51. Marshall Jewell to Washburne, December 5, 1874, EBW-LC.

52. *CR,* 43-2, 985–992.

53. *CR,* 43-2, 1001, 1002, 1005, 1009; Garfield, *Diary,* 3:21.

54. *CR,* 43-2, 938, 999, 1010–1011; McPherson, *Hand-Book of Politics for 1876,* 4–7; Donald Bruce Johnson and Kirk H. Porter, comps., *National Party Platforms, 1840–1972* (Urbana: University of Illinois Press, 1975), 41, 44.

55. Dawes to Bowles, February 2, 1875, SB-Yale; House Report No. 127, 43rd Cong., 2nd sess.

56. Hamilton Fish, diary, November 17, December 4, 1874, January 22, 1875, HF-LC; August H. Garland to Grant, January 13, 1875 (telegram), USG-LC; *CR,* 43-2, 1034; House Report No. 127, 43rd Cong., 2nd sess., 15–16; *NYT,* February 7, 1875.

57. Richardson, *Messages,* 7:319.

58. Hamilton Fish, diary, February 9, 11, 1875, HF-LC; Harlan to Bristow, February 16, 1875, BHB-LC.

59. Richardson, *Messages,* 7:319; Hamilton Fish, diary, February 9, 21, March 9, 1875, Fish to L. J. Jennings, March 3, 1875, HF-LC; *CR,* 43-2, 2086, 2093, 2117–2118; McPherson, *Hand-Book of Politics for 1876,* 20–21.

60. *CR,* 43-2, 1645–1652; McPherson, *Hand-Book of Politics for 1876,* 36–38, 200–201; Otten, "Wheeler Adjustment," 361–364; Garfield, *Diary,* 3:34.

61. *CR,* 43-2, 1453; *NYT,* February 15, 1875; Garfield to Burke Hinsdale, February 13, 1875, JAG-WRHS.

62. *NYT,* February 15, 1875; *CR,* 43-2, 1823–1834, 1847, 1907.

63. *CR,* 43-2, 1852, 1907, 1925, appx., 127.

64. *CR,* 43-2, 1838, 1839, 1885.

65. *CR,* 43-2, 1885; Garfield to W. C. Howells, January 17, 1875, JAG-LC; Medill to Washburne, January 17, 1875, EBW-LC; Medill to James G. Blaine, February 14, 1875, JGB-LC; H. Clay Trumbull to Joseph R. Hawley, January 6, 1875, JRH-LC.

66. *CR,* 43-2, 1853, 1855.

67. *CR,* 43-2, 1935; McPherson, *Hand-Book of Politics for 1876,* 18; Garfield to Hinsdale, March 8, 1875, JAG-WRHS.

68. *CR,* 43-2, 1791–1798, 1867–1870; McPherson, *Hand-Book of Politics for 1876,* 8.

69. For press reaction, see Gillette, *Retreat from Reconstruction,* 273–275; James M. McPherson, "Abolitionists and the Civil Rights Act of 1875," *JAH* 52 (December 1965): 508–509.

70. McPherson, *Hand-Book of Politics for 1876,* 8–11; *NYTr,* April 1, 1875.

71. Pierrepont to Fish, March 10, 1875, HF-LC.

72. *NYT,* March 13, April 3, 1875.

73. *NYT,* April 7, 1875; Marshall Jewell to Washburne, April 23, 1875, EBW-LC.

74. Jewell to Washburne, April 23, 1875, Elliot C. Cowdin to Washburne, February 20, 1875, EBW-LC; William Faxon to William E. Chandler, December 3, 1874, D. E. Sickles to Chandler, April 23, May 30, 1875, WEC-LC; Garfield, *Diary,* 3:6; Hamilton Fish, diary, May 30, 1875, HF-LC; A. T. Wikoff to Grant, May 18, 1875, Grant to Harry White, May 29, 1875, O. E. Babcock to White, May 30, 1875 (telegram), Frederick Douglass to Babcock, May 31, 1875, USG-LC; McPherson, *Hand-Book of Politics for 1876,* 154–155.

75. *NYT,* April 8, September 9, 1875; Garfield speech at Warren, Ohio, August 31, [1875], unidentified newspaper clipping, JAG-LC; Sherman, *Selected Speeches,* 491; Garfield, *Diary,* 3:119–120, 143, 155; John Sherman, *Recollections of Forty Years in the House, Senate and Cabinet* (Chicago: Werner, 1895), 1:520–521.

76. Sherman, *Recollections,* 1:520; *Harper's Weekly,* April 3, 1875; Steven K. Green, "The Blaine Amendment Reconsidered," *American Journal of Legal History* 36 (1992): 41–47; Harry Barnard, *Rutherford B. Hayes and His America* (Indianapolis: Bobbs-Merrill, 1954), 272–273; Reginald Charles McGrane, *William Allen: A Study in Western Democracy* (Columbus: Ohio State Archaeological and Historical Society, 1925), 229–231; McPherson, *Hand-Book of Politics for 1876,* 227.

77. Garfield speech at Warren, Ohio, August 31, [1875], unidentified newspaper clipping, JAG-LC; Garfield, *Diary,* 3:120; *Diary and Letters of Rutherford B. Hayes,* ed. Charles Richard Williams (Columbus: Ohio State Archaeological and Historical Society, 1922), 3:274, 276, 283, 285, 286, 290.

78. Oliver P. Morton, *Record and Platforms of the Democratic Party. Speech of Senator Morton, at Urbana, Ohio, Aug. 7, 1875* (n.p., 1875).

79. *Harper's Weekly,* August 28, 1875; *NYTr,* August 30, 1875; Bristow to Harlan, August 27, 1875, BHB-LC.

80. *The Papers of U. S. Grant*, ed. John Y. Simon (Carbondale: Southern Illinois University Press, 1967–), 26:342–344, 349n.

81. Blanche Ames Ames, *Adelbert Ames, 1835–1933: General, Senator, Governor* (New York: Argosy-Antiquarian, 1964), 419, 443; Rable, *But There Was No Peace*, 154–156; Levi P. Luckey to Edwards Pierrepont, September 9, 1875, EP-Yale; McPherson, *Hand-Book of Politics for 1876*, 42–43.

82. *ANB*, 17:506–507; Pierrepont to Alphonso Taft, June 29, 1875, WHT-LC; Fish to Pierrepont, September 10, 1875, EP-Yale; Pierrepont to Fish, September 10 (telegram), 11 (telegram), 1875, HF-LC; *NYT*, June 25, 1874, September 10, 11, 1875; McPherson, *Hand-Book of Politics for 1876*, 40–42.

83. Grant to Pierrepont, September 13, 1875, EP-Yale.

84. McPherson, *Hand-Book of Politics for 1876*, 42–43; Pierrepont to Grant, September 16, 1875 (telegram), USG-LC; *NYT*, September 9, 16, 1875.

85. Ames, *Ames*, 431–434.

86. Ibid., 440–441; G. K. Chase to Pierrepont, May 4, 1877, EP-Yale.

87. Finis H. Little to Bristow, November 6, 1875, BHB-LC; Rable, *But There Was No Peace*, 158–161; Ames, *Ames*, 442–444.

88. Garfield, *Diary*, 3:176; Pierrepont to Washburne, November 3, 1875, EBW-LC; Horace Maynard to Fish, November 11, 1875, HF-LC; Bristow to J. K. Gant, December 2, 1875, BHB-LC; Richardson, *Messages*, 7:332–356.

89. *NYT*, September 13, 1875; Blaine to Morton, August 21, 1875, Blaine to A. T. Wikoff, October 2, 1875, JGB-LC.

90. Blaine to Whitelaw Reid, November 29, 1875, WR-LC; *NYT*, November 29, 1875; Marie Carolyn Klinkhamer, "The Blaine Amendment of 1875: Private Motives for Political Action," *Catholic Historical Review* 42 (April 1956): 28–32; Richardson, *Messages*, 7: 334, 356.

91. *CR*, 44-1, 205, 5189; McPherson, *Hand-Book of Politics for 1876*, 240–241.

CHAPTER 4: The Southern Question Revived: The Campaign of 1876

1. Henry L. Dawes, diary, January [misdated March] 14, 1876, HLD-LC; *The Diary of James A. Garfield*, ed. Harry James Brown and Frederick D. Williams (East Lansing: Michigan State University Press, 1967–1981), 3:192, 204.

2. *CR*, 44-1, 224, 323–326, 382–388.

3. James G. Blaine, *Twenty Years of Congress* (Norwich, Conn.: Henry Bill Publishing, 1884, 1886), 2:554; Garfield to Blaine, January 13, 1876, JAG-LC; *CR*, 44-1, 545–551, 387.

4. Garfield, *Diary*, 3:218; Dawes, diary, January [misdated March] 14, 1876, HLD-LC.

5. Dawes, diary, January [misdated March] 14, 1876, HLD-LC; Carl Schurz to Samuel Bowles, January 16, 1876, SB-Yale; *CR*, 44-1, 408–410; R. J. Griffin to Nathaniel Banks, January 14, 1876, B. B. Johnson to Banks, January 19, 1876, B. F. Clough to

Banks, January ?, 1876, Gideon J. Pillow to Banks, February 2, 1876, Herbert Radclyffe to Banks, January 17, 1876, NPB-LC.

6. John E. Russell to Bowles, January 16, 1876, James G. Blaine to Bowles, January 22, 1876, Charles Nordhoff to Bowles, January 16, 1876, SB-Yale; Whitelaw Reid to Blaine, January 23, 1876, WR-LC; John Hay to Blaine, January 27, [1876], JGB-LC; *NYTr,* February 7, 8, 1876; James A. Garfield to Burke Hinsdale, January 18, 1876, Garfield to Austin Harmon, January 16, 1876, JAG-LC.

7. John W. Forney to Elihu B. Washburne, February 5, 1876, EBW-LC; Garfield to Hinsdale, April 4, 1876, JAG-LC.

8. *CR,* 44-1, 239, 497, 2101–2104, 2119.

9. *Appletons' Annual Cyclopaedia and Register of Important Events of the Year 1876* (New York: D. Appleton, 1877), 601.

10. *U.S. v. Cruikshank,* 92 U.S. 542 (1876).

11. *U.S. v. Reese,* 92 U.S. 214 (1876); *CR,* 44-1, 2149, 3098, 4057–4075; *Revised Statutes of the United States,* 2nd ed. (Washington, D.C.: Government Printing Office, 1878), 353, 1067–1068.

12. *Speeches, Correspondence and Political Papers of Carl Schurz,* ed. Frederic Bancroft (New York: G. P. Putnam's Sons, 1913), 3:242; *Record of Benjamin H. Bristow,* pamphlet (Boston, 1876); Bristow to W. B. Belknap, June 8, 1875, BHB-LC.

13. Garfield, *Diary,* 3:254; *Official Proceedings of the National Republican Conventions of 1868, 1872, 1876, and 1880* (Minneapolis: Charles W. Johnson, 1903), 279–281.

14. *Official Proceedings . . . 1868, 1872, 1876, and 1880,* 290–294, 295, 299–301.

15. E. Bruce Thompson, "The Bristow Presidential Boom of 1876," *MVHR* 32 (June 1945): 3–30; David Saville Muzzey, *James G. Blaine: A Political Idol of Other Days* (New York: Dodd, Mead, 1934), 83–99; *Official Proceedings . . . 1868, 1872, 1876, and 1880,* 299–301, 327, 330.

16. Ari Hoogenboom, *Rutherford B. Hayes: Warrior and President* (Lawrence: University Press of Kansas, 1995), 196–201, 204–208; *Diary and Letters of Rutherford B. Hayes,* ed. Charles Richard Williams (Columbus: Ohio State Archaeological and Historical Society, 1922), 3:147, 269, 286.

17. Schurz, *Speeches,* 3:249, 251, 254.

18. Edward McPherson, *A Hand-Book of Politics for 1876* (Washington, D.C.: Solomons & Chapman, 1876), 212–213; Schurz, *Speeches,* 3:260; George William Curtis to Hayes, July 13, 1876, RBH-HPC.

19. Hayes, *Diary and Letters,* 3:340.

20. Amos Akerman to John Sherman, June 17, 1876, Akerman to George Friedley, August 22, 1876, ATA-UVA.

21. Senate Executive Document No. 85, 44th Cong., 1st sess., 5, 6; *CR,* 44-1, 4645, 4711.

22. *CR,* 44-1, 5087–5094.

23. *The Works of James Abram Garfield,* ed. Burke A. Hinsdale (Boston: James R. Osgood, 1882), 2:353–387.

24. Hayes to Garfield, August 5, 1876, JAG-LC; *CR,* 44-1, 5275–5281; Hayes, *Diary and Letters,* 3:343.

25. Hayes, *Diary and Letters,* 3:343, 358, 360; *CR,* 44-1, 5191–5192, 5595; McPherson, *Hand-Book of Politics for 1876,* 240–241.

26. *Confederate Leaders in the Forty-Fourth Congress. Who They Are—Their Aims and Opinions. A Democratic Counter Rebellion. Conquering the Union They Failed to Destroy,* and *Record of the Democratic Speaker. Hon. Michael C. Kerr, A Representative Bourbon. The Rebel South Victorious,* both in *Documents Issued by the Union Republican Congressional Committee, Campaigns of 1875–76* (Washington, D.C., 1877); *Indianapolis Journal,* August 19, 24, 1876; *NYT,* September 19, 1876.

27. Washburne to Aaron F. Perry, September 7, 1876, Edwards Pierrepont to Washburne, August 31, October 14, 1876, EBW-LC; Murat Halstead to Hayes, September 19, 1876, RBH-HPC.

28. Gail Hamilton, *Biography of James G. Blaine* (Norwich, Conn.: Henry Bill Publishing, 1895), 422; William A. Wheeler to Whitelaw Reid, October 17, 1876, WR-LC; George S. Boutwell to James Redpath, September 12, 1876, George S. Boutwell Papers, HPC.

29. Hayes to Halstead, October 14, 1876, Murat Halstead Papers, Cincinnati Historical Society; *NYT,* October 26, 1876; John Sherman, *Selected Speeches and Reports on Finance and Taxation, from 1859 to 1878* (New York: D. Appleton, 1879), 552.

30. Sherman, *Selected Speeches,* 554, 555; George C. Rable, *But There Was No Peace: The Role of Violence in the Politics of Reconstruction* (Athens: University of Georgia Press, 1984), 172–176; Hamilton Fish, diary, October 12, 17, 1876, HF-LC; James D. Richardson, *A Compilation of the Messages and Papers of the Presidents, 1789–1902* (Washington, D.C.: Bureau of National Literature and Art, 1903), 7:396–397; *Appletons' Annual Cyclopaedia . . . 1876,* 720–721.

31. Carl Schurz, *To Business Men. Address of Hon. Carl Schurz, before the Union League Club, of New York, Saturday Evening, October 21, 1876* (New York: Republican National Committee, 1876), 7; *NYT,* November 4, 1876.

32. Garfield, *Diary,* 3:377–378; Hayes, *Diary and Letters,* 3:373.

CHAPTER 5: Rescuing the Republic: The Electoral Crisis of 1876–1877

1. See, for example, Paul Leland Haworth, *The Hayes-Tilden Disputed Presidential Election of 1876* (Cleveland: Burrows Brothers, 1906); C. Vann Woodward, *Reunion and Reaction: The Compromise of 1877 and the End of Reconstruction* (Boston: Little, Brown, 1951); Keith Ian Polakoff, *The Politics of Inertia: The Election of 1876 and the End of Reconstruction* (Baton Rouge: Louisiana State University Press, 1973); Allan Peskin, "Was There a Compromise of 1877?" *JAH* 60 (June 1973): 63–75; Michael Les Benedict, "Southern Democrats in the Crisis of 1876–1877: A Reconsideration of *Reunion and Reaction,*" *JSH* 46 (November 1980): 489–524; George C. Rable, "Southern Interests

and the Election of 1876: A Reappraisal," *Civil War History* 26 (December 1980): 347–361; Brooks D. Simpson, "Ulysses S. Grant and the Electoral Crisis of 1876–77," *Hayes Historical Journal* 11 (Winter 1992): 5–22; Ari Hoogenboom, *The Presidency of Rutherford B. Hayes* (Lawrence: University Press of Kansas, 1988), chap. 2; Mark Wahlgren Summers, *The Era of Good Stealings* (New York: Oxford University Press, 1993), chap. 20; Brooks D. Simpson, *The Reconstruction Presidents* (Lawrence: University Press of Kansas, 1998), 192–196. Recent popular treatments add nothing of significance to the historiographic debate: Roy Morris Jr., *Fraud of the Century: Rutherford B. Hayes, Samuel Tilden, and the Stolen Election of 1876* (New York: Simon & Schuster, 2003); William Rehnquist, *Centennial Crisis: The Disputed Election of 1876* (New York: Alfred A. Knopf, 2004).

2. Zachariah Chandler to Edward Wade, December 1, 1876, ZC-LC; Edwards Pierrepont to Rutherford B. Hayes, December 7, 1876, RBH-HPC.

3. Jerome L. Sternstein, ed., "The Sickles Memorandum: Another Look at the Hayes-Tilden Election-Night Conspiracy," *JSH* 32 (August 1966): 342–357. Although it turned out that Hayes had clearly carried Oregon, the parties disputed the election of a single elector there on a technicality. Polakoff, *Politics of Inertia*, 225–228.

4. [William E.] C[handler] to Hayes, November 9, 1876, John Mercer Langston to Hayes, November 9, 1876 (telegram), RBH-LC.

5. Hamilton Fish, diary [November 9, 10, 1876], HF-LC; Edward McPherson, *A Hand-Book of Politics for 1878* (Washington, D.C.: Solomons & Chapman, 1878), 57; T. Harry Williams, *Hayes: The Diary of a President, 1875–1881* (New York: David McKay, 1964), 52; Polakoff, *Politics of Inertia*, 207–210, 219; Hoogenboom, *Presidency of Hayes*, 27–31.

6. Hoogenboom, *Presidency of Hayes*, 31; Haworth, *Hayes-Tilden Disputed Presidential Election*, 176–186; Polakoff, *Politics of Inertia*, 223–225.

7. E. W. Winkler, ed., "The Bryan-Hayes Correspondence, VII," *Southwestern Historical Quarterly* 26 (1923): 311.

8. Murat Halstead to Hayes, November 30, 1876, RBH-HPC; Williams, *Hayes: Diary of a President*, 52–53; *NYH*, December 4, 1876.

9. W. B. Williams to James A. Garfield, December 11, 1876, Garfield to Hayes, December 12, 1876, RBH-HPC; *NYH*, December 4, 1876; Hayes to Garfield, December 16, 1876, JAG-LC; *The Diary of James A. Garfield*, ed. Harry James Brown and Frederick D. Williams (East Lansing: Michigan State University Press, 1967–1981), 3:395.

10. Hoogenboom, *Presidency of Hayes*, 33–35; Polakoff, *Politics of Inertia*, 248–254; "Col. Kellar," memorandum, 1876, H. V. Boynton to William Henry Smith, December 20, 26, 1876, WHS-IHS; Smith to Hayes, December 14, 1876, Halstead to Hayes, December 21, 1876, RBH-HPC.

11. William Henry Smith to Hayes, December 22, 1876, RBH-HPC. Smith's letter quoted Medill.

12. Edward McPherson, *Hand-Book of Politics for 1876* (Washington, D.C.: Solomons & Chapman, 1876), 142–143; Donald Bruce Johnson and Kirk H. Porter, comps., *National Party Platforms, 1840–1972* (Urbana: University of Illinois Press, 1975), 47, 54; Boynton to W. H. Smith, December 20, 1876, WHS-IHS; Garfield, *Diary*, 3:397–399, 414; James M. Comly to Hayes, January 8, 1877, RBH-HPC; House Report No.

139, 44th Cong., 2nd sess. See also speech by C. G. Williams, June 13, 1878, in *CR*, 45-2, Appendix, 487.

13. *Diary and Letters of Rutherford B. Hayes,* ed. Charles Richard Williams (Columbus: Ohio State Archaeological and Historical Society, 1922), 3:393, 396–397, 399; John A. Kasson to Hayes, December 17, 27, 1876, William E. Chandler to Hayes, December 29, 1876, E. F. Noyes to Hayes, December 30, 1876, January 2, 1877, RBH-HPC; Williams, *Hayes: Diary of a President,* 61–62; *Speeches, Correspondence and Political Papers of Carl Schurz,* ed. Frederic Bancroft (New York: G. P. Putnam's Sons, 1913), 3:354–355.

14. Hayes to William K. Rogers, December 31, 1876, RBH-LC; Hayes, *Diary and Letters,* 3:395; Samuel Shellabarger to Hayes, December 30, 1876, John D. Defrees to Hayes, December 26, 1876, RBH-HPC.

15. E. D. Morgan to Hayes, December 2, 1876, Garfield to Hayes, December 9, 1876, John Sherman to Hayes, December 12, 1876, RBH-HPC; Williams, *Hayes: Diary of a President,* 54.

16. T. C. Platt to Hayes, December 11, 1876, Sherman to Hayes, December 12, 1876, Albert D. Shaw to Hayes, December 16, 22, 28, 1876, Hayes, diary, December 17, 1876, RBH-HPC

17. *NYH,* December 4, 1876; Alphonso Taft to Hayes, December 4, 24, 27, 31, 1876, William Dennison to Hayes, December 9, 1876, RBH-HPC; Hayes to U. S. Grant, December 25, 1876, USG-LC; Polakoff, *Politics of Inertia,* 263.

18. Hayes, *Diary and Letters,* 3:393; *Letters and Literary Memorials of Samuel J. Tilden,* ed. John Bigelow (New York: Harper and Brothers, 1908), 2:491–492; Comly to Hayes, January 8, 1877, RBH-HPC.

19. Schurz, *Speeches,* 3:339–348, 351, 353, 354–361.

20. Joseph Medill to W. H. Smith, January 3, 1877, WHS-IHS; Smith to Hayes, December 30, 1876, Sherman to Hayes, January 3, 1877, Charles Foster to Hayes, January 21, 1877, RBH-HPC; Hoogenboom, *Presidency of Hayes,* 38; Norman Kuntz, "Edmunds' Contrivance: Senator George F. Edmunds of Vermont and the Electoral Compromise of 1877," *Vermont History* 38 (Autumn 1970): 308–312; Edmunds to Schurz, January 2, 1877, CS-LC; *CR*, 44-2, 713–714.

21. Garfield, *Diary,* 3:419; Garfield to Hayes, January 19, 1877, William Dennison to Hayes, January 20, 1877, RBH-HPC.

22. Hayes, *Diary and Letters,* 3:404, 406; *CR*, 44-2, 820–822; Polakoff, *Politics of Inertia,* 278.

23. *CR*, 44-2, 824; Sherman to Hayes, January 8, 1877, RBH-HPC.

24. Garfield, *Diary,* 3:419; *The Works of James Abram Garfield,* ed. Burke A. Hinsdale (Boston: James R. Osgood, 1882), 2:408–433.

25. *CR*, 44-2, 799–801, 893–898; E. A. Fulton to Oliver P. Morton, January 27, 1877, OPM-ISL; McPherson, *Hand-Book of Politics for 1878,* 2, 10.

26. Hayes, *Diary and Letters,* 3:404; Hamilton Fish, diary, January 20, 1877, HF-LC; George W. Childs, *Recollections* (Philadelphia: J. B. Lippincott, 1890), 79–80; *CR*, 44-2, 825–831.

27. Garfield to Hayes, January 19, 1877, RBH-HPC; *CR*, 44-2, 713, 878.

28. *CR*, 44-2, 907, 1023; John P. Jones to Mrs. Jones, January 21, 1877, JPJ-HL.

29. Shellabarger to Hayes, January 8, 1877, William E. Chandler to Hayes, January 16, 1877, Sherman to Hayes, January 26, 1877, James N. Tyner to J. M. Comly, January 26, 1877, Boynton to Comly, January 25, 1877, RBH-HPC; Harman Yerkes to Samuel J. Randall, January 20, 1877, Samuel Dickson to Randall, January 18, 19, 1877, George Vickers to Randall, December 5, 1876, SJR-HSP.

30. Andrew J. Kellar to W. H. Smith, January 26, 1877, February 2, 1877, Boynton to Smith, January 14, 30, 1877, WHS-IHS; *CR*, 44-2, 913, 1050; McPherson, *Hand-Book of Politics for 1878,* 9, 10; Boynton to Comly, January 25, 1877, RBH-HPC.

31. *CR*, 44-2, 913, 1050; McPherson, *Hand-Book of Politics for 1878,* 9, 10; W. B. Lawrence to Samuel J. Tilden, January 27, 1877 SJT-NYPL.

32. James D. Richardson, *A Compilation of the Messages and Papers of the Presidents, 1789–1902* (Washington, D.C.: Bureau of National Literature and Art, 1903), 7:422–424; Hayes, *Diary and Letters,* 3:410.

33. Sherman to Hayes, January 30, 1877, Chandler to Hayes, January 31, February 4, 1877, Dennison to Hayes, February 1, 1877, RBH-HPC.

34. *Electoral Count of 1877. Proceedings of the Electoral Commission* (Washington, D.C.: Government Printing Office, 1877), 195; James G. Blaine to Hayes, February 14, 1877, Chandler to Hayes, February 9, 1877, Shellabarger to Hayes, February 10, 1877, Halstead to Hayes, February 11, 1877, RBH-HPC.

35. Grant to Edwards Pierrepont, February 11, 1877, Alfred W. Van Sinderen Collection, Yale University Library; *Electoral Count of 1877,* 201–202; *CR*, 44-2, 1486; *NYT,* February 11, 12, 1877; Sherman to Hayes, February 10, 1877, Stanley Matthews to Hayes, February 13, 1877, RBH-HPC.

36. Boynton to "Dear Mr. Smith," February 11, 1877, WHS-IHS. This letter apparently went to Richard Smith, Boynton's editor at the *Cincinnati Gazette,* who forwarded it to Hayes, who sent it to William Henry Smith. The letter bears Hayes's characteristic notation of sender and city of origin.

37. Boynton to William Henry Smith, February 11, 1877 (with Hayes's notation of sender, city of origin, and date), WHS-IHS. Smith forwarded this letter to Hayes and kept a copy for himself. Hayes returned the original to Smith.

38. *CR*, 44-2, 1486, 1488–1502; McPherson, *Hand-Book of Politics for 1878,* 13; Tyner to Comly, February 12, 1877, RBH-HPC.

39. *Electoral Count of 1877,* 416–423; John P. Jones to Mrs. Jones, February 19, 1877, JPJ-HL; Hayes, *Diary and Letters,* 3:416.

40. *CR*, 44-2, 1664–1665; McPherson, *Hand-Book of Politics for 1878,* 16; *NYTr,* February 19, 1877; Garfield, *Diary,* 3:443; Dennison to Hayes, February 17, 1877, Sherman to Hayes, February 18, 1877, RBH-HPC; *NYH,* February 18, 1877; A. H. Coffroth to Randall, February 20, 1877, George M. Dallas to Randall, February 19, 1877, SJR-HSP.

41. Boynton to W. H. Smith, February 18, 1877, WHS-IHS; *NYH,* February 18, 1877; Shellabarger to Hayes, February 18, 1877, RBH-HPC; J. S. Robinson to Sherman, February 20, 1877, JS-LC.

42. Hayes, *Diary and Letters,* 3:416–417.

43. Jacob D. Cox to Hayes, January 31, 1877, RBH-HPC.

44. Hayes to Cox, February 2, 1877, quoted in Polakoff, *Politics of Inertia*, 295; Hayes to Schurz, February 4, 1877, CS-LC.

45. Hayes, *Diary and Letters*, 3:417.

46. Under a decision of Florida's state supreme court, the Democrats had retaken control of that state and inaugurated their candidate for governor on January 1. Grant and the national administration posed no interference. Polakoff, *Politics of Inertia*, 230; Simpson, *Reconstruction Presidents*, 193.

47. Untitled typescript, n.d., Edward A. Burke Papers, Special Collections, Tulane University Library.

48. McPherson, *Hand-Book of Politics for 1878*, 60–61; Alphonso Taft to Hayes, February 14, 1877, RBH-HPC; Hamilton Fish, diary, January 17, 1877, HF-LC; *Presidential Election Investigation*, House Miscellaneous Document No. 31, 45th Cong., 3rd sess., 3:605, 607, 609, 613, 616.

49. Thomas C. W. Ellis to "Dear Meart," February 19, 1877, EF-LSU; *Presidential Election Investigation*, 1:962–963, 1044–1045.

50. *Presidential Election Investigation*, 1:970–971, 3:614, 631–632.

51. *Presidential Election Investigation*, 1:964, 967.

52. Hoogenboom, *Presidency of Hayes*, 42; *NYH*, February 18, 1877; Benedict, "Southern Democrats," 512, 516, 520–523; J. P. Bishop to Hayes, February 19, 1877, RBH-HPC.

53. *House Journal*, 44-2, 484–485; Benedict, "Southern Democrats," 521; Halstead to Hayes, February 19, 1877, RBH-HPC; Boynton to W. H. Smith, February 22, 1877, WHS-IHS; Hayes, *Diary and Letters*, 3:415.

54. Benedict, "Southern Democrats," 521; *NYH*, February 20, 1877; *NYTr*, February 20, 1877; Polakoff, *Politics of Inertia*, 304–305; *House Journal*, 44-2, 491–492; Williaim D. Kelley to Mrs. William D. Kelley, February 21, 1877, WDK-HSP; Grant to Hayes, February 20, 1877, RBH-HPC.

55. Charles Foster to Hayes, February 21, 1877, RBH-HPC; Benedict, "Southern Democrats," 521; *House Journal*, 44-2, 491–492; *CR*, 44-2, 1708.

56. Foster to Hayes, February 21, 1877, RBH-HPC; *House Journal*, 44-2, 500–501; Benedict, "Southern Democrats," 521; *Presidential Election Investigation*, 1:957, 973–974; 3:595, 616.

57. *Presidential Election Investigation*, 598–601; *NYH*, February 24, 1877; *House Journal*, 44-2, 520–521; Benedict, "Southern Democrats," 521.

58. *NYH*, February 24, 1877, *NYTr*, February 24, 1877; Tyner to Comly, February 23, 1877 (telegram), Sherman to Hayes, February 24, 1877, RBH-HPC.

59. *CR*, 44-2, 1905–1915; Benedict, "Southern Democrats," 521; W. W. H. Davis to Randall, February 26, 1877, SJR-HSP; Garfield, *Diary*, 3:447–448; John P. Jones to Mrs. Jones, February 24, 1877, JPJ-HL; Sherman to Hayes, February 25, 1877, RBH-HPC.

60. E. John Ellis to E. P. Ellis, February 25, 1877, EF-LSU.

61. *Presidential Election Investigation*, 1:990, 992, 3:618; Garfield, *Diary*, 3:448.

62. *NYH*, February 26, 1877; *Presidential Election Investigation*, 3:618.

63. *Presidential Election Investigation*, 1:974–975, 3:619–620.

64. *NYT,* March 29, 1877.

65. *House Journal,* 44-2, 547–548, 553; Benedict, "Southern Democrats," 521; Jones to Mrs. Jones, February 26, 1877, JPJ-HL; Boynton to W. H. Smith, February 26, 1877, 7:30 P.M. (telegram), WHS-IHS.

66. Boynton to W. H. Smith, February 26, 1877, 9:45 (telegram), February 26, 1877, 7:30 (telegram), WHS-IHS.

67. Sherman to Hayes, February 21 (telegram), 24, 25, 1877, RBH-HPC. The unspecified "expedient" that Sherman mentioned in his February 25 letter may have been the sort of commission that Hayes used to conclude the Louisiana controversy early in his presidency. A letter of March 25 from Kellar to William Henry Smith included the sentence, "The Louisiana Commission is a very wise movement, and one, as you know the president's mind approved some weeks ago." Kellar to Smith, March 25, 1877, WHS-IHS.

68. Garfield, *Diary,* 3:448–449.

69. *Presidential Election Investigation,* 1:983, 3:596–597, 621–623. See also S. P. Packard to Hayes, April 5, 1877, RBH-HPC.

70. *Presidential Election Investigation,* 1:1034–1037, 3:621–622; Hayes, *Diary and Letters,* 3:421.

71. *Presidential Election Investigation,* 3:623, 624; *NYT,* March 29, 1877.

72. *Presidential Election Investigation,* 3:623; *House Journal,* 44-2, 558–561, 573–579; Benedict, "Southern Democrats," 522; *Selected Writings of Abram S. Hewitt,* ed. Allan Nevins (New York: Columbia University Press, 1937), 177; J. P. Crozer's Sons to Randall, February 28, 1877, SJR-HSP.

73. Charles Devens to George F. Hoar, February 27, 1877, GFH-MHS; William D. Kelley to Mrs. Kelley, February 28, 1877, WDK-HSP; Barclay Gallagher to W. H. Smith, March 1, 1877 (telegram), WHS-IHS; *NYTr,* March 2, 1877; *CR,* 44-2, 2047; *Electoral Count of 1877,* 728.

74. *Appletons' Annual Cyclopaedia and Register of Important Events of the Year 1877* (New York: D. Appleton, 1883), 456–457; McPherson, *Hand-Book of Politics for 1878,* 67–68; Hamilton Fish, diary, March 1, 1877, HF-LC; *Presidential Election Investigation,* 3:626–630.

75. *NYT,* March 15, 1877; Charles Richard Williams, *The Life of Rutherford Birchard Hayes* (Columbus: Ohio State Archaeological and Historical Society, 1928), 2:43–44; *Presidential Election Investigation,* 3:631.

CHAPTER 6: Conciliation Is Not Mutual: Republicanism and the Southern Policy of Rutherford B. Hayes

1. Hamilton Fish, diary, January 17, 1877, HF-LC; Adam Badeau to Rutherford B. Hayes, March 2, 1877, RBH-HPC.

2. James D. Richardson, *A Compilation of the Messages and Papers of the Presidents, 1789–1902* (Washington, D.C.: Bureau of National Literature and Art, 1903), 7:442–447.

3. William Henry Smith to Hayes, February 17, 1877, Joseph Medill to Richard

Smith, February 17, 1877, W. H. Smith to Richard Smith, February 19, 1877, RBH-HPC; Andrew J. Kellar to W. H. Smith, February 16, 1877, WHS-IHS; *NYTr,* March 5, 1877; Hamilton Fish to J. C. B. Davis, March 22, 1877, HF-LC; Henry L. Dawes to Mrs. Dawes, March 7, 9, 1877, HLD-LC.

4. Medill to Richard Smith, February 17, 1877, W. H. Smith to Richard Smith, February 19, 1877, RBH-HPC.

5. *CR,* 45th Cong., Special Session of the Senate, 16; Hamilton Fish, diary, March 6, 1877, HF-LC.

6. *Diary and Letters of Rutherford B. Hayes,* ed. Charles Richard Williams (Columbus: Ohio State Archaeological and Historical Society, 1922), 3:427–429.

7. *NYT,* March 24, April 4, 11, 1877; D. H. Chamberlain, Jno. J. Patterson, and D. T. Corbin, undated memorandum [circa April 1877], Wade Hampton to Hayes, March 29, 31, 1877, RBH-HPC; Edward McPherson, *A Hand-Book of Politics for 1878* (Washington, D.C.: Solomons & Chapman, 1878), 81.

8. "Josie" to "My darling sister," March 21, 1877, EF-LSU; Francis T. Nicholls to R. L. Gibson, E. J. Ellis, and W. M. Levy, March 26, 1877 (letterpress), FTN-LSU; L. Q. C. Lamar to Hayes, March 22, 1877, Stanley Matthews to Hayes, March 23, 1877, RBH-HPC.

9. Hamilton Fish, diary, March 27, 1877, HF-LC; McPherson, *Hand-Book of Politics for 1878,* 70–71.

10. Nicholls to Gibson, Ellis, and Levy, March 26, 1877 (letterpress), FTN-LSU; John Marshall Harlan to Benjamin Bristow, April 13, 1877, BHB-LC; Andrew J. Kellar to D. M. Key, April 14, 19, 1877, RBH-HPC; *NYT,* April 17, 20, 1877; McPherson, *Hand-Book of Politics for 1878,* 69–70.

11. Kellar to W. H. Smith, March 25, April 26, 1877, WHS-IHS.

12. Hayes, *Diary and Letters,* 3:430.

13. *NYT,* March 24, 1877.

14. James G. Blaine to the Editor of the *Boston Herald,* April 10, 1877, JGB-LC; Blaine to Whitelaw Reid, April 12, 1877, WR-LC; Benjamin Wade to U. H. Painter, April 9, 1877, in *NYT,* April 23, 1877; Zachariah Chandler to William E. Chandler, July 26, 1877, WEC-NHHS.

15. Edwards Pierrepont to Hayes, April 22, 1877, Benjamin Harris Brewster to Hayes, April 19, 1877, RBH-HPC; Murat Halstead to William E. Chandler, May 31, 1877, WEC-NHHS.

16. Walter Q. Gresham to Thomas Slaughter, May 20, 1877, Walter Q. Gresham Papers, Indiana State Library, Indianapolis; R. R. Hitt to Oliver P. Morton, June 9, 1877, R. R. Hitt Papers, LC; Marshall Jewell to Bristow, May 17, 1877, BHB-LC.

17. John W. Foster to Morton, April 16, 1877, OPM-ISL; *NYT,* May 26, 1877.

18. *NYT,* May 24, 26, June 12, 1877; John Sherman to L. Q. C. Lamar, June 2, 1877, JS-LC; James M. Wells, *The Chisolm Massacre: A Picture of "Home Rule" in Mississippi* (Washington, D.C.: Chisolm Monument Association, 1878); Green B. Raum, *The Existing Conflict between Republican Government and Southern Oligarchy* (Washington, D.C.: Charles M. Green Printing, 1884), 337–345; Robert M. Goldman, *"A*

Free Ballot and a Fair Count": The Department of Justice and the Enforcement of Voting Rights in the South, 1877–1893 (New York: Fordham University Press, 2001), 52–53.

19. Sherman to J. Madison Wells, July 7, 1877, JS-LC.

20. *Independent,* July 12, 1877; Daniel Hall to Chandler, July 5, 1877, WEC-NHHS.

21. Sherman to Willard Warner, October 4, 1877, JS-LC.

22. John Sherman, *Selected Speeches and Reports on Finance and Taxation, from 1859 to 1878* (New York: D. Appleton, 1879), 571–574.

23. Thurlow Weed to Sherman, August 18, 1877, JS-LC; William E. Chandler to Edward McPherson, August 22, 1877, EM-LC; Zachariah Chandler to William E. Chandler, August 7, 1877, WEC-NHHS.

24. W. E. Stevens to W. E. Chandler, August 24, 1877, WEC-NHHS; *NYT,* September 18, 20, 1877.

25. Charles Richard Williams, *The Life of Rutherford Birchard Hayes* (Columbus: Ohio State Archaeological and Historical Society, 1928), 2:248; *NYT,* September 23, 1877.

26. *NYT,* September 21, 23, 1877.

27. *NYT,* September 18, 20, 23, 1877; R. B. Avery to W. E. Stevens, January 10, 1878, WEC-LC.

28. *NYT,* September 12, 13, 26, 1877.

29. Samuel Bowles to Henry L. Dawes, August 26, 1877, HLD-LC.

30. Henry L. Dawes, manuscript election speech, n.p., n.d. [1877], HLD-LC.

31. Hayes, *Diary and Letters,* 3:444; Timothy Howe to Grace Howe, October 15, 1877, TOH-WHS; Donald Bruce Johnson and Kirk H. Porter, comps., *National Party Platforms, 1840–1972* (Urbana: University of Illinois Press, 1975), 53–54; Edward McPherson, ed., *The Tribune Almanac and Political Register for 1878* (New York: Tribune Association, 1878), 22–28.

32. *The Diary of James A. Garfield,* ed. Harry James Brown and Frederick D. Williams (East Lansing: Michigan State University Press, 1967–1981), 3:529, 532, 535.

33. Warner Bateman to Sherman, October 11, 1877, JS-LC; McPherson, *Hand-Book of Politics for 1878,* 233.

34. Chandler's letters to newspapers were published in *Letters of Mr. William E. Chandler Relative to the So-Called Southern Policy of President Hayes, Together with a Letter to Mr. Chandler of Mr. William Lloyd Garrison* (Concord, N.H.: Monitor and Statesman Office, 1878). Quotation from 54.

35. *NYT,* November 9, 1877.

36. Sherman to Wm. A. Newall, January 8, 1878, JS-LC; Howe to Grace Howe, November 16, 1877, TOH-WHS; Richardson, *Messages,* 7:459; Fish to John L. Cadwalader, January 25, 1878, HF-LC; *NYT,* December 22, 1877.

37. Garfield, *Diary,* 4:19; *NYT,* February 12, 1878; Sherman to Hayes, February 9, 1878, RBH-HPC; *CR,* 45-2, 1194.

38. Hayes, *Diary and Letters,* 3:459, 471, 4:280; *NYT,* February 13, 18, March 19, 1878; Winfield S. Hancock to W. T. Sherman, February 14, 15, March 4, 1878, RBH-

HPC; David M. Jordan, *Winfield Scott Hancock: A Soldier's Life* (Bloomington: Indiana University Press, 1988), 265.

39. *CR*, 45-2, 2000–2008; T. Harry Williams, *Hayes: The Diary of a President, 1875–1881* (New York: David McKay, 1964), 133.

40. Howe to Grace Howe, April 4, 11, 1878, TOH-WHS; John Kimball to Justin S. Morrill, March 12, 1878, JSM-LC; C. A. Boutelle to Chandler, April 12, 1878, WEC-NHHS.

41. Hayes to Guy M. Bryan, July 27, 1878, RBH-HPC; Williams, *Hayes: Diary of a President*, 141–142; *NYT*, May 29, 1878; Williams, *Life of Hayes*, 2:155n.

42. *NYTr*, May 22, 1878, and October 1878, passim; Richard Smith to Hayes, June 8, 1878, RBH-HPC; *NYT*, May 29, 1878; McPherson, *Hand-Book of Politics for 1878*, 192–194; Williams, *Hayes: Diary of a President*, 145; Ari Hoogenboom, *Rutherford B. Hayes: Warrior and President* (Lawrence: University Press of Kansas, 1995), 368; Williams, *Life of Hayes*, 2:161–169.

43. *NYT*, August 26, 1878; McPherson, *Hand-Book of Politics for 1878*, 159–167, 219–222; Edward McPherson, ed., *The Tribune Almanac and Political Register for 1879* (New York: Tribune Association, 1879), 20–26; Chandler to James S. Clarkson, August 1, 1878, WEC-LC.

44. Hayes, *Diary and Letters*, 3:496; *NYT*, August 22, September 6, 1878.

45. Chandler to Reid, September 14, 1878, WR-LC; Blaine to Chandler, September 29, 1878, George C. Gorham to Chandler, October 26, 1878, E. Hinds to Chandler, October 28, 1878, WEC-LC; *NYT*, October 14, 1878.

46. Hayes, *Diary and Letters*, 3:501–502, 505; Charles Devens to Hayes, October 4, 1878, with enclosure, RBH-HPC; Goldman, *"Free Ballot,"* 54–56.

47. Kenneth C. Martis, *The Historical Atlas of Political Parties in the United States Congress, 1789–1989* (New York: Macmillan, 1989), 130–133; Garfield, *Diary*, 4:143–144; E. F. Noyes to Hayes, November 8, 1878, RBH-HPC; Hayes, *Diary and Letters*, 3:509.

48. Hayes, *Diary and Letters*, 3:509, 510; Washington *National Republican*, November 13, 1878; Sherman to Thomas G. Baker, November 26, 1878, JS-LC.

49. *NYT*, November 15, 1878; Washington *National Republican*, November 19, 1878; Hayes, *Diary and Letters*, 3:509.

50. Richardson, *Messages*, 7:493–495; Williams, *Hayes: Diary of a President*, 175; Goldman, *"Free Ballot,"* 56–73.

51. E. W. Winkler, ed., "The Bryan-Hayes Correspondence, XI," *Southwestern Historical Quarterly* 27 (1924): 323, 324–325; *CR*, 45-2, 75; Hayes, *Diary and Letters*, 3:516.

52. W. A. Wheeler to Hayes, November 21, 1878, RBH-HPC; Boutelle to Reid, December 6, 17, 1878, WR-LC.

53. *CR*, 45-2, 2, 84–87, 243.

54. Washington *National Republican*, November 19, 1878.

55. Boutelle to Reid, November 20, 1878, WR-LC; D. H. Chamberlain, "Reconstruction and the Negro," *North American Review* 128 (February 1879): 161–173.

56. James G. Blaine et al., "Ought the Negro to Be Disfranchised? Ought He to Have Been Enfranchised?" *North American Review* 128 (March 1879): 225–283, quotations at 242, 279, 246, 248.

57. Angus Cameron to Blaine, January 14, 1879, JGB-LC; *Louisiana and South Carolina in 1878*, 45th Cong., 2nd sess., Senate Report No. 855, xxvii, xliii, xlv, xlvi; Edward McPherson, *A Hand-Book of Politics for 1880* (Washington, D.C.: James J. Chapman, 1880), 78–79.

58. McPherson, *Hand-Book of Politics for 1880*, 55–56; Richardson, *Messages*, 7:520; Hayes, *Diary and Letters*, 3:528.

59. *Supplement to the Revised Statutes of the United States, 1874–1891* (Washington, D.C.: Government Printing Office, 1891), 190; Hayes, *Diary and Letters*, 3:544–547, 561; *Revised Statutes of the United States*, 2nd ed. (Washington, D.C.: Government Printing Office, 1878), 352, 1071.

60. C. R. Brayton to Nelson Aldrich, April 8, 1879, NWA-LC; *CR*, 46-1, 118, 415; McPherson, *Hand-Book of Politics for 1880*, 117; Garfield, *Diary*, 4:207; Xi Wang, *The Trial of Democracy: Black Suffrage and Northern Republicans, 1860–1910* (Athens: University of Georgia Press, 1997), 172–173.

61. *CR*, 46-1, 144, 166, 232, 234.

62. *CR*, 46-1, 214, 266, 805–806; Hayes, *Diary and Letters*, 3:543.

63. *CR*, 46-1, 439, 441, Appendix, 10; *NYTr*, March 27, 1879.

64. John Sherman, manuscript speech fragment [July 1879], JS-LC; *CR*, 46-1, 115–118, 235; *Garfield-Hinsdale Letters: Correspondence between James Abram Garfield and Burke Aaron Hinsdale*, ed. Mary L. Hinsdale (Ann Arbor: University of Michigan Press, 1949), 403–404.

65. Hayes, *Diary and Letters*, 3:529, 530, 532; Hayes to William Henry Smith, March 27, 1879, RBH-HPC.

66. Richardson, *Messages*, 7:523–536.

67. Richardson, *Messages*, 7:536–544, 545–547; McPherson, *Hand-Book of Politics for 1880*, 112–113; Hayes, *Diary and Letters*, 3:561; Hoogenboom, *Rutherford B. Hayes*, 402; *Annual Report of the Attorney General of the United States for the Year, 1879*, 15.

68. Garfield, *Diary*, 4:233, 234, 243, 281–283; *Garfield-Hinsdale Letters*, 416, 417; *The Works of James Abram Garfield*, ed. Burke A. Hinsdale (Boston: James R. Osgood, 1882), 2:713, 719. For treatments of the growth of the conciliatory spirit that aroused Garfield's skepticism, see Nina Silber, *The Romance of Reunion: Northerners and the South, 1865–1900* (Chapel Hill: University of North Carolina Press, 1993); David W. Blight, *Race and Reunion: The Civil War in American Memory* (Cambridge, Mass.: Harvard University Press, 2001).

69. S. M. Cullom to Hayes, May 5, 1879, RBH-HPC.

70. Hayes, *Diary and Letters*, 3:564; *Garfield-Hinsdale Letters*, 429; *Appletons' Annual Cyclopaedia and Register of Important Events of the Year 1879* (New York: D. Appleton, 1883), 603, 679, 703.

71. *NYTr*, September 18, 1879.

72. Garfield, *Works*, 2:760–768.

73. Elihu Washburne to Blaine, July 25, 1879, JGB-LC; John Sherman, *Speech of Hon. John Sherman, of Ohio, on the Financial and Other Issues of the Times, Delivered at Steubenville, Ohio, August 20, 1879* (n.p., n.d. [1879]).

74. Hayes, *Diary and Letters*, 3:575; Richardson, *Messages*, 7:557–581.

75. Sherman to A. J. Dumont, November 10, 1879, Sherman to B. D. Fearing, November 1, 1879, JS-LC; *NYTr*, October 28, 1879; *Garfield-Hinsdale Letters*, 430–431.

76. Hamilton Fish to Nicholas Greusel, November 24, 1879, HF-LC; *NYTr*, October 4, 22, 1879.

77. Zachariah Chandler, *Last and Greatest Speech of Zach. Chandler, Late U.-S. Senator from Michigan, Delivered at McCormick Hall, Chicago, Oct. 31, 1879* (Chicago: Fergus Printing, 1879), 17, 21, 26–27.

78. Edwards Pierrepont to Zachariah Chandler, February 25, 1879, ZC-LC; William Chandler to Reid, November 22, 1879, WR-LC.

CHAPTER 7: Confrontation with a Solid South: New Directions under Garfield and Arthur

1. D. W. Voyles to Walter Q. Gresham, November 3, 1879, NCB-IHS; Whitelaw Reid to James G. Blaine, December 20, 1879, WR-LC.

2. *Chicago Tribune*, November 13, 1879; Adam Badeau, *Grant in Peace* (Hartford: S. S. Scranton, 1887), 321; Henry L. Dawes to Mrs. Dawes, December 15, 1879, HLD-LC; H. Wayne Morgan, *From Hayes to McKinley: National Party Politics, 1877–1896* (Syracuse: Syracuse University Press, 1969), 59–62.

3. Morgan, *From Hayes to McKinley*, 62; John Sherman to W. C. McFarland, January 2, 1880, Sherman to T. C. Jones, February 23, 1880, JS-LC.

4. C. H. Grosvenor to Sherman, March 27, 1880, W. S. Furay to Sherman, March 21, 1880, Sherman to John W. Bremmer, March 27, 1880, JS-LC; *NYT*, April 1, 1880.

5. Morgan, *From Hayes to McKinley*, 69–71; David Saville Muzzey, *James G. Blaine: A Political Idol of Other Days* (New York: Dodd, Mead, 1934), 155–157; *NYT*, January 22, 1880.

6. *CR*, 46-2, 2641–2643, 2647–2648. Vice President William A. Wheeler ruled Blaine's amendment out of order because it proposed general legislation in an appropriations bill.

7. *Appletons' Annual Cyclopaedia and Register of Important Events of the Year 1880* (New York: D. Appleton, 1883), 172; *Diary and Letters of Rutherford B. Hayes*, ed. Charles Richard Williams (Columbus: Ohio State Archaeological and Historical Society, 1922), 3:561.

8. Edward McPherson, *A Hand-Book of Politics for 1880* (Washington, D.C.: James J. Chapman, 1880), 22–32; *CR*, 46-2, 1516–1517, 1703. The Supreme Court's split in the *Siebold* case was actually 7 to 2.

9. *CR*, 46-2, 1600, 1639–1640; James D. Richardson, *A Compilation of the Messages and Papers of the Presidents, 1789–1902* (Washington, D.C.: Bureau of National Literature and Art, 1903), 7:591–592.

10. George S. Boutwell, "General Grant and a Third Term," *North American Review* 130 (April 1880): 384; *Appletons' Annual Cyclopaedia . . . 1880*, 558, 706.

11. *NYTr*, April 9, 19, 1880; *NYT*, March 26, April 1, 11, 12, 16, May 5, 6, 1880; Timothy Howe to Blaine, April 14, 1880, JGB-LC; *The Diary of James A. Garfield*, ed. Harry James Brown and Frederick D. Williams (East Lansing: Michigan State University Press, 1967–1981), 4:422.

12. *Proceedings of the Republican National Convention, Held at Chicago, Illinois . . . 1880* (Chicago: Jno. B. Jeffrey Printing and Publishing House, 1881), 6, 160; Donald Bruce Johnson and Kirk H. Porter, comps., *National Party Platforms, 1840–1972* (Urbana: University of Illinois Press, 1975), 62.

13. *Republican National Convention . . . 1880*, 180–182, 183, 186, 188, 189.

14. *The Works of James Abram Garfield*, ed. Burke A. Hinsdale (Boston: James R. Osgood, 1882), 2:734; Garfield, *Diary*, 4:385, 404.

15. Sherman to Richard Smith, June 14, 1880, JS-LC; Richardson, *Messages*, 7:592–598; Hayes note, June 16, 1880, JAG-LC.

16. *Letters and Literary Memorials of Samuel J. Tilden*, ed. John Bigelow (New York: Harper and Brothers, 1908), 2:599–600; *Chicago Tribune*, June 26, 1880; *Cincinnati Gazette*, June 29, 1880; David M. Jordan, *Winfield Scott Hancock: A Soldier's Life* (Bloomington: Indiana University Press, 1988), 200–227; *Boston Evening Transcript*, July 1, 1880.

17. *Boston Evening Transcript*, July 1, 1880; John D. Defrees to Garfield, June 28, 1880, JAG-LC.

18. *Republican National Convention . . . 1880*, 298–299.

19. William E. Chandler to Hayes, July 3, 1880, RBH-HPC. Chandler's analysis assumed that Garfield would win all the other normally Republican northern and western states.

20. *Cincinnati Gazette*, July 2, 1880; Hayes, *Diary and Letters*, 3:615.

21. For instance, Herbert Clancy, *The Presidential Election of 1880* (Chicago: Loyola University Press, 1958), 185–192; Morgan, *From Hayes to McKinley*, 108–110; Robert Marcus, *Grand Old Party: Political Structure in the Gilded Age, 1880–1896* (New York: Oxford University Press, 1971), 44–47; Allan Peskin, *Garfield* (Kent, Ohio: Kent State University Press, 1999), 488–490. Stanley Hirshson notes the discussion of the southern question but claims that "the sectional theme was used to cover up the true story of the Fifth Avenue Hotel conference." Hirshson, *Farewell to the Bloody Shirt: Northern Republicans and the Southern Negro, 1877–1893* (Bloomington: Indiana University Press, 1962), 80–81. Kenneth Ackerman offers a similar treatment in *Dark Horse: The Surprise Election and Political Murder of President James A. Garfield* (New York: Carroll & Graf, 2003), 166–173.

22. *NYTr*, August 6, 1880.

23. *NYTr*, August 7, 1880.

24. John Hay, *The Balance Sheet of the Two Parties, A Speech Delivered by John Hay, at Cleveland, Ohio, July 31, 1880* (Cleveland: Leader Printing, 1880), 15–16; *CR*, 46-2, 528, 1702; Hayes, *Diary and Letters*, 3:616; *Cincinnati Gazette*, August 12, 1880; *Boston Evening Transcript*, July 22, 1880.

25. Edward McPherson to Garfield, September 21, 1880, JAG-LC; *The Republican Campaign Textbook for 1880* (Washington, D.C.: Republican Congressional Committee, 1880); Edward McPherson and Jay Hubbell, *Union Republican Congressional Committee Documents* (Washington, D.C.: Republican Congressional Committee, 1880); *Boston Evening Transcript*, July 29, 1880; Schuyler Colfax to Edward McPherson, September 18, 1880, EM-LC; U. S. Grant to E. F. Beale, October 22, 1880, USG-LC.

26. John Sherman, *Is a Change Necessary? Speech of Hon. John Sherman, Secretary of the Treasury, Delivered at Cincinnati, Ohio, Monday, August 30, 1880* (Washington, D.C.: Republican Congressional Committee, 1880), 7.

27. Marshall Jewell to Garfield, September 14, 1880, Joseph Nimmo Jr. to Garfield, September 15, 1880, with clipping from Washington *National Republican*, September 15, 1880, Geo. W. Hooker to Garfield, September 13, 1880 (telegram), Garfield and D. G. Swaim to J. C. Keffer, September 13, 1880 (telegram), A. L. Morrison to Garfield, September 14, 1880, JAG-LC; Garfield, *Diary*, 4:455; Garfield to Sherman, September 25, 1880, JS-LC.

28. This incident, probably apocryphal, was recounted by William C. Hudson, *Random Recollections of an Old Political Reporter* (New York: Cuples & Long, 1911), 112, and cited in Morgan, *From Hayes to McKinley*, 116; Peskin, *Garfield*, 494.

29. Jewell to Reid, August 16, 23, 26, 1880, WR-LC; *Protection or Free Trade?* (New York: New York Republican State Committee, 1880), 3.

30. *Great Republican Speeches of the Campaign of 1880* (Stapleton, N.Y.: Staten Island Publishing, 1881), 41, 44; John Sherman, *Recollections of Forty Years in the House, Senate and Cabinet* (Chicago: Werner, 1895), 2:780–782; Geo. C. Tichenor to Sherman, October 20, 1880, JS-LC.

31. *Great Republican Speeches . . . 1880*, 8, 10–11.

32. *NYTr*, October 1, 1880.

33. *Indianapolis Journal*, August 21, 1880; Hancock interview in *Paterson Guardian* (New Jersey), quoted in *Cincinnati Gazette*, October 11, 1880; *Great Republican Speeches . . . 1880*, 42; *NYTr*, October 19, 21, 1880.

34. *Great Republican Speeches . . . 1880*, 50.

35. *Cincinnati Gazette*, July 24, October 9, 1880; *Boston Evening Transcript*, July 1, 1880; Edwards Pierrepont, *Speech of the Hon. Edwards Pierrepont, Delivered before the Republican Meeting, at the Hall of Cooper Institute, October 6th, 1880* (New York: Cornwell Press, 1880), 10.

36. *Great Republican Speeches . . . 1880*, 44, 66; R. G. Ingersoll, *Free Speech and an Honest Ballot* (Chicago: L. W. Blaisdell, 1880), 4; *Cincinnati Gazette*, September 30, 1880.

37. Garfield to Sherman, November 4, 1880, JS-LC.

38. Hamilton Fish to Nicholas Greusel, November 11, 1880, HF-LC.

39. Richardson, *Messages,* 7:601–602; Robert M. Goldman, *"A Free Ballot and a Fair Count": The Department of Justice and the Enforcement of Voting Rights in the South, 1877–1893* (New York: Fordham University Press, 2001), 85–86.

40. Chandler to Garfield, November 1, 1880, February 17, 1880, JAG-LC.

41. Vincent P. De Santis, *Republicans Face the Southern Question—The New Departure Years, 1877–1897* (Baltimore, Md.: Johns Hopkins University Press, 1959), 140–141; Justus D. Doenecke, *The Presidencies of James A. Garfield and Chester A. Arthur* (Lawrence: Regents Press of Kansas, 1981), 34; *Garfield-Hinsdale Letters: Correspondence between James Abram Garfield and Burke Aaron Hinsdale,* ed. Mary L. Hinsdale (Ann Arbor: University of Michigan Press, 1949), 490; R. C. McCormick to Chandler, April 1, 1881, E. H. Rollins to Chandler, May 15, 17, 1881, H. W. Blair to Chandler, May 20, 1881, WEC-NHHS; Leon Burr Richardson, *William E. Chandler: Republican* (New York: Dodd, Mead, 1940), 268–271; Goldman, *"Free Ballot,"* 88–89.

42. *Garfield-Hinsdale Letters,* 469; *NYT,* January 18, 1881; Albion W. Tourgée to Garfield, December 14, 1880, D. H. Chamberlain to Garfield, December 28, 1880, Garfield to Chamberlain, January 15, 1881, JAG-LC.

43. *Garfield-Hinsdale Letters,* 431; "Memorandum" with Chandler to Garfield, November 22, 1880, JAG-LC.

44. *CR,* 47th Cong., 1st Special Session of the Senate, 33–34. A Democratic filibuster blocked the election of Mahone's choices for officers of the Senate.

45. Garfield, *Diary,* 4:516–517, 540–541, 583; Garfield to Whitelaw Reid, December 30, 1880, WR-LC; Garfield to John Hay, May 29, 1881, JAG-LC; De Santis, *Republicans Face the Southern Question,* 146–147.

46. *Garfield-Hinsdale Letters,* 469–470.

47. *Republican National Convention . . . 1880,* 161, 299.

48. Richardson, *Messages,* 7:56; *CG,* 41-2, appx., 478, 479, 485; Gordon Canfield Lee, *The Struggle for Federal Aid: First Phase: A History of the Attempt to Obtain Federal Aid for the Common Schools, 1870–1890* (New York: Teachers College, Columbia University, 1949), 42–55.

49. *CG,* 42-2, 794, 862; Edward McPherson, *A Hand-Book of Politics for 1872* (Washington, D.C.: Philp & Solomons, 1872), 122–124; Lee, *Struggle for Federal Aid,* 81–84.

50. Richardson, *Messages,* 7:152, 203, 296, 334, 356, 411, 479, 506, 579; *Cincinnati Gazette,* August 12, 1880.

51. Richardson, *Messages,* 7:602–603; Edward McPherson, *A Hand-Book of Politics for 1882* (Washington, D.C.: James J. Chapman, 1882), 37–39; *CR,* 46-3, 147–151, 229; Frederick Douglass to Justin Morrill, January 4, 1881 [misdated 1880], JSM-LC.

52. *NYT,* January 15, 1881.

53. Garfield, *Works,* 2:791–792.

54. McPherson, *Hand-Book of Politics for 1880,* 210A–210B; Richardson, *Messages,* 8:58.

55. Goldman, *"Free Ballot,"* 90–124; Xi Wang, *The Trial of Democracy: Black Suffrage and Northern Republicans, 1860–1910* (Athens: University of Georgia Press, 1997), 199, 208.

56. Thomas C. Reeves, *Gentleman Boss: The Life of Chester Alan Arthur* (New York: Alfred A. Knopf, 1975), 308–312.

57. *NYT,* September 19, 1882.

58. Chandler to Blaine, October 2, 1882, WEC-LC; Reeves, *Gentleman Boss,* 310–311.

59. Richardson, *Messages,* 8:59–60, 95–96; George C. Tichenor to Sherman, January 28, 1882, JS-LC; *Appletons' Annual Cyclopaedia and Register of Important Events of the Year 1881* (New York: D. Appleton, 1883), passim; *Appletons' Annual Cyclopaedia and Register of Important Events of the Year 1882* (New York: D. Appleton, 1883), passim; Edward McPherson, ed., *The Tribune Almanac and Political Register for 1882* (New York: Tribune Association, 1882), 16–22; Edward McPherson, ed., *The Tribune Almanac and Political Register for 1883* (New York: Tribune Association, 1883), 22–25; Carl Schurz, "Party Schisms and Future Problems," *North American Review* 134 (May 1882): 433.

60. Kenneth C. Martis, *The Atlas of Political Parties in the United States Congress, 1789–1989* (New York: Macmillan, 1989), 134–137; Edmund Meisenhelder to Edward McPherson, December 13, 1882, EM-LC.

61. Richardson, *Messages,* 8:143–144; John J. Mott to Sherman, January 23, 1883, JS-LC.

62. James R. Randall to Nelson Aldrich, April 9, 1883, NWA-LC; Benjamin Harrison, speech at Des Moines, September 21, 1883, unidentified newspaper clipping, BH-LC; *Garfield-Hinsdale Letters,* 470.

63. *NYT,* September 26, 27, 28, October 6, 1883.

64. Civil Rights Cases, 109 U.S. 3 (1883); *The Frederick Douglass Papers,* series 1, ed. John W. Blassingame and John R. McKivigan (New Haven, Conn.: Yale University Press, 1979–1992), 5: 111, 112, 121.

65. *The Works of Robert G. Ingersoll* (New York: Dresden Publishing, 1912), 11:9–10, 11, 41.

66. *NYTr,* November 20, 1883.

67. Unidentified newspaper clipping, October 1883, BH-LC.

68. W. M. Dickson to Sherman, November 22, 1883, Henry Hurd to Sherman, January 3, 1884, JS-LC; Louis T. Michener to Gresham, October 27, 1883, WQG-LC.

69. Hirshson, *Farewell to the Bloody Shirt,* 119–120; Senate Reports 512 and 579, 48th Cong., 1st sess.; Green B. Raum, *The Existing Conflict between Republican Government and Southern Oligarchy* (Washington, D.C.: Charles M. Green Printing, 1884), 384–426; *NYTr,* October 20, November 20, 1883; Warner Bateman to Sherman, December 28, 1883, JS-LC.

70. Richardson, *Messages,* 8:188; *NYT,* December 13, 1883; Chandler to Reid, December 17, 26, 1883, WR-LC.

71. Edward McPherson, *A Hand-Book of Politics for 1884* (Washington, D.C.: James J. Chapman, 1884), 106, 108, 110, 111; *CR,* 48-1, 11–12, 249, 288.

72. *CR,* 48-1, 715, 717; Senate Reports 512 and 579, 48th Cong., 1st sess.

73. *CR*, 48-1, 2000.

74. *CR*, 48-1, 2062, 2106, 2151, 2253; T. J. Porter to Sherman, March 22, 1884, J. D. Cox and E. E. White to Sherman, March 24, 1884 (telegram), JS-LC.

75. *CR*, 48-1, 2000, 2009–2010, 2693–2707, 2724; McPherson, *Hand-Book of Politics for 1884*, 147; Henry W. Blair, *The Education Bill* (Washington, D.C.: n.p., 1887), 47.

76. House Report No. 495, 48th Cong., 1st sess.; James A. Barnes, *John G. Carlisle: Financial Statesman* (New York: Dodd, Mead, 1931), 152–153; Lee, *Struggle for Federal Aid*, 158; Allen J. Going, "The South and the Blair Education Bill," *MVHR* 44 (September 1958): 282.

77. George C. Davies to Sherman, November 21, 1883, JS-LC.

CHAPTER 8: The Fundamental Question in a Republic: Republicanism, Economics, and Electoral Stalemate in the 1880s

1. John J. Mott to John Sherman, January 8, 1884, Wm. R. Moore to Sherman, January 24, 1884, B. Nesbitt to Sherman, May 19, 1884, JS-LC.

2. James G. Blaine, *Twenty Years of Congress* (Norwich, Conn.: Henry Bill Publishing, 1884, 1886), 1:46, 121, 559; M. Woodhull to William E. Chandler, September 9, 1884, WEC-LC.

3. *Official Proceedings of the Republican National Convention Held at Chicago, June 3, 4, 5, and 6, 1884* (Minneapolis: Charles W. Johnson, 1903), 141–142.

4. *Republican National Convention . . . 1884*, 91–95.

5. *Republican National Convention . . . 1884*, 105, 106, 117, 122, 127.

6. *Republican National Convention . . . 1884*, 141–163, 181.

7. *Republican National Convention . . . 1884*, 182; James G. Blaine, *Political Discussions: Legislative, Diplomatic, and Popular, 1856–1886* (Norwich, Conn.: Henry Bill Publishing, 1887), 430.

8. Newark *Daily Advertiser*, July 19, 1884, quoted in Stanley Hirshson, *Farewell to the Bloody Shirt: Northern Republicans and the Southern Negro, 1877–1893* (Bloomington: Indiana University Press, 1962), 124; C. A. Boutelle to Blaine, July 17, 1884, JGB-LC.

9. T. B. Boyd, *The Blaine and Logan Campaign of 1884* (Chicago: J. L. Reagan, 1884), 104, 146.

10. W. B. Allison to John A. Logan, September 15, 1884, JAL-LC; Charles E. Buell to Sherman, October 31, 1884, JS-LC; Green B. Raum, *The Existing Conflict between Republican Government and Southern Oligarchy* (Washington, D.C.: Charles M. Green Printing, 1884); Green B. Raum to Nelson Aldrich, July 31, 1884, NWA-LC.

11. Walter Q. Gresham to A. C. Harris, June 30, 1884, Gresham to G. I. Reed, July 19, 1884, WQG-LC; Boyd, *Blaine and Logan Campaign*, 103, 104–105.

12. *Appletons' Annual Cyclopaedia and Register of Important Events of the Year 1884* (New York: D. Appleton, 1885), 631–632, 806; Boyd, *Blaine and Logan Campaign*, 127, 138, 142, 176.

13. Edward McPherson, *A Hand-Book of Politics for 1886* (Washington, D.C.: James J. Chapman, 1886), 236.

14. Blaine, *Political Discussions*, 467, 468, 469, 470; Albion W. Tourgée to Blaine, November 20, 1884, JGB-LC.

15. Hirshson, *Farewell to the Bloody Shirt*, 131; *Speeches, Correspondence and Political Papers of Carl Schurz*, ed. Frederic Bancroft (New York: G. P. Putnam's Sons, 1913), 4:294; M. Woodhull to Chandler, November 19, 1884, WEC-LC.

16. Edward Squire to Sherman, November 22, 1884, John Hopley to Sherman, November 20, 1884, JS-LC.

17. *Independent*, July 9, 1885, 3–4; John Sherman, *Fair Elections and an Honest Count. Speeches of Hon. John Sherman in Ohio and Virginia during the Campaign of 1885* (n.p., n.d.), 4, 6, 9, 12, 23.

18. Sherman, *Fair Elections and an Honest Count*, 51–52.

19. Charles Holstein to Sherman, October 1, 1885, J. C. F. Beyland to Sherman, October 14, 1885, JS-LC.

20. Benjamin Harrison to W. W. Slaughter, March 14, 1885, BH-LC; McPherson, *Hand-Book of Politics for 1886*, 158–164; Lawrence Grossman, *The Democratic Party and the Negro: Northern and National Politics, 1868–92* (Urbana: University of Illinois Press, 1976), 117–118.

21. George Hoar to Blaine, September 1, 1886, JGB-LC; *NYT*, September 7, 1886; Kenneth C. Martis, *The Atlas of Political Parties in the United States Congress, 1789–1989* (New York: Macmillan, 1989), 138–141.

22. Warner Bateman to Chandler, June 11, 1887, WEC-NHHS; Chandler to Bateman, July 15, 1887, Warner Bateman Papers, Western Reserve Historical Society, Cleveland.

23. Sherman to M. W. Cramer, February 15, 1887, JS-LC; *NYTr*, March 25, 1887.

24. *NYTr*, March 27, 1887; John Hay to Sherman, March 26, 1887, R. W. Thompson Jr. to Sherman, April 20, 1887, JS-LC.

25. J. P. Osterhout to Sherman, April 29, 1887, John W. Finnell to Sherman, May 24, 1887, Raum to Sherman, May 9, 27, 1887, suggestions for Sherman's speech [misdated June 1888], JS-LC.

26. John Sherman, *Speech of Hon. John Sherman, Delivered before the Legislature of Illinois at the City of Springfield, June 1, 1887* (Columbus: Ohio State Journal Job Printing Establishment, 1887), 9, 12, 16.

27. *NYTr*, June 3, 1887; J. W. Dimmick to "Dear General," June 16, 1887, JS-LC; William E. Chandler, *Speech of Mr. William E. Chandler, at Concord, N.H., June 9th, 1887, on Accepting the Nomination of U.S. Senator* (n.p., n.d. [1887]).

28. Wm. Henry Smith to Sherman, June 8, 1887, Sherman to George B. Wright, June 4, 1887, Sherman interview quoted in unidentified newspaper clipping, dateline Cincinnati, June 17, [1887], JS-LC; *Nation*, June 9, 1887, 479; Sherman interview quoted in John Sherman, *Recollections of Forty Years in the House, Senate and Cabinet* (Chicago: Werner, 1895), 2:987.

29. Mary R. Dearing, *Veterans in Politics: The Story of the G.A.R.* (Baton Rouge: Louisiana State University Press, 1952), 342–351; Richard E. Welch Jr., *The Presidencies*

of Grover Cleveland (Lawrence: University Press of Kansas, 1988), 62–64; Sherman, *Speech at Springfield*, 9; John F. Gowey to Sherman, June 24, 1887, Warner Miller to Sherman, July 19, 1887, JS-LC.

30. Joseph B. Foraker to Sherman, June 21, 1887, JS-LC; J. B. Foraker, "The Return of the Republican Party," *Forum* 3 (August 1887): 544, 546, 557–558.

31. Sherman to Samuel Sewall, September 27, 1887, JS-LC.

32. H. H. Leavitt to James P. Foster, October 19, 1887, enclosed in Leavitt to Sherman, October 24, 1887, Sherman to "My Dear Sir," [November 1887] (letterpress), JS-LC

33. *NYTr,* December 8, 1887; John Spooner to W. S. Stanley, December 9, 1887, JCS-LC.

34. Willie D. Halsell, "The Appointment of L. Q. C. Lamar to the Supreme Court," *MVHR* 28 (December 1941): 399–412; James B. Murphy, *L. Q. C. Lamar: Pragmatic Patriot* (Baton Rouge: Louisiana State University Press, 1973), 260–263; Arnold Paul, "Lucius Quintus Cincinnatus Lamar," in *The Justices of the Supreme Court, 1789–1978,* ed. Leon Friedman and Fred Israel (New York: Chelsea House, 1980), 2:1443–1444; Allan Nevins, *Grover Cleveland: A Study in Courage* (New York: Dodd, Mead, 1932), 339.

35. Chandler to Whitelaw Reid, December 26, 1887, WR-LC.

36. Edward McPherson, *A Hand-Book of Politics for 1880* (Washington, D.C.: James J. Chapman, 1880), 78–79; Spooner to Frank Avery, January 7, 1888, Spooner to George C. Ginty, January 10, 1888, JCS-LC; *NYTr,* January 10, 1888.

37. L. S. Fish to Sherman, January 9, 1888, JS-LC; Murphy, *Lamar,* 263.

38. James S. Clarkson quoted in *Nation,* January 26, 1888, 64, 65; James S. Clarkson et al., "Permanent Republican Clubs," *North American Review* 146 (March 1888): 260–261.

39. Foraker to Murat Halstead, June 8, 1888, JBF-CHS.

40. *CR,* 50-1, 29, 402–406.

41. P. B. Thompkins to Sherman, January 16, 1888, JS-LC.

42. Wm. B. Merchant to Sherman, April 24, 1888, P. F. Herwig to Sherman, April 23, 1888, JS-LC; *CR,* 50-1, 5136, 3086. Sherman quoted Eustis's speech.

43. J. W. Gordon to Sherman, May 15, 1888, Frederick Douglass to Sherman, April 25, 1888, JS-LC.

44. *Official Proceedings of the Republican National Convention Held at Chicago, June 19, 20, 21, 22, 23, and 25, 1888* (Minneapolis: Charles W. Johnson, Publisher, 1903), 13–14, 22, 109.

45. *Republican National Convention . . . 1888,* 144, 145–146.

46. *Republican National Convention . . . 1888,* 159–199, 209, 226, 232–233.

47. *Indianapolis Journal,* October 2, 1876, December 21, 1887; *Speeches of Benjamin Harrison,* comp. Charles Hedges (New York: United States Book Company, 1892), 16, 21, 22.

48. T. B. McKearney to Harrison, June 26, 1888, Clarkson to Harrison, July 25, 1888, BH-LC; M. S. Quay to James M. Swank, July 17, 1888, James M. Swank Papers, Historical Society of Pennsylvania, Philadelphia; James A. Kehl, *Boss Rule in the Gilded*

Age: Matt Quay of Pennsylvania (Pittsburgh: University of Pittsburgh Press, 1981), 94–95; Joanne Reitano, *The Tariff Question in the Gilded Age: The Great Debate of 1888* (University Park: Pennsylvania State University Press, 1994); Clarkson to Allison, September 24, 1888, WBA-SHSI.

49. John A. Roche to Harrison, September 28, 1888, BH-LC; Foraker to C. L. Edwards, September 10, 1888, JBF-CHS; Spooner to J. V. Quarles, October 10, 1888, Spooner to O. L. Rosenkrans, October 11, 1888, JCS-LC; *CR*, 50-1, 8523–8534, 8536–8541, 9315.

50. *CR*, 50-1, 7818–7830, 7865–7878; William E. Chandler, "Our Southern Masters," *Forum* 5 (July 1888): 518.

51. Ben Butterworth to Harrison, July 13, 1888, A. E. Bateman to Harrison, July 17, 1888, William Henry Wood to Harrison, June 30, 1888, with note from T. Platt, T. C. Platt to Harrison, July 3, 1888 (telegram), BH-LC.

52. Wood to Harrison, June 30, 1888, Whitelaw Reid to Harrison, September 25, 1888, BH-LC; Harrison to Reid, September 27, 1888, WR-LC; Harrison, *Speeches*, 56, 59, 65–66, 108–115.

53. Carl H. Moneyhon, *Arkansas and the New South, 1874–1929* (Fayetteville: University of Arkansas Press, 1997), 87; Clifton Paisley, "The Political Wheelers and Arkansas' Election of 1888," *Arkansas Historical Quarterly* 25 (Spring 1966): 17–18; Kenneth C. Barnes, *Who Killed John Clayton? Political Violence and the Emergence of New South, 1861–1893* (Durham, N.C.: Duke University Press, 1998), 62–64; Reid to Harrison, September 25, 1888, Logan H. Roots to J. S. Fassett, September 18, 1888, BH-LC.

54. Harrison to Reid, September 27, 1888, WR-LC.

55. Reid to Harrison, October 6, 1888, BH-LC; Harrison, *Speeches*, 162–163.

56. William G. Shade and Ballard C. Campbell, eds., *American Presidential Campaigns and Elections* (Armonk, N.Y.: M. E. Sharpe, 2003), 2:536; Martis, *Atlas of Political Parties*, 140–143.

CHAPTER 9: Republicanism Defeated: The Lodge Federal Elections Bill

1. A. B. Williams to Benjamin Harrison, November 10, 19, 1888, BH-LC; *NYT*, November 19, 28, 1888.

2. Joseph B. Foraker to Harrison, November 24, 1888, William E. Chandler to Harrison, December 22, 1888, BH-LC.

3. Two somewhat different versions of Harrison's GAR remarks appear in *Speeches of Benjamin Harrison*, comp. Charles Hedges (New York: United States Book Company, 1892), 190, and *NYT*, January 3, 1889.

4. Henry Booth to Harrison, December 4, 1888, Robert A. Hill to Harrison, December 18, 1888, BH-LC.

5. *The Frederick Douglass Papers*, series 1, ed. John W. Blassingame and John R. McKivigan (New Haven, Conn.: Yale University Press, 1979–1992), 5:399–403; John

Mercer Langston to Harrison, November 10, 1888, BH–LC; *NYT,* January 24, February 15, 1889; *Indianapolis Journal,* February 15, 1889.

6. Typescript of John Sherman's speech to the John Sherman Republican League, December 21, 1888, JS–LC; *CR,* 50-2, 576; *Indianapolis Journal,* January 28, 1889.

7. Willard Warner to Sherman, January 10, 1889, JS–LC; Augustus E. Willson to Harrison, February 4, 1889, John Marshall Harlan to Harrison, December 25, 1888, BH–LC.

8. *Diary and Letters of Rutherford B. Hayes,* ed. Charles Richard Williams (Columbus: Ohio State Archaeological and Historical Society, 1922), 4:437, 450; *ANB,* 16:469–470.

9. James D. Richardson, *A Compilation of the Messages and Papers of the Presidents, 1789–1902* (Washington, D.C.: Bureau of National Literature and Art, 1903), 9:8, 9, 13.

10. Benjamin Harrison, manuscript draft of inaugural address, BH–LC; *Annual Report of the Attorney-General of the United States for the Year 1889,* xiv–xv; *NYT,* April 27, 1890; Robert M. Goldman, *"A Free Ballot and a Fair Count": The Department of Justice and the Enforcement of Voting Rights in the South, 1877–1893* (New York: Fordham University Press, 2001), 145–169, 177–178 n61.

11. *Annual Report of the Attorney-General . . . 1889,* xxii–xxiii; Richardson, *Messages,* 9:54.

12. *CR,* 51-1, 100; Edward McPherson, *A Hand-Book of Politics for 1888* (Washington, D.C.: James J. Chapman, 1888), 122–125; John C. Covert to Sherman, January 9, 1890, JS–LC; H. W. Blair to Harrison, February 10, 1890, BH–LC.

13. *CR,* 51-1, 1073.

14. *CR,* 51-1, 1868, 1875, 1939.

15. *CR,* 51-1, 2075, 2339, 2340, 2389.

16. Mrs. Frances W. Leiter to Sherman, February 19, 1890, Mrs. Henriett L. Monroe to Sherman, February 19, 1890, A. C. Cowan to Sherman, March 12, 1890, JS–LC; Chauncey M. Depew to "Dear Sir," October 11, 1889, Mortimer C. Addoms to "Dear Sir," January 11, 1890, NPB–LC; Daniel W. Crofts, "The Black Response to the Blair Education Bill," *JSH* 37 (1971): 56–58; *CR,* 51-1, 1068–1069.

17. [Edward P. Clark], *A Bill To Promote Mendicancy* (New York: Evening Post Publishing, 1888); Stanley Hirshson, *Farewell to the Bloody Shirt: Northern Republicans and the Southern Negro, 1877–1893* (Bloomington: Indiana University Press, 1962), 194–200; *Chicago Tribune,* March 22, 1890; Otto Olsen, *Carpetbagger's Crusade: The Life of Albion Winegar Tourgée* (Baltimore, Md.: Johns Hopkins University Press, 1965), 304; *CR,* 51-1, 2436; Edward McPherson, *A Hand-Book of Politics for 1890* (Washington, D.C.: James J. Chapman, 1890), 194; Daniel Wallace Crofts, "The Blair Bill and the Elections Bill: The Congressional Aftermath of Reconstruction" (Ph.D. diss., Yale University, 1968), 210–211. Blair switched his vote to "nay" in order to be able to move a reconsideration.

18. Blair to William E. Chandler, July 17, 1890, WEC–NHHS; William M. Evarts to John Jay, April 4, 1890, WME–Yale; Crofts, "Black Response," 59, 60.

19. J. A. Berry to Sherman, May 1, 1890, JS-LC; *CR*, 51-1, 2200; John C. Spooner to J. F. Dudley, March 16, 1890, JCS-LC.

20. For a complete treatment of the Clayton episode, see Kenneth C. Barnes, *Who Killed John Clayton? Political Violence and the Emergence of the New South, 1861–1893* (Durham, N.C.: Duke University Press, 1998).

21. *NYTr*, February 15, 1889; Chandler to W. Scott Smith, March 1, 1889, WEC-NHHS; Richardson, *Messages*, 9:12.

22. *NYTr*, May 6, September 14, 1889; E. E. Baldwin to Sherman, May 9, 1889, JS-LC; *Indianapolis Journal*, September 26, October 11, 1889.

23. J. B. Cheadle to E. W. Halford, October 15, 1889, Cheadle to Harrison, October 22, November 16, 1889, BH-LC; Crofts, "Blair Bill and Elections Bill," 238–239.

24. Louis T. Michener to Halford, October 1, 1889, BH-LC.

25. Richardson, *Messages*, 9:55–56.

26. John A. Garraty, *Henry Cabot Lodge: A Biography* (New York: Alfred A. Knopf, 1965), 12–13; *New York Herald*, November 30, December 24, 1889; Henry Cabot Lodge to Anna Cabot Lodge, December 21, 1889, HCL-MHS; Harrison Kelley to Albion W. Tourgée, January 7, 1890, AWT-CCHS; J. R. Hawley to Andrew W. DeForrest, August 14, 1890, JRH-LC.

27. Untitled, undated typescript [James S. Clarkson], JSC-LC; J. S. Clarkson to Michener, May 29, 1890, LTM-LC.

28. Powell Clayton to George F. Hoar, July 21, 1890, GFH-MHS; William Moore to Sherman, March 17, 1890, Cyrus Drew to Sherman, August 8, 1890, L. J. Gartrell to Sherman, July 24, 1890, Sherman to Gartrell, July 26, 1890, JS-LC.

29. Crofts, "Blair Bill and Elections Bill," 243–250; Hirshson, *Farewell to the Bloody Shirt*, 203.

30. *CR*, 51-1, 96; Sherman to Gartrell, July 26, 1890, JS-LC; *A Bill to Make and Alter Regulations as to the Times, Places, and Manner of Holding Elections for Representatives in Congress*, S 2, 51st Cong., 1st sess. Sherman's bill was identical to one he had introduced at the end of the previous Congress, S 3783, 50th Cong., 2nd sess.

31. William E. Chandler, "Memorandum for Mr. Speaker Reed concerning Mr. Tourgée's objections to Senator Hoar's bill for national elections," April 29, 1890, WEC-LC; Spooner to A. J. Turner, December 11, 1889, JCS-LC.

32. *A Bill to regulate elections of Representatives in Congress*, HR 8242, 51st Cong., 1st sess.; *CR*, 51-1, 2285; *National Control of Elections. Remarks of Hon. A. W. Tourgée before the Committee on the Election of President, Vice-President, and Representatives in Congress* (Washington, D.C.: Government Printing Office, 1890), 3; *A Bill to Provide for the Election of Members of the House of Representatives*, HR 8286, 51st Cong., 1st sess.; Tourgée to Lodge, March 31, 1890, HCL-MHS.

33. Richardson, *Messages*, 9:56.

34. George F. Hoar, *Autobiography of Seventy Years* (New York: Charles Scribner's Sons, 1903), 2:151–152; Spooner to Tourgée, April 23, 1890, AWT-CCHS; *A Bill to Provide for the More Efficient Enforcement of the Laws of the United States Relating to Elections at Which Representatives or Delegates in Congress are to be Voted For*, S 206, *A Bill to Punish*

Offenses Committed at Elections at Which Representatives or Delegates in Congress are to be Voted For, S 207, *A Bill to Regulate Elections of Representatives in Congress.* HR 8242, *A Bill to Amend and Supplement the Election Laws of the United States and to Provide for the More Efficient Enforcement of Such Laws,* S 3652, all 51st Cong., 1st sess.

35. Tourgée to Spooner, April 29, 1890, T. B. Reed to Tourgée, May 14, 1890, AWT-CCHS; Tourgée to Harrison, May 2, 1890, BH-LC; *NYTr,* April 27, 1890; Chandler, "Memorandum for Mr. Speaker Reed concerning Mr. Tourgée's objections to Senator Hoar's bill for national elections," April 29, 1890, WEC-LC.

36. John I. Davenport to Hoar, April 27, 1890, GFH-MHS; *A Bill to Amend and Supplement the Election Laws of the United States and to Provide for the More Efficient Enforcement of Such Laws,* HR 10084, *A Bill to Amend and Supplement the Election Laws of the United States and to Provide for the More Efficient Enforcement of Such Laws,* HR 10958, *A Bill to Amend and Supplement the Election Laws of the United States and to Provide for the More Efficient Enforcement of Such Laws,* HR 11045, all 51st Cong., 1st sess.; *CR,* 51-1, 4362, 6114, 6286; House Report No. 2493, 51st Cong., 1st sess.; Harrison Kelley to Tourgée, June 13, 1890, AWT-CCHS; Lodge to Anna Cabot Lodge, June 8, 15, 1890, HCL-MHS; William E. Chandler, "National Control of Elections," *Forum* 9 (July 1890): 705–709; George F. Hoar, "The Fate of the Election Bill," *Forum* 11 (April 1891): 129–130; *NYT,* June 17, 1890; Xi Wang, *The Trial of Democracy: Black Suffrage and Northern Republicans, 1860–1910* (Athens: University of Georgia Press, 1997), 232–237; Richard E. Welch Jr., "The Federal Elections Bill of 1890: Postscripts and Prelude," *JAH* 52 (December 1965): 512–513.

37. This latter provision for judicial certification seems to have originated in an earlier bill submitted by Rowell. HR 11045 (June 19, 1890; July 7, 1890); *A Bill to Regulate the Method of Procedure in Contested Elections,* HR 3828, 51st Cong., 1st sess.

38. *Sections of Revised Statutes and Acts of Congress Repealed, Re-enacted, or Amended by H. R. 11045* (Washington, D.C.: Government Printing Office, 1890), 5–6; Spooner to George Farnam, May 8, 1890, JCS-LC.

39. Stephen Cresswell, *Multiparty Politics in Mississippi, 1877–1902* (Jackson: University Press of Mississippi, 1995), 94–96; *CR,* 51-1, 804.

40. *CR,* 51-1, 6553, 6554, 6677, 6684.

41. *Frank Leslie's Illustrated Newspaper,* May 3, 1890, 274; *CR,* 51-1, 407, 428, 6538–6540, 6694, 6709, 6886–6887.

42. *CR,* 51-1, 6541–6543, 6544–6547, 6774, 6886.

43. *CR,* 51-1, 6543, 6544, 6593, 6613, 6710, 6723, appx., 432. In a treatment that says little about the Republicans' arguments in favor of the bill, Heather Richardson, focusing mostly on press opinion, argues that northerners tended to denounce it as a scheme to put power in the hands of dangerous working-class blacks. Haugen's and Kerr's arguments suggest otherwise. Heather Cox Richardson, *The Death of Reconstruction: Race, Labor, and Politics in the Post–Civil War North, 1865–1901* (Cambridge, Mass.: Harvard University Press, 2001), 202–208.

44. *CR,* 51-1, 6556, 6686, 6897.

45. *CR*, 51-1, 6538, 6592, 6607–6608, 6610, 6723.

46. *CR*, 51-1, 6694, 6706, 6720, 6848, 6893, appx., 491.

47. *CR*, 51-1, 6688–6691, 6772–6773.

48. *CR*, 51-1, 6934, 6940–6941; McPherson, *Hand-Book of Politics for 1890*, 218–219; Kelley to Mrs. Albion W. Tourgée, July 4, 1890, AWT-CCHS; Chandler to Lodge, July 7, 1890, HCL-MHS.

49. Lodge to Chandler, July 10, 1890, Eugene Hale to Chandler, July 24, 1890, WEC-LC; Spooner to John A. Johnson, July 13, 1890, Spooner to Henry C. Payne, July 23, 1890, JCS-LC.

50. J. C. Dusk to Sherman, July 24, 1890, Daniel J. Ryan to Sherman, July 8, 1890, JS-LC.

51. *CR*, 51-1, 7835–7836; Warner Bateman to Sherman, August 5, 1890, M. D. Harter to Sherman, July 25, 1890, JS-LC. Harter was a Democrat from Sherman's hometown.

52. *American Grocer* quoted in *NYT*, July 24, 1890; Hirshson, *Farewell to the Bloody Shirt*, 218.

53. *Chicago Tribune*, July 13, 1890; *NYTr*, July 14, 19, 1890; Charles P. Taylor to Sherman, July 10, 1890, JS-LC.

54. Spooner to Henry Fink, July 27, 1890, Spooner to J. M. Smith, July 21, 1890, Spooner to W. A. Barber, July 13, 1890, JCS-LC.

55. HR 11045 (August 7, 1890), 51st Cong., 1st sess.; *CR*, 51-2, 723; Lodge to E. B. Haskell, August 8, 1890, HCL-MHS.

56. Senate consideration of the McKinley Bill had also been delayed by western silver state senators who had held the bill hostage until passage of the Sherman Silver Purchase Act on July 14. H. Wayne Morgan, "Western Silver and the Tariff of 1890," *New Mexico Historical Review* 35 (April 1960): 118–128.

57. Theodore Justice to William B. Allison, July 24, 30, 1890, WBA-SHSI; Samuel Lee to Sherman, August 4, 1890, JS-LC.

58. Crofts, "Blair Bill and Elections Bill," 289–293; A. R. Spofford to Nelson Aldrich, July 11, 1890, NWA-LC; O. H. Platt to Chandler, July 22, 1890, WEC-LC; *CR*, 51-1, 8355, 8422, 8440; Louis A. Coolidge, *An Old-Fashioned Senator: Orville H. Platt of Connecticut* (New York: G. P. Putnam's Sons, 1910), 1:232–233.

59. James A Kehl, *Boss Rule in the Gilded Age: Matt Quay of Pennsylvania* (Pittsburgh: University of Pittsburgh Press, 1981), 128–133; *CR*, 51-1, 8466.

60. Spooner to W. W. Lockwood, August 18, 1890, Spooner to Payne, August 13, 1890, JCS-LC; *NYT*, August 14, 1890; *CR*, 51-1, 8488–8489, 8678; *Chicago Tribune*, August 15, 16, 1890; *Philadelphia Press*, August 16, 1890; Charles Foster to Sherman, August 16, 1890, JS-LC.

61. *Philadelphia Press*, August 20, 1890.

62. Elijah W. Halford diary, August 14, 15, 1890, Harrison to Mame Dimmick, August 16, 1890, BH-Walker; *NYT*, August 19, 1890; *Chicago Tribune*, August 18, 1890.

63. James G. Blaine to Harrison, August 30, 1890, BH-LC; Blaine to Mrs. Henry Cabot Lodge, August 31, 1890, HCL-MHS; *Indianapolis Journal*, August 17, 1890.

64. *Philadelphia Press,* August 19, 21, 1890; Henry F. Downing to Sherman, August 18, 1890, Moore to Sherman, August 21, 1890, JS-LC; Albert Clarke to Hoar, August 21, 1890, GFH–MHS.

65. *CR,* 51-1, 8842–8848.

66. Spooner to G. W. Hazelton, August 23, 1890, JCS-LC; *NYT,* August 22, 24, 1890; *Chicago Tribune,* August 23, 1890; J. R. Hawley to N. T. Adams, August 26, 1890, JRH-LC; signed pledge, "Washington, D.C., August 22, 1890," Eugene Hale and John C. Spooner to "My Dear Sir," August 25, 1890, GFH–MHS.

67. Hawley to H. C. Dwight, August 29, 1890, JRH-LC; *CR,* 51-1, 9943, 10333; Spooner to G. W. Hazelton, August 23, 1890, Spooner to Captain E. Enos, September 6, 1890, JCS-LC; Evarts to Collins Arnold, August 25, 1890, WME-Yale.

68. *Indianapolis Journal,* September 4, 1890; Chas. A. Klinefelter to Chandler, September 8, 1890, WEC-LC; Frederick Douglass to Hoar, September 2, 1890, GFH–MHS.

69. William P. Frye to Harrison, September 8, 11, 1890, O. H. Platt to Harrison, September 13, 19, 1890, BH-LC; George F. Edmunds to Justin S. Morrill, September 9, 1890, JSM-LC.

70. L. T. Michener to E. W. Halford, November 8, 1890, James S. Clarkson to Halford, November 20, 1890, BH-LC; W. I. Ewart to Sherman, November 13, 1890, JS-LC; Spooner to N. T. Martin, November 19, 1890, JCS-LC; Robert W. Cherny, *American Politics in the Gilded Age, 1868–1900* (Wheeling, Ill.: Harlan Davidson, 1997), 104–108; Paul Kleppner, *The Cross of Culture: A Social Analysis of Midwestern Politics, 1850–1900* (New York: Free Press, 1970), 143–171; Richard Jensen, *The Winning of the Midwest: Social and Political Conflict, 1888–1896* (Chicago: University of Chicago Press, 1971), 122–153.

71. Kenneth C. Martis, *The Atlas of Political Parties in the United States Congress, 1789–1989* (New York: Macmillan, 1989), 142–145; J. H. Purnell to M. S. Quay, December 19, 1890, JS-LC.

72. Edward C. Wade to Sherman, November 30, 1890, C. L. Poorman to Sherman, December 12, 1890, JS-LC; Harrison Reed to E. W. Halford, November 26, 1890, BH-LC.

73. Harrison to Howard Cale, November 17, 1890, BH-LC; Richardson, *Messages,* 9:128–129.

74. *NYTr,* December 2, 1890; Tourgée to Harrison, December 2, 1890, Clarkson to Harrison, December 2, 1890 (telegram), BH-LC.

75. *CR,* 51-2, 18–26; Henry Cabot Lodge, journal, December 20, 1890, Lodge to Anna Cabot Lodge, December 8, 1890, HCL-MHS.

76. *CR,* 51-2, 245, 459, and passim; Thomas Adams Upchurch, *Legislating Racism: The Billion Dollar Congress and the Birth of Jim Crow* (Lexington: University Press of Kentucky, 2004), 129–150.

77. *CR,* 51-2, 713–730, 858.

78. *CR,* 51-2, 729, 857, 861, 1421–1422; George F. Hoar, *Speech of Hon. George F. Hoar, of Massachusetts, in the Senate of the United States, Monday, December 29, and Tuesday, December 30, 1890* (Washington, n.p., 1891), 33–34, 45.

79. *ANB*, 6:712–713, 8:941–942; *CR*, 51-2, 520.

80. *CR*, 51-2, 520, 521.

81. *CR*, 51-2, 873.

82. *NYT*, December 30, 1890; Kelley to Mr. and Mrs. Albion W. Tourgée, January 1, 1891, AWT-CCHS; *CR*, 51-2, 819–820, 852.

83. *CR*, 51-2, 906–913, 1324; *NYTr*, January 3, 1891; John R. Lambert Jr., *Arthur Pue Gorman* (Baton Rouge: Louisiana State University Press, 1953), 159; Edward McPherson, *A Hand-Book of Politics for 1892* (Washington, D.C.: James J. Chapman, 1892), 24, 27; Jones to Mrs. Jones, January 10, 1891, JPJ-HL.

84. Spooner to C. W. Porter, January 11, 1891, JCS-LC; Fred Wellborn, "The Influence of the Silver-Republican Senators. 1889–1891," *MVHR* 14 (March 1928): 478–479; *CR*, 51-2, 678–684.

85. *CR*, 51-2, 1462–1463.

86. William M. Stewart to E. A. Angier, February 2, 1891, Stewart to A. P. K. Safford, March 7, 1891, WMS-NHS.

87. *CR*, 51-2, 1564–1568, 1651-1655, 1738–1740; Crofts, "Blair Bill and Elections Bill," 327–334.

88. Spooner to J. M. Bundy, January 27, 1891, JCS-LC; Evarts to Platt, February 12, 1891, WME-Yale; *NYTr*, January 28, March 17, 1891; Stewart to J. T. Leonard, February 19, 1891, WMS-NHS; *Reminiscences of Senator William M. Stewart of Nevada*, ed. George Rothwell Brown (New York: Neale Publishing, 1908), 297–307, 310.

89. Hoar to Ledyard Bill, January 29, 1891, L. S. Metcalf to Hoar, February 17, 1891, GFH-MHS; Hoar, "Fate of the Election Bill," 127–136.

90. Hoar, "Fate of the Election Bill," 137; Spooner to G. L. Chapin, March 8, 1891, JCS-LC; Stewart to J. Taylor Ellyson, February 19, 1891, WMS-NHS.

CHAPTER 10: Surrender of the New Republic: Reconstruction Undone and the Nationalism of Reconciliation

1. *Appletons' Annual Cyclopaedia and Register of Important Events of the Year 1890* (New York: D. Appleton, 1891), 559–560; *CR*, 51-2, 727, 894; George F. Hoar, *Speech of Hon. George F. Hoar, of Massachusetts, in the Senate of the United States, Monday, December 29, and Tuesday, 30, 1890* (Washington, D.C.: n.p., 1891), 28; Michael Perman, *Struggle for Mastery: Disfranchisement in the South, 1888–1908* (Chapel Hill: University of North Carolina Press, 2001).

2. *NYTr*, March 17, 1891; *Speeches of Benjamin Harrison*, comp. Charles Hedges (New York: United States Book Company, 1892), 302, 305, 309, 493; Edward Frantz, "A March of Triumph? Benjamin Harrison's Southern Tour and the Limits of Racial and Regional Reconciliation," *Indiana Magazine of History* 100 (December 2004): 293–320.

3. *Independent,* July 9, 1891, 7, 8.

4. *NYTr*, June 18, July 2, September 10, 1891; William E. Chandler to T. Thomas Fortune, September 2, 1891 (draft), WEC-LC; Harrison, *Speeches*, 528, 529, 543.

5. James D. Richardson, *A Compilation of the Messages and Papers of the Presidents, 1789–1902* (Washington, D.C.: Bureau of National Literature and Art, 1903), 9:210–211.

6. Frederick Douglass, "Lynch Law in the South," *North American Review* 155 (July 1892): 17–24; Benjamin Harrison to Mrs. H. Davis, April 1, 1892, Harrison to Albion W. Tourgée, April 21, 1892, BH-LC; *Washington Post*, May 14, 1892; *NYT*, May 28, 1892; Harry J. Sievers, *Benjamin Harrison: Hoosier President* (Indianapolis: Bobbs-Merrill, 1968), 183–190; *Public Papers and Addresses of Benjamin Harrison, Twenty-Third President of the United States* (Washington, D.C.: Government Printing Office, 1893), 293–294.

7. Hoar to Nathan Appleton, January 23, 1892, GFH-MHS; *CR*, 51-1, appx., 427; *Proceedings of the Tenth Republican National Convention Held in the City of Minneapolis, Minnesota, June 7, 8, 9 and 10, 1892* (Minneapolis: Harrison & Smith, 1892), 65; Fortune to Harrison, June 10, 1892, BH-LC.

8. William Henry Smith to Joseph B. Foraker, June 15, 1892, JBF-LC; E. P. Branch to John Sherman, June 20, 1892, JS-LC; Joseph R. Hawley to Harrison, August 3, 1892, BH-LC.

9. S. B. Elkins to Whitelaw Reid, June 17, 1892, WR-LC; Donald Bruce Johnson and Kirk H. Porter, comps., *National Party Platforms, 1840–1972* (Urbana: University of Illinois Press, 1975), 86–87; New York *Sun*, June 24, July 8, 24, 1892; *NYT*, July 14, 19, 1892.

10. V. D. Groner to Harrison, August 17, 1892, Harrison to E. W. Halford, August 20, 1892, BH-LC; *NYTr*, August 24, 1892.

11. Vincent De Santis, *Republicans Face the Southern Question—The New Departure Years, 1877–1897* (Baltimore, Md.: Johns Hopkins University Press, 1959), 227–232, 234–235; C. Vann Woodward, *Origins of the New South, 1877–1913* (Baton Rouge: Louisiana State University Press, 1951, 1971), 262; Groner to Harrison, August 17, 1892, B. W. Walker to E. W. Halford, August 12, 13, 1892, BH-LC.

12. Harrison to Halford, August 20, 1892, BH-LC; *Republican National Convention . . . 1892*, 141.

13. Harrison to Halford, August 20, 1892, BH-LC; *Republican National Convention . . . 1892*, 149–150.

14. Republican National Committee, *The Republican Campaign Text-Book for 1892* (New York: Brodix Publishing, 1892), 197–199; James P. Boyd, *Men and Issues of '92* (n.p.: Publishers Union, 1892), 58–59.

15. William G. Shade and Ballard C. Campbell, eds., *American Presidential Campaigns and Elections* (Armonk, N.Y.: M. E. Sharpe, 2003), 2:536, 552.

16. P. C. Cheney to Harrison, November 19, 1892, Thomas W. Palmer to Harrison, November 16, 1892, with clipping, Harrison to Palmer, November 19, 1892, BH-LC; Theodore Roosevelt to Benjamin F. Tracy, November 20, 1892, Benjamin F. Tracy Papers, LC.

17. Richardson, *Messages*, 9:331–332.

18. George F. Hoar, *Autobiography of Seventy Years* (New York: Charles Scribner's Sons, 1903), 2:181–183; *NYT,* February 3, 1893.

19. Irving Schiffman, "Howell E. Jackson," in *Justices of the United States Supreme Court, 1789–1978,* ed. Leon Friedman and Fred Israel (New York: Chelsea House, 1980), 2:1607–1611; *ANB,* 11:749–750; Harrison to George L. Pullman, February 3, 1893, BH–LC.

20. Stanley Hirshson, *Farewell to the Bloody Shirt: Northern Republicans and the Southern Negro, 1877–1893* (Bloomington: Indiana University Press, 1962), 246–248; *Washington Post,* February 5, 6, 7, 1893; James S. Clarkson to Shelby M. Cullom, February 3, 1893 (telegram), Shelby M. Cullom Papers, Illinois State Historical Library, Springfield; *NYT,* February 5, 1893.

21. Harrison to Howell E. Jackson, February 4, 1893, BH–LC.

22. *NYT,* February 19, 1893; *ANB,* 11:750; Richard E. Welch Jr., *The Presidencies of Grover Cleveland* (Lawrence: University Press of Kansas, 1988), 67–68; Richardson, *Messages,* 9:391.

23. James S. Clarkson, Speech "By JSC Delivered at Louisville KY as Prest of Natl League of Clubs at Annual Meeting," [May 10, 1893], typescript, JSC-LC.

24. *Washington Post,* May 12, 1893; William S. Ball to John C. Spooner, July 5, 1893, JCS-LC.

25. *CR,* 53-1, 1395, 1811–1813; 2378, 53-2, 1999; House Report No. 18, 53rd Cong., 1st sess.; Senate Report No. 113, 53rd Cong., 2nd sess.; Edward McPherson, *A Hand-Book of Politics for 1894* (Washington, D.C.: Robert Beall, 1894), 142.

26. Chandler to William P. Frye, October 9, 1893, WEC-LC.

27. *CR,* 53-1, 2228, 53-2, 1982; Senate Report No. 113, Part 2, 53rd Cong., 2nd sess., 37.

28. *CR,* 53-1, 1820, 2228, 2280, 53-2, 1314, 1230.

29. *CR,* 53-1, 1952, 1822, 53-2, 1320.

30. *CR,* 53-1, 1815, 53-2, 1586, 1978; William Chandler to "My dear sir," December 26, 1893, J. H. Manley to Chandler, December 22, 1893, WEC-LC; Senate Report No. 113, Part 2, 53rd Cong., 2nd sess., 27–32.

31. *CR,* 53-1, 2147, 2275, 53-2, 1861, 1862.

32. John A. Garraty, *Henry Cabot Lodge: A Biography* (New York: Alfred A. Knopf, 1965), 141–145; Henry Cabot Lodge, *Historical and Political Essays* (Boston: Houghton, Mifflin, 1892), 138–168.

33. *CR,* 53-2, 1316–1317.

34. *CR,* 53-1, 1820, 2235, 53-2, 1588, 1589; Senate Report No. 113, Part 2, 53rd Cong., 2nd sess., 32.

35. *CR,* 53-1, 2343–2345; 53-2, 1859; Richardson, *Messages,* 9:332.

36. *CR,* 53-1, 2088.

37. *CR,* 53-2, 1588, 1860; McPherson, *Hand-Book of Politics for 1894,* 140, 142. In the Senate, William Stewart, an erstwhile Republican who voted for repeal, had assumed the Populist label.

38. *CR*, 53-1, 2343, 2345, 53-2, 1979; George Edmunds to Justin Morrill, September 16, 1893, JSM-LC.

39. *CR*, 53-1, 1817, 1820, 2159, 53-2, 1863; Senate Report No. 113, Part 2, 53rd Cong., 2nd sess., 3.

40. *CR*, 53-2, 1316; John Sherman, *Recollections of Forty Years in the House, Senate and Cabinet* (Chicago: Werner, 1895), 1:450–451.

41. Hoar, *Autobiography*, 1:258–259; J. E. Bruce to Hoar, February 20, 1895, Hoar to Bruce, February 25, 1895, GFH-MHS.

42. *The Booker T. Washington Papers*, ed. Louis R. Harlan (Urbana: University of Illinois Press, 1972–1989), 3:583–587, 4:26n, 111.

43. Richard B. Sherman, *The Republican Party and Black America from McKinley to Hoover, 1896–1933* (Charlottesville: University Press of Virginia, 1973), 4; *NYTr*, March 25, 28, April 1, May 8, 1896.

44. *Plessy v. Ferguson*, 163 U.S. 537 (1896); Charles A. Lofgren, *The Plessy Case: A Legal-Historical Interpretation* (New York: Oxford University Press, 1987), 196–197.

45. Sherman, *Republican Party and Black America*, 5–6; Jeffrey Nelson, "The Rhetoric of the 1896 Republican National Convention at St. Louis," *Missouri Historical Review* 77 (1983): 403–408; *Official Proceedings of the Eleventh Republican National Convention Held in the City of St. Louis, Mo., June 16, 17, and 18, 1896* (n.p., 1896), 44, 84–85; Joseph Benson Foraker, *Notes of a Busy Life* (Cincinnati: Stewart & Kidd, 1916), 1:463–486.

46. *Republican National Convention . . . 1896*, 137, 139, 140.

47. *Republican National Convention . . . 1896*, 159; *NYT*, September 9, 16, October 10, 1896; A. P. Funkhouser to William McKinley, October 6, 1896, WM-LC; *Richmond Times*, October 6, 1896.

48. Joseph P. Smith, comp., *McKinley, the People's Choice* (Canton, Ohio: Repository Press, 1896), 39–40; *McKinley's Speeches in August*, comp. Joseph P. Smith (n.p.: Republican National Committee, 1896), 86–87; *NYT*, September 29, 1896.

49. Shade and Campbell, *American Presidential Campaigns*, 2:568; *NYTr*, November 29, 1896.

50. Richardson, *Messages*, 10:15, 18. For brief treatments of McKinley's conciliatory policy, see Nina Silber, *The Romance of Reunion: Northerners and the South, 1865–1900* (Chapel Hill: University of North Carolina Press, 1993), 179–180; David W. Blight, *Race and Reunion: The Civil War in American Memory* (Cambridge, Mass.: Harvard University Press, 2001), 351–352.

51. Lewis L. Gould, *The Presidency of William McKinley* (Lawrence: Regents Press of Kansas, 1980), 153–155; Sherman, *Republican Party and Black America*, 8–11; McKinley to M. A. Hanna, November 24, 1897, B. K. Bruce to McKinley, February 10, 1898, WM-LC.

52. Richardson, *Messages*, 10: 23, 52, 146–148, 179, 205–206, 234, 236.

53. *Speeches and Addresses of William McKinley from March 1, 1897 to May 30, 1900* (New York: Doubleday & McClure, 1900), 32, 39, 88, 121, 141.

54. John P. Green to McKinley, June 29, 1899, McKinley to Elihu Root, August 19, 1899, R. C. Ransom to Green, June 27, 1899, WM-LC; Gould, *Presidency of McKinley*, 155–158.

55. For the Wilmington riot, see H. Leon Prather Sr., *We Have Taken a City: Wilmington Racial Massacre and Coup of 1898* (Cranbury, N.J.: Associated University Presses, 1984); Prather, "We Have Taken a City: A Centennial Essay," in *Democracy Betrayed: The Wilmington Race Riot of 1898 and Its Legacy*, ed. David S. Cecelski and Timothy B. Tyson (Chapel Hill: University of North Carolina Press, 1998), 15–41.

56. Executive Mansion Telegrams, Wilmington, N.C., November 10, 1898, WM-LC; Prather, "We Have Taken a City," 152, 154–157; Glenda Elizabeth Gilmore, *Gender and Jim Crow: Women and the Politics of White Supremacy in North Carolina, 1896–1920* (Chapel Hill: University of North Carolina Press, 1996), 113.

57. Hoar to Rev. Louis H. Taylor, November 30, 1898, GFH-MHS; *NYT*, December 23, 1898.

58. Prather, "We Have Taken a City," 158; John E. Milholland to McKinley, November 14, 1898, WM-LC; Richardson, *Messages*, 10:82–123; McKinley, *Speeches and Addresses*, 158, 159, 160.

59. McKinley, *Speeches and Addresses*, 168, 169, 177–178.

60. Booker T. Washington to McKinley, December 22, 1898, WM-LC; Washington, *Papers*, 4:530–531; Emma Lou Thornbrough, *T. Thomas Fortune: Militant Journalist* (Chicago: University of Chicago Press, 1972), 182–183; *NYT*, December 21, 1898.

61. Xi Wang, *The Trial of Democracy: Black Suffrage and Northern Republicans, 1860–1910* (Athens: University of Georgia Press, 1997), 260–261; J. Morgan Kousser, *The Shaping of Southern Politics: Suffrage Restriction and the Establishment of the One-Party South, 1880–1910* (New Haven, Conn.: Yale University Press, 1974); Perman, *Struggle for Mastery*, 91–194; *Williams v. Mississippi*, 170 U.S. 213 (1898) at 225.

62. *CR*, 55-3, 1124–1126; Kousser, *Shaping of Southern Politics*, 190–195; *Appletons' Annual Cyclopaedia and Register of Important Events of the Year 1899* (New York: D. Appleton, 1900), 566; *Appletons' Annual Cyclopaedia and Register of Important Events of the Year 1900* (New York: D. Appleton, 1901), 444–445; *Journal of the House of Representatives of the General Assembly of the State of North Carolina at Its Session of 1899* (Raleigh: E. M. Uzzell, 1899), 655; *Journal of the Senate of the General Assembly of the State of North Carolina, Session 1899* (Raleigh: Edwards and Broughton, 1899), 494–495.

63. *CR*, 56-1, 674, 1027–1038, 1172, 1173, 6370.

64. Kousser, *Shaping of Southern Politics*, 192; McKinley, *Speeches and Addresses*, 304, 313; *CR*, 56-1, 674, 1035.

65. McKinley, *Speeches and Addresses*, 245, 254, 314.

66. Johnson and Porter, *National Party Platforms*, 123; Sherman, *Republican Party and Black America*, 17; *NYT*, September 10, 1900; Richardson, *Messages*, 10:241.

67. Hoar, *Autobiography*, 1:261.

68. Albion W. Tourgée to McKinley, November 23, 1898, WM-LC.

INDEX

45- Frederick Douglas,
50- Wishful thinking in Giant's and Jnaguard
52- Benjamin Borsten - 14 th Amendment